NATIONAL IDENTITY AND EUROPE IN TIMES OF CRISIS
Doing and Undoing Europe

NATIONAL IDENTITY AND EUROPE IN TIMES OF CRISIS
Doing and Undoing Europe

EDITED BY

CHRISTIAN KARNER
University of Nottingham, Nottingham, UK

MONIKA KOPYTOWSKA
University of Łódź, Łódź, Poland

United Kingdom – North America – Japan
India – Malaysia – China

Emerald Publishing Limited
Howard House, Wagon Lane, Bingley BD16 1WA, UK

First edition 2017

Copyright © 2017 Emerald Publishing Limited

Reprints and permissions service
Contact: permissions@emeraldinsight.com

British Library Cataloguing in Publication Data
A catalogue record for this book is available from the British Library

ISBN: 978-1-78714-514-6 (Print)
ISBN: 978-1-78714-513-9 (Online)
ISBN: 978-1-78714-956-4 (Epub)

Printed and bound by CPI Group (UK) Ltd, Croydon, CR0 4YY

ISOQAR certified
Management System,
awarded to Emerald
for adherence to
Environmental
standard
ISO 14001:2004.

Certificate Number 1985
ISO 14001

INVESTOR IN PEOPLE

CONTENTS

ABOUT THE AUTHORS

Fabienne Baider received her PhD at the University of Toronto and is Associate Professor in Linguistics at the University of Cyprus, Cyprus. She works on contrastive linguistics, semantics and discourse from a socio-cognitivist perspective on English, French and Greek. She is particularly interested in issues related to conceptual metaphors, emotions, extremist and violent discourse, language and identity construction. Her work has been published in peer-reviewed journals such as the *International Journal of Lexicography* and *Modern and Contemporary France*. She has co-edited several special issues and volumes, both in language and gender (Intersexion, 2012; John Benjamins, 2016) and in linguistic approaches to emotions (Langage et l'homme, 2015, John Benjamins, 2014; Presses de la Sorbonne, 2013). She is the author of a volume on semantics, gender and the French languages (Hommes galants, 2004). Her recent research focuses on journalistic and political discourse and CMC (forums, blogs) and she coordinated a two-year EU programme dedicated to hate speech in the European space (2015–2017, CONTACT).

Maria Constantinou received her PhD in Language Sciences from the University of Franche-Comté in 2006, France. She has been teaching foreign languages and communication-related courses in private academic institutions of Cyprus (since 2007) and linguistics (since January 2012) at the University of Cyprus. Her research interests include critical discourse analysis, contrastive linguistics and translation studies. She is particularly interested in issues related to conceptual metaphors, emotions, extremist and violent discourse, irony and identity construction through discourse and symbolism. Her recent research focuses on journalistic and political discourse, computer-mediated communication (CMC) (forums, blogs) and translation mainly from the viewpoint of narrative theory and Critical Discourse Analysis. She has participated in various conferences and published articles and chapters in and on English, French and Greek mainly from a contrastive and translational perspective in refereed and peer-reviewed journals and volumes.

Łukasz Grabowski is Associate Professor at the Institute of English, University of Opole, Poland. His research interests include corpus linguistics, phraseology, formulaic language, translation studies and lexicography. He is also interested in computer-assisted methods of text analysis. He has published internationally in *International Journal of Corpus Linguistics and English for Specific Purposes*, among other journals. He is also Managing Editor of the journal *Explorations: A Journal of Language and Literature*.

Christian Karner is Associate Professor of Sociology at the University of Nottingham, UK. He has previously worked as a Leverhulme Special Research Fellow and as a Research Associate in the Center for Austrian Studies at the University of Minnesota. Christian's research focuses on memory studies, the politics of national identity in Austria and on urban sociology. His books include *Ethnicity and Everyday Life* (2007), *Negotiating National Identities* (2011), *The Use and Abuse of Memory: Interpreting World War II in Contemporary European Politics* (co-edited with Bram Mertens, 2013) and *The Commonalities of Global Crises* (co-edited with Bernhard Weicht, 2016).

Monika Kopytowska received her PhD from the University of Łódź, Poland, where she is currently affiliated with the Department of Pragmatics. Her research interests revolve around identity, media discourse and the pragma-rhetorical aspects of the mass-mediated representation of conflict/terrorism, ethnicity and religion. She has published internationally in linguistic journals and volumes (e.g. with Yusuf Kalyango (eds.), *Why Discourse Matters*, Peter Lang Publishers, 2014) and is now working on the dynamics of proximization in news discourse (*Creating Context, Shaping Cognition: Africa, Conflict and the Media*, Amsterdam: Benjamins, forthcoming) and the mediatization of religion (with Paul Chilton (eds.), *Religion, Language and Human Mind*, New York: Oxford University Press, forthcoming). She is the co-editor of *Łódź Papers in Pragmatics* (de Gruyter), the associate editor of *Moral Cognition & Communication* (Benjamins), the assistant editor of *CADAAD Journal* and editorial board member of *The University of Nairobi Journal of Language and Linguistics*. She is the board member of the European Network for Intercultural Education Activities.

Zinovia Lialiouti is Researcher at Panteion University of Social and Political Sciences, Athens, Greece, and Research Fellow at the National Research Foundation. Her current research projects involve American cultural diplomacy in post-war Greece and ideological trends in Greek society in the crisis context. She has conducted three-year post-doctoral research on the ideology of Americanism and the image of Greece during the period 1947–1967. She holds a PhD from the Department of Politics and History, Panteion University, Athens. The title of her thesis is *Greek anti-Americanism, 1947–1989*. She has published papers on the phenomenon of anti-Americanism, American studies, cold war culture, as well as the study of political discourse and Greek political culture.

James Moir is Senior Lecturer in Sociology at the Abertay University, Dundee, Scotland, UK. He has a research interest in the application of discourse analysis across a wide range of topics including discourses of occupational identities, health-related discourse, the discursive construction of nationalism and identity, education policy and citizenship discourse, political discourse in the media and in this volume pro- and anti-immigration discourse in the European context.

Maja Muhic is Associate Professor of Cultural Studies, Multiculturalism, Post-Colonial Theory and Culture of the English-speaking countries at the South East European University in Tetovo, Macedonia. She holds a PhD in Philosophy from Ss Cyril and Methodius University, Skopje, and an MPhil in Cultural Anthropology from Cambridge University, UK. During 2007–2008, Muhic spent a semester at the Department of Anthropology at the University of California, Berkeley. In the previous years, she has also visited and did research at other renowned universities, such as The University of Santa Barbara, California, where she earned a fellowship to study religious pluralism and diversity in the USA. As a result of her stay there and her cooperation with the Department of Religious Studies, Muhic has shown up as the co-author of the *Encyclopedia of Global Religion* (2011) edited by Mark Juergensmeyer and Wade Clark Roof. She has also published her work in *After Yugoslavia: Identities and Politics within the Successor States* (2011) edited by Robert Hudson and Glenn Bowman and published by Palgrave Macmillan. In addition to this, Muhic has published a number of articles in philosophical and anthropological journals focusing primarily on issues of diversity, ethnicity and identity formation. She participated as a guest speaker in a number of conferences throughout Europe, Japan and USA.

Chiara Nasti is currently temporary Lecturer in the Department of Languages, Literature and Comparative Studies at the University of Naples L'Orientale, Italy. She is also working as temporary Lecturer at the University of Naples Federico II for the Department of Statistical Science and Economics. She has been a Postdoctoral Research Fellow working on Uniweb and English as Lingua Franca within the project FORGIARE funded by the University of Naples Federico II. In 2011 she completed her PhD in *Lingua Inglese per Scopi Speciali* (English for Special Purposes), for which she was awarded a three-year studentship. From 2011 to 2013 she worked as temporary Lecturer in the Department of Architecture at the University of Naples Federico II. She is a member of the RaAM (Researching and Applying Metaphor association) and she also has participated in international conferences and symposiums. Her research interests are English as Lingua Franca in the institutional academic domain, corpus linguistics, metaphor analysis, news discourse and evaluation.

Christian Nestler, MA, is Research Assistant at the University of Rostock, Germany, Department of Comparative Politics at the Institute for Political Science. His research focuses among other topics on the history of science and system change in 20th-century Germany.

Magdalena Nowicka-Franczak is Assistant Professor of Sociology in the Department of Research on Social Communication at the Institute of Sociology, University of Łódź, Poland. In 2014–2015, she was Junior Visiting Fellow at the Institute for Human Sciences in Vienna. Her academic interests focus on the current public debate in Central and Eastern Europe, collective memory of Shoah and World War II, post-Foucauldian discourse analysis and post-colonial studies. A book based on her dissertation 'Niechciana debata. Spór o ksiażki Jana Tomasza Grossa' was published in December 2016 (in Polish).

Alexandra Pinto is Assistant Professor in the Arts Faculty of University of Porto, Portugal and PhD in Linguistics, with a thesis about aspects of the advertising textualization. She is responsible for the teaching of several chairs in Linguistics in graduation and post-graduation and specialized in discourse analysis, pragmatics and sociolinguistics. She is a member of the Scientific Committee of CLUP — Linguistics Centre of University of Porto, where she participates in several international investigation projects and networks, such as Es.Por.Atenuación — Atenuación en el español y el portugués; MEMITA — Memory, identity, integration to identify analysis models in media communication; International Cooperation Agreement I&D USP/U.Porto, on the Discourse of Science. She is the main organizer, since 2011, of JADIS — Annual International Conferences on Discourse Analysis and editor in chief of REDIS — Discourse Studies Review, an online publication by the Arts Faculty of University of Porto. She is also author of several works in national and international publications in the area of Discourse Studies, having focused on aspects of the discursive functioning of advertising discourse, of media opinion discourse, of political discourse and also of scientific discourse.

Jan Rohgalf is Research Assistant at the University of Rostock, Germany, Department Political Theory and History of Ideas at the Institute for Political Science. His research focuses on the political imaginary, the theory of late modern societies and protest movements.

Franco Zappettini (PhD, Applied Linguistics University of London) is Adjunct Professor of English in the Department of Education, University of Genoa, Italy. He is also a Honorary Research Associate in the School of Management, Royal Holloway, University of London, UK. His research interests focus on the application of critical linguistic approaches to political and organisational discourses.

INTRODUCTION: DISCURSIVELY DOING AND UNDOING EUROPE

Christian Karner and Monika Kopytowska

On 7 July 2015, writing in the German paper *Die Welt*, columnist Thomas Straubhaar warned that following Greek Prime Minister Alexis Tsipras' surprise call of a referendum leading to Greeks' resounding 'no' to more austerity, Tsipras was 'not to be trusted'. The latter, Straubhaar postulated, was a tactically astute radical seeking to install a neo-Marxist regime within the European Union (EU), which would, so Straubhaar continued, embolden the far left across the continent and could purportedly threaten Europe — or, more accurately, Europe as seen and defined by the journalist in question and with him, undoubtedly, significant sections of the German public. A few days earlier, Alexis Tsipras had left negotiations with his Eurozone partners, shortly before calling the referendum, declaring that 'the European Union was founded on principles of democracy, solidarity, equality and mutual respect', not on 'blackmail and ultimatums', and that no one, especially 'in these crucial times', had the right to compromise Europe's values (e.g. Maltezou & Ponthus, 2015). In the period between the Greek referendum and 'last-minute' talks widely seen to 'decide Greece's fate' whether inside or out of the Eurozone, German Chancellor Angela Merkel invoked the notion of a 'good European', suggesting that the latter 'respects the European treaties and national laws' and helps 'ensure the stability of the Eurozone' (e.g. Levine, 2015).

These were but some of the near-daily recent invocations of what Europe is taken to be, by a multitude of social actors, from politicians to public intellectuals, academics, journalists, to 'ordinary citizens'. As such examples

National Identity and Europe in Times of Crisis: Doing and Undoing Europe, 1–12
doi:10.1108/978-1-78714-513-920171001

powerfully illustrate, there is not only long-standing disagreement over Europe's boundaries and polysemy (e.g. Jenkins, 2008), but Europeans continually reflect and speak from a diversity of historical, structural and ideological positions about the continent's past, present and future. The present volume captures and analyses such reflections and positions on Europe in a variety of national and local contexts. Several key observations and underlying premises will accompany us throughout the following chapters: first, discourses about Europe, its limits, meanings, values, histories and future trajectory are inescapably varied and conflictual, both within and across national boundaries; second, none of the competing positions examined can be understood without thorough contextualisation in their local and national histories of ideas, political conflicts and their enduring legacies; third, disagreements over Europe are also inescapably future-oriented, revealing clashes between competing models and answers as to *which Europe* — or, in some prominent formulations, which post-European institutional configurations — the political actors in question have in mind and argue for or against. Further, we discover in what follows that discussions about Europe are the most prominent in moments or periods of crisis (also see Krzyżanowski, Triandafyllidou, & Wodak, 2009), when established positions are called into question and possible alternatives suggested. Moving backwards, so-to-speak, from an anticipation of our findings to our premises, all our contributions, their different and mutually complementary methodological and theoretical trajectories notwithstanding, share important ontological and epistemological ground: the conviction that linguistic and semiotic realms — what we say, write, read and hear as well as how it gets said and communicated — play a crucial role in the reproduction or transformation of existing social and political relations (e.g. Reisigl & Wodak, 2001); and that illuminating these interfaces of the discursive with the political requires the kinds of approaches outlined and utilised in the following chapters.

This book is the outcome of intellectual debate, exchange and refinement that has preoccupied its editors and contributors for more than 2 years, having started with a conference organised at the University of Warsaw in May 2014 and dedicated to examining questions of *doing and undoing Europe* from the inter-disciplinary perspectives of political linguistics.[1] This volume contains a selection of the theoretically most sophisticated and empirically most thorough papers first presented in Warsaw and subsequently refined by their authors. What is more, we have made sure to select contributions that, taken together, stretch across as much geographical space and as diverse a set of historical and contemporary experiences as possible. Consequently, the chapters that follow cover, collectively, large parts of Western, Central and Eastern Europe, the continent's North as well as its Mediterranean South. To state and repeat the obvious: historical memories, and their perceived relevance today, as well as perceptions and experiences of current crises inevitably differ enormously both within and across the different national contexts examined by our contributors. Before turning to our individual chapters and their examinations of the different kinds of political work performed by multiple discursive engagements with 'Europe' currently evident across the continent, important preliminary ground needs to be covered. We thus proceed with outlines of the empirical circumstances, out of which this volume emerges and which it in turn seeks to illuminate, and the conceptual foundations, on which we build and which we hope to further refine.

1. SETTING THE SCENE

The European project, under which we here subsume the EU and its now long-standing attempts to work towards greater integration of its currently 28 (but soon, following a now materialising Brexit, 27) constitutive member states, is on the brink. The centrifugal forces currently threatening to unravel this historically unique political project that has ensured peace, economic and political collaboration between nation states − whose inter-relations had historically been defined by warfare, intense competition, border disputes, mutual distrust and dislike − are varied and many.

When we first commenced the editorial work for this collection of essays in July 2015, the long-standing 'Greek debt crisis', which in actual fact is a much-deeper and wider crisis reflecting the incompleteness of the political structures of the common currency used by the 19 members of the 'Eurozone', was at the forefront of public debate and concern across and beyond the continent. More accurately, the spectre of a possible 'Grexit', or Greece's exit from the common currency, had haunted Europeans for several years. More than a year later, such a scenario continues to be a distinct possibility, even if the previous peak of the difficulties faced by ordinary Greeks who were having to live with capital controls on top of Europe's highest unemployment figures, tough austerity, and a chronically stagnating economy, has arguably, if only temporarily, been displaced by other epicentres of crises. And if a 'Grexit' was to materialise, this would undoubtedly do great damage to both the Eurozone's and, more widely, the EU's credibility vis-à-vis the markets, European citizens and the world at large. This is not to even mention the spectre of Italy opting out of the Eurozone, which following the rejection of Matteo Renzi's proposed constitutional reform in December 2016 is no longer considered to lie outside the realm of possibility. Even without any of these worst-case scenarios, recent events within the Eurozone and the EU more widely have revealed new − or arguably merely revived − chasms, power dynamics and inequalities between its member states that provide ample reason for grave concern that the European project could be undone from within. As we conclude our work on this edited collection at the end of 2016, Europeans are awaiting at least three major elections in the year ahead, in the Netherlands, France and Germany, each of which with considerable potential to further exacerbate the crises jeopardising (further) European integration.

Meanwhile, the United Kingdom's referendum in June 2016 determined that long-standing and over recent years growing British opposition to EU membership will in due course culminate in a 'Brexit', whether a 'hard' or 'soft' version thereof is yet to be seen, taking one of Europe's largest economies outside of the EU and casting further doubt on whether, or how enduringly, the continent's historical wounds have indeed healed and if the majority of European citizens and politicians can, or are willing to, look beyond national frames and institutions. Concurrently, the appeal and success of populist, often unapologetically neo-nationalist, EU-sceptical or explicitly EU-phobic parties have also increased elsewhere, and often dramatically, over recent years, as evidenced particularly by the most recent elections to the European Parliament in May 2014. All along, on the other side of but very close to the EU's current boundaries, and at least in the Ukrainian case very much on what is widely considered to be European territory, human lives are lost in a number of armed conflicts on a near-daily basis.

Nor do Europe's profound and deep contemporary challenges and problems stop there: since 2015, a dramatic increase in the number of asylum-seekers crossing the Mediterranean has pushed several receiving countries to or beyond their infrastructural capabilities, while not many of their often larger, richer, northern European 'partners' show a definitive commitment to sharing the practical and ethical responsibility of handling this humanitarian crisis. On the contrary, and to repeat what readers will remember well, the much-discussed 'refugee crisis' since 2015 has also led to the re-building, renewed patrolling and closure of fences and borders on the European continent, which the historical shifts and institutional developments of the previous two decades had (at least partly) dismantled. Moreover, in the post-9/11 era a succession of vicious terrorist attacks has cost hundreds of lives across a number of European countries. These most violent and tragic episodes in Europe's recent history have also caused as yet hard-to-estimate damage to inter-religious relations and are commonly interpreted — by politicians, journalists and other opinion-makers, as well as growing numbers of so-called 'ordinary European citizens' — as purported signs that Europe's ethnic and religious pluralism constitutes a problem rather than an asset. This, in turn, not only leaves the continent's recent histories of migration, its various multicultural policies and their often exclusionary logics and effects (e.g. Baumann, 1999; Castles, 2000) unscrutinised, it also stands in the way of Europe discovering and sharpening its arguably historically demanded mission: to institutionalise and represent collective responsibility and respect for the rights the dignity of 'the other' (Bauman, 2004), the subaltern, whose oppression European societies have historically enabled and benefited from, and critical opposition to which is at the same time demanded by the legacy and moral imperatives of the Enlightenment.

Arguably, the list of profound, systemic crises currently shaking Europe is longer still. One, for instance, may wish to add current demographic shifts, commonly described as the ageing of populations, and consider the difficult questions those shifts pose about the long-term sustainability of welfare systems and social contracts, from which three generations in at least (Western) Europe's more affluent nation states have benefitted. Further, environmental degradation and climate change are, in Europe as elsewhere, providing ample reason for serious concern and immediate action. Added to all this is a subtle, though undeniable state of collective nostalgia afflicting significant proportions of Europe's populations, which sense or fear that the continent is increasingly struggling to compete on what are now irrevocably global markets, where production costs are always and inevitably lower elsewhere (e.g. Beck, 2000), leading to local, national or ultimately continental losses of industry and all it provides, while post-industrial, service-driven economies never seem to 'catch' all those now finding themselves 'surplus to requirements' (Bauman, 2005). In the context of these multiple and mounting crises, one also discerns a re-opening and retrenchment of 'older' ideological chasms, as neoliberal and neo-Keynesianist positions clash in the struggle for what may come to constitute a new (or old) economic orthodoxy for the twenty-first century, and as social inequalities — both continentally and globally — reach levels not known for much of the last 70 years (e.g. Piketty, 2014). With political power now also exercised transnationally, and the EU the quintessential 'network state' trying to come to terms with the multiple challenges of contemporary globalisation (Castells, 2000), such economic struggles do not always map onto the classical political spectrum and ideological categories quite as straightforwardly as one may predict; thus, for example, political science research (Halikiopoulou, Nanou, & Vasilopoulou, 2012) has demonstrated that the European project is currently called into question both by the far left and the far right, though for the contrasting ideological reasons of class solidarity and ethnic nationalism respectively, with only parties near the centre of the classical political spectrum showing a relatively reliable and consistent commitment to the EU and its integrative efforts.

Such and similar contemporary crises could be further multiplied at will. This book casts light on how such shifts, challenges (and political responses to them) that presently threaten — or are perceived to threaten — life-worlds, identities, institutional structures and present- or future life chances, manifest across a range of national contexts and, both within and across them, in a range of pertinent discursive domains. This calls for an outline of the conceptual backdrop to our individual analyses.

2. CRISIS TALK

Crises have long been recognised for their politicising effects. In one of his earliest and most seminal contributions to social theory, Pierre Bourdieu (1977, pp. 168−169) discusses the effects of 'objective crisis' on people's cultural common-sense (i.e. shared dispositions, cognitive categories, practices and ways of living), or the 'universe of the undiscussed', which Bourdieu subsumes under his central concepts of the *habitus* and *doxa* respectively. It is in moments of crisis, Bourdieu postulates, that a previously taken-for-granted cultural universe undergoes a profound transformation: everything formerly seen as self-evidently true and hence merely backdrop to the ordinary course of events is suddenly called into question and debated; *doxa* thereby turns into a 'universe of opinion[s]', a domain of competing political positions. While describing the consciousness-raising effects of profound social change, Bourdieu's model is underpinned by his acute − and characteristic − awareness of the impact of power, inequality and hierarchy on social actors' thought and behaviour. Or in Bourdieu's own words (1977, p. 169), while 'crisis is a necessary condition for the questioning of doxa ... the dominated classes have an interest in ... exposing the arbitrariness of the taken for granted; the dominant classes have an interest in defending the integrity of doxa'.

Existing literature has employed Bourdieu's argument to cast light on the politicising effects of, for instance, migratory experiences or on perceptions of crises affecting cherished symbols of national identity (e.g. Karner, 2005, 2007; Vertovec, 2000). The present volume also connects with this conceptual strand, by illuminating the contrasting politics − and their competing discursive uses of the category 'Europe' − formulated in contexts of, and often polarised responses to, various crises. That said, we also here extend Bourdieu's relatively narrow crisis definition. While very significant parts of Europe are currently undergoing their most severe, systemic crises for generations, which by any definition clearly qualify as 'objective crises', other parts of Europe continue to enjoy what are by global standards remarkable levels of affluence and security. However, as we also discover in some of our later chapters, a *perceived sense of crises* perfectly suffices to trigger similar processes of collective soul-searching, debate, disagreement and political antagonism. Indeed, in some of the more prosperous European contexts examined below the mere perceived contrast with a nostalgically (mis)constructed recent past, purportedly before the onset of social decline bemoaned in the here and now, gives rise not only to nationalist identity politics, but also to alternative ideological reactions in increasingly contested discursive fields. The centrality of objective/ structural or perceived crises to contemporary social life also provides a plausible explanation for the rise of neo-nationalisms (e.g. Gingrich & Banks, 2006; McCrone, 1998) witnessed over the last 20 years. After all, nationalist historiography (e.g. Hutchinson, 1987) − with its distinctive discursive structure juxtaposing an alleged 'golden age' located in the past to a present found to be deeply unjust or unsatisfactory, and to a future premised on a nation-focused revival and return to purported 'order' − often prove themselves to be widely appealing interpretative and political reactions to crisis-stricken contexts. In the settings examined by our respective contributors, this raises the crucial question as to how nationalist responses to crises react to the idea and structures of 'Europe'. To repeat our earlier point, however, the following analyses also corroborate Bourdieu's observation that the political responses to crises are seldom, if ever, uniform; instead, crises give rise to internally heterogeneous and strongly contested discursive realms. In our specific cases, we thus ask *how Europe is being discursively both done and undone* under the particular historical circumstances and in the particular political fields being examined.

Rather than offering an extensive literature review of the large, multi-disciplinary and steadily growing bodies of scholarship examining current forms of pro- and anti-European politics, a task that is best left to our contributors and their nationally focused discussions, there are two competing, existing hypotheses that also form a crucial part of the theoretical backdrop to this book and therefore need to be summarised in this introduction. The first hypothesis, as, for example, formulated by Montserrat Guibernau (2007, pp. 112–118) even before the financial crisis of 2008 and its serious fallout on Europeans and their identifications, postulates that at present the EU can, at best, offer instrumental, 'embryonic', 'non-emotional' identities that are secondary to more immediate and much stronger national identifications; consequently, Guibernau articulates serious doubt if such weak European identifications could withstand a serious economic crisis. Arguably, these were prophetic fears that anticipated precisely the discursive 're-nationalisation' (e.g. Hartleb, 2012) witnessed over recent, indeed crisis-stricken years.

The alternative hypothesis was, interestingly, first explicitly formulated after the effects of the financial crises on Europe in general, and the Eurozone more particularly had already become apparent. In an extension of Michael Billig's (1995) seminal notion of 'banal nationalism' – describing the countless daily, largely unnoticed semiotic and discursive ways of performing and thus reproducing national identities – Laura Cram (2009) observes forms of 'banal Europeanism': national and European identifications, she postulates, are not mutually exclusive, but increasingly sit alongside one another, in mutually complementary rather than contradictory fashion, in many Europeans' life-worlds; Cram refers to the waving of European flags, passports and driving licences, where the EU appears alongside national ascriptions, as indications of such a banal Europeanism. As we discover in some of our contributions, these are indeed some, though not the only ways of *doing Europe* in our era of multiple crises.

All along, there is of course – as we discover throughout this book – ample evidence of the corrosive political tendencies that invest much of their discursive energy in *undoing Europe*. To reiterate our empirical and conceptual focus, however, our collective attention here rests on the *competing politics* vis-à-vis Europe and other scales and categories of identification that are currently (re-)shaping a variety of local, national and transnational contexts. In exploring such contexts, we further build on seminal work examining Europe's experiences of the interfaces of crises, ethics and political struggles:

> [M]oments/ events of crisis are crucial for the ethically based negotiation of Europe and/or the nation(-state). It is within these crises that values are sometimes violated (e.g. values of freedom, or human rights) while different actors also use those crises to express (in/ through the media) their defence of other values (e.g. democracy, social justice or peace) with a view to legitimizing their ideas about the existing social, political and economic order … It is within those crises, understood here as disruptive moments of history, that sensitive perceptions of different common objects of reference (e.g. 'Europe', 'nation-state' and relations between them) become particularly salient and vibrant, and open for a context-dependent (re-)negotiation and (re-)appropriation. (Krzyżanowski et al., 2009, p. 6, original italics)

Krzyżanowski, Triandafyllidou and Wodak also provide vital methodological impetus for the present volume, in alerting us to the centrality − in moments of crisis and ethical/ political debate − of discursive negotiations taking place within 'European public spheres' and, yet more particularly, within the media. As we discover in the ensuing chapters, these are precisely some of the key domains, within which our contributors locate today's defining political battles.

Before providing a somewhat more explicit anticipation of our book's constitutive chapters, a little more definitional groundwork is needed. Given that 'crisis talk' is central to our concerns, more needs to be said about what the broad category of 'talk' is here taken to include and what its wider significance is.

3. IDEOLOGY AND LANGUAGE

The notion of discourse, central to our entire analytical endeavour, has already informed our introductory elaborations on contemporary Europe's multiple crises and, conceptually, on the consciousness-raising effects of crisis and the political negotiations they give rise to. By way of a working definition, we here follow Bo Stråth and Ruth Wodak critical discourse analytical (CDA) understanding of discourse as 'social practice', recognising that 'speaking and writing always represent, produce and reproduce attitudes, beliefs, opinions and ideologies' (2009, p. 28). Our contributors approach their respective contexts of investigations from a variety of (often mutually complementary) methodological and theoretical perspectives. Each chapter provides an outline of the methods and theoretical premises underpinning it, which therefore require no separate outline here. However, and such conceptual and methodological diversity notwithstanding, our contributors also share more implicit ontological and epistemological common ground. The latter does warrant further preliminary commentary.

Concepts of ideology and discourse lie at the heart of much scholarship in each of the intellectual (sub)disciplines represented in this volume, including (political) linguistics, sociology, cultural studies, anthropology, history and political science. In each of these scholarly settings, and arguably even more so in an inter-disciplinary project such as ours, 'ideology' and 'discourse' need to be approached with definitional clarity, particularly since both terms are of course also part of everyday language and political rhetoric, where they are often left undefined, invoked vaguely, yet put to a range of subtle though important argumentative purposes. To avoid complicity in such un-reflected rhetorical trickery, let us turn to ideology first. Its use in the present volume is that proposed by Martha Augoustinos (1998) who defines as 'ideological' all language and (other) social practices that contribute to the *reproduction or contestation of existing relations of power*. We ought to note that, thus defined, the concept avoids pronouncing on the veracity or otherwise of what people say and do; ideology, in this definition, can be either dominant or resistant, either way it is understood as words or actions that are socially situated and politically consequential.

Discourse, though overwhelmingly tied to language (as we see below), has also been conceptualised somewhat more broadly, as going beyond the merely linguistic. Thus, for example, Rom Harré (1998, p. 132) defines 'discursive activity [as] the work we severally or jointly engage in when we make use of a common system of signs for the accomplishment of some task or project'. This is evidently relevant to some of the images or ethnographic observations that some of our later chapters examine alongside more typical 'language-based' data.

The central ontological terrain occupied by this volume is arguably most accurately delineated by the aforementioned approach of critical discourse analysis. Condensing an internally varied, complex and continually expanding body of work to its conceptual core-assumptions, CDA defines all discourse, that is, written and spoken language of any form and in any register, as forms of 'social practice' (e.g. Fairclough, 1989; Weiss & Wodak, 2003) that emerge from, and hence need to be understood in relation to wider social and political contexts, which discourse in turn feeds back into either as a contribution to structural reproduction or as a force of ideological resistance. Put differently, discourse is both shaped by and in turn (potentially re-)shapes its wider contexts (e.g. Chouliaraki & Fairclough, 1999; Weiss & Wodak, 2003). All language therefore needs to be understood in relation to the institutional surroundings that give rise to it, as well as in relation to the social effects language in turn has. While CDA has born particularly impressive fruit in illuminating the discursive 'construction, perpetuation or justification, transformation … or dismantling' of national identities (Wodak, de Cillia, Reisigl, & Liebhart, 1999, p. 33), we here examine similar processes of reasserting, negotiating or at times refusing various identifications on several geographical scales simultaneously, most centrally in relation to 'the nation' and 'Europe' respectively. What is more, collectively we here trace such discourses in different national contexts both within and outside the current and regularly shifting external boundaries of the EU, across a wide range of social and cultural domains, and as they are articulated by a diversity of (structurally and ideologically differently positioned) social and political actors.

We consider it to be one of this volume's other great assets that, taken in its entirety, it offers and utilises a range of approaches to understanding language in context. Yet, CDA, in particular, helpfully points towards our shared epistemological core: that is, our underlying assumption that in paying close analytical attention to the contexts, meanings and workings of written and spoken language and other sign systems, one can help to cast light on wider political processes of institutional reproduction and transformation and on the implicated self-identifications and boundary negotiations.

Thus, we turn to a very brief anticipatory outline of the chapters to follow. As already mentioned, this volume stretches across considerable geographical distances and displays formidable and productive methodological flexibility and diversity. Fittingly, we thus start with an analysis by Franco Zappettini of some transnational, indeed 'trans-European' discourses. Most of our subsequent contributions, however, focus on particular and current member states of the EU, including Austria, France, Germany, Greece, Portugal and Poland. At the same time, we also — in and through Muhic's chapter on Macedonia — examine a national context that currently lies politically outside the EU, yet, for example, in relation to the refugee crisis shares a central European challenge of our time. The migrant crisis itself, along with its media representation and the implications it has had for perceptions of European solidarity and security, is taken under scrutiny too in Kopytowska and Grabowski's study. What is more, our collection also includes two chapters with different British foci, examining UK responses to Bulgarian and Romanian migrants and to the Lisbon Treaty respectively, which help interpret the political and discursive developments that had paved the way towards the Brexit decision in June 2016. In other words, this volume also makes considerable space for analyses of a national context where the discursive processes of *undoing* EU membership have progressed the furthest.

While we are here empirically focused on Europe in some of its historical and geographical diversities, the theoretical implications of the present volume go much further, for we illustrate and analyse how political institutions and social relations are continually being done, re-done and — particularly in periods of crisis — partly undone. Moreover, we pay particular attention to the roles played by linguistic and other semiotic practices in such crucial, albeit widely taken-for-granted processes of ongoing social reproduction and (occasional) transformation. In empirical terms, our selection of chapters has had to be precisely that — a selection that reflects the process and its particular participants, as well as their respective areas of expertise, that have given shape to our international and inter-disciplinary project. It is stating the obvious that numerous other contexts not addressed here, that is, other local, national and transnational settings, are equally pertinent to the questions explored in what follows.

While we can obviously make no claims to exhausting these questions in their timeliness and full geographical spread and relevance, we very much hope to help pave the way towards future work on some of the most pressing issues confronting our continent and its shifting political structures in the early twenty-first century.

NOTE

1. Professor Anna Duszak was the driving force behind the conference organised in Warsaw in 2014 and behind the early editorial work for this edited collection resulting from it. Sadly, Professor Duszak passed away in December 2015. Her imagination, organisation and kindness are greatly missed. Without her, this book would never have seen the light of day. It is to her memory that this volume is dedicated. The editors hope that the present work will also reflect and do justice to Anna's lasting legacy within political linguistics.

REFERENCES

Augoustinos, M. (1998). Social representations and ideology. In U. Flick (Ed.), *The psychology of the social* (pp. 156–169). Cambridge: Cambridge University Press.

Bauman, Z. (2004). *Europe*. Cambridge: Polity Press.

Bauman, Z. (2005). *Work, consumerism and the new poor*. Maidenhead: Open University Press.

Baumann, G. (1999). *The multicultural riddle*. New York, NY: Routledge.

Beck, U. (2000). *What is globalization?* Cambridge: Polity Press.

Billig, M. (1995). *Banal nationalism*. London: Sage.

Bourdieu, P. (1977). *Outline of a theory of practice*. Cambridge: Cambridge University Press.

Castells, M. (2000). *End of millennium*. Oxford: Blackwell.

Castles, S. (2000). *Ethnicity and globalization*. London: Sage.

Chouliaraki, L., & Fairclough, N. (1999). *Discourse in late modernity*. Edinburgh: Edinburgh University Press.

Cram, L. (2009). Introduction. *Nations and Nationalism, 15*(1), 101–108.

Fairclough, N. (1989). *Language and power*. London: Longman.

Gingrich, A., & Banks, M. (2006). *Neo-nationalism in Europe and beyond*. New York, NY: Berghahn.

Guibernau, M. (2007). *The identity of nations*. Cambridge: Polity Press.

Halikiopoulou, D., Nanou, K., & Vasilopoulou, S. (2012). The paradox of nationalism: the common denominator of radical right and radical left Euroscepticism. *European Journal of Political Research, 51*, 504–539.

Harré, R. (1998). The epistemology of social representations. In U. Flick (Ed.), *The psychology of the social* (pp. 129–137). Cambridge: Cambridge University Press.

Hartleb, F. (2012). European project in danger? Understanding precisely the phenomena 'Euroscepticism, Populism and Extremism' in times of crisis. *Review of European Studies, 4*(5), 45–63.

Hutchinson, J. (1987). *The dynamics of cultural nationalism*. London: Allen and Unwin.

Jenkins, R. (2008). The ambiguity of Europe. *European Societies, 10*(2), 153–176.

Karner, C. (2005). National doxa, crises and ideological contestation in contemporary Austria. *Nationalism and Ethnic Politics, 11*(2), 221–263.

Karner, C. (2007). *Ethnicity and everyday life*. New York, NY: Routledge.

Krzyżanowski, M., Triandafyllidou, A., & Wodak, R. (2009). Introduction. In A. Triandafyllidou, R. Wodak, & M. Krzyżanowski (Eds.), *The European public sphere and the media: Europe in crisis* (pp. 1–12). Basingstoke: Palgrave.

Levine, E. (2015). Just what makes a 'good European'? Retrieved from http://foreignpolicy.com/2015/07/08/just-what-makes-a-good-european-greece-germany-eurozone/. Accessed 15 July 2015.

Maltezou, R., & Ponthus, J. (2015). Tsipras denounces 'blackmail'; EU warns of 'game over'. Retrieved from http://www.cnbc.com/2015/06/26/reuters-america-wrapup-2-tsipras-denounces-blackmail-eu-warns-of-game-over.html. Accessed 15 July 2015.

McCrone, D. (1998). *The sociology of nationalism*. New York, NY: Routledge.

Piketty, T. (2014). *Capital in the twenty-first century*. Cambridge, MA: Belknap/Harvard.

Reisigl, M., & Wodak, R. (2001). *Discourse and discrimination*. London: Routledge.

Stråth, B., & Wodak, R. (2009). Europe-discourse-politics-media-history: Constructing 'crises'? In A. Triandafyllidou, R. Wodak, & M. Krzyżanowski (Eds.), *The European public sphere and the media: Europe in crisis* (pp. 15–33). Basingstoke: Palgrave.

Straubhaar, T. (2015). Man darf Tsipras nicht ein zweites Mal unterschätzen. Retrieved from http://www.welt.de/wirtschaft/article143662668/Man-darf-Tsipras-nicht-ein-zweites-Mal-unterschaetzen.html. Accessed 7 July 2015.

Vertovec, S. (2000). *The Hindu diaspora*. London: Routledge.

Weiss, G., & Wodak, R. (2003). Introduction. In G. Weiss & R. Wodak (Eds.), *Critical discourse analysis* (pp. 1–31). Basingstoke: Palgrave.

Wodak, R., de Cillia, R., Reisigl, M., & Liebhart, K. (1999). *The discursive construction of national identity*. Edinburgh: Edinburgh University Press.

TRANSNATIONALISM AS AN INDEX TO CONSTRUCT EUROPEAN IDENTITIES: AN ANALYSIS OF 'TRANSEUROPEAN' DISCOURSES

Franco Zappettini

ABSTRACT

Transnationalism is a multi-faceted phenomenon which has impacted on society and challenged, inter alia, the paradigm of national affiliations. The transnationalisation of the European field has arguably contributed to a political arena where embryonic post-national identities and new forms of belonging are being negotiated, challenged and legitimised. By investigating the discourses of members of a transnational NGO of 'active' citizens, this chapter seeks to understand how current European identities are discursively constructed from bottom up in the public sphere. Appropriating CDA, this chapter offers insights into how discursive strategies and linguistic devices used by the speakers and predicated on the indexicality of transnational frames, construct Europe and patterns of belonging to it. This chapter suggests different conceptual dimensions of transnationalism enacted by members in discourse which are conveniently summarised as nation-centric, Euro-centric and cosmopolitan.

Keywords: Discursive construction of European identities; transnationalism; citizens' initiative; indexicality; European public sphere; critical discourse analysis

National Identity and Europe in Times of Crisis: Doing and Undoing Europe, 13–35
doi:10.1108/978-1-78714-513-920171002

1. INTRODUCTION

In the last two decades the growing complexity, diversification and context-dependency of European identities has been the focus of much academic interest in a number of disciplines including politics, sociology, psychology, philosophy, linguistics, critical and cultural studies (cf. for example Balibar, 2004; Cerutti & Lucarelli, 2008; Checkel & Katzenstein, 2009; DeBardeleben & Achim, 2011; Delanty & Rumford, 2005; Eder, 2009; Fligstein, 2008; Friedman & Thiel, 2012; Herrmann, Risse-Kappen, & Brewer, 2004; Krzyżanowski, 2010; Mole, 2007; Morin & Carta, 2014; Oberhuber, 2007; Stråth, 2010; Wodak & Weiss, 2005; Wodak, 2004). Although such body of literature has provided significant insights on the many fluid transformations of Europe (anness), very few studies have illuminated how European identities are being negotiated and transformed among social actors vis-à-vis global changes and increasingly transnationalised societies which 'make obsolete conventional understandings of identity formation and its processes' (Haller & Landolt, 2005, p. 1183).

The general aim of this chapter is thus to contribute to an interdisciplinary and transnational approach to the gamut of European identities emerging and transforming in late modernity. By focusing on the discourses of a transnational association of 'active' citizens, this chapter strives to illuminate a specific locus of negotiation of Europeanness where social imaginaries of Europe interplay with wider transnational discourses. Furthermore, this chapter aims to provide qualitative insights on the construction of Europeanness from a bottom-up/grassroots perspective subscribing to Kraus' view (2006, p. 205) that 'a common European identity cannot simply be created "from above"' and taking up Krzyżanowski's (2010, p. 201) call for research to 'turn to social action as the main force driving the dynamics of contemporary identities'.

The chapter is structured as follows. First, it argues the case for exploring (European) identities from a transnational perspective in the wake of processes of late modernity. It then provides some background on the organisation investigated and the methodology used. Second, it outlines a theoretical framework for the examination of European discourses that takes into account indexicality as an entry point for the interpretation of different 'social imaginaries' of Europe and/in the world. Third, the chapter engages with a Critical Discourse Analysis of the data, focusing on the illustrations of some linguistic realisations and suggesting their indexical valence in the construction of members' Europeanness. It then introduces a taxonomy of European imaginaries constructed by members around different 'deictic centres'. This chapter will finally conclude with some considerations on the relevance of findings.

2. A TRANSNATIONAL[1] APPROACH TO IDENTITIES

Identity has been a major topic of investigation and debate in social sciences especially in the last few decades. Whilst social psychology has substantially conceptualised identity as a salient link between the individual and a social group (Jenkins, 2004; Tajfel & Turner, 1979) or an 'imagined community' (Anderson, 2006), social constructivism has underscored how identities should be accounted for as dynamic, multiple and fluid constructs that emerge, inter alia, from discursive negotiation rather than existing in reified forms (see for example Hall, 1996a, 1996b, 1997). For most critical linguists, therefore, discourses of identity must be seen as dialogically related with and mutually constitutive of social structures and their transformation (Fairclough & Wodak, 1997). Whilst nation-states have represented a major source of identification in the last three centuries (Hobsbawm, 1997) and, in some cases, they can still provide powerful identity anchors (Wodak, 2012), national affiliations should no longer be taken for granted as stable identitarian parameters in late modernity. Beck, Giddens, and Lash (1994) define late modernity as a socio-historical context characterised, inter alia, by processes of globalisation, the expansion of networks, the decline of grand narratives and the emergence of post-national powers – including the EU – that have profoundly impacted on how individuals conceive the organisation of social orders and political communities (cf. also Castells, 1997; Habermas, 2001; Held, 1999; Lyotard & Benjamin, 1989). In this vein, Beck (1996) has drawn attention to the emergence of a global or cosmopolitan reflexivity in modern polities contending that there is 'a new dialectic of global and local questions which do not fit into national politics' (p. 29) and which can only be 'properly posed, debated and resolved' (*ibid*) in a transnational framework which increasingly involves non-state actors.

In many cases, the de-territorialisation of cultural practices has allowed for new forms/opportunities of membership, social solidarity and civic participation to emerge across unbounded 'habitats of meaning' (Hannerz, 1996) which must take into account influences and variables brought about by multiple cultural and social contexts of 'translocality' and 'glocal' practices (Appadurai, 1995). For example, much literature has noted how *transnational social fields*[2] have redefined traditional referents of groupness (such as citizenship, ethnicity and language), established political actors (such as national institutions) and their roles in the imagination of civic and cultural communities and their solidarity ties (see for example Albert, Jacobson, & Lapid, 2001; Bauböck & Faist, 2010; Blommaert, 2013; Kastoryano, 2002; Sassen, 1996).

Hence, in investigating (European) identities in 'late modernity' this chapter recognises the need to move away from 'methodological nationalism' (Wimmer & Schiller Glick, 2002) and it aligns itself with a transnational perspective that makes sense of social interaction beyond the 'container theory of society' (Beck, 2008). At the same time, transnational dynamics cannot be

assumed as a linear process that will eventually lead to the formation of a unified world identity (Rumford, 2008; Shani, 2011). In fact the complexity of
transnationalism lies in the interplay of global and local forces resulting in
diversified 'glocal' instantiations of identity (Robertson, 1992). To adequately
capture the complexity of such dynamics Levitt and Glick Schiller (2004,
p. 1010) argue for the adoption of 'a transnational social field approach to the
study of social life that distinguishes between the existence of transnational
social networks and the consciousness of being embedded in them'. Levitt and
Glick Schiller suggest that it is possible for individuals in transnational fields to
engage in a simultaneity of connections spanning from routines and daily activities, to the production of (cultural) identities that reflect their multiple locations. From this perspective Levitt and Glick Schiller, define 'ways of being' in
social fields as opposed to 'ways of belonging' referring to the former as

> *the actual social relations and practices that individuals engage in rather than to the identities*
> *associated with their actions*

and to the latter as

> practices that signal or enact an identity which demonstrates a conscious connection to a
> particular group [...] and an awareness of the kind of identity that action signifies. (Levitt &
> Glick Schiller, 2004, p. 1010)

Whilst for Levitt and Glick Schiller local and transnational connections can
occur simultaneously, ways of being and ways of belonging are often dependant
on the specific context upon which they are enacted and therefore they suggest
that whilst individuals embedded in a social field have the potential to identify
with any label associated with that field not all choose to do so.

2.1. Europe as a Transnational Social Field and the European Public Sphere

Europe (inclusive of its geographical, social, political and economic aspects)
represents a transnational field of its own where processes of transnationalisation have been significantly compounded by the post-national integration project started by the EU institutions. Such project has manifested itself at many
different levels, for example in supranational forms of governance and the free
circulation of goods, capital, services, and people within Member States.
Moreover, as well as the site of incoming diaspora and exogenous migration
patterns, Europe has become to represent a site of 'desirable' internal mobility
for many EU citizens.[3] Whilst these practices have not necessarily resulted in a
full post-national 'consciousness' at mass level, they have nonetheless contributed to a stratified society where transnational elements have filtered down to
citizens differently (Hanquinet & Savage, 2013). Moreover, whilst patterns of
economic and political convergence have increased, the 'European field' has
also amplified the antimonies between the 'global' and the 'local', the 'universal'

and the 'particular' dimensions of the EU project (Wodak & Weiss, 2005). These tensions are often reflected in multifarious, fragmented, and 'in-between' forms of European identifications which, as most recent 'snapshots' have highlighted, are emerging between agentive, structural, individual, and collective dimensions (Biebuyck & Rumford, 2011; Checkel & Katzenstein, 2009; Krzyżanowski, 2010; McEntee-Atalianis & Zappettini, 2014).

Following on Delanty's (2013, p. 265) suggestion that European identity 'is best evidenced in specific sites of communication [such as] debates about Europe' (p. 265) this chapter regard the European public sphere (EPS) as one significant locus of investigation for the emergence and negotiation of 'new' transnational European identities. Put succinctly, the public sphere is 'a network for communicating information and points of view' (Habermas, 1998, p. 360), to discuss and deliberate on public issues which, in modern and deliberative democracies, is seen as a forum for civic participation and the formation of public opinion (Wodak & Koller, 2008). Habermas sees the EPS as a transnational site of participation in the democratic debate on European issues which must exist for a European civic identity to emerge and for the European project to be fully legitimised. Although there is little consensus as to whether (and to which extent) the EPS exist in transnational forms (see, inter alia, Closa, 2001; Eriksen & Fossum, 2001; Risse, 2010; Salvatore, Schmidtke, & Trenz, 2013; Splichal, 2006; Triandafyllidou, Wodak, & Krzyżanowski, 2009) an increasing number of European social actors – such as non-governmental organisations (NGOs) and (in)formal networks – have emerged in recent years which are focused on transnational clusters of interests (Della Porta & Tarrow, 2005; Kaiser, Leucht, & Gehler, 2010). It is to one of such organisations, called European Alternatives (EA),[4] that this chapter now turns to investigate how its members make sense of their Europeanness in relation to transnational practices and their imagination of community.

3. FOCUS: BACKGROUND AND DATA

EA, which characterises itself as a transnational association of citizens, has been campaigning since 2007[5] to influence European policies beyond national remits and it is part of a larger umbrella of organisations of the civil society.[6] The organisation has, to date, 19 local offices across Europe and is run on a voluntary basis by ordinary citizens[7] who share an ideological commitment to the grassroots development of a 'more just and open' social Europe. Transnational meetings are held on a rotational basis and activities are run simultaneously across branches. Typical activities consist of (on and offline) campaigns, cultural events, seminars, debates, and proposals to the EU organs with recent activities including a citizens' manifesto and several proposals under the Citizens' initiative programme.[8] The salience of investigating EA lies therefore in the NGO's cross-border set up and, most of all, in its advocacy for framing the debate over European issues within the construction of a transnational (civic) community. Taking *indexicality* (see Section 4) as an 'entry point' for the investigation of members' belonging to such an 'imagined community', the specific objective of this chapter is to identify how European identities are represented, constructed, and negotiated in the member's discourses and how the imagination of European and transnational affiliations interplay. The research questions are articulated as follows:

- Which frames do speakers construct and draw from in representing themselves as Europeans?
- How is transnationalism conceptualised in the discourses of members?
- What is the role of nationhood in members' constructions of Europeanness?

Data were collected via four focus groups and nine individual interviews conducted with EA's members in seven locations across Europe between 2010 and 2013 (see Appendices A and B for details). The focus groups were moderated and attended by 17 participants in total. All interviews were conducted in English, except the focus group in Bologna (Italy) and Cluj (Romania) which were conducted in Italian and Romanian respectively and the interview with BE2 which was conducted in Italian.[9] All participants represent a self-selecting sample of members who responded to an initial call sent via each branch's gatekeepers. Due to mixed national make-up of each local group [10] and the transnational approach to the design of this study, certain variables of participants (i.e. their nationality, residency and patterns of mobility) were not controlled. However, participants were profiled for these and other socio demographics through a questionnaire distributed at the end of each interview (see table 1 for a summary of results). Group and individual discussions were initiated with open questions derived from the literature review on transnationalism and from familiarisation with the organisational literature (e.g. newsletters, website and Facebook pages). Examples of questions asked include: 'Do you consider yourself European?'; 'What does transnationalism mean to you?'; 'Can you describe Europe from a transnational perspective?'; 'What are your organisational/personal objectives as a member of EA?'. Furthermore, in some cases, members voluntarily initiated personal narratives through which they developed 'secondary' topics (Jones & Krzyżanowski, 2008) such as, for example, their own family history, experience abroad, and their engagement in other associations or with other interests.

4. ANALYTICAL FRAMEWORK

The analytical framework largely draws on Critical Discourse Analysis (CDA) that sees discourse and society as mutually constitutive (Fairclough & Wodak,

1997). For CDA, language does more than the mere communication of information, for in and through discourses we also construct social meanings. In CDA discourses therefore describe the world as much as they constitute 'situations, objects of knowledge, and the social identities of and relationships between people and groups of people' (Fairclough, Mulderrig, & Wodak, 1997, p. 358). From this perspective, the construction of identities can be seen as enacted in and through discursive acts in which social actors articulate one's 'situatedness' (Hall, 1997) by representing themselves and others. Trading on the dialogical nature of discourse, CDA sees linguistic resources used by speakers to construct their 'locations' encoding larger ideological stances on 'ways of being' in and 'ways of belonging' in the world. As Davies and Harré (2001, p. 262) argue: '[t]he words the speaker chooses inevitably contain images and metaphors which both assume and invoke the ways of being that the participants take themselves to be involved'.

In this sense, for example, linguistic realisations of national groupness can be achieved, inter alia, via metaphorical/metonymical inferences to 'family' and 'home', via the personification/agentification of nation as 'motherland/fatherland' and, furthermore, via the inclusiveness/exclusiveness of certain pronouns or possessive adjectives (e.g. *we/us/our*) (cf. Wodak, de Cillia, Reisigl, & Liebhart, 2009). At the same time, these ways of talking about nationhood can crystallise in socially shared frames which become available for one to draw upon to discursively reproduce her or his nationality (Billig, 1995).

With regard to the specific organisation examined in this study, McEntee-Atalianis and Zappettini (2014) have offered insights on members' metaphorical realisations suggesting how speakers often challenged established conceptualisations of nationhood. McEntee-Atalianis and Zappettini (2014) have suggested that members made sense of their Europeanness and their transnational activities through the metaphorical scenario of *spatial dynamics* and how such scenario represented a salient referent for members' sense of community especially in relation to entailments of *network* and *interconnectedness*. Building on the insights of this previous study, this chapter develops a further line of analysis which interprets the data through the lens of *indexicality* as explained in the next section below.

4.1. Indexicality

Indexicality refers to the property of certain elements of language (called *deixis*[11]) of 'pointing' to meanings like we would physically point our finger to objects (index is in fact the Latin word for finger). Deixis, more than other words, encode 'the relation between objects and contexts' (Hanks, 1999, p. 124) as they can only be interpreted in relation to specific referents or situations. In a narrow sense, pronouns such as *I* and *she*, demonstrative such as *this* and *that,* and adverbs such as *here* and *now* always exist in dual indexical forms (Kaplan, 1979) or, in other words, as 'types' with semantic meaning and 'tokens' with denotational meaning. Furthermore, in broader terms, indexicality can be interpreted as 'the pervasive context-dependency of natural language utterances' (Hanks, 1999, p. 124) and it can be realised in discourse through different means. Whilst for example a regional accent can index a speaker's identity (Johnstone, 2013), this can generate different orders of indexicalities (Silverstein, 2003) if an ideological evaluation is associated with a social connotation (i.e. if the regional accent is associated with a specific social practice which then becomes to be regarded as an index of 'authenticity'). Further realisations of indexicality can be achieved through specific perspectivisation of a message (Renkema, 2004), by means of labels, implicatures and epistemic orientations (Bucholtz & Hall, 2005) which can reveal the speaker's stance towards 'objects' (e.g. a topic, a person or a relationship).

Chilton (2004) highlights how positioning and indexical anchoring can be typically realised along temporal spatial, personal, and ideological dimensions. For Chilton through deictic expressions speakers can metaphorically construct a 'deictic centre' that defines their ontological orientation to the world and their relationship with society. Indexical anchoring and positioning vis-à-vis the 'deictic centre' can ultimately be interpreted as the speaker's representation of their social identity through time, space and personal relations, that is, their 'situatedness'. As noted earlier, the use of personal pronoun *we, us* and possessive adjective *our* can signal (dis)alignment with one particular group identity. At the same time, as they index inclusion/exclusion, personal deixis can point to a cognitive frame that encodes a 'conventional shared understandings about the structure of society, groups and relations with other societies' (Chilton, 2004, p. 56). Likewise, temporal deictic expressions such as 'after the fall of the Berlin Wall' can be understood in terms of a particular historical frame involving wider ideologies beyond the temporal event itself. Similar considerations apply to spatial representations where, for example, the adverb *here* and the demonstrative *this country* can symbolically embody a frame entertained by the speaker about geo-political relations rather than simply proximity.

Building on the theoretical framework outlined above, the analysis has been primarily concerned with: (a) identifying and interpreting indexical expressions that could point to different frames of transnationalism; and (b) developing insights on how such conceptualisations contributed to members' identification as European. Decoding the indexical 'value' of certain utterances and linguistic items was achieved via contextual cues and operationalised at different levels of context as proposed by Wodak (2009, p. 67) namely: (a) the immediate, language or text internal co-text; (b) the intertextual and interdiscursive relationship between utterances, texts, genres and discourses; (c) the extra-linguistic social/sociological variables and institutional frames of a specific 'context of situation'; and (d) the broader socio-political and historical contexts, within which the discursive practices are embedded'. For example, the analysis has interpreted the indexicality of *now* in expressions such as '*let's have a break now*', '*now, this is the issue!*' or '*it's difficult to get a job anywhere in Europe now*' on different contextual cues and it has consequently derived different insights into the temporal positioning of the speaker.

The next section will offer some examples of how different temporal, spatial, personal and ideological deixis were deployed by members in their discourses, focusing specifically on their indexical interplay with wider transnational discourses, as made relevant to this study in the two previous sections.

5. CONSTRUCTIONS OF EUROPEANNESS IN DISCOURSES OF TRANSNATIONALISM: USE OF TEMPORAL, SPATIAL, PERSONAL AND IDEOLOGICAL DEIXIS

The temporal dimension was conspicuous in the focus group conducted in Cluj, Romania where the topic of mobility introduced by the moderator gave some members the opportunity to place much emphasis on the 'freedom of movement' that Romanians can now enjoy following their country joining the EU in 2007 as exemplified by the following extract:

Extract 1

Moderator: [...] would you define yourselves as Europeans? and if you could tell me what this means to each one of you?

CL3: The right we have now, I don't know, well, I think, that we can travel more freely now, and somehow we were given more rights to do what we want, to do what we like [...] we took some distance from something that bound us, we are not bound anymore, it isn't hard to dream of something anymore, like it used to be, now you can learn more easily, as you can be with people more easily, you can interact with strangers more easily, it's more ... it's more ok than before.

In this case the speaker constructs his Europeanness through a discursive frame revolving around Romania's accession to the EU in 2007, a key date that defines the now and before in his discourse and allows him to juxtaposes his current status of European citizen[12] ('now') with what it used to be in the past ('before'). Significantly these temporal deixis point further to the historical frame of 'mobility in the Communist era'. Under the Communist regime (1947–1989) severe restrictions applied to Romanian citizens who wanted to travel abroad. Passports were held by the police and visas were subject to government approval. Furthermore, citizens who applied to emigrate had their civic and economic rights revoked and they were systematically disparaged by authorities. The relevance of being able to travel freely therefore must be interpreted in the light of such political and historical contingencies. From this perspective, the speaker sees his new status of European as an opportunity to overcome the constraints of the past communist regime that kept Romanians 'captive' in an ideological 'container' bounded by the 'iron curtain' and limiting their civic rights. Becoming a European citizen for CL3 therefore seems to index the imagination of his emancipation from slavery ('we are not bound anymore') and his validation as a free citizen. In this sense for CL3 Europe (embodied by its institutions) represents a new salient referent for renegotiating his civic affiliation away from national institutions whilst claiming his Europeanness as his membership in a community of relevance.

A different use of temporal deixis emerged from the interview with RO1 (Rome, individual interview) when the speaker constructed an argument for using English in transnational communication in Europe:

Extract 2

RO1: 'Well, I think that my dream, my vision is that Europe be united politically and for this to happen […] we need to have a language in common […] I'm really a fan of English not because I see this as a sort of cultural imperialism, because by now English has nothing to do with England any more or with the UK […] I don't see it as an imposition of cultural imperatives from the Brits, you know, by now English is the language of Eur... by now, you know, if aliens came to the Earth, by now, they'd probably try and talk to us in English... it's the language of old England it is the language of the US but it is the language of the EU too...'

Appealing to the universality and modernity of English, RO1 realised his argument along a temporal axis (signalled by the expressions 'by now' and 'anymore') which allowed him to represent a socio-historical evolution of English language towards the 'de-territorialisation' and the decoupling of specific cultural/identitarian connotations from communicative functions in line with a 'quasi-diglossic' scenario envisaged for European languages by most members (cf. Zappettini & Comănaru, 2014). Furthermore, RO1 appealed to a cognitive schema of universality of the English language through the hyperbolic and futuristic imagery of 'aliens' expected to be able to communicate with humans, an effective linguistic device that allowed him to contextualise issues of communication among Europeans in a global, indeed universal, context of unbounded interaction.

In an individual interview conducted in Valencia (Spain), the speaker used temporal and spatial indexes to suggest the specific conditions of Spanish society and more generally of European youth:

Extract 3

VA1: for me belonging means not only a place you know (.) it's also belonging to a society belonging to a certain group of people that have similar values to yours (..) I mean I could say yeah I am Spanish [..] but this doesn't mean I belong to Spain (..) I don't know if I want to to to grow my roots or something like that (..) I don't know if I want to stay here you know I don't know I don't know if I want to be in South America or in the north of Europe it's not only the city or the buildings but is also the people is what you give to this society with what you contribute you know (.) I don't know where I belong (...) if you ask me now I belong to my family at the moment and no at the moment I'm not independent yet (.) I don't have a job I don't have my own house and now I don't have more options than belonging here'.

Through her narrative VA1 reflexively positioned herself 'in-between' identities highlighting how her different sources of attachments had yet to fully develop into firmer feelings of belonging and groupness. VA1 represented her (European) identity as a process of 'rooting' herself in a wider social space, a process which, however, she depicted as a struggle between personal choices and external constraints. VA1 constructed her difficulty to locate herself in relation to a meta-space comprising of different dimensions: a geographical dimension (specific world locations such as South/America/North Europe, or objects such buildings); an affective dimension (family, band); a social dimension of groupness (defined by the sharing of values and the moral obligation to give to society); and the historical difficult social-economic conjuncture of Spain (and more generally of Europe).

Amid this scenario the member used the spatial deictic 'here' and the temporal clause 'at the moment' to mark her precarious situatedness − a topic that VA1 discussed repeatedly in the interview and clearly echoed wider discourses of 'social precariousness'.[13] It was thus inferable that for VA1 the contingencies of 'here' and 'now' (i.e. the lack of certainties about the future) were preventing her from emancipation and a full realisation of meaningful social identities through firm ties undermining the 'ontological security' (Giddens, 1991) of her identity. The gap between an ideal sense of belonging and the social and economic constraints was realised through the comparative '*I don't have more options than belonging here*' which presents her current choice of belongings in negative terms.

Personal deixis were also frequently deployed by members. The pronoun *we* and *us* and the possessive adjective *our*, for example, were inferable in several different meanings. In some cases, the indexicality of 'we' pointed to the organisational groupness, whether at the level of the local branch or the whole organisation (e.g. 'our events' and 'our work'). In a similar way, the 'we-citizens' (e.g. in the expressions 'our institutions') was often realised from the perspective of a local administration, the national apparatus, or the EU system. Furthermore, some members anchored the meaning of the 'we-group' to a generational belonging (e.g. 'our generation), an awareness of a socio-historical condition (e.g. 'our situation') or simply the condition of being humans (e.g. 'our emotions'). Of particular interest was the indexical use of pronouns and adjectives as used in representations of the interplay between Europeanness and national referents. For example, German national BE1 (Berlin individual interview) constructed her location 'outside' Germany via personal and spatial deixis as exemplified by the following extract:

Extract 4

BE1: yes I think for me I don't really identify as being German .. no not at all but this is also because of the German [...] history, they really don't have many good things to talk about .. [it] is quite strange because now, in the crisis it happens quite often that if you are German people say 'come on, but you're in Germany, and you've got money, and you can find a good job, so come on' but really, I can't be proud of it because I see the crisis from outside more than inside

BE1 used both personal and spatial deixis to distance herself from her Germanness and to invest into a transnational social location. Initially, BE1 invokes the *topos of history* and, through the moral evaluation of the German past, she clearly dissociates herself from the negative connotations of 'being German'. The speaker's use of the pronoun *they* in this case suggest the negative perception of nationhood as a historical 'other'. Moreover, the 'otherisation' of nationhood was made discursively relevant by the speaker through the context of the current economic crisis. In this case, whilst the member could potentially identify with a positively connoted German referent, she chooses not to do so through her spatial positioning 'outside' the perspective of a national 'container' which suggests her alignment and empathy with other fellow Europeans.

In contrast to BE1, CA1 and CA3 (both from the Cardiff focus group) used personal and spatial deixis to construct more ambivalent interplay between national and European affiliations. CA1 drew on the *topos of Turkey straddling across continents/cultures* to position herself as (partly) non-European as a consequence of her Turkish identity. Likewise, CA3 invoked the *topos of the UK insularity* to constructing a metaphorical positioning of Britain on the edge of Europe and the ambivalent marginality of her own Europeanness.

Extract 5

CA1: I'm not a part of Europe because I'm from Turkey [rising tone] (.) actually it's both part of Europe and at the same time (..) it still isn't in the European Union and (..) yes, I've always been keen on studying about Europe because of its diversity there's a lot of cultures a lot of languages [...]) I think the common point is history, European history, European tradition, [...] and I think this is the point that makes us European, they share the same history

Extract 6

CA3: I like to think of Europe as...ehm ...yeah the experience of living in Europe as being transnational because I think it's very easy to move about and to exchange culture. I think living in the UK our experience is slightly different obviously being an island we are that much further away from it but I think by studying languages that, ehm that sort of distance is bridged because you spend a year abroad and obviously by speaking a foreign language you can sort of go and live in that country, and I think it becomes a lot easier [...] I think yeah certainly like the way the UK is concerned people that only speak English I think... there is definitely a distance that they don't feel European or even maybe they don't speak a foreign language but if they are sort of really interested in European cultures ....it's probably as well a political thing some people are very sort of anti-Europe I think it is based on you know the fact that we are separate and people are very keen to guard that whereas other people are much more open to integrating ourselves into Europe and I think in Europe we are also viewed differently [...] I think that the UK is in quite a unique position as being part of Europe I think.

In extract 5 the speaker realised her ambivalent European identity by simultaneously affiliating with and dissociating from the European group through the conflictual use of the pronouns *us* and *they* contextually referring to the generic 'Europeans'. CA1's extract highlights crucial tensions. In CA1's torn positioning in and out of the European space, one can recognise wider discourses of inclusion and exclusion surrounding the long-debated Turkish membership of the EU and more generally of Turkish identity as Europe's historical 'other' (cf. Rumford, 2011). These tensions appear to shape and constrain CA1's discourse and to be internalised by the speaker in an almost 'schizophrenic' pattern of binary belongings and shifting inclusiveness/exclusiveness. In this case, rather than compatibly integrated, European and national identities were represented as intersecting whilst also functioning as antagonists.

A similarly ambivalent self-collocation in and out of Europe was achieved in extract 6 by CA3, a British national who characterised Europeanness primarily in relation to an understanding of transnationalism as mobility and intercultural encounters. Although she evaluated positively her engagement in transnational practices, in her discourse she appeared to index her belonging to national more than European referents. Her stance was signalled by her use of personal pronouns ('we/ourselves') and possessive adjectives ('our experience') that clearly suggest her main group affiliation as British and a general British-centric perspective of social interaction (cf. expressions such as 'a year abroad', 'a foreign language', and 'go and live in that country'). Furthermore through the *topos of the UK insularity*[14] CA3 emphasised the geo-cultural 'uniqueness' of Britain and constructed a marginality of its relationship with Europe, appealing to both geographical and cultural arguments. The *topos of insularity* was further used by the speaker as a warrant for her representation of views of the European project in the British society split between what have often been characterised as 'Eurosceptic' and 'Europhile' attitudes. Although CA3 offered a neutral representation of these two sides through the lexical choice of 'people', she consistently aligned her group membership with the British referent and its distinctiveness (her in-group positioning for example supported by the expression 'we are viewed differently'). At the same time, in her final proposition, CA3, discursively placed the UK within Europe albeit through the disclaimer on its 'uniqueness', a representation that, in relation to the extract, seems to reinforce a metaphorically peripheral positioning of Britain in relation to Europe and the speaker's own ambivalent location 'on the edge' of European identification.

5.1. Transnational Europe: Poly-Centric Social Imaginaries

Overall the data have suggested that members drew on (and the same time constructed) different conceptualisations of transnationalism. By and large these were oriented towards interpreting transnationalism as:

- An opportunity for the bottom-up (re)definition of civic/political community;
- The 'natural'/historical process of the demise of nationhood;

- A site of global practices of consumption, mobility, cultural exchange, and (negative/positive) economic integration.

These transnational frames seemed to operate as ideological lenses that provided members with critical and reflexive perspectives on the meaning of their activities and their social locations. Amid these frames, spatial, temporal, personal, and ideological deixis were deployed by members to position themselves and negotiate their (European) identities 'glocally'. Furthermore, different imaginaries of Europe (related to different conceptualisations of transnationalism) were recognisable which were evoked by members in relation to discursive deictic centres. As a convenient conceptualisation, three notable interpretations of how the transnational European field was imagined by members are suggested as follows: nation-centric; Euro-centric and cosmopolitan.

5.1.1. Transnational Europe as a Nation-Centric Field

From a nation-centric perspective (which was invoked by a minority of members) transnationalism is the ability to interconnect across borders through different practices of mobility, cultural exchange, and so on. Intra-state mobility and the 'coming together' of different peoples/cultures are valued positively; however, they mainly represent 'ways of being' whilst belonging remains primarily indexed to reproduction of national identities albeit projected on a European trajectory. In other words, this vision accepts/validates the world order of states and it conceives of EU-rope as the sum of its parts, that is a 'Union of states' or a 'family of peoples'. In this respect the nation-centric vision of the transnational European field corroborates Risse's (2010) findings on the 'Europeanisation' of national identities, that is, their recontextualisation at a European level. From a nation-centric perspective, the interplay between European and national affiliations in members' discourses was somewhat consistent with the 'Russian Doll' conceptualisation of hierarchically stacked identities (Herrmann et al. 2004) working in 'non zero-sum' dynamics.

5.1.2. Transnational Europe as a Euro-Centric Field

The imagination of Europe from a Euro-centric perspective supported ambivalent definition of the European field as an open/closed geo-political and social container. On the one hand, internal (physical and ideological) borders were often discursively deconstructed by members who emphasised the unboundedness of the European *inside* and its interconnectedness with the *outside* thus suggesting an open and cosmopolitan interpretation of Europe (see below). On the other hand, however, some members invoked the (cultural, social, economic, and political) boundaries of Europe and its outside to construe Europeans as a cohesive group vis-à-vis other groups (typically the Americans) and to portray EU-rope as a political entity of its own, a geo-political body that pursues 'European' rather than national interests. For most members, identification as European occurred through interpretations of transnationalism as both a *way of being* and a *way of belonging*. Through the latter interpretation, transnational practices such as mobility were often seen as indexes of emancipation from nationalistic ideologies and as positive social progress. Europeanness was often interpreted in its dual nature of 'brought along' heritage and as the transformation of ethnic/national identities into civic identities 'brought about' by the EU project. The Euro-centric perspective suggested an overall interplay of national and European identities whereby the former were seen as transiting into the latter in a 'zero sum' logic.

5.1.3. *Transnational Europe as a Cosmopolitan Field*

Finally, through the conceptualisation of the European field enacted from a cosmopolitan perspective, members conceived of transnational dynamics as a consequence of the 'natural' interconnectedness of the (social) world. They defined their European identities reflexively and emphatically through polycentric 'locations' and often rejected the 'container theory of society'. In this case Europeanness could be seen as a 'node' or a 'gateway' capable of interconnecting individuals with(in) a wider cosmopolitan 'network' of relations, an intermediate but not exclusive stage linking the local with the global. However, whilst in a cosmopolitan perspective Europeanness can represent a salient way of belonging, members appeared to relativise the overall salience of identities especially those derived from formal membership. Instead, for most members, the meaning of their Europeanness seemed to lay in their perception as social actors participating in a political experiment of transnational democracy that could eventually be expanded and replicated in the wider world.

6. CONCLUSIONS

Trading on a transnational perspective and on the indexicality of different linguistic realisations, this chapter has provided insights on how EA members constructed their Europeanness. It has been argued that, rather than representing an identity *per se*, transnationalism operated as an overarching ideological lens through which members were able to negotiate global and local dimensions often (re)constructing multiple and overlapping affiliations with Europe. Furthermore, members evoked different 'imaginaries' of Europe through indexical expressions and through the construction of their social locations in relation to different 'deictic centres'. These constructions were conveniently summarised as nation-centric, Euro-centric, and cosmopolitan conceptualisations of Europe as a transnational field. By and large, the nation-centric dimension conceives of Europe as a field of transnational practices more than of belonging. This perspective projects national identities on a European trajectory and corroborates finding on the Europeanisation of national identities in discourse. The Euro-centric conceptualisation of transnationalism deconstructed Europe's internal borders and reconstructed the European field as an internally open space of belonging. However, such space was also defined in relation to its outer boundaries to assimilate its inside and dissimilate its outside. From a Euro-centric perspective, therefore, the European field emerged ambivalently conceived as an open/close space and was discursively associated/dissociated with the EU project. Finally, a cosmopolitan conceptualisation of the transnational European field emerged in members' discourses that, whilst rejecting nations as incongruous containers of social interaction, saw individuals networked worldwide and conceptualised the European space as immersed within a wider cosmopolitan frame. From this stance, Europe was interpreted as a site of political experimentation that could be replicated worldwide. Consequently, European identity was often seen by members as a 'node' interconnecting individuals with a cosmopolitan 'network' of practices and ties, seamlessly and simultaneously occurring at local and global levels.

The data have suggested that transnationalism can represent a powerful referent in the imagination of Europe as a space and as a community between various dimensions. Transnational narratives could drive the construction of Europeanness from bottom-up and towards post-national forms of membership alternative to institutional identity projects. The analysis has also suggested that, whilst national referents can still interplay in the imagination of Europeanness, nationhood becomes increasingly volatile as national identity referents were recontextualised, deterritorialised, represented in transition or rejected altogether by members. Of course, this study has only been able to draw a partial picture of the complex dynamics at play in the articulation of (European) identities and it would welcome further investigation on similar sites of production of Europeanness.

NOTES

1. In this chapter I use the term transnationalism to conveniently refer to 'multiple ties and interactions linking people across the borders of nation-states' Vertovec (1999, p. 447) which have impacted on several dynamics of 'nationhood'. I acknowledge that terms such as transnationalism, post-nationalism ad cosmopolitanism are not necessarily synonyms (see Roudometof, 2005 for a distinction).

2. For Levitt and Glick-Schiller (2004) a transnational field typically contains 'institutions, organizations, and experiences, within their various levels, that generate categories of identity that are ascribed to or chosen by individuals or groups' (p. 1010).

3. However, see Balibar (2009) for a critique of 'Fortress Europe'.

4. See www.euroalter.com for further details.

5. EA originated in 2006 from the initiative of a few activists who received some funding under the 'PLAN D for Democracy, Dialogue and Debate'. This scheme was launched by the Commission to address the 'communication gap' between institutions and citizens in the wake of the failed European Constitution in 2004/5. Since then EA has been increasingly reliant on private sponsors and membership fees.

6. see http://euplus.org/ for further details.

7. The physical location of branches is not necessarily correlated to members' nationality (e.g. Italian, French, German, Turkish as well as British nationals are based at the London office).

8. Introduced under the Treaty of Lisbon the European Citizens' initiative is a legal provision that allows EU citizens to put forward legislation proposals to the European Commission (for details and legal requirements see http://www.citizens-initiative.eu/?page_id = 2). Accessed 13 March 2014.

9. All interviews in Romanian and Italian were translated in English. All excerpts presented later in the analysis are in the English version. All focus groups were conducted in situ at the local branch of EA. All individual interviews were conducted over Skype, except RO1 who was interviewed at EA Rome office and LO3 who was interviewed at a public location in London.

10. Local groups across Europe are open to all EU and third-country citizens regardless of their nationality or residency. Geographical locations of branches therefore do not necessarily reflect members' variety.

11. Sometimes also referred to as *deictic* or *indexical expressions*.

12. Following 2007 enlargement, Romanians and Bulgarians acquired European citizenship granting rights of movement and residence in any EU member states (albeit restrictions have been applied at different times by different states).

13. In the past few years there have been different movements in Spain which have campaigned in support of the right to affordable housing (VdeVivienda) and against the lack of certainty (*precariedad*) in employment and social welfare (Precarios en movimiento); cf. also *Juventud Sin Futuro* (Youth without a Future) which have campaigned under the slogan 'no house, no job, no pension, no fear'. In general the deregulation of the job markets in the 1990s and 2000s has resulted in more temporary jobs being available at the expense of long-term and fixed jobs and the emergence as the 'Precariat' as a new social class (Standing, 2011). EA has run a number of campaigns to demand radical changes to the current job situation and VA1 has been personally involved in these activities.

14. Cf. 'the myth of Anglo-Saxon exceptionalism' (Marcussen & Roscher, 2010).

ACKNOWLEDGMENT

It must be acknowledged that this contribution has previously appeared under the same title as Zappettini, F. (2017). *Russian Journal of Linguistics, 21*(2), 260–281.

REFERENCES

Albert, M., Jacobson, D., & Lapid, Y. (2001). *Identities, borders, orders: Rethinking international relations theory*. Minneapolis, MN: University of Minnesota Press.

Anderson, B. (2006). *Imagined communities: Reflections on the origin and spread of nationalism*. New York, NY: Verso.

Appadurai, A. (1995). The production of locality. In R. Fardon (Ed.), *Counterworks: Managing the diversity of knowledge* (pp. 204–225). London; New York, NY: Routledge.

Balibar, E. (2004). *We, the people of Europe?: Reflections on transnational citizenship*. Princeton, NJ: Princeton University Press.

Balibar, E. (2009). Europe as borderland. *Environment and Planning D: Society and Space, 27*(2), 190–215.

Bauböck, R., & Faist, T. (2010). *Diaspora and transnationalism: Concepts, theories and methods.* Amsterdam: Amsterdam University Press.

Beck, U. (1996). The cosmopolitanism manifesto. In G. W. Brown & D. Held (Eds.), *The cosmopolitanism reader* (pp. 213–228). Cambridge: Polity.

Beck, U. (2008). The cosmopolitan perspective: Sociology of the second age of modernity. *The British Journal of Sociology, 51*(1), 79–105.

Beck, U., Giddens, A., & Lash, S. (1994). *Reflexive modernization: Politics, tradition and aesthetics in the modern social order.* Stanford, CA: Stanford University Press.

Biebuyck, W., & Rumford, C. (2011). Many Europes: Rethinking multiplicity. *European Journal of Social Theory, 15*(1), 3–20.

Billig, M. (1995). *Banal nationalism.* London: Sage.

Blommaert, J. (2013). Citizenship, language and superdiversity: Towards complexity. *Tilburg Papers in Cultural Studies University of Tilburg, February*(45). 1–4.

Bucholtz, M., & Hall, K. (2005). Identity and interaction: A sociocultural linguistic approach. *Discourse Studies, 7*(4-5), 585–614.

Castells, M. (1997). *End of millennium.* Malden, MA: Blackwell.

Cerutti, F., & Lucarelli, S. (2008). *The search for a European identity: Values, policies and legitimacy of the European Union.* Abingdon, UK; New York, NY: Routledge.

Checkel, J. T., & Katzenstein, P. J. (2009). *European identity.* Cambridge: Cambridge University Press.

Chilton, P. (2004). *Analysing political discourse: Theory and practice.* London; New York, NY: Routledge.

Closa, C. (2001). Requirements of a European public sphere: Civil society, self, and the institutionalization of citizenship. In K. Eder & B. Giesen (Eds.), *European citizenship between national legacies and postnational projects* (pp. 180–201). Oxford, UK; New York, NY: Oxford University Press.

Davies, B., & Harré, R. (2001). Positioning: The discursive production of selves. In M. Wetherell, S. Taylor, & S. J. Yates (Eds.), *Discourse theory and practice: A reader* (pp. 261–271). London; Thousand Oaks, CA: Sage.

DeBardeleben, J., & Achim, H. (2011). *Transnational Europe: Promise, paradox, limits.* Houndmills, Basingstoke, Hampshire, UK; New York, NY: Palgrave Macmillan.

Delanty, G. (2013). *Formations of European modernity: A historical and political sociology of Europe.* New York, NY: Palgrave Macmillan.

Delanty, G., & Rumford, C. (2005). *Rethinking Europe: Social theory and the implications of Europeanization.* Abingdon, Oxford: Routledge.

Della Porta, D., & Tarrow, S. G. (2005). *Transnational protest and global activism.* Lanham, MD: Rowman & Littlefield.

Eder, K. (2009). A theory of collective identity: Making sense of the debate on a 'European Identity'. *European Journal of Social Theory, 12*(4), 427–447.

Eriksen, E. O., & Fossum, J. E. (2001). Democracy through strong publics in the European Union? *ARENA Working Paper* 01/16.

Fairclough, N., Mulderrig, J., & Wodak, R. (1997). Critical discourse analysis. In T. A. van Dijk (Ed.), *Discourse studies: A multidisciplinary introduction* (pp. 357–378). London; Thousand Oaks, CA: Sage.

Fairclough, N., & Wodak, R. (1997). Critical discourse analysis. In T. van Dijk (Ed.), *Introduction to discourse analysis Vol. 2. Discourse as social interaction* (pp. 258–284). London: Sage.

Fligstein, N. (2008). *Euroclash: The EU, European identity, and the future of Europe: The EU, European identity, and the future of Europe.* Oxford: Oxford University Press.

Friedman, R., & Thiel, M. (2012). *European identity and culture: Narratives of transnational belongings.* Farnham: Ashgate.

Giddens, A. (1991). *Modernity and self-identity: Self and society in the late modern age.* Stanford, CA: Stanford University Press.

Habermas, J. (1998). *Between facts and norms: Contributions to a discourse theory of law and democracy.* Cambridge, MA: MIT Press.

Habermas, J. (2001). *The postnational constellation political essays.* Cambridge, MA; London: MIT Press.

Hall, S. (1996a). The question of cultural identity. In S. Hall, D. Held, D. Hubert, & K. Thompson (Eds.), *Modernity: An introduction to modern societies.* Malden, MA: Blackwell.

Hall, S. (1996b). Who needs identity? In S. Hall & P. D. Gay (Eds.), *Questions of cultural identity* (pp.1–17). London; Thousand Oaks, CA: Sage.

Hall, S. (1997). *Representation: Cultural representations and signifying practices.* London; Thousand Oaks, CA: Sage in association with the Open University.

Haller, W., & Landolt, P. (2005). The transnational dimensions of identity formation: Adult children of immigrants in Miami. *Ethnic and Racial Studies, 28*(6), 1182–1214.

Hanks, WF. 1999. Indexicality. *Journal of Linguistic Anthropology, 9*(1–2), 124–126.

Hannerz, U. (1996). *Transnational connections: Culture, people, places.* London: Taylor & Francis Group.

Hanquinet, L., & Savage, M. (2013). The Europeanisation of everyday life: Cross-Border practices and transnational identifications among EU and third-country citizens. *Eucross working papers series* 6 (Eucross research project funded by the EC 7th Framework programme).

Held, D. (1999). *Global transformations: Politics, economics and culture.* Stanford, CA: Stanford University Press.

Herrmann, R. K., Risse-Kappen, T., & Brewer, M. B. (2004). *Transnational identities: Becoming European in the EU.* Oxford: Rowman & Littlefield.

Hobsbawm, E. (1997). *Nations and nationalism since 1780: Programme, myth, reality.* Cambridge: Cambridge University Press.

Jenkins, R. (2004). *Social identity.* London: Routledge.

Johnstone, B. (2013). *Speaking Pittsburghese: The story of a dialect.* New York, NY: Oxford University Press.

Jones, P., & Krzyżanowski, M. (2008). Identity, belonging and migration: Beyond describing 'others'. In G. Delanty, R. Wodak, & P. Jones (Eds.), *Identity, belonging and migration* (pp. 38–53). Liverpool: Liverpool University Press.

Kaiser, W., Leucht, B., & Gehler, M. (2010). *Transnational networks in regional integration: Governing Europe 1945-83.* New York, NY: Palgrave Macmillan.

Kaplan, D. (1979). On the logic of demonstratives. *Journal of Philosophical Logic, 8*(1), 81–98.

Kastoryano, R. H. B. (2002). *Negotiating identities.* Princeton, NJ: Princeton University Press.

Kraus, P. (2006). Legitimacy, democracy and diversity in the European Union. *International Journal of Multicultural Societies, 8*(2), 203–224.

Krzyżanowski, M. (2010). *The discursive construction of European identities: A multi-level approach to discourse and identity in the transforming European union.* Frankfurt am Main: Peter Lang.

Levitt, P., & Glick Schiller, N. (2004). Conceptualizing simultaneity: A transnational social field perspective on society. *International Migration Review, 38*(3), 1002–1039.

Lyotard, J. F., & Benjamin, A. E. (1989). *The Lyotard reader.* Oxford, UK; Cambridge, MA: Blackwell.

Marcussen, M., & Roscher, K. (2010). Europe and the other and Europe as the other. In B. Stråth (Ed.), *The social construction of 'Europe': Life-cycles of nation-state identities in France, Germany and great Britain* (pp. 325–358). Brussels: Peter Lang.

McEntee-Atalianis, L., & Zappettini, F. (2014). Networked identities. *Critical Discourse Studies, 11*(4), 397–415.

Mole, R. C. M. (2007). *Discursive constructions of identity in European politics.* Basingstoke and New York, NY: Palgrave Macmillan.

Morin, J.-F., & Carta, C. (2014). *EU foreign policy through the lens of discourse analysis: Making sense of diversity.* Aldershot; Farnham: Ashgate.

Oberhuber, F. (2007). Legitimating the European Union: The contested meanings of an EU constitution. *EUI Working Papers RCAS* 2007, 25.

Renkema, J. (2004). *Introduction to discourse studies.* Amsterdam; Philadelphia, PA: John Benjamins.

Risse, T. (2010). *A community of Europeans?: Transnational identities and public spheres.* New York, NY: Cornell University Press.

Robertson, R. (1992). *Globalization: Social theory and global culture.* London: Sage.

Roudometof, V. (2005). Transnationalism, cosmopolitanism and glocalization. *Current Sociology,* *53*(1), 113–135.

Rumford, C. (2008). *Cosmopolitan spaces: Europe, globalization, theory.* New York, NY: Routledge.

Rumford, C. (2011). Editorial: New perspectives on Turkey–EU relations. *Journal of Contemporary European Studies, 19*(4), 459–462.

Salvatore, A., Schmidtke, O., & Trenz, H.-J. (2013). *Struggling with the concept of a public sphere, rethinking the public sphere through transnationalizing processes: Europe and beyond.* Basingstoke: Palgrave Macmillan.

Sassen, S. (1996). *Losing control?: Sovereignty in an age of globalization.* New York, NY: Columbia University Press.

Shani, G. (2011). Identity-politics in the global age. In A. Elliott (Ed.), *Routledge handbook of identity studies* (pp. 380–396). Abingdon, Oxon; New York, NY: Routledge.

Silverstein, M. (2003). Indexical order and the dialectics of sociolinguistic life. *Language and Communication, 23*(3/4), 193–229.

Splichal, S. (2006). In search of a strong European public sphere: Some critical observations on conceptualizations of publicness and the (European) public sphere. *Media, Culture & Society, 28*(5), 695–714.

Standing, G. (2011). *The precariat the new dangerous class.* London; New York, NY: Bloomsbury Academic.

Stråth, B. (2010). *Europe and the other and Europe as the other.* Frankfurt am Mein: Peter Lang.

Tajfel, H., & Turner, J. (1979). An integrative theory of intergroup conflict. In W. G. Austin & S. Worchel (Eds.), *The social psychology of intergroup relations.* Monterey, CA: Brooks/Cole Publication Co.

Triandafyllidou, A., Wodak, R., & Krzyżanowski, M. (2009). *The European public sphere and the media: Europe in crisis.* Basingstoke: Palgrave Macmillan.

Vertovec, S. (1999). Conceiving and researching transnationalism. *Ethnic and Racial Studies, 22*(2), 447–462.

Vertovec, S. (2009). *Transnationalism.* Oxford; New York, NY: Taylor & Francis.

Wimmer, A., & Schiller Glick, N. (2002). Methodological nationalism and beyond: Nation-state building, migration and the social sciences. *Global Networks, 2*(4), 301–334.

Wodak, R. (2004). National and transnational identities: European and other identities constructed in interviews with EU officials. In R. K. Herrmann, T. Risse-Kappen, & MB. Brewer (Eds.), *Transnational identities: Becoming European in the EU* (pp. 97–128). Lanham, MD: Rowman & Littlefield.

Wodak, R. (2009). The discourse-historical approach. In R. Wodak & M. Meyer (Eds.), *Methods of critical discourse analysis* (2nd ed., pp. 63–94). London: Sage.

Wodak, R. (2012). Reinventing nationalism: Recontextualising traditional themes in glocal politics. First International Conference on the Discourse of Identity Santiago de Compostela, 13th–15th June 2012.

Wodak, R., de Cillia, R., Reisigl, M., & Liebhart, K. (2009). *The discursive construction of national identity.* Edinburgh: Edinburgh University Press.

Wodak, R., & Koller, V. (2008). *Handbook of communication in the public sphere.* Berlin; New York, NY: Mouton De Gruyter.

Wodak, R., & Weiss, G. (2005). Analyzing European Union discourses: Theories and applications. In R. Wodak & P. Chilton (Eds.), *A New Agenda in (Critical) discourse analysis: Theory, methodology and interdisciplinarity* (pp. 121–133). Amsterdam: J. Benjamins.

Zappettini, F., & Comănaru, R. (2014). Bottom-up perspectives on multilingual ideologies in the EU: The case of a transnational NGO. *Journal of Contemporary European Research, 10*(4), 402–422.

APPENDICES

Appendix A. Summarising Socio-Demographic Data Collected through Questionnaires at Focus Groups.

Focus Group	Cardiff – UK			Cluj – Romania						Bologna-Italy						London (pilot)-UK	
Date	22/04/2012			14/09/2011						21/04/2011						06/04/2011	
Duration (mins)	65			84						70						36	
Participant Code	CA1	CA2	CA3	CL1	CL2	CL3	CL4	CL5	CL6	BO1	BO2	BO3	BO4	BO5	BO6	LO1	LO2
Age Group																	
18–24	X	X	X	X	X	X	X	X	X								
25–34										X	X	X	X	X	X	X	X
35+																	
Male/Female	F	F	F	F	M	M	F	M	F	F	F	M	F	F	M	M	M
Occupation	Student	Student	Student	Student	Unemployed	Employee	Student	NGO Coordin	Youth Worker/Student	Journalist	Researcher	Student	Student	Employee	Employee	Researcher	Employee
Nationality	Turkin	Romanian	British	Romanian	Hungarian	Romanian	Romanian	Romanian	Romanian	Italian	Italian	Italian	German/Russian	Italian	Italian/French	Italian	British
Current Country of Residence	UK	Wales	Wales	Romania	Romania	Romania	Romania	Romania	Romania	Italy	Italy	Italy	Germany	Italy	Italy	UK	UK
Lived Abroad	Cyprus 4 yrs; UK 2 yrs	Sweden 6 mths	France 9 mths	Belgium 7 mths; Greece 3 mths	Germany 3 mths; Netherlands 1 mth	Italy 8 mths	France 4mths; Austria 3 wks			France 9 mths; Tanzania 3 mths	Spain 1yr; Belgium 9 mths; UK 6 mths	Germany 1 mth	Russia 13yrs; Spain 2 yrs; Italy 1 yr; Slovakia 1 mth	France 6 mths	UK 4 mths; Ireland 4 mths; France 9 mths	Ireland 1 mth; France 4 mths; USA 5 mths	France 1 yr; Spain 6 mths; Lebanon 1 yr

Appendix A. *(Continued)*

	CA1	CA2	CA3	CL1	CL2	CL3	CL4	CL5	CL6	BO1	BO2	BO3	BO4	BO5	BO6	LO1	LO2
Focus Group	Cardiff – UK			Cluj – Romania						Bologna-Italy						London (pilot)-UK	
Date	22/04/2012			14/09/2011						21/04/2011						06/04/2011	
Duration (mins)	65			84						70						36	
Participant Code	CA1	CA2	CA3	CL1	CL2	CL3	CL4	CL5	CL6	BO1	BO2	BO3	BO4	BO5	BO6	LO1	LO2
First Language	Turkish	Romanian	English	Romanian	Hungarian	Romanian	Romanian	Romanian	Romanian	Italian	Italian	Italian	Russian	Italian	Italian	Italian	English
Other Languages; Self-Reported Proficiency	ENG 5 FR3	ENG 5 SW 4 FR1	FR 5	FR 5 ENG 4 GER 2.5 GR 2 IT 1	GER 5 ROM 5 ENG 4	ENG 3 IT 3	ENG 5 FR 5 IT 4 GER 2 SP 2 HUN 1	FR 5 ENG 5 IT 4 SP 3 RU 2 GR 2	ENG 4 FR 2 SP 1	ENG 4 FR 3	ENG 5 FR 3 SP 4	ENG 5 GER 1 FR 1	GER 5 SP 4 IT4 ENG 3 FR 2 POR 1	ENG 5 FR 4.5 SP 3	FR 5 ENG 3	ENG 3 FR 3	GER 5 FR 4

Note: ENG, English; FR, French; GER, German; GR, Greek; HUN, Hungarian; IT, Italian; POR, Portuguese; ROM, Romania; RU, Russian; SP, Spanish; SW, Swedish.

Appendix B. Summary of socio-demographic data collected through questionnaires at individual interviews.

Interview	Rome-Italy	Berlin-Germany	Berlin-Germany	London-UK	Prague-Czech Republic	Prague-Czech Republic	Sofa-Bulgaria	Valencia - Spain	Amsterdam-Netherlands
Date	20/04/2010	16/02/2013	08/02/2013	18/01/2013	24/01/2013	27/01/2013	21/01/2013	24/01/2013	09/02/2013
Duration	36	52	41	45	65	42	61	56	80
Participant Code	RO1	BE1	BE2	LO3	PR1	PR2	SO1	VA1	AM1
Age Group									
18–24									
25–34	X	X		X	X	X	X	X	X
35+			X						
Male/Female	F	F	M	F	F	F	M	F	F
Occupation	NGO Worker	Unemployed	Cultural Manager	Student	Human Rights officer	Admin/education sector	PhD Student	Journalists	Temp clerk
Nationality	Italian	German	Italian	British	French	American	Bulgarian	Spanish	Dutch
Country Of Residence	Italy/UK	Germany	Germany	UK	Czech Republic	Czech Republic	Slovenia	Spain	Netherlands
Lived Abroad	Canada 2 yrs; UK 8 yrs; Spain 1 yr	Italy 9 mths	Spain 6 mths; Austria 3 yrs; Germany 7 yrs	Germany 3 yrs; UK 1 yr; Romania 8 mths; Czech Republic 2 yrs	Czech Republic 5 yrs		Croatia 3 mths; Malta 6 mths; Macedonia 3 yrs	Netherlands 2 yrs; Hungary 1 mth; Russia 1 mth; Finland 1 mth	Sweden 1 yr; Australia 2 mths
First Language	Italian	German	Italian	English	French	English	Bulgarian	Spanish	Dutch
Other languages; Self-reported Proficiency	ENG 5, SP5, POR 2	ENG 4, IT3, FR 2, SP 1, TUR 1	ENG 4, GER3, SP 2	GER 2, FR 1, SP 1	ENG 5, GER 5, ROM 3, IT 3, CZ 2	SP 3, CZ 3	ENG 5, MAC 5, SB-CR 4, RU 3	ENG 3, IT 1, CAT 5	ENG 5, GER 4, FR 2, SP 1

Note: CAT, Catalan; CZ, Czech; ENG, English; FR-French; GER, German; GR, Greek; HUN, Hungarian; IT, Italian; MAC, Macedonian; POR, Portuguese; ROM, Romanian; RU, Russian; SB-CR, Serbo-Croatian; SP, Spanish; SW, Swedish; TUR, Turkish.

DISCURSIVELY 'UNDOING' AND 'DOING EUROPE' THE AUSTRIAN WAY

Christian Karner

ABSTRACT

Literature on European and national identities displays a tension between occasional observations of an emerging 'banal Europeanism' (Cram, 2009) and a dominant strand (e.g. Guibernau, 2007; Toplak & Šumi, 2012) that questions the viability of European identifications vis-à-vis historically entrenched nationalisms, particularly in the context of the debt crisis and the resulting (re)nationalization of European politics. This chapter builds on recent work on Austrian European Union (EU) scepticism and its contestation (Karner, 2013) to examine instances — in diverse media coverage, readers' letters to the editor of Austria's most widely read newspaper, internet platforms, political essays and party political positions — of national identity negotiations in relation to the EU and as articulated in the context of successive European crises and the most recent elections to the European Parliament. The qualitative, thematic analysis of these wide-ranging materials developed here draws on two key concepts in critical discourse analysis, the notions of deixis *(Billig, 1995) or 'rhetorical pointing' and of the* topos *or 'structure of argument' (e.g. Reisigl & Wodak, 2001), which are complemented by a third theoretical tool, namely the anthropological concept of 'grammars of identity' (Baumann & Gingrich, 2004). The resulting discussion reveals the uneasy coexistence of (critical) Europeanisms and various national reassertions in Austria's public sphere and their respective discursive features. Further, the theoretical approaches synthesized cast light on internal diversities within political positions that are often too monolithicly*

National Identity and Europe in Times of Crisis: Doing and Undoing Europe, 37–59
doi:10.1108/978-1-78714-513-920171003

classified as being 'simply' pro- or anti-European respectively. Instead, the analysis presented here reveals a spectrum of (at least five) competing positions.

Keywords: EU scepticism; critical discourse analysis; deixis; public sphere; Austria; media

1. INTRODUCTION

Three months after the most recent European Union (EU) elections had resulted in some dramatic swings to the EU-sceptical (or hostile) populist right across the continent, Austria's governing coalition comprising the Social Democrats (SPÖ) and the country's center-right People's Party (ÖVP) announced a plan for 'more Europe in [Austria's] Parliament': The proposed steps included granting members of the European Parliament (MEPs) the right to speak in both chambers of the Austrian Parliament, which would also spend more time discussing EU-level plans and invite high-level EU functionaries, including the Commission President, to relevant sessions; moreover, the level of cooperation between Austrian MPs and MEPs would be stepped up. Austria's opposition parties were divided in their reactions to the government's plans, with the generally pro-European Greens and NEOS welcoming the initiative, and the decidedly more EU-sceptical Freedom Party (FPÖ) and Team Stronach criticizing what they portrayed as a confusion of political competencies (http://www.orf.at/stories/2243125).

This empirical snippet provides an apt illustration of the kinds of discursive and institutional efforts at both 'doing' and − often much more prominently − 'undoing' Europe that are in evidence across the EU today. The Austrian context is particularly pertinent here, as the country has often ranked amongst the EU's most sceptical member states, leading a commentator to argue that 15 years after Austria's EU accession Austrians had not yet 'arrived in Europe' (Filzmaier, 2010, p. 121, my translation). A more recent survey by IMAS (*Institut für Markt- und Sozialanalysen*) suggested that, increasingly vocal and widespread criticism of − and disillusionment with − the EU notwithstanding, the majority of Austrians pragmatically still favoured continued membership (quoted in Gnam, 2014). Other polls have revealed widespread indifference, as in March 2014 when 50% of Austrian respondents to another survey defined the EU as 'insignificant' or 'not very important' (quoted in Rainer, 2014; http://ooe.orf.at/news/stories/2637458). The juxtaposition of the above-mentioned governmental initiative for 'more Europe' to prominent, grassroots EU scepticism and a widespread lack of identification with the European project confirms that studies of national and European identification, their interrelations and potential overlaps, need to span those different 'scales': the top-down political, as well as the bottom-up, quotidian. This chapter therefore casts its eye widely, capturing diverse discursive engagements with the EU as encountered across a wide range of domains within Austria's public sphere, including party political positions and statements, political essays by public intellectuals, the country's diverse media (i.e. the public broadcasting network, the tabloid and broadsheet press), readers' letters to newspapers editors (i.e. particularly in the country's most widely read paper, the EU-sceptical tabloid *Kronen Zeitung*) and relevant citizens' initiatives. This discussion thereby focusses on empirical materials collected in, and covering, a period of several years up until the 2014 EU elections. The data analysed below thus predate the more recent national and European crises that have shaped 2015 and 2016 — including the escalating Greek debt and austerity crisis and the Eurozone's response, the ongoing 'refugee crisis' and the processes of political fragmentation and re-nationalization seen in its wake, the Brexit referendum and the much-discussed Austrian presidential election during 2016. The findings presented and the argument developed below thus provide important insights into a hotly contested discursive field that has seen further changes, and considerable polarization, since. It is my hope and claim that the analysis presented here provides a necessary, indeed vital step towards capturing yet more recent and currently unfolding political developments in and beyond Austria.

As shown below, Austria's internally much-debated relationship with the rest of the EU, and the latter's present and future trajectory, provides more than an empirical case study and illustration of the political tension, revealed in recent literature, between the forces of EU-sceptical, national reassertion (e.g. Lubbers & Scheepers, 2007; Schiedel, 2011; Startin & Krouwel, 2013; Toplak & Šumi, 2012) and an emerging 'banal Europeanism' (Cram, 2009) respectively. Instead, the analysis offered here reveals that both positions — opposition to the EU and a more or less taken-for-granted identification with (parts of) the European project — are in turn internally complex, varied and in need of closer analysis. The application of theoretical key tools provided by critical discourse analysis (CDA), complemented by the anthropological notion of 'grammars of identity' (Baumann & Gingrich, 2004), is shown here to pay the analytical dividends needed.

The argument developed in what follows unfolds in a succession of steps. Following an outline of the historical, methodological and theoretical contexts to the discussion, thematic analysis of the data underpinning it reveals five broad positions, each of which is examined for its defining argumentative structures and discursive features. Rather than being reducible to an anti- versus pro-Europe binary, these five discursive positions are best sketched along a spectrum of publicly available and mutually contesting political alternatives that are here described and analysed under the following headings: *undoing Europe, re-doing Europe sceptically, doing Europe critically, doing Europe, celebrating cosmopolitanism.* We begin, however, by contextualizing this discussion empirically, methodologically and conceptually.

2. CONTEXTS

The suggestion that Europe can, at most, evoke 'embryonic' and hence fragile identifications unlikely to withstand serious economic turmoil (Guibernau, 2007, pp. 115−116) poses an open empirical question to be addressed in specific contexts. Recent years have seen the very socio-economic conditions postulated by Guibernau become a reality. Yet, there is also a counterargument: The idea that, the continuing dominance of the nation state with regard to most Europeans' self-understanding notwithstanding, there is also some evidence of an emerging, albeit 'banal Europeanism' that in its symbolic manifestations and provision of the cognitive-discursive category of 'Europe' complements − rather than necessarily competes with − national identifications (e.g. Cram, 2009). There is now an urgent need, and ample opportunity, to put such alternative suggestions to the empirical test. Doing so requires prior empirical and epistemological contextualization.

2.1. Austria and Europe

While present constraints of space leave insufficient room for a *longue durée* discussion of the complex history of political identifications in Austria during the Habsburg era, passing mention must be made of the long rivalries between distinctly Austrian, pan-Germanic, and occasionally European discourses of identity since at least the 18th century (e.g. Heer, 2001, pp. 115−320). Condensing the deeply troubled history of Austria's subsequent post-imperial era, it suffices − for present purposes − to stress that the time between 1918 and 1945 was, in terms of ethnic self-understandings, a period of ideological dominance exercised by different forms of pan-Germanism that defined Austrians as ethnically German, were encountered across much of the political spectrum and hence shared among many from what were in all other respects party political enemy camps (i.e. the Christian Social Party, the Social Democrats and National Socialists) (e.g. Hanisch, 1994, pp. 126−127). As is well-documented (e.g. Karner, 2005; Thaler, 2001), it was only in the post-1945 era that a discourse of Austrian particularism became the hegemonic discourse of national identity, with the Second Austrian Republic henceforth commonly portrayed in clear distinction from a newly defined 'German other'. This was reflected in longitudinal changes recorded in a periodically conducted survey, which has been since then a much-quoted survey, that showed a steep increase between the late 1940s and the 1980s in the proportion of Austrians who defined themselves as 'a separate people' rather than as ethnically German (e.g. see Bruckmüller, 1996; Reiterer, 1988). Simultaneously, the post-war discourse of Austrian distinctiveness derived considerable political momentum from its propagation of the myth of Austrian World War II victimhood, which was premised on a highly selective reading of the Moscow declaration of 1943 (e.g. Thaler, 2001, p. 27) and was reluctant to acknowledge Austrians' co-responsibility for World War II and the Holocaust (e.g. Uhl, 2006).

While Austria's post-war economic and ideological reconstruction eventually led to some of the highest levels of patriotic attachment recorded anywhere (e.g. Rathkolb, 2005, pp. 25–26), the period since the mid-1980s has also been a time of profound changes. These have included a long overdue critical re-examination of Austrian World War II history; the end of the communist regimes just across Austria's (south-)easterly borders; increasingly, the local effects of global economic forces and markets, often perceived as disrupting and dislocating a previous state of purported harmony and reflected in the much-repeated trope and nostalgic (mis)portrayal of Austria of the 1960s and 1970s as an 'island of the blessed' (Liessmann, 2005); and EU membership since 1995. At a referendum held in June 1994, 66.6% of Austrians voted for accession to what was then still the European Community. Since then, Austrian EU-approval rates have fluctuated considerably, reaching a low point in 2000, when Austria's then 14 European partners reacted to the inclusion of the controversial, nationalist FPÖ in a coalition government with Austria's People's Party with a series of temporary 'sanctions' (e.g. Merlingen, Mudde, & Sedelmeier, 2001). As already mentioned, subsequent years saw comparatively pronounced levels of EU scepticism in the Alpine Republic. For example, successive crises since 2008 manifested in the 2010 spring Eurobarometer, when a mere 36% of Austrian respondents – compared to 49% across the EU – defined EU membership as 'a good thing' (Eurobarometer, 2010). Yet, more recently, 2 months prior to the 2014 elections to the European Parliament, another survey revealed 64% of Austrians supporting continued membership, 24% favouring a (hypothetical) exit, and the rest professing to be undecided (http://www.orf.at/stories/2223976).

Conceptually and empirically relevant scholarship on Austrian national identifications has included some of the most widely cited, theoretically most influential studies of the 'discursive construction', 'reproduction' and occasional 'dismantling' of national identities in public, semi-public and semi-private text and talk (Wodak, de Cillia, Reisigl, & Liebhart, 1999) of discriminatory discourses (Reisigl & Wodak, 2001) and of a 'new', anti-immigration racism (Krzyżanowski & Wodak, 2009). With regard to the discursive negotiation of national identities in relation to the EU, recent literature has shown that Austrian EU scepticism and its (pro-European) counter-discourses revolve around four main areas of thematic concern and debate: the EU's relationship to global markets; a 'spectrum of competing identifications' offering different geographical scales of identifications (i.e. localities, the nation, Europe);

memory and future predictions premised on projections based on particular interpretations of the past; discussion of existing EU structures and institutions in relation to competing political visions (Karner, 2013; also see Karner, 2011). The following discussion builds on this literature, while also making analytical use of select concepts borrowed from Ruth Wodak et al.'s 'discourse-historical approach' (1999, pp. 7–8) and other forms of CDA.

2.2. Method and Data

As shown by Bo Stråth and Ruth Wodak (2009, pp. 15, 17), '"Europe" has no essence *per se*, but it is a discursive construct and a product of many overlapping discourses', subject to 'various understandings' that are continually 'proposed, confronted and negotiated'. Of course, something very similar can be – and often has been (e.g. Anderson, 1983; Bell, 2003) – said about nation states and nationalisms as their ideologies of legitimation. However, the crucial difference lies in the relative novelty or longevity of European and national institutions respectively, and, consequently, in the very different degrees to which they are, or are not, embedded – and taken-for-granted (see Billig, 1995) – as part of people's life-worlds.

Krzyżanowski, Triandafyillidou, and Wodak's (2009, pp. 4–5) argue that the national media are 'key carriers' – particularly in contexts of crises – of different conceptions of Europe (and indeed of nation states); from this they derive a much-needed analytical focus on 'different discursive patterns of "talking about Europe" in the national media over time'. Taking my methodological cue, to a significant extent, from this, the bulk of the data underpinning this chapter draws on a large corpus of Austrian media discourse collected over the past decade: This includes, first, coverage by Austria's public broadcasting network (ORF); second, the country's most widely read paper – the usually strongly EU-sceptical *Kronen Zeitung* (or *Krone*), known for its extraordinarily high circulation figures (i.e. consistently reaching around or even above 40% of Austrians) and for both reflecting and shaping populist sentiments (e.g. Hanisch, 1994, p. 467; Rittberger, 2009) and third, Austria's ideologically heterogeneous quality press (e.g. *Die Presse, Der Standard, Profil, Falter*). While the media materials collected span considerable time and political diversity, my focus here lies on how these diverse media have 'talked about Europe' in the context of recent crises since 2008 and, yet more particularly, in the run up to and aftermath of the 2014 European elections.

However, returning to my starting observation of the need to examine different domains of national identity negotiation vis-à-vis the EU, this chapter also captures some of what lies outside of what Hall, Critcher, Jefferson, Clarke, and Roberts (1978, pp. 57–60) describe as a discursive realm dominated by politicians and the media as 'primary and secondary definers'. Following Lynn and Lea's rationale (2003, p. 430) for a complementary examination of readers' letters to newspaper editors as revealing 'ordinary actors'' positions on 'sensitive topics' as articulated in the 'intersections' of media- and everyday discourse, I also examine such readers' letters — published particularly, though not only, in the *Kronen Zeitung* — as a means of capturing receptions and appropriations of dominant discourse and bottom-up identity negotiations. Finally, the materials examined below also include other public assessments of the nation state in relation to the European 'network state' (Castells, 2000) as formulated in political essays by public intellectuals (e.g. Menasse, 2012; Portisch, 2011), by party political statements and electoral slogans or by citizen initiatives.

2.3. Theoretical 'Drivers'

As anticipated earlier, thematic analysis of this wide-ranging data — driven by initial 'open coding' that subsequently leads to the discernment of recurring themes within the materials examined (e.g. Esterberg, 2002, pp. 158–161) — reveals five broad discursive alternatives, which together sketch a continuum of competing stances with regard to the EU: (a) outright opposition (i.e. *undoing Europe*); (b) calls for fundamental changes to European structures (i.e. *re-doing Europe sceptically*); (c) criticisms aimed at improving existing EU institutions (i.e. *doing Europe critically*); (d) a broad commitment to the political status quo and distrust of many of its critics' claims (i.e. *doing Europe*); (e) transnational identity formations (i.e. *celebrating cosmopolitanism*). To illuminate the argumentative workings of these five, internally heterogeneous positions, this analysis makes use of three theoretical tools, two of which are borrowed from CDA and the third from social anthropology.

In terms of conceptual momentum provided by CDA, the first key tool utilized below is the notion of 'rhetorical pointing' or *deixis* (e.g. Billig, 1995, pp. 11, 94), achieved by the use of personal pronouns or the distinction between 'here' and 'there', through which identities are (re)produced and, in the context at hand, the relationship between the nation state and the European 'network state' (Castells, 2000) is negotiated. While 'deictic expressions' (e.g. 'we', 'us', 'ours', 'they', 'them', 'their') have long been recognized as instrumental to the discursive construction of 'sameness' and difference (e.g. Wodak et al., 1999, pp. 45–47), they are here particularly suited to illuminating the relative (in)significance of the nation and Europe in a social actor's identity negotiations.

CDA's second key concept to be employed below is that of the *topos*, or 'structure of argument' (e.g. Krzyżanowski et al., 2009, p. 9): i.e. those 'parts of argumentation', the 'explicit or inferable premises ... [that] connect the argument ... with the ... claim' (e.g. Reisigl & Wodak, 2001, pp. 74–75). Also described as 'obligatory premises', *topoi* (e.g. of purported threats, dangers, decline, etc.) are 'central to ... seemingly convincing fallacious arguments ... widely adopted in prejudiced discourse' (Krzyżanowski & Wodak, 2009, p. 22). Relying on *a priori* assumptions and assertions, rather than open-minded engagement with all available evidence and counter-evidence, topoi affect circular, ideologically 'naturalized' arguments.

The third theoretical driver is derived from Baumann and Gingrich's (2004) *grammars of identity* offering anthropological insights into three different patterns, in which categories of *self* and *other* and their interrelationship are discursively defined and culturally practiced: first, a grammar of diametrical opposition or 'orientalising' (i.e. 'we' and 'they' are mutually and perpetually exclusive); second, sliding scales of context-specific inclusion and exclusion or 'segmentation' (i.e. local foes becoming allies when facing external 'others'); third, relative inclusion or 'encompassment' (i.e. an overarching category of inclusion with internal, relative degrees of hierarchically arranged [dis] similarity).

Jointly, these three key concepts (i.e. deixis, topoi, grammars of identity) help illuminate: the categories of self-identification (e.g. Austria, the EU) available and debated in the data; the claims being made about them; and the discursively postulated and contested interrelationships between different categories of self-understanding (i.e. the nation state, Europe). With our analytical framework thus outlined, we turn to the first of the five discursive positions evident in the data.

3. UNDOING EUROPE

Starting on one end of a spectrum of available positions, one discerns frequently made claims that present national interests as diametrically opposed to, and hence threatened by, the EU. Such discursive strategies tie and reduce the EU to a series of negatively connoted phenomena, ranging from bureaucratic over-regulation, corrosive effects of lobbyists purportedly shaping European politics, to imminent environmental and social disaster. Writing in *Profil* about widespread opposition to the ratification of the Lisbon Treaty in 2008, Otmar Lahodynsky summarized such topoi of European threats, before juxtaposing them to counter-evidence:

> Citizen initiatives on both the left and the right are hoping to prevent the EU reform-treaty's ratification with demonstrations and court-cases. Many rely mainly on the Kronen Zeitung, its daily complaints about Brussels and calls for a referendum. The paper presents the EU as a veritable monster ... allegedly threatening neutrality, water, energy, traffic, or "our precious health system". It even postulates a European compulsion towards genetically modified food. (Lahodynsky, 2008, p. 26, my translation)

Many of the positions described here conform to André Gingrich's description (2006) of a 'culturally pessimistic' and 'economically protectionist' neo-nationalist populism. Part of its discursive workings is a process of dual 'othering' — internally with regard to political elites, and externally in relation to Brussels and through topoi of (other) foreign threats. The *Kronen Zeitung*'s readers' letter pages articulate such sentiments, of which the following is a case in point, on a near-daily basis:

> The EU opposes the ecologically sustainable production of electricity, supporting the nuclear lobby instead. The EU opposes old, non-GM seeds, and it supports large agri-business, thereby destroying *our* small farmers. The EU forbids the policing of *our* borders, thereby supporting criminal foreign gangs. We can only look across to Switzerland in envy, for they still have real democracy. (*Kronen Zeitung* reader's letter, 18 February 2014, p. 29, my translation, *italics added*)

A general pessimism concerning the EU's future has become commonplace also beyond the tabloid press and the nationalist right. It manifested, to name but one of numerous continually produced examples, in a *Profil* cover (3 March 2010, my translation) — published against the backdrop of the then escalating Greek debt crisis — of a coffin draped in a European flag, the headline alongside which read: 'Is this Europe's end? No — unless Spain, Portugal and Italy are next'.

Meanwhile, the rigid, nation-centred deixis contained in the *Krone* reader's letter quoted above (i.e. '*our* borders'), coupled with topoi of external threats, internal disempowerment, and of envy of Switzerland's non-EU status (see Karner, 2011, p. 101), resonates with growing numbers of voters, particularly amongst those most (likely to be) directly affected by the manifestations of successive European crises. Hans-Peter Martin, former independent MEP who self-describes as a pro-European critical of current EU structures, explained his decision not to stand in 2014 — despite his European electoral successes in 2004 and 2009 — with reference to 'a dangerous shift to the right', which he felt no longer able to counteract. Martin detected a more salient anti-Europeanism and xenophobia (often underpinned by fears about declining living standards and insecure employment) and a disconcerting, renewed yearning for scapegoats and simplistic political solutions; and while linking growing inequalities to globalization, rather than the EU (as its most outspoken critics have it), Martin also insisted that the EU continued to suffer from a 'massive democratic deficit' and had 'failed to regulate the financial markets' (quoted in Thurnher, 2014a, p. 10).

Prominent discursive strategies aimed at *undoing Europe* indeed featured in the 2014 European election campaigns. It is here that Baumann and Gingrich's conceptualization of different 'grammars of identity' — capturing competing, discursively constructed relationships between identity-bestowing categories of 'self' and 'other' — bears first analytical dividends, enabling us to pinpoint structural features of alternative positions, which we may describe as deep EU hostility, EU scepticism and relative indifference respectively. In terms of the former, the most rigidly oppositional position, premised on unambiguously 'positive self- and negative other-presentation' (e.g. Wodak, 2007, p. 662), informed the electoral platform 'EU Stop': calling for Austria's 'soonest possible EU exit', 'direct democracy' and a commitment to Austrian neutrality, EU Stop received 2.76% of Austrian votes at the recent EU elections; the platform defines an EU exit as necessary for 'Austria to regain her sovereignty' and the spending of Austrian taxes exclusively on Austria as a means of protecting 'Austrian prosperity' (http://www.eustop.at/programm.html, my translations). Topoi of external, European threats and nostalgic (mis)portrayals of the recent national past (Karner, 2010; Liessmann, 2005) here furnish a binary, 'orientalist' grammar of identity, which connotes the national 'self' in overwhelmingly positive, the European 'other' in exclusively negative terms.

The FPÖ's current positions on the EU, though also premised on strong criticisms of what the party portrays as 'too much Europe' and an oppositional grammar of identity (i.e. a nationalist logic of rigid external boundaries), show somewhat more nuance than EU Stop's basic Manicheanism (see http://orf.at/stories/2225818). For its 2014 EU election campaign the FPÖ used slogans with clearly nation-centred *deixis*, interpellating voters as Austrians, not as Europeans (i.e. 'We understand your rage', 'Austria changes her mind', 'Too much Europe doesn't do anyone any good'). Having received 19.72% of the Austrian vote, the FPÖ's head Heinz-Christian Strache recently insisted that his party was 'not anti-European' but opposed current developments in the EU, wanted a 'federal, not centralist EU' and new negotiations to change Austria's purported role as 'a permanent net-contributor' (*permananter Nettozahler*) (http://orf.at/stories/2244035/2244037).

The SPÖ (24.09% of the subsequent votes) and ÖVP (26.98%), meanwhile, campaigned for the European elections with slogans indicative of 'encompassment' (Baumann, 2004, pp. 25−26) of sorts: a grammar of identity that hierarchically subsumes various 'layers' under a singular, 'encompassing' category of identification, while, crucially, defining these different layers as differently salient or − in this case − more or less emotionally charged. While the SPÖ's electoral posters included slogans to the effect of 'Austria at heart, Europe on my mind', the ÖVP's lead candidate was depicted declaring that 'because I love Austria, I am working for a better Europe'. Such positions present the EU in terms of pragmatic calculation, as a means to an end for the more immediate, central, loyalty-demanding, emotionally significant national context. Although the very different positions portrayed here and above must − of course − not be conflated, it can be argued that the relative, emotional indifference vis-à-vis the EU conveyed by the SPÖ's and ÖVP's electoral posters − and their 'hierarchical subsumption' of Europe within an encompassing identity clearly centred on the nation state − also fed into a wider 'climate', in which European issues did not receive the urgent attention they needed. Journalist Eva Linsinger (2014) thus predicted that the 'trivial' approach to the EU communicated by some of the above-mentioned slogans would further strengthen right-wing populism and political apathy. Put differently: Although ideologically and argumentatively they differ enormously, the various positions mentioned here arguably all contribute, in different ways, to a wider discursive 'undoing of Europe' – either through outright opposition, deep scepticism or relative indifference.

4. RE-DOING EUROPE SCEPTICALLY

Ulrike Haider-Quercia – daughter of Jörg Haider, the controversial former head of the FPÖ and the *Bündnis Zukunft Österreich* (BZÖ) who died in a car crash in 2008 – briefly led the BZÖ's European election campaign, before withdrawing her candidature. She described her positions as being 'very critical' of the EU's status quo, as 'wanting Europe to remain unified' but as calling for 'fundamental reforms' of the EU, and as 'sensing that the Euro cannot be saved' (http://kaernten.orf.at/news/stories/2633249). While the BZÖ's electoral performance was extremely poor (i.e. 0.47%), versions of such strong EU scepticism, coupled with pessimistic prognoses and concomitant calls for far-reaching reforms of current EU structures are common across large stretches of the ideological spectrum. On the (far) right, they are encountered in the BZÖ's position, in the FPÖ's above-mentioned calls for a 'less centralist, more federal' EU, and in the trope – common to the far right more generally (e.g. Schiedel, 2011, p. 91) – of a 'Europe of distinctive homelands' (*Europa der Vaterländer*), purportedly threatened by the forces of European integration.

On the left, meanwhile, there have also been recurring calls to 're-do Europe', premised on deep opposition to neoliberalism. One encounters this, for instance, in the discursive position occupied by Attac (Austria), an NGO critical of economic globalization, and a European platform – called *Europa geht anders* ('Europe can work differently') – against the EU's 'pact for competitiveness'. One of their key organizers, writing in the Viennese weekly *Falter*, has argued that the EU's commitment to competitiveness would create a 'Troika for everyone': the socially disastrous austerity politics 'tested' on Greece and Portugal would thereby be extended across Europe, depleting workers' rights, privatizing water, traffic, health care and education, while further disempowering national parliaments (Strickner, 2013). The platform's website elaborates:

> Instead of changing the neo-liberal prescription, they are increasing the dosage. The so-called 'pact for competitiveness' is a plan for the decline of wages and social welfare and for privatisation. Troika for everyone … We reject this plan by the European Commission. We urge people who want a different Europe to put pressure on their governments … so that as many heads of government as possible reject the pact at the upcoming European Council meeting. We need a democratic, social and ecological Europe. (http://www.europa-geht-anders.eu, my translation)

Importantly, we here encounter first evidence of a distinctly European deixis (i.e. the frame of identification communicated here is distinctly supranational), tied to a topos of neoliberal conspiracy. Also writing in *Falter*, economist Markus Marterbauer offers a similarly damning assessment of the EU's austerity-driven status quo: European Commissioner for Economic and Monetary Affairs Olli Rehn, Marterbauer argues, continues to follow a 'perilous economic path' – mass unemployment, an increase in deprivation, social exclusion and widening inequalities notwithstanding; Rehn's 'politics of structural reform' are here further tied to massive reductions in public spending, declining wages, shrinking public sectors, weakening trade unions, decline in consumer spending and a concomitant loss in tax revenue. Marterbauer then calls, also employing a European deixis, for a 'radical change of direction' away from Rehn's neoliberal course: such an alternative is to be premised on a joint 'fight against unemployment, particularly amongst the young', on securing social welfare as 'an essential European project', on taxing the financial sector and the super-rich, and on policies of redistribution (Marterbauer, 2014, pp. 6–7, my translations). *Falter* editor Armin Thurnher arguably pinpoints the wider context to the current neoliberal hegemony within the EU when articulating concern that the EU could degenerate into a 'transnational association led by financial oligarchies', where the 'ritually invoked' financial markets trump all other social and political considerations (Thurnher, 2014b, my translation).

As suggested earlier, topoi of 'market fundamentalism' and environmental irresponsibility also appear in ideologically very differently positioned media. Writing in the *Kronen Zeitung*, Monika Langthaler has outlined her version of why a 'new Europe' was urgently required:

> GM-corn, [negative] changes in energy policy, nuclear energy being funded – one currently gets the impression that the European Commission is doing everything possible to win a "worst-of-the-bad" award … It is hardly surprising that there is growing distrust among Europe's populations in these decision-makers … This is why the upcoming European elections are so important, as our chance to elect alternatives that may put a stop to the above-mentioned nonsense. (Langthaler, 2014, my translation)

The *Kronen Zeitung*'s recent calls for fundamental changes to the EU's assumed political trajectory have been most prominent in relation to the paper's vocal opposition to the controversial plans for a Transatlantic Trade and Investment Partnership (TTIP). While the *Krone* is far from alone in articulating deep concern about the purportedly negative consequences a potential free trade agreement with the United States might have on European environmental-, health- and consumer protection standards, the paper's strategies of opposition are noteworthy: They have included the publication of regular petitions, for readers to sign and return to the paper, which by mid-August 2014 had resulted in 500,000 signatures calling on Austrian MEPs to veto TTIP (*Kronen Zeitung*, 12 August 2014, p. 1).

The second set of discursive positions, examined in this section, is thus highly heterogeneous and includes ideological stances that in most other respects are diametrically opposed and mutually exclusive. As we have seen, however, in relation to the EU some of the left's most pronounced criticisms of neoliberalism and the (far) right's trope of a 'Europe of distinctive homelands' (premised on a topos of the threat of integration) share *some* discursive terrain: on the 'diagnostic' level, they both oppose what they perceive as the EU's 'direction of travel' and call for a far-reaching re-doing of European structures and re-definition of the EU's purpose. Conversely, in terms of their respective 'prognoses' and recommendations, the positions on the left and the right examined above of course differ profoundly: as shown by the very different forms of deixis they employ, the former call for a pan-European U-turn on socio-economic policy, while the latter envisage a retrenchment of national boundaries.

5. DOING EUROPE CRITICALLY

The third set of discursive positions is also encountered across a range of public, argumentative domains. They differ from calls for fundamental reforms of the EU, such as the ones examined above, insofar as they formulate more moderate criticisms of the status quo, look upon existing EU institutions in more nuanced terms, consider them capable of implementing necessary reforms or even detect significant, positive changes to be already afoot. Put simply: the positions to be examined next are neither overly pessimistic or damning, nor uncritically enthusiastic about the EU; instead, they formulate often carefully argued criticisms aimed at improving existing EU institutions broadly within existing institutional parameters.

The manifestations of such more nuanced discourses include attempts to challenge and rectify common, often entirely negative misperceptions of the EU. For example, against the backdrop of the 2009 European elections and the then early stages of the Eurozone crisis, weekly news magazine *Profil* presented a far more 'mixed balance sheet' concerning the economic and ecological impact of EU membership than its most outspoken opponents had predicted; while the latters' near-apocalyptic predictions had not materialized, *Profil* summarized that membership and the EU's eastwardly expansion had translated into additional economic growth and employment in Austria, while at the same time 'lorry traffic transiting Austria' − one of the common complaints of the EU's local critics − had indeed also increased, albeit of technologically more advanced lorries with less environmental impact (*Profil*, 29 May 2009, p. 36). In other words, simplistic topoi and earlier prognoses of impending doom were here confronted with more nuanced realities. *Profil* also quoted survey evidence suggesting that the crisis had triggered some of the highest EU-approval rates since Austria's accession in 1995, and revealed a very substantial majority (i.e. 70% of Austrian respondents) who thought a collective, European response to the crisis was more likely to succeed than a national one (*Profil*, 29 May 2009, p. 36).

Perhaps more surprisingly, there have been recent traces of an arguably inadvertent, partial Europeanism, albeit a still sceptical one certainly grounded in national (rather than supranational) interests, in some of the *Kronen Zeitung*'s coverage. For example, in the context of escalating violence in the Ukraine and the trade embargos between Russia and the EU, the *Krone* reported that the EU Commission had agreed to support 'our farmers' – in distinctly national deixis – financially and in locating alternative markets, more quickly than Austria's industry of agriculture (Vettermann, Hauenstein, & Ebeert, 2014). In the context of British prime minister Cameron's opposition to Jean-Claude Juncker as the Commission's next president, *Kronen Zeitung* coverage showed no sympathy for Cameron, depicting his 'anti-EU show' as premised on emotional outbursts – Cameron was described as angry ('*polterte wütend*', '*wetterte*') – and as squarely pitted 'against the rest of Europe' (Vettermann, 2014): this is noteworthy, for although this generally EU-sceptical paper stopped short of aligning itself explicitly with a European deixis (i.e. it did not present Cameron explicitly in opposition to 'us'), it also clearly disapproved of what was presented as an unreasonable, anti-EU position.

Elsewhere, firm criticism of particular aspects of the EU is coupled with suggestions or hopes that some of the required steps are about to be taken. For instance, reflecting on voters' disenchantment with the EU both in the debt-stricken Mediterranean South and the more prosperous North, *Profil* columnist Ulla Kramar-Schmid (2014) has suggested that the EU-sceptics' electoral gains would have to shake up the pro-European parties: The latter would need to dissuade their electorates from the mistaken assumption that nation states were more likely to succeed in a globalized world than the EU by pushing for Tobin Tax, pan-European minimum wages, transnational projects against unemployment and by fighting tax evasion. Not dissimilarly, Christoph Hofinger – from a Viennese social research institute – has detected both profound structural weaknesses and attempts to rectify those on EU level: Hofinger postulated that the EU could only 'survive' if Europeans could truly vote their representatives into- and out of office; thus far, the argument continued, there was no clarity as to where European power truly resides, depriving voters of a chance to 'personalize' discontent, which was consequently channelled against the EU in its entirety; Hofinger concluded that the working assumption at the 2014 EU elections that the leading candidate of the strongest faction would become then next Commission president was a long overdue step in the right direction (Hofinger, 2014).

Perhaps most prominently, two of Austria's best-known public intellectuals' recent contributions to debates about the EU's future need to be mentioned. Articulated through political essays, both acknowledge the EU's profound achievements to date and argue for the ethical and practical need for its continued success. Yet, both essays also call for urgent changes, which they define as necessary prerequisites for the EU's future. Historian and journalist Hugo Portisch has thus forcefully argued against anti-EU populism, calling for more (or rather a renewed) commitment to European redistribution from the rich to the poor as part of further economic and financial integration, but also criticizing a continuing 'lack of transparency' in parts of the EU's institutions and sometimes insufficient subsidiarity (i.e. the principle, enshrined in EU treaties, that 'whatever can be solved on national or regional level, should be solved there') (Portisch, 2011, pp. 56−62, my translations).

Writer and public intellectual Robert Menasse, meanwhile, employs an unambiguously European deixis, defining the EU's historical *raison d'être* as the transcendence of nationalism − an ideology that 'will never be innocent again' (Profil, 26 May 2014, p. 24). Yet, Menasse's book is not an uncritical celebration of all things European. Instead, it is based on a serious research effort, an institutional ethnography conducted in Brussels. Menasse's findings are perhaps surprising, yet also critical of parts of the status quo. With regard to the EU's opponents, Menasse argues that their complaints about a 'democratic deficit' merely reflect disquiet about the loss of (national) identities that were always 'imaginary' (*eine Chimäre*), while what is accepted as legitimate politics on national level (i.e. legislation) is discursively misrepresented by the widespread topos of the EU's purported 'over-regulation' (*Regulierungswut*) when involving EU institutions (Menasse, 2012, pp. 13, 15). Contrary to their detractors' other central topoi, Menasse (2012, pp. 21−22, my translations) has found the European Commission to be 'open and transparent' and Brussel's bureaucracy 'extremely slim … thrifty, modest and cheap'. Menasse analysis revolves around the idea of 'post-national' politics, in relation to which the European Commission and Parliament are found to be 'genuinely supranational institutions'. However, Menasse also detects a central 'construction error' hampering the EU's post-national development, namely the European Council as a 'bulwark' of national(ist) self-interest (Menasse, 2012, pp. 49−50). With the Council thus identified as the crux of the EU's problems, Menasse calls for a genuinely post-national democracy, a 'post-national' Europe of the regions and subsidiarity (2012, pp. 84, 95). In our theoretical terms, Menasse speaks through a normative 'grammar of encompassment', different from the one mentioned earlier, in which post-national Europe subsumes and ideally empowers its regions, while transcending nation states and their self-legitimizing ideologies.

6. DOING EUROPE

There are, of course, many ways of discursively *doing Europe*. They include what existing literature, based on analyses of interview data and political rhetoric respectively, has shown to be attitudes of 'critical approval' of, but also 'ostensible disappointment' with, the EU (Wodak et al., 1999, p. 170), often coupled with an ambivalent pragmatism (e.g. Bushell, 2013, pp. 231–233) that sees membership as economically necessary though ideologically unconvincing or problematic. As shown earlier with reference to some of Austria's political parties' recent electoral slogans, there is a case that an instrumentalism that reduces the EU to rational calculations, without investing in its symbolic and historical significance, can inadvertently strengthen a wider discursive shift from *doing* to *undoing Europe*.

In distinction from such (more or less) ambivalent stances, this section draws attention to explicitly pro-EU positions that have recently been articulated in active opposition to some of the EU's most vocal detractors. In the run-up to the EU elections, for instance, Green party candidate Ulrike Lunacek – who subsequently received 14.52% of the Austrian vote – employed an unambiguously and positively connoted European deixis when stating that 'Europe is not somewhere out there, it is *our* home' (*Der Standard*, 29 April 2014, p. 8, my translation, *italics added*). Other commitments to discursively doing Europe have included attempts to meet common (mis)perceptions of the EU head-on, by confronting them with counter-evidence. Thus, Otmar Lahodynsky (2014a, pp. 19–20) has challenged the earlier-mentioned, much-repeated topos of the EU's purported over-regulation of European citizens' life-worlds by revealing that European regulation presupposes national politicians' involvement and, often, their initiative, that some of the most controversial regulations (such as those pertaining to the size of bananas or the shape of cucumbers) have been withdrawn, and by quoting José Manuel Barroso's position: that while 'the EU still had to become more pre-occupied with big issues, and less so with smaller matters', common rules where nonetheless preferable to 28 separate bureaucracies, particularly in safeguarding the economic interests of smaller countries in the common European market. Similarly, some pre-election *Falter* coverage (Gepp, 2014) demonstrated that some claims encountered in Austrian and German tabloids, in this particular case concerning an allegedly planned EU ban on Bavarian beer jugs, had no basis in facts and were seemingly figments of some critics' imagination. With regard to the potential Transatlantic Trade Investment Partnership, meanwhile, Anna Gulia Fink and Robert Treichler (2014) have argued that its opponents' topoi/fears of a likely 'assault' on Europeans' 'health, environment and democracy' were not justified and ignored the economic growth TTIP would create.

In a related vein, some journalistic commentators suggested that the high-point of anti-EU populism had now passed or, a little less optimistically, that what was needed was more top-down political commitment, on national level, to doing Europe positively. The already mentioned Otmar Lahodynsky (2014b) thus quoted post-EU election Eurobarometer data suggesting that the wave of anti-European sentiment triggered since the 2009 crisis had been stopped, as reflected in growing EU-approval rates, renewed belief in the Euro's future and increasing proportions of respondents who again profess to identify with the EU. *Profil* columnist Peter Michael Lingens (2014), meanwhile, juxtaposed the EU's very considerable recent achievements (as manifest particularly in its central regulation of the banking sector) to (Austria's) national politicians' − almost across the entire political spectrum − reluctance to acknowledge, let alone convey those accomplishments to their widely EU-sceptical electorates. Such discursive (counter-) positions thus *do Europe* by stressing that the EU does indeed work well − despite what are portrayed as counterproductive (/anachronistic) national politics.

As already hinted, there are many other public arenas, in which Europe is being discursively done. Those include less overtly political, primarily symbolic investments in supranational identifications and ties. Sometimes, as in Vienna's 2015 city marathon under the motto of 'We are Europe' (*Wir sind Europa*), such symbolic Europeanism indeed transcends the EU in its current membership (http://insider.vienna-marathon.com/?url = news&newsDetail = 1981). As we discover in the next section, there are other positive invocations of Europe that arguably operate with distinctive 'identity grammars' and topoi requiring separate discussion.

7. CELEBRATING COSMOPOLITANISM

The final set of positions to be analysed here provides the strongest counter-discourses to anti-EU populism. Articulated through explicitly European deixis, they overlap significantly with some of the arguments for *doing Europe* and *doing Europe critically* discussed above. Yet, the positions outlined next also display distinctive features of their own − explicit celebration of a European cosmopolitanism and particular forms of encompassing and, occasionally, also orientalizing grammars of identity.

NEOS, Austria's new liberal and pro-European party, was founded in 2012 and obtained 8.14% of the Austrian vote at the 2014 elections to the European Parliament. The party's '9 1/2' programmatic points 'for a new Austria' include calls to 'embrace Europe': this is, nonetheless, a critical 'embrace' that envisages far-reaching reforms 'of the greatest project of peace', including 'a stronger European Parliament, a directly elected Commission, more budgetary discipline, common economic policies, a democratic Europe of the regions rather than of rivalling nation-states, and European citizenship' (http://www.neos.eu/ programm/9-europa-umarmen/, my translation). The NEOS detailed 2014 electoral manifesto elaborates on its vision 'for a new Europe': premised on a 'love for a united and diverse Europe', this includes an active, educational fostering of European consciousness and identification; a common European army; willingness to shape globalization; more complete integration but also significant reforms of the EU's existing institutions (e.g. more transparency, subsidiarity, preservation of Europe's cultural diversity); significantly, NEOS see Europe at decisive crossroads: 'Either people can be persuaded of the need for further political integration, or current trends towards re-nationalization will have drastic consequences for all Europeans. Also: Europe's economic future and the sustainability of our part of the world for future generations require decisive ecological and social steps'. (NEOS, 2014, pp. 5, 10–11, 22, 26–27, 17–18, 6, my translations). NEOS discourse on the EU is thus defined by an active, cosmopolitan Europeanism (in clear distinction from the merely pragmatic, firmly nation-centred approach to EU membership discussed earlier). Yet, its argumentative topoi also detect far-reaching current crises, which only joint European action – diametrically opposed to the forces of a nationalist retrenchment – can overcome.

An application of Baumann and Gingrich's grammars of identity casts additional light on the discursive workings of pro-European cosmopolitanism. In some instances (also see Karner, 2013, p. 260), the latter is premised on yet another grammar of encompassment:

> The question is sometimes posed whether we Europeans actually exist. Well, I am Viennese! ... And I am of course Austrian! ... But of course I am a European! And I am proud of that! Never before ... have 500 million people declared peace. And never before have 500 million people enjoyed our levels of social security. (*Krone* reader, 22 July 2009, p. 19, my translation)

This calls for several observations. First, this reader's letter constitutes a noteworthy instance of cosmopolitan counter-discourse in what is a generally strongly EU-sceptical newspaper. Second, context matters and changes of course, and it is therefore debatable if, several years of austerity politics later, the social security provided particularly in the Eurozone's most debt-stricken member states can be assessed quite so optimistically. Third, and most important for present analytical purposes, this reader operates with a deictic frame that is simultaneously local, national and European; such encompassment thus defines Europe as self-evidently and comfortably subsuming its various constitutive local/regional and national scales of identification.

In other formulations, however, pro-EU cosmopolitanism can also include elements of a national, internally strongly differentiating deixis:

> It is embarrassing how some of us Austrians are not prepared to look beyond narrow self-interest and fall prey to populist Eurosceptics. The creation of this project of peace was a quantum leap in European history. Despite existing weaknesses, one should be aware of that. Europe comprises 7% of the world's population, generates a quarter of the world's total economic output and half of the world's total social spending. (*Profil* reader, 31 March 2014, p. 7, my translation)

This reader's letter celebrates its European cosmopolitanism, in part, through clear self-differentiation from a carefully defined (internal) 'other': i.e. those co-nationals perceived and portrayed as misrecognizing the accomplishments of, and need for, the EU. Arguably also at work in the NEOS (2014) electoral slogan *Wir schauen über den Tellerrand*, loosely translated as 'We look beyond narrow self-interest' (http://orf.at/stories/2225818), such cosmopolitan articulations – perhaps somewhat paradoxically – also exhibit features of an orientalizing grammar of identity: in their oppositional self-demarcation from (the majority of) their purportedly non-cosmopolitan co-nationals, they perhaps point towards a contemporary version of what Ernest Gellner (1998) famously detected as a hallmark of the final decades of the Habsburg empire: a clash between cosmopolitan rationalism and romantic nationalism.

8. CONCLUDING COMMENTS

In June 2014, a post-election analysis suggested that Austria's tabloid press had considerable impact on the Austrian vote, confirming especially the *Krone Zeitung*'s continuing influence on widespread 'perceptions and interpretations of social and political realities' (http://news.orf.at/stories/2234555). Subsequent attempts to make sense of the European results cast their analytical nets more widely: *Falter* editor Armin Thurnher (2014c), for instance, invoked Perry Anderson's assessment of a European 'malaise', the purported symptoms of which included democratic deficits, corruption and the unresolved global economic crisis. Further afield, writing already prior to the EU elections in the German daily *Die Welt*, economist Thomas Straubhaar (2014) had argued that neo-nationalisms driven by recent economic crises mis-portrayed the EU as a scapegoat for all contemporary ills and thereby posed a very serious threat to the European project of peace and prosperity. All of this, to reiterate an earlier point, pre-dated the escalating Greek crisis in 2015 (see Lialiouti, this volume), the ongoing 'refugee crisis', the Brexit referendum in June 2016, as well as their joint impact on Austrian EU discussions, positions and anxieties since.

The spectrum of discursive positions vis-à-vis the EU revealed here helps analyse the many recent (trans)national debates concerning the EU's present and future. In particular, the delineation of five internally heterogeneous discursive stances – here discussed under the headings of *undoing Europe*, *re-doing Europe sceptically*, *doing Europe critically*, *doing Europe* and *celebrating cosmopolitanism* respectively – helps break the empirically relatively unilluminating binary between supposed 'pro-EU-' and 'EU-skeptical' perspectives. As we have seen, Austrian debates are considerably more varied than such a binary acknowledges. What is more, there are complex ideological entanglements and overlaps that require a more nuanced conceptual grid of the kind developed here. Thus, for example, in the run-up to the EU elections, Austria's pro-European Greens and the highly EU-sceptical FPÖ showed – all their profound ideological differences and contrasting suggestions as to *how* the EU ought to change notwithstanding – some overlap in their respective criticisms of the European status quo: those concerned the alleged influence of economic lobbies on EU politics, a commitment to non-GM food, TTIP's (and, since then, CETA's) purported dangers, and the need for some structural reforms on EU level (http://orf.at/stories/2229514/2229515). Through its close attention to the specific discursive characteristics and argumentative structures underpinning any of the competing arguments, this discussion has extrapolated more fine-grained, not always binary distinctions between the claims (or *topoi*), frames of identification (or types of *deixis*) and suggested self-other category relations (or *grammars of identity*) involved. While this has resulted in an extrapolation of heterogeneous discursive positions and ideological motivations, more research is needed both to measure the relative salience of the five broad stances (and the various sub-positions within them) across Austria's population and political spectrum, and to trace both individuals' and groups' negotiations of — and potential switches between — the different positions over time.

The conceptual frame developed here has potential applications far beyond Austria. For example, statements of the kind made by former British PM David Cameron, who declared that his country's EU exit 'would not break [his] heart' since, he claimed, 'things aren't really working for us' (http://www.orf.at/stories/2247737), yield themselves to the type of analysis proposed above: in deictic terms, Cameron's statement was unambiguously premised on a national 'us'; further, it transported various topoi of Britain's purported disadvantages incurred by virtue of its EU membership and the country's widely assumed economic viability without the EU and continuing global political standing; finally, Cameron — as the majority of his co-nationals — here operated with an orientalizing grammar of identity, defining the nation and 'Europe' as mutually exclusive, rigidly separate categories of identification.

Such orientalizing grammars — whether articulated by a British PM, in some of the Austrian examples discussed earlier or elsewhere — are the most explicit and direct way of discursively *undoing* Europe. As we have seen, however, there are also numerous other arguments, claims and ideological dispositions that contribute to the current tide of sentiments threatening to undo the European project. Meanwhile, attempts to discursively and productively *do* Europe are themselves internally varied and, in many of their formulations, far from uncritical in relation to existing institutional realities.

REFERENCES

Anderson, B. (1983). *Imagined communities*. London: Verso.
Baumann, G. (2004). Grammars of identity/alterity: A structural approach. In G. Baumann & A. Gingrich (Eds.), *Grammars of identity/alterity* (pp. 18–50). New York, NY: Berghahn.
Baumann, G., & Gingrich, A. (Eds.), (2004). *Grammars of identity/alterity*. New York, NY: Berghahn.

Bell, D. S. (2003). Mythscapes: Memory, mythology, and national identity. *British Journal of Sociology, 54*(1), 63–81.

Billig, M. (1995). *Banal nationalism*. London: Sage.

Bruckmüller, E. (1996). *Nation Österreich*. Vienna: Böhlau.

Bushell, A. (2013). *Polemical Austria*. Cardiff: University of Wales Press.

Castells, M. (2000). *End of millennium*. Oxford: Blackwell.

Cram, L. (2009). Introduction. *Nations & Nationalism, 15*(1), 101–108.

Der Standard (2014). *Der Standard*, 29 April 2014, p. 8.

Esterberg, K. (2002). *Qualitative methods in social research*. Boston, MA: McGraw Hill.

Eurobarometer (2010). Standard EB 73, Spring 2010. http://ec.europa.eu/public_opinion/archives/eb/eb73/eb73_fact_at_en.pdf (Accessed on February 7, 2011).

Filzmaier, P. (2010). *Der Zug der Lemminge*. Salzburg: Ecowin.

Fink, A. G., & Treichler, R. (2014). Ein Pakt mit dem Chlorhühnchen. *Profil, 3*(13), January, 52–55.

Gellner, E. (1998). *Language and solitude*. Cambridge: Cambridge University Press.

Gepp, J. (2014). Am Apparat: warum will die EU Bierkrüge verbieten, Herr Corazza?. *Falter, 11*, 9.

Gingrich, A. (2006). Nation, status and gender in trouble. In A. Gingrich & M. Banks (Eds.), *Neo-nationalism in Europe and beyond* (pp. 29–49). New York, NY: Berghahn.

Gnam, P. (2014). Leere Versprechen der Politiker ärgern Österreicher am meisten. *Kronen Zeitung, 15*, August, 5.

Guibernau, M. (2007). *The identity of nations*. Cambridge: Polity.

Hall, S., Critcher, C., Jefferson, T., Clarke, J., & Roberts, B. (1978). *Policing the crisis*. Basingstoke: Macmillan.

Hanisch, E. (1994). *Der lange Schatten des Staates*. Vienna: Ueberreuter.

Heer, F. (2001 [1981]). Der Kampf um die österreichische Identität. Vienna: Böhlau.

Hofinger, C. (2014). Wahlrecht für den Groll auf Europa. *Falter, 12*, 6–7.

http://insider.vienna-marathon.com/?url = news&newsDetail = 1981, Accessed on October 14, 2014.

http://kaernten.orf.at/news/stories/2633249, (26 February 2014), "EU-Wahl: Haiders Tochter will Vater verteidigen", Accessed on February 26, 2014.

http://news.orf.at/stories/2234555, (18 June 2014), "EU-Wahl-Nachlese: 'Boulevard' hatte großen Einfluss", Accessed on June 18, 2014.

http://ooe.orf.at/news/stories/2637458, (25 March 2014), "Österreicher skeptisch gegenüber EU", Accessed on March 25, 2014.

http://orf.at/stories/2225818, (12 May 2014), "FPÖ und NEOS präsentierten EU-Wahlplakate", Accessed on May 12, 2014.

http://orf.at/stories/2229514/2229515, (12 May 2014) "Nur wenige Überschneidungen", Accessed on May 12, 2014.

http://orf.at/stories/2244035/2244037, (9 September 2014), "Strache hält an Neuwahlforderung fest: 'Anstand keine Frage der Herkunft'", Accessed on September 9, 2014.

http://www.europa-geht-anders.eu, "Europa geht anders. Verhindern wir die 'Troika für alle' – Nein zum Wettbewerbspakt", Accessed on May 30, 2013.

http://www.neos.eu/programm/9-europa-umarmen/, Accessed on October 16, 2014.

http://www.orf.at/stories/2223976, (3 March 2014), "Umfrage: 64 Prozent für Verbleib in der EU", Accessed on October 30, 2014.

http://www.orf.at/stories/2243125, (25 August 2014) "Koalition will Rederecht für EU-Abgeordnete im Nationalrat", Accessed on August 26, 2014.

http://www.orf.at/stories/2247737, (30 September 2014), "EU-Austritt würde Cameron 'nicht das Herz brechen'", Accessed on September 30, 2014.

http://www.eustop.at/programm.html, Accessed on October 30, 2014.

Karner, C. (2005). The 'Habsburg dilemma' today: Competing discourses of national identity in contemporary Austria. *National Identities, 7*(4), 411–434.

Karner, C. (2010). The uses of the past and European integration: Austria between Lisbon, Ireland and EURO 08. *Identities, 17*(4), 387–410.

Karner, C. (2011). *Negotiating national identities*. Farnham: Ashgate.

Karner, C. (2013). Europe and the Nation: Austrian EU-scepticism and its contestation. *Journal of Contemporary European Studies*, *21*(2), 252–268.

Kramar-Schmid, U. (2014). Undankbares Volk. *Profil*, *23*(2), June, 11.

Kronen Zeitung, various dates and page numbers as in text.

Krzyżanowski, M., Triandafyillidou, A., Wodak, R. (2009). Introduction. In A. Triandafyillidou, R. Wodak, & M. Krzyżanowski (Eds.), *The European public sphere and the media* (pp. 1–12). Basingstoke: Palgrave.

Krzyżanowski, M., & Wodak, R. (2009). *The politics of exclusion*. New Brunswick: Transaction.

Lahodynsky, O. (2008). Allianz der Angstmacher. *Profil*, *15*(7), April, 26–29.

Lahodynsky, O. (2014a). Verordnungshalber. *Profil*, *4*(20), January, 16–20.

Lahodynsky, O. (2014b). Starke Ansagen. *Profil*, *32*(4), August, 54.

Langthaler, M. (2014). Ein neues Europa. *Kronen Zeitung*, *20*, February, 20.

Liessmann, K. (2005). *Die Insel der Seligen*. Innsbruck: Studienverlag.

Lingens, P. M. (2014). 'Gurkenkrümmung' vs. 'Bankenunion'. *Profil*, *19*(5), May, 128.

Linsinger, E. (2014). Alle Menschen samma zwider. *Profil*, *21*(19), May, 18–20.

Lubbers, M., & Scheepers, P. (2007). Explanations of political Euro-scepticism at the individual, regional and national levels. *European Societies*, *9*(4), 643–669.

Lynn, N., & Lea, S. (2003). A 'phantom menace' and the 'new apartheid'. *Discourse & Society*, *14*(4), 425–452.

Marterbauer, M. (2014). Die Schreckensbilanz des EU-Kommissars. *Falter*, *8*, 6–7.

Menasse, R. (2012). *Der europäische Landbote*. Vienna: Zsolnay.

Merlingen, M., Mudde, C., & Sedelmeier, U. (2001). The right and the righteous? European norms, domestic politics and the sanctions against Austria. *Journal of Common Market Studies*, *39*(1), 59–77.

NEOS. (2014). *Wahlprogramm 2014: Pläne für ein neues Europa*. Vienna: Das Neue Österreich und liberales Forum. Retrieved from http://www.neos.eu. Accessed on May 1, 2014.

Portisch, H. (2011). *Was jetzt?* Salzburg: Ecowin.

Profil, various dates and page numbers as in text.

Rainer, C. (2014). EU. Nicht wichtig. *Profil*, *13*(24), March, 11.

Rathkolb, O. (2005). *Die paradoxe Republik*. Vienna: Zsolnay.

Reisigl, M., & Wodak, R. (2001). *Discourse and discrimination*. London: Routledge.

Reiterer, A. (Ed.), (1988). *Nation und Nationalbewußtsein in Österreich*. Vienna: VWGÖ.

Rittberger, M. (2009). Wie kommt die Ausländerfeindlichkeit in die Kronen Zeitung?. In Bardakçi, S. et al. (Eds.), *Dazugehören oder nicht?* (pp. 40–57). Innsbruck: Studienverlag.

Schiedel, H. (2011). *Extreme Rechte in Europa*. Vienna:Steinbauer.

Startin, N., & Krouwel, A. (2013). Euroscepticism re-galvanized: the consequences of the 2005 French and Dutch rejection of the EU constitution. *Journal of Common Market Studies*, *51*(1), 65–84.

Stråth, B., & Wodak, R. (2009). Europe-discourse-politics-media-history: constructing 'crises'?. In A. Triandafyillidou, R. Wodak, & M. Krzyżanowski (Eds.), *The European public sphere and the media* (pp. 15–33). Basingstoke: Palgrave.

Straubhaar, T. (2014). Der neue Nationalismus stürzt Europa in den Abgrund. Retrieved from http://m.welt.de/article.do?id=wirtschaft/article125451311/Der-neue-Nationalismus-st...... (Accessed on March 11, 2014).

Strickner, A. (2013). Der EU-Wettbewerbspakt bedroht den sozialen Frieden Europas. *Falter*, *44*, 6.

Thaler, P. (2001). *The ambivalence of identity*. West Lafayette, IN: Purdue University Press.

Thurnher, A. (2014a). Interview. *Falter*, *13*, 10–12.

Thurnher, A. (2014b). Hypo Alpe Adria: nicht systemrelevant, aber sie stellt das System in Frage. *Falter*, *8*, 5.

Thurnher, A. (2014c). Was Europa krank macht. Was wir dagegen tun können. *Falter*, *22*, 5.

Toplak, C., & Šumi, I. (2012). Europe(an Union): Imagined community in the making?. *Journal of Contemporary European Studies*, *20*(1), 7–28.

Uhl, H. (2006). From victim myth to co-responsibility thesis. In R. Lebow, W. Kansteiner, & C. Fogu (Eds.), *The politics of memory in postwar Europe* (pp. 40–72). Durham, NC: Duke University Press.

Vettermann, D. (2014). Briten-Premier zieht Anti-EU Show ab!. *Kronen Zeitung, 28*, June, 2–3.

Vettermann, D., Hauenstein, C., & Ebeert, C. (2014). Russisches Importverbot: EU-Soforthilfe für unsere Bauern. *Kronen Zeitung, 9*, August, 2–3.

Wodak, R. (2007). Discourses in European Union organizations. *Text & Talk, 27*(5–6), 655–680.

Wodak, R., de Cillia, R., Reisigl, M., & Liebhart, K. (1999). *The discursive construction of national identity*. Edinburgh: Edinburgh University Press.

BRITAIN, BULGARIA AND BENEFITS: THE POLITICAL RHETORIC OF EUROPEAN (DIS)INTEGRATION

James Moir

ABSTRACT

This chapter considers the political controversy in Britain over the lifting of restrictions of freedom of movement on European Union (EU) citizens from Bulgaria and Romania in January 2014. The response of the then Conservative-Liberal Democrat Coalition Government centred on altering the rules on the payment of welfare benefits to potential new EU immigrants such that they would not be entitled to claim these benefits for 3 months after entry to the United Kingdom. This policy led to a split in the coalition, with the Liberal Democrat leadership claiming that it was a panicked move by the majority Conservative coalition partner, and moreover that it was a blatant attempt to appeal the electorate in an effort to be seen to be doing something to stop the welfare benefit system from being abused by 'foreigners'. The backdrop to this political fracas centred on the economic contribution of East European immigrants to Britain and the claim and counterclaim over the issues jobs, welfare benefits and services such as English language support in schools. These contentious issues are examined in terms of an analysis of online comments to posted in reaction to a political interview with Vince Cable, the Liberal Democrat business secretary, who claimed that the

National Identity and Europe in Times of Crisis: Doing and Undoing Europe, 61–82
doi:10.1108/978-1-78714-513-920171004

Conservatives were attempting to placate public disquiet over immigration as a response to the rising popularity of the United Kingdom Independence Party.

Keywords: Europe; Bulgaria; Romania; immigration; United Kingdom; discourse

1. INTRODUCTION

Lesińska (2014) has charted the rise of anti-immigration discourse accompanied by tighter immigration controls across Europe in recent years, and in particular since the 'Great Recession' and economic crisis of 2008. However, this critical discourse pre-dates the recession and is part of a larger pattern featuring the 'immigration debate'. As Braidotti (2011, p. 242) has pointed out European expansion has also occurred at a time of fragmentation and rising nationalist sentiment and sectarianism:

> Unification coexists with the closing down of borders; the common European citizenship and common currency coexist with increasing internal fragmentation and regionalism; a new allegedly postnationalist identity exists with the return of xenophobia, racism and anti-Semitism.

Political reaction to these contradictions and schisms within the European Union (EU) has occurred at the level of both fringe and mainstream party politics as well as through governmental policies aimed at limiting immigration. However, from the perspective of the study presented in this chapter, it is 'down' at the level of the general population where people represent themselves and others in terms of ethnic and national identifications that such matters are brought to the fore. It is at this level where these issues become problematical in the face of rising levels of immigration. 'Labour market' immigrants from within the EU are considered as far less problematic than that of other categories such as those who are regarded as seeking nothing more than access to state benefits or who are associated with petty crime, and perceived as 'failed citizens' (Anderson, 2013). Nevertheless, as Lesińska points out, in the post-9/11 world, there has been a rival of concerns about 'foreigners' and these have merged with concerns about immigration in general. A new climate of opinion has given 'right-authoritarian' parties purchase amongst the electorate in a number of counties, and particularly in the context of the EU and its enlargement through the accession of countries in 2004 and 2007 (Berezin, 2009; Mudde, 1999, 2012). This has gathered pace in the post-2008 economic recession with increasing numbers of migrants from crisis-hit counties seeking work in the relatively stronger Western European economies (Barslund & Busse, 2014, pp. 10–11).

Although this backlash against immigration has also found some populist support, its effects upon political leaders have for the most part resulted in defensive policies. This resulted in attempts to curb immigration in some way or other by placing restrictions and limits on those seeking to enter into a country. This has taken the form of citizenship tests (e.g. obligatory integration courses and language tests) or restrictions on rights to welfare benefits (Currie, 2008; Dwyer & Scullion, 2014; Lesińska, 2014). As a result the thrust of EU reform strategies in relation the liberalization of the labour market has largely remained intact, notwithstanding concerns about 'cheap labour' and job competition in host countries. However, there has also been a rising tide of critical discourse in Europe that has sought to undermine ideas of 'multiculturalism' with claims of threats to national culture, identity and community cohesion (e.g., Kymlicka, 2010). These 'traditional' objections to immigration have merged with economic concerns over jobs, welfare costs and fiscal burdens giving rise to the status of immigrants as major political issue in a number of EU states (Lesińska, 2014).

In the United Kingdom (UK) this has resulted in the increasing popularity of the UKIP, the United Kingdom Independence Party (Ford & Goodwin, 2014; Martin & Smith, 2014). This political party advocates withdrawal from the EU as well as claiming that immigration is 'out of control' in the UK. For example, one of their 2013 posters read 'Next year, the EU will allow 29 million Bulgarians and Romanians to come to the UK'. 'The Government have admitted there's nothing we can do about it, while we're in the EU'. ('And Labour say they don't want to do anything anyway'.) Another poster in relation to the European Parliamentary elections of May 2014 showed what was supposed to be a native British construction worker 'begging' in the street with the caption 'EU Policy at Work'. 'British Workers are hit hard by unlimited cheap labour'. 'Take control of our country'. 'Vote UKIP on May 22nd'.

Mintchev (2014) has examined the ways in which UKIP and its leader Niger Farage have constructed an anti-immigration stance against Bulgarians and Romanians settling in the UK. There are several strands to their arguments but taken together they create exclusionary discourses that, although ostensibly being culturally and ethnically neutral, seek to present the potential negative impact of *all* such immigrants. One line of argument suggests that they are a threat to jobs that otherwise would be taken by young British people whilst another claims that they are 'benefit seekers' based on the presentation of differences in the relative economic wealth between the UK and Eastern Europe. Such seemingly rational arguments lend themselves to being more persuasive given that they are not couched in an overtly racist manner and steer clear of asserting cultural or national superiority. However, another argument presented does rely on the notion of challenges to cultural cohesion and integration through the claim that immigration needs to be curbed lest communities find themselves facing increasing disruption. Although such arguments often rely on making the case through drawing upon language differences they are

also tinged with negative cultural stereotypes of criminality associated with
East European Roma gypsies.

It against this backdrop that the British Broadcasting Corporation (BBC)
ran a story on 22 December 2013 in which Vince Cable the Liberal Democrat
Party Business Secretary within the Liberal Democrat-Conservative Coalition
Government claimed the Conservatives were 'in a bit of a panic because of
UKIP' and that any proposed 75,000-a-year cap on the number of EU migrants
to the UK would not happen. The Government had previously indicated that
it would place a curb on immigrant claiming welfare benefits for the first
3 months of residency but the Home Secretary, Theresa May, has not ruled out
a possible future cap on numbers. In response to these measures the BBC article cited comments made by the Bulgarian President Rosen Plevneliev who
warned that Prime Minister David Cameron's plans curb immigration could
damage the UK's image as a 'great global power that pioneered integration'.
Proposals seeking to curb immigrants' rights to welfare benefits in the UK has
remained on both on the national and EU agenda. For example, Prime
Minister Cameron 'passionately urged other EU leaders to support his "reason-
able" proposals for far-reaching curbs on welfare benefits for migrants' (BBC,
28/11/14: http://www.bbc.co.uk/news/uk-politics-30224493). This is linked to
his party's policy on an in/out referendum on the EU in the post-2015 general
election landscape with the argument being made that the UK will be more
likely to vote to stay in if such measures are adopted.

This chapter analyses the comments posted in reaction to original news story
when such plans were first mooted. The analysis examines what these comments
reveal about the rhetorical ground on which claims are made by those who
wish to curb immigration or those who support it. In order to do this I draw
upon the work of Billig (Billig, 1991; Billig et al., 1988) who argues that
nationalism is dilemmatic in nature in that it makes use of universalism and
particularism; one nation within a world of nations. Billig and his colleagues
further argue that this related to 'ideological dilemmas' that characterize common-sense thinking in that contrary views and themes require that people must
construct a rhetorical position that is in actual, or potential opposition, to 'the
other side of the coin'.

Condor et al. have shown the analytical power of these ideas in relation the
strategic construction of national identities in the UK. For example, this
includes an examination of the ways in which opposing themes such as multiculturalism and Anglo-centrism, or national diversity and tolerance, are pitted
against cultural homogeneity (Condor, 2011; Verkuyten, 2004). Such oppositional themes can sometimes be constructed together in such a way as to allow
for the existence of multiple and conflicting positions to be adopted in relation
to self and the other and to suppress the attribution of any negative in-group
stereotype (Andreouli, 2013). And, in contemporary work that has a bearing
on the present study, Andreouli and Dashtipour (2014) found that citizenship
officers in London constructed the UK as humanitarian and tolerant on the

one hand whilst on the other as being threatened by increasing numbers of immigrants. This often involved talking about immigrants in terms of being either 'good' or 'bad', or as 'deserving' or 'undeserving', in relation to criteria for the process of inclusion or exclusion as citizens.

The data reported upon in the chapter is analysed with this dilemmatic nature of argumentation in mind with respect to the comments posted on the BBC news story outlined above. However, unlike this previous work, the analysis undertaken is more concerned with the rhetorical ground on which arguments rest and where a 'stand is made'.

2. DATA AND METHODOLOGY

The story provoked a considerable reaction on the BBC news website with 1417 comments being posted in total (see http://www.bbc.co.uk/news/uk-politics-25484456). As anticipated most of the comments posted were made as a negative reaction to the Cable's comments contained in news story. These varied from what may be regarded as overtly hostile to more 'reasoned' positions. Any offensive posts were removed under BBC house rules pertaining to comments that are 'racist, sexist, homophobic, sexually explicit, abusive or otherwise objectionable'. There were also a number of comments made that were in agreement with a liberal UK immigration policy or that challenged other's ultra-right-wing or 'racist' comments.

In a similar approach to Andreouli and Dashtipour (2014), these comments were analysed in a theoretically guided thematic manner using the notion of 'latent thematic analysis' (Braun & Clarke, 2006). This permitted an analysis in which arguments and counter-arguments, themes and counter-themes, could be examined as within a dialectical relationship with each other. However, the analytical focus in this chapter differs in emphasis from that of Andreouli and Dashtipour's work in that it seeks to show how each opposing 'side in the debate' draws upon particular rhetorical constructions to shore up and bolster its position. In other words, the focus of the analysis is the rhetorical act of winning the argument and of making a position that is credible and persuasive. No attempt has been made to quantify these comments given that the analysis focuses on rhetorical forms and is not concerned with distributions of views across the data. Moreover, it was anticipated that most of the comments would be reactive against Cable's remarks about the illegality of the proposed cap on EU immigrants and Bulgarian President's intervention. In other words, the people tend to post comments in a period of heightened political activity with the result that this would not permit any kind of distributive sampling to evaluate relative strengths of opinion (Boczkowski & Mitchelstei, 2012). Themes were identified in an inductive manner through organizing the comments in terms of their rhetorical strategies (e.g. resource-based arguments, employment, cultural issues) in either supporting or arguing against Cable and his remarks, as well as more broadly the issue of East European immigration to the UK. Also borne in mind was van Dijk's (1998, p. 33) concept of the 'ideological square' in which the twin strategies of positive 'ingroup' description and negative 'outgroup' description manifest themselves through lexical choice and other linguistic features to emphasize and 'us' and 'them' ideological framework. The themes were then examined further in considering the deployment of assertions and/or supporting 'evidence'.

The comments presented below in the analysis have had all identifiers removed, save their comment number. Typographical errors have been corrected, and where comments contained 'texting-language' these have also been corrected to enable readability. In all other respects the comments presented are as posted with no amendments to content.

3. FINDINGS

3.1 The Rhetoric of Resources

As noted above, it is not the purpose of this chapter to politically side with these reactions in one way or another but rather to examine their rhetorical construction. One of the most common themes present in the data was the 'rhetoric of resources'. This was particularly drawn upon by those objecting to the liberalization of UK immigration in relation immigrants coming from Eastern Europe. Such people are positioned as being an actual or potential source of 'competition' for resources that are presented as being finite or constrained in some way or other. This type of comment came in various forms ranging from a simple statement about overcapacity and resources to more elaborate formulations that countered claims of racism.

Examples of relatively 'straightforward' claims about resource constraints are presented in comments 541, 772 and 472 below. Their rhetorical force is constructed in different ways although they all make much the same point. In comment 541 the rhetorical impact derives from its brief assertive sentences and by ending on a 'plea' to political leaders. Comment 772 also appeals those in 'authority' to recognize that the UK is 'grossly overcrowded' and hints at the effects on the 'army' of 'young unemployed'. The juxtaposition of immigrants coming with their 'wives and children in tow' with that 'unemployed youth' is a powerful rhetorical claim for curbing immigration. Comment 472 uses the familiar technique of a rhetorical question ('Why would we need more unskilled workers?') in relation to prior resource shortage claims. Note the assertion that immigrants are 'unskilled'.

Comment number 541

We are over-populated.

Our schools are full.

Our roads are full.

Our trains are full, with no seats left.

Hospitals are overflowing.

The skies are jam-packed.

… and much more!

Mr Clegg and Mr Cable − our infrastructure cannot take more people!

Comment number 772

Does no one in authority realize that the UK is grossly overcrowded as it is without even more people being allowed to come here with their wives and children in tow. We've got no spare capacity in houses, schools, health care and both trains and roads are bursting at the seams. Plus the fact that we can't provide jobs for the army of unemployed, especially the young.

Comment number 472

The country is overcrowded, we have a shortage of houses, hospital beds and the classrooms are full. Why would we need more unskilled workers?

Examples of comments that countered claims of racism are presented below. These were given either directly in response to another participant's comment or in more general terms. Comment 1256 adopts the more general response by arguing that a concern with resources is not 'racism'. The simplicity of this contrast structure differs from comment 1385 which turns the argument into an environmental concern and the need to maintain a 'pleasant country'.

Comment number 1256

Re the 'racist' argument − disagreeing with mass immigration is not racist. I am sure that more Eastern Europeans are hard-working people who are simply wanting to improve their standard of living. The problem is the sheer numbers coming to the UK − at a time when we have a housing crisis, a shortage of primary school places, an overstretched National Health Service (NHS), crowded roads, etc. This is not racism!

Comment number 1385

In response to Comment number 1372.

> Immigration can work if we are willing to spend on infrastructure − massive house, school, hospital and transport building programmes. But not if we shy away from these issues.

And then more, and then more... You can't keep adding to infrastructure indefinitely, and in the mean time you end up with a less pleasant country than one that needs less infrastructure to cope.

Although those who argued against such views were in a minority, the counter-rhetorical stance to the focus on resources shortages was to redirect the criticism at previous UK government policy decisions. Comments 1404 and 1093 represent examples of this redirection back to politicians. In the case of comment 1404 the issue of housing shortages back to a previous Conservative government policy whilst comment 1093 makes a more general point about resources being exploited for the few.

Comment number 1404
If your objections to immigration is based in a housing shortage, then cast your mind back to the 1980s when Mrs T forced the sell-off of council housing but stopped any replacement of the housing stock to turn a house from somewhere you lived to a speculative commodity.

As for UKIP simply a one trick pony party whose leader decries the EU yet carries on drawing his Member of European Parliament (MEP) pay − A tad hypocritical.

Comment number 1093
Politicians of this country have made people to believe that reason behind all the problems is immigration, not exploitation of country's resources for the advantage of few.

3.2 Constructing the Citizen-Contributor

The immigrant as a citizen-contributor was also a common theme within the corpus of comments. As might be anticipated there were a number of comments that juxtaposed the immigrant with the taxpayer-citizen or the 'good' immigrant as a skilled person who works hard and pays their taxes with the 'benefit tourist' or unskilled migrant worker. Examples of these kinds of rhetorical construction are presented below. The simplicity of this contrast structure is that it set up the issue as a simple either/or. Metaphors such as 'fling the gates open' or humorous quips such as referring to the UK as 'Treasure Island' serve to strengthen these contrasts by heightening the problematization of immigration. However, as can be seen later, such a construction is open to being easily countered because of this very one-dimensional simplicity and sometimes undisguised stereotyping of immigrants.

Comment number 1096
So what's happening at our borders.

Well we have Labour and the Lib Dems wanting to fling the gates open so anyone can come in and claim benefits. Meanwhile you have taxpayers and the Tories calling for the gates to be closed.

Taxpayers (the few of us left), we know which way to vote now, don't we?

Comment number 1038

Nothing wrong with immigration if it's controlled.

But!

Any country that accepts immigrants, should be able to pick and choose who comes in.

It they don't offer anything to benefit the people who already live here then they shouldn't qualify.

Skilled people YES please.

Benefit tourists NO thanks.

Comment number 956

You don't have to cap immigration. Just REMOVE the benefits for 12 months. They won't come then.

Vince Cable you are wrong. Ask yourself why come to UK when passing all other EU countries, it's because UK offer best benefits. No wonder they call us Treasure Island.

Comment number 389

Immigrants who come to this country to work are welcome. Those who arrive, expecting immediate handouts of UK taxpayers' money are not. It really is that simple. The PM is right to introduce rules governing benefits paid to new immigrants. If the EU do not like it, then we should leave.

Comment number 362

If you have a job lined up then I don't think it's so much of a problem.

However if you have no job, why should you be entitled to the benefit system and NHS? It's not paid for by the EU it's paid for by taxpayers of the UK who in these austere times are struggling to foot the bill for those who already live at present in the UK. Free movement ok.

Freeloading?

Definitely not.

Comment number 216

An educated and skilled American who will not claim a penny in benefits and contribute positively to the economy will basically find it impossible today to get a visa as they are non-EU citizens. An uneducated, non-English speaking Romanian who is here for the sole purpose of claiming benefits only — welcome to the UK, here's some free money! Good for the economy Lib Dems? You haven't a clue.

Comment number 54
Polish people are mainly single, came here to work and got jobs and don't use/abuse public services and pay into the system. BUT – it'll be a completely different demographic from Romania and Bulgaria – purely benefit/health tourism. These countries are corrupt. Has to be a restriction – ONLY PEOPLE WITH JOBS WHO WILL PAY INTO THE SYSTEM. This influx will further decimate health services.

As noted above these comments lend themselves to being easily countered either directly by pointing out the 'good' immigrant-contributor (comments 1380, 741, 210) or by drawing attention to the one-dimensional nature of the 'blame the immigrant' argument (comments 1279, 1287, 823, 779).

Comment number 1380
Overall immigration is a good thing. New blood, new skills, ideas, etc. we are after all a nation of immigrants. The difficult thing is that there seems to be little in the way of (a) helping immigrants adapt to UK life; (b) stopping those with a criminal record from entering the UK; (c) having some control over the deportation of those who seek to undermine our way of life.

It is a complex issue...

Comment number 741
The fact is that those EU migrants come here to WORK. Almost all of them. They ARE good for Britain. If one thinks they lose their jobs to foreigners then how miserable they have to be to lose a job to a foreign guy who doesn't speak the language properly? One must be ashamed to say so. Moreover most of those who claim having lost their job seemingly have never even had one.

Comment number 210
Immigration has been the bedrock on which our countries have been built, since before our little group of islands could even call themselves countries.

Immigrants throughout the ages have enriched the UK in all matters financial, cultural and spiritual, and they continue to do so today.

We should welcome any and all who wish to call our home their own, and together reap the benefits that follow.

Comment number 1279
I don't have a job – Blame it on immigrants. I can't raise my kids – Blame it on immigrants.... I don't have a good education – Blame it on immigrants... My Health is poor – Blame it on immigrants. Stop these xenophobic attacks on immigrant... Having studied and worked with Eastern Europeans, I must

say they are a lovely people and work hard unlike some of our own people here.

Comment number 1287
Most immigrants are hard workers, that scares the bone idle Brits to death.

Comment number 823
The British view of the average immigrant is disproportional. Working immigrants is exactly what this country needs; more tax to pay for our ageing population. Most of the immigrants are skilled, filling jobs that Britain doesn't have enough of. The rest are students, who spend billions per year.

If you're unemployed, I would suggest you take the initiative of these immigrants, and look elsewhere.

Comment number 779
I think it's a myth that large numbers come over for benefits as I work with quite a few Eastern Europeans, they come over as they can earn more money here than they can at home and they either settle and pay tax like the rest or pay tax while working and then leave.

We should be asking ourselves why people from Eastern Europe who rarely speak English are better candidates for jobs than locals.

3.3 Constructing Politicians and the Populace

Another form of rhetorical construction present in the posts is the connection, or lack of connection, between politicians and the populace. Anti-immigration rhetoric within the data most commonly alluded to the political elite being out of touch with the 'ordinary' voters. Examples of this kind of construction are presented below and in each case draw attention to the alleged political consequence/backlash. Such constructions vary in their rhetorical force by drawing on name calling, references to being politically correct, or deluded. Nevertheless all present the case that politicians should be in touch and reactive to voters' concerns or otherwise face the political consequences.

Comment number 1400
Cable is an idiot if he doesn't understand by now that this is a serious issue for voters. Arrogantly describing it as panic is just another pseudo-intellectual conceit from the 'right on' PC establishment that allowed unrestrained immigration in the first place. You are not listening to the votes Cable and you will reap the whirlwind in the next General Election.

Comment number 1360
Cable is completely mad if he thinks remaining passive in the face of open borders with Romania and Bulgaria is the best way to allay people's fears. This issue will cause the overthrow of the political class, who are in the grip of a delusion.

Comment number 1040
The apathy to address the British people's concerns about mass uncontrolled immigration will be the downfall of the political parties currently in Westminster. Is it any wonder UKIP are on the rise? They are the only political party that isn't afraid to pussy foot around this issue. What the Tories are proposing is all smoke and mirrors.

Comment number 1014
The Lib Dems are reading this one very badly. The majority of the public are frustrated and upset by the rapid culture change being forced onto the country placing a burden on its infrastructure and people. All this is, rightly or wrongly, bringing us closer to leaving the EU. The libs need to be more in tune with public thinking and legitimate worries... But I suppose it doesn't affect them?

These kinds of comments were countered by claiming that populist extremism has taken hold and that this is 'beyond reason', threatening and disturbing. What is striking about these claims is the extent to which they mirror academic critiques as a rhetorical counter to anti-immigration.

Comment number 1295
The depressing thing is the lack of willingness of the mainstream parties to tackle such issues, or even admit that they are issues. By avoiding serious issues that have a bit of political danger about them a disturbing number of people start turning towards the more unhinged parties (who mostly want curbs for all the wrong reasons). Scary times.

Comment number 1267
So now the Tories are swinging to the xenophobic to placate the drift of their support to UKIP. It wasn't that long ago that Cameron referred to UKIP as swivel-eyed loons so if they are swivel-eyed loons by implication the Tories are too?

Comment number 635
There seems to be a lot of pride in how 'nasty' we are becoming as a nation; towards immigrants, the unemployed, pensioners, the disabled, towards those needing the help of food banks. These days we follow the likes of Nigel Farage, the former investment banker who 'talks our language' and therefore

CLEARLY is 'one of us' and anyone with a shred of empathy left for others is a leftie, communist, etc.

3.4 The Voice of Experience

Some contributors posted comments based upon personal circumstances and knowledge. These drew upon through largely the same rhetorical structure as those advocating anti- or pro-immigration positions. The voice of experience is presented in these accounts as verification for the position being argued for – it is rooted in what the person has encountered. These sorts of accounts are taken as being literally self-evident in that they are not based upon a more generalizable argument. This is both a strength and a weakness – to claim that your experience has taught you this or that is easily countered by someone else's contrary experience. Comments 1175, 843 and 802 are examples of an anti-immigration stance whilst comments 1327, 1273, 417 and 85 are examples of pro-immigrant rhetoric.

Comment number 1175
I've worked in Bucharest for 2 years, and I can completely understand why Romanians would want to escape their country. I've also visited Bulgaria and they are even poorer, considerably poorer. There is a total disregard from their own government for their own welfare, security and safety. I'm against mass immigration, but actually don't think they will arrive en masse. Many do work hard there.

Comment number 843
My young nephew is sick and tired of having his job applications turned down point blank because local employers have a policy of taking on immigrant workers – no questions asked! If local employers recruit immigrants they don't have to pay the minimum wage and also can get away with ignoring a whole load of legal requirements. It's got absolutely nothing to do with British workers being lazy!

Comment number 802
Come down to Luton in Chatham Kent. See the groups of Eastern Europeans, mostly Roma, who do not work, wander the streets in gangs, schools up to 50% Roma, Medway Maritime Hospital maternity unit struggling with their women turning up 9 months pregnant as their 1st appearance … . yeah, tell me unlimited migration is a good thing, all you goody goodys come and live amongst it.

Comment number 1327
Each summer, a lecturer at the local university would phone me and ask if I would take students on work experience during the holiday. Having interviewed five of them I had to say no because they had been taught nothing of our key processes. I have retired now but my previous position and others are now filled by brilliant young Europeans. Our problems would seem to stem from our own inabilities.

Comment number 735
We have just tried to employ eleven people on £24 a year we got just under a 100 apply most failed the entrance exam. We are now interviewing educated Poles who have almost all passed the exams.

Comment number 417
I happen to be one of the 'East European' migrants in UK. Part of my job is to hire people at my workplace. I give preference to native British but you may be shocked how hard that might be. Try explaining the importance of timekeeping to an ordinary 'working class' Brit. Or even importance of turning up at work at all. So nope we don't take their jobs. They just refuse to take them themselves.

Comment number 85
I know this will get a lot of likes but does anyone know any 'benefit tourists' personally. I worked as a cleaner alongside a staff which was majority Polish and I've never met a harder working people. We are scapegoating outsiders in times of economic hardship because that's a natural but very bigoted human reaction. Every benefit scrounger case I've heard of has been white and totally British.

3.5 Comparing Countries

Given UK's traditional links with Commonwealth countries and the United States, a number of posts made direct comparisons with immigration policies in Canada, Australia and the United States where there are points-based systems. Somewhat like the personal experience comments these types of comments drew their rhetorical force in equal measure by either advocating an immigration policy similar to those countries (comments 1376, 1286 and 497) or in pointing to the different reception of people from these countries in the UK in comparison to East Europeans (comments 1128, 585, 548). It is also notable that the pro-immigrant rhetoric extended to comparisons that pointed to hypocritical claim in relation to the status UK immigrant in other counties (comments 904 and 815).

Comment number 1376
I think we need to adopt a points-based migration system. If you are not skilled and you cannot contribute adequately then the subject migrant will inevitably become a drain/burden (welfare, public services, NHS etc...) and hence should not be allowed in. Free movement is all well and good in a single state/country, but that's not what the EU is (yet...).

Comment number 1268
Maybe we should take the standpoint of countries such as Australia whereby criteria for immigration into their country is strict, i.e. immigrants need a profession or trade useful to their economy/country and if I'm not wrong money in the bank to support their initial move. This said it seems outrageous that the UK as a smaller country with a bigger population continues to burden itself!

Comment number 497
We need immigration for certain high skilled areas and they contribute to our education system. However, that doesn't mean that access to this country should be a free-for-all and immigration should be reflected by economic needs. Over 2 million have come here since the recession. Modern liberal democracies like Australia and Canada have made access harder. Why can't we?

Comment number 1128
It amazes me that people are blaming immigration on the EU. The UK has been taking immigrants for cheap labour since the 1900s, India, Jamaica, etc. Why is it suddenly a problem? Governments have been happy for years with the situation, suddenly they make a fuss because they think it's a vote winner. Shameful.

Comment number 904
Er – I think you will find that Brits DID go to most countries and built their own churches, and created ghettos with different cultures, etc. It was called the British Empire, and yes, we DID get kicked out.

Comment number 815
For heaven's sake get a grip you commenters! under the same laws YOU have the total right to buy a farm in France, open a B&B in Bulgaria, manage a hotel in sunny Spain or retire to Rhodes. Look for Work anywhere! You can send your kids to university in Holland, tuition is £200 a term. You can get a major op done in France quicker than here. At least 700,000 of us live in Spain, 200,000 live in France.

Comment number 585
I've only see the little Englanders moaning about Eastern Europeans nobody
ever complains about the number of South Africans, Australians, Americans,
New Zealanders in the UK. They are all made welcome as they should be. pick-
ing on just Eastern Europeans is racist.

Comment number 548
Funny that many people who don't like immigrants (well, some kinds of immigrants – they probably think Australians, etc. are fine, but they're not being
racist, no…) are the same people who will be cared for by immigrants and will
rely on immigrant tax revenue.

   With the demographic 'bubble' of baby-boomers, low childbirth rates and
perpetual economic 'growth' immigration is the sensible solution.

3.6 Formulating Figures

A number of comments made reference to statistical information in some way
or other. These formulations tended to be used, as would be expected, to support a rhetorical claim. Those arguing against tended to used figures relating to
unemployed British nationals (e.g. comment 1381), the cost of living in the UK
being too high for most immigrants (e.g. comment 1107) or figures relating to
net immigration and the rising numbers within the UK relative 'dissatisfied
Britons' leaving (e.g. comment 1035).

Comment number 1381
Some in the media are stating working immigrants contribute to the UK government through their taxes – that is because in the majority of cases they are
taking jobs that could be filled by UK nationals. We have 965,000 unemployed
16–24 year olds and a total of 2.47 million unemployed. I see many Eastern
European workers locally in jobs traditionally taken by our youth. This can't
continue.

Comment number 1107
Most immigrants cannot afford to live in this country. To live in the south
without any assistance from the government requires an income of £50,000
a year. To buy a bog standard house requires an income of £60,000 a year.
A monthly food bill for a family of four is £400 + My basic point is that 90%
of immigrants should not move here unless they can earn the above…

Comment number 1035
It is not just the numbers immigrating (503,000) but the number of dissatisfied
Britons leaving (321,000). These are not the rich nor the poor, but the normal

British people. So the proportions of foreign to native-born is increasing more rapidly than the 'net immigration' figures imply with an increasingly detrimental effect on the British culture. good-bye GB.

Those in favour of a liberal immigration policy tended to support their argument through 'official' statistics. This kind of quoted use of statistics lends an external evidential basis to the claims being made in favour of immigration (comments 1407, 1032 and 471).

Comment number 1407
Facts: Between 2001 and 2011 EEA immigrants contributed to the fiscal system 34% more than they took out, with a net fiscal contribution of about 22.1 billion GBP. In contrast, over the same period, natives' fiscal payments amounted to 89% of the amount of transfers they received, or negative fiscal contribution of 624.1 billion Great British Pound (GBP).

http://www.cream-migration.org/publ_uploads/CDP_22_13.pdf

Comment number 1032
A study last year by the Office for Budget Responsibility (OBR) said that Gross Domestic Project (GDP) would grow by 2.3% in a decade under a scenario of high migration, 0.2% higher than if there was zero migration, and said the gap would widen in succeeding decades.

The OBR also said that migrants would have a beneficial effect on national debt. By 2062, with high migration, debt would be 50% of GDP; with low migration 90%.

Comment number 471
A recent Department for work and Pensions (DWP) report found that overall 16.6% of working age UK nationals were claiming a DWP working age benefit compared to 6.6% of working age non-UK nationals. So, based on data from National Insurance numbers, UK nationals are around two-and-a-half times as likely to be claiming working age benefits than non-UK nationals.

3.7 Asserting Motives

A number of posts addressed the issue through asserting unstated or underlying political motives. Those who took an anti-immigration line directed these assertions at EU or accession country political leaders. In other words, they were directed at drawing attention to sinister motives outwith the UK (comments 1388, 1310 and 610).

Comment number 1388
In response to comment number 1283

Why do the EU want freedom of movement?

They see it as an essential part of free trade, without it they reckoned some countries would deliberately maintain a low wage environment to undercut other members but with freedom of movement (free trade in Labour) then the best workers would get jobs in the higher wage countries leaving the undercutters with 'the dross'.

Comment number 1310

In response to comment number 1283

The EU wants free movement in order to destroy national identities and create on big European superstate modelled on the United States. It's about diluting cultures by breaking down boundaries. The intent is to spread wealth for which we won't benefit and prevent another world war. Problem is that it will start one.

Comment number 610

Why is the Bulgarian President keen for all his skilled workers to migrate to the UK? He knows the type of citizens that will want to move and it certainly won't be the high earners. Cable says that immigrants pay more tax than claim in benefits, but who does Mr Cable think that these migrants are taking available UK jobs from?

Comments made in favour of immigration asserted the underlying motives of the UK Government Conservative politicians with an eye on the populist vote and electoral advantage. Their rhetorical construction is based upon pointing out that political leaders are seeking to manipulate the masses through 'facing up' to the EU (comment 1391) or by keeping in step with the populist media (comments 1391, 1390, 1052 and 64).

Comment number 1391

Here we have a Government acting irresponsibly,

We, the people, are being fed misinformation and propaganda, for that's what it is.

All this engenders fear among the unthinking masses.

We are no more at risk from floods of 'immigrants' – (awful word) it's a government with nothing positive to do except pretend to be bossy with the rest of the EU.

It does us no favours, and makes us look idiotic!

Comment number 1390

Many frightened Tories citing the demise of the liberals – do they think the shambles of a Clown Party harbouring large factions of swivel-eyed tea party acolytes is likely to fare any better? Really?

Cameron is a u-turning marketeer with less substance than candy floss – his tenure is characterized by utter subservience to corporate interests and media posturing as a replacement for action.

Comment number 1052
What we need is truth speaking from Cameron and his party. If the Sun poll shows people think more than half of immigrants are on benefits, he needs to tell the truth – it is nowhere near that. He needs to say business loves cheap hard-working East Europeans, prepared to live 6 to a 2 bedroom house and send their wages home. He won't, he's a coward.

Comment number 64
Here we go again. Another chance for everyone to vent their anger against immigration. This is all part of the Tories re-election campaign orchestrated by their new strategist Lynton Crosby aided and abetted by the Sun and the Mail among others. Vote for the nasty party. They will give you plenty of scapegoats to blame for your problems while making sure their friends in the City are protected.

4. DISCUSSION

This chapter has provided an analysis of the thematic rhetorical construction of comments about UK immigration policy in relation to Business Secretary Vince Cable's remarks about the illegality of capping EU immigrant numbers. The themes emerging from the data – resources, the citizen-contributor, voices of experience, politicians and the populace, comparing counties, using figures and asserting motives – provide a means of charting the rhetorical strengths and weakness of either pro- or ant-immigration supporters. In the case of arguments about resources the power of this construction favours an anti-immigration stance. The claims made appeal to aspects such as housing, education and health and how these have been the subject of cutbacks during the recession such that increased immigration is claimed to add to an already worsening resources situation. This is constructed as a rational argument that is neutral in its political stance and is in effect, just 'telling it like it is'. In the context of EU enlargement this can be seen as a legitimate argument without any of the negative connotations of cultural or national superiority.

The citizen-contributor theme is addressed in different ways by each side of the argument. Anti-immigration comments draw their rhetorical strength from focusing upon the UK national as contributing to the taxation system and thereby being able to legitimately claim benefits. Immigrant as positioned in a dichotomous way as either skilled contributors or as benefit tourists. Such discursive constructions cohere to rule out Eastern European immigrants from coming to the UK: They are positioned as either they taking UK citizens' jobs or taking benefits. This kind of rhetoric is countered in two ways: (i) through constructing immigrants as necessary for the economic and cultural benefit of the country and (ii) by alluding to the easy-to-blame rhetoric of those who either through misfortune or their own failings are struggling economically or who are out of work.

Comments based upon the personal experience are the weakest rhetorical construction of either side of the argument. Whilst they attest to actual lived experience and circumstance this amounts to simply that a person's own experience. It can both be seen as sincere and authentic but at the same time seen as being less than representative. Nevertheless, this kind of rhetorical construction lends a personalized and experiential dimension.

A number of comments were directed at the portraying politicians as 'out of touch' with the populace or as extremists who were whipping up irrational fears. The rhetorical force of the 'out of touch' construction is that it asserts the views and experiences of the 'ordinary citizen' as opposed to the political elite. This in effect creates a dichotomy between the 'reality' of everyday life versus the world of political discourse. Those who argue that extremism has taken hold construct a rhetoric of irrationality and fear and that the public has unthinkingly gone along with this. Both sets of constructions trade upon the notion of reality versus fantasy.

The comparison of countries is a familiar rhetorical move when discussing immigration policy. Those arguing in favour of curbing immigration drew parallels with familiar and popular countries for those with relative who may have emigrated from the UK. Hence it was no surprise to see Canada and Australia mentioned the points-based immigration system they operate. Of course these countries are not part of the EU and therefore their mention sidesteps the issue of EU freedom of movement policy. This also leaves open the implication that the UK should not be part of the EU. Others countered such a view by drawing attention to the fact that UK nationals have moved in large numbers to other EU countries such as Spain, Bulgaria or France for different reasons and often related to retirement, second homes and leisure. It is also the case that comparisons are made with Australians, Canadians and American moving to the UK where there is little questioning of such immigration. Pointing out these sorts of inconsistencies is a powerful rhetorical strategy in countering anti-immigration discourse.

It was also interesting to see the different use made of statistical information on both sides of the argument. Anti-immigration arguments did not rely upon 'official' immigration statistics but instead pointed to figures such as numbers of UK unemployed. Pro-immigration arguments in almost all cases drew upon official immigration statistics to make the case for a liberal policy. By drawing upon external sources in this way the agency of the person making the comment is removed and the figures left to 'speak for themselves'.

Finally, in asserting the unstated motives of politicians anti-immigration arguments adopted a 'them and us' rhetorical construction in which the 'real' motives of 'them' — the EU or Bulgarian President — were somehow underhand and being 'hidden' from us (the 'British'). The counter rhetoric to this was constructed in terms of Conservative Government politicians of covering up the truth about immigration in order to appeal to populist sentiment as a means of securing electoral advantage.

In each of these themes the rhetorical force of the arguments deployed adopts a particular stance on the British citizen versus other (East) European immigrant in a dialectical manner. In the context of EU enlargement it is therefore evident that the discourse of integration is met with a range of populist representations that seek to counter this with an anti-immigration stance based rational argument rather than of rooted in xenophobia. Those who support immigration therefore find it difficult to challenge these arguments on racist grounds and are left in the position of having to engage on an evidential basis rather than through the expression of approval towards an integrationist EU position. The findings lend support to the Mintchev's (2014) view that the rhetoric of immigration as posing a threat to community cohesion is now used to justify calls to curb entry to East Europeans entering the UK. Based on the simple argument that there are now too many immigrants to cope with and that some communities are now stretched, it is easy to see how this argument seeks to evade any charge of racism. However it is also evident that the 'us' and 'them' nature of this discourse (Van Dijk, 1998, p. 33) betrays any sense of a common European citizenship. The findings also provide more detail on the sort of rhetorical constructions Andreouli and Dashtipour (2014) found in their examination of immigration officers. As they note, the ambivalence between 'good immigrant' rhetoric which shows Britain as a place of tolerance, freedom and humanitarian values is counter-posed in a binary way that of the 'bad immigrant' who is seeking to exploit the welfare system and where Britain needs to be protected from cultural threats and being drained economically.

REFERENCES

Anderson, B. (2013). *Us and them?: The dangerous politics of immigration control*. Oxford: Oxford University Press.

Andreouli, E. (2013). Identity and acculturation: The case of naturalised citizens in Britain. *Culture & Psychology, 19*, 165–183.

Andreouli, E., & Dashtipour, P. (2014). British citizenship and the 'other': An analysis of the earned citizenship discourse. *Journal of Community & Applied Social Psychology, 24*, 100–110.

Barslund, M., & Busse, M. (2014). *Making the most of EU labour mobility*. CEPS Task Force Reports. Retrieved from http://papers.ssrn.com/sol3/papers.cfm?abstract_id=2507228. Accessed on December 2, 2015.

Berezin, M. (2009). *Illiberal politics in neoliberal times*. Cambridge: Cambridge University Press.

Billig, M. (1991). *Ideology and opinions: Studies in rhetorical psychology*. London: Sage.

Billig, M., Condor, S., Edwards, D., Gane, M., Middleton, D., & Radley, A. (1988). *Ideological dilemmas: A social psychology of everyday thinking*. London: Sage.

Boczkowski, P. J., & Mitchelstei, E. (2012). How users take advantage of different forms of interactivity on online news sites: Clicking, e-mailing, and commenting. *Human Communication Research, 38*, 1−22.

Braidotti, R. (2011). *Nomadic theory: The portable Rosi Braidotti*. New York, NY: Columbia University Press.

Braun, V., & Clarke, V. (2006). Using thematic analysis in psychology. *Qualitative Research in Psychology, 3*, 77−101.

Condor, S. (2011). Rebranding Britain? Ideological dilemmas in political appeals to "British Multiculturalism". In M. D. Barrett, C. Flood, & J. Eade (Eds.), *Nationalism, ethnicity, citizenship: Multidisciplinary perspectives* (pp. 101−134). Newcastle upon Tyne: Cambridge Scholars Publishing.

Currie, S. (2008). *Migration, work and citizenship in the enlarged European Union*. Farnham: Ashgate.

Dwyer, P., & Scullion, L. (2014). *Conditionality Briefing: Migrants*. Welfare Conditionality: Sanctions, Support and Behaviour Change. Retrieved from http://www.welfareconditionality.ac.uk/wp-content/uploads/2014/09/Briefing_Migrants_14.09.10_FINAL.pdf. Accessed on December 2, 2015.

Ford, R., & Goodwin, M. (2014). Understanding UKIP: Identity, social change and the left behind. *The Political Quarterly, 85*, 277−284.

Kymlicka, W. (2010). The rise and fall of multiculturalism? New debates on inclusion and accommodation in diverse societies. *International Social Science Journal, 61*, 97−112.

Lesińska, M. (2014). The European backlash against immigration and multiculturalism. *Journal of Sociology, 50*, 37−50.

Martin, K., & Smith, K. (2014). UKIP and the rise of populist politics. *Anthropology Today, 30*, 1−2.

Mintchev, N. (2014). Logics of exclusion: Culture, economy and community in British anti-immigration discourses. In S. Wiseman (Ed.), *Assembling identities* (pp. 99−144). Newcastle upon Tyne: Cambridge Scholars Publishing.

Mudde, C. (1999). The single-issue party thesis: Extreme right parties and the immigration issue. *West European Politics, 22*, 182−197.

Mudde, C. (2012). *The relationship between immigration and nativism in Europe and North America*. Washington, DC: Migration Policy Group. Retrieved from http://works.bepress.com/cgi/viewcontent.cgi?article=1100&context=cas_mudde. Accessed on December 2, 2015.

Van Dijk, T. (1998). Opinions and ideologies in the press. In A. Bell & P. Garrett (Eds.), *Approaches to media discourse* (pp. 21−63). Oxford: Blackwell.

Verkuyten, M. (2004). Everyday ways of thinking about multiculturalism. *Ethnicities, 4*, 53−74.

EUROPEAN SECURITY UNDER THREAT: MEDIATING THE CRISIS AND CONSTRUCTING THE OTHER

Monika Kopytowska and Łukasz Grabowski

ABSTRACT

Departing from the assumption that discourse is both socially constituted and constitutive, and that social reality is co-constructed by the institutions of mass communication, this chapter takes under scrutiny media representation of the recent refugee crisis in Europe. The objective behind it is to maximise the validity of the Media Proximization Approach (MPA), drawing on the insights from Critical Discourse Studies, cognitive linguistics and corpus linguistics, in explicating how the media can potentially impact on the salience of issues and thus on public perception of problems and threats along with measures to be taken to deal with them. Examining the data from Poland, a European Union member state from Central Europe, criticised for its anti-refugee stance and refusal to accept the assigned quotas of migrants, and, importantly, the country 'experiencing' migrant crisis without refugees, we look at the role of word co-occurrence patterns in the discursive representation of refugees and immigrants in Rzeczpospolita *daily and* Niezależna. pl, *the Polish right-wing press. The analysis, of both quantitative and qualitative nature, focuses on lexical associations of two nouns,* uchodźca *'refugee' and* imigrant *'immigrant', and their role as epistemic, axiological and emotional proximization triggers in the process of mediated construction of crisis and European security.*

Keywords: Media Proximization Approach (MPA); Critical Discourse Analysis; corpus linguistics; Polish media; refugee crisis; Europe

National Identity and Europe in Times of Crisis: Doing and Undoing Europe, 83–112
doi:10.1108/978-1-78714-513-920171005

1. INTRODUCTION

Since summer 2015 Europe has been in the throes of what is interchangeably referred to as 'the refugee' or 'migrant crisis'. Only in 2015 over 1 million people made their way to the Old Continent in search of security and better economic prospects. Such a massive influx, coupled with sociopolitical tensions — growing nationalism and xenophobia, threat of terrorism, radicalization and violent extremism — resulted in the polarization of the political arena and created a rift among the European Union (EU) states struggling with the resettlement process. The European Commission's request to the block's member states to accept quotas of migrants further undermined the political and economic integrity of the EU and sparked a debate over Eastern and Western Europe (Dragostinova, 2016; Lulle & Ungure, 2015; Veebel, 2015). Should EU solidarity and humanitarianism take priority over national security concerns and member states' self-determination? Does Schengen still have *raison d'être*? Is Central and Eastern Europe more xenophobic and racist than the rest of the continent? These are some of the questions that surfaced in the discussion on European integrity and stability.

The media, depending on their political affiliations and ideological orientation, have bombarded the public either with images of suffering, bravery and sacrifice or stories of 'Islamic invasion', 'Europe under siege', or 'swarms of migrants'. Political elites and journalists alike have expressed concerns about the integration of migrants in economic and cultural terms (e.g. the incompatibility of the Islamic faith with European values) along with fears of terrorism and violence (including violence against women). Social media users joined in to offer sympathy and call for 'open doors' for refugees, or, to the contrary, to label migrants as potential terrorists, sub-humans and a threat to European cultural and religious heritage. Clearly, as it is often the case in times of crisis, the questions of 'who are we?', 'where do we belong?', 'what rights and responsibilities do we have?' have come to the fore, resulting in new alliances and new divisions, and bringing about new nationalisms and Us versus Them dynamics. With anti-refugee, anti-EU and nationalistic sentiments, and torn between humanitarianism on the one hand and concerns about internal safety and economic conditions on the other, the European Self has reached the point where 'Europeanness' has to be redefined anew (see Dzenovska, 2016).

Starting from the premise that social reality, relations and identities are — to a large extent — discursively constituted (Fairclough & Wodak, 1997, p. 273), and so is the current refugee crisis with its political, economic and cultural consequences, this chapter takes under scrutiny the mediated construction of this crisis in the Polish right-wing online press. Poland deserves attention for at least two reasons. First, similarly to other Central European and Baltic states (Hungary, Czechia, Slovakia, Lithuania, Latvia, Estonia), it has vocally opposed the EU refugee quota proposal requiring the acceptance of a designated number of migrants from front-line Mediterranean countries, namely Greece and Italy. Second, it is an interesting example of an EU state 'experiencing' the refugee crisis without refugees. The discursive construction of the crisis by the country's ruling Law and Justice (PiS) party, with its right-wing stance, has evolved along two lines: presenting the EU quota requirement as something that undermines the sovereignty of Poland as an EU member state, and construing the refusal to accept potential migrants as a manifestation of the state's responsibility to protect its own citizens (on three levels: security, economy and cultural/religious values). The anti-immigration sentiment has also been reflected (and validated) in the right-wing media. An analysis of data collected by the Polish Public Opinion Research Center in 2015 and early 2016 shows that in April 2016, only 25% of Poles thought that the country should take refugees from the Middle East and Africa (60% were prepared to accept Ukrainians) (Bachman, 2016). While the direct link between media representation and public attitudes cannot be empirically proven here,[1] the assumption inherent in CDA that discourse is socially constituted and constitutive (Fairclough & Wodak, 1997) and constructivist approach to language and social reality give us grounds to hypothesise that the media construction of the crisis and main social actors involved in it is likely to both reflect and trigger public fears concerning refugees and impact on the perception of security and measures necessary to preserve it.

Accordingly, our aim in this chapter is to demonstrate why and how discursive construction of this phenomenon and its implications may potentially influence public attitudes through affecting both the salience of issues and the way groups, individuals and problems are conceptualised (and their quasi-status functions established). The structure of the chapter looks as follows. Section 2 provides background information about migration crisis and its peculiar form in Central and Eastern Europe. Section 3 offers a brief overview of previous research on the media representation of migration and refugees. Section 4 presents the theoretical foundations of our new integrated approach – Media Proximization Approach (MPA) – drawing on the insights from Critical Discourse Analysis (CDA), constructivism and cognitive linguistics in order to explicate how certain phenomena, events, groups or individuals acquire their axiologically and emotionally imbued representations, often with real life implications within the sphere of collective consciousness. Section 5 is a corpus-based study of Polish online newspaper coverage of migration crisis. We make an attempt here to demonstrate how lexical and grammatical choices act as proximization triggers and impact on the salience of issues thereby promoting certain interpretations and perceptions and validating the anti-refugee stance.

2. MIGRATION CRISIS IN EUROPE

What triggered the current refugee crisis in summer 2015 is primarily the on-going civil war in Syria, which has left 22 millions of Syrians homeless and vulnerable. This conflict, along with critical situation in Iraq, Afghanistan, Libya and Eritrea, has resulted in an unprecedented migration flow, exceeding even the scale of World War II forced displacement (Alfred, 2015). Faced with the impossibility to get decent legal conditions and permanent residence in countries like Lebanon, Jordan and Turkey, refugees started to consider Europe a new possible destination, choosing Italy and Greece as the main entry points. Most of them, however, upon arrival in these countries set out for Germany, Austria, Sweden or Norway, western European countries offering generous social benefits. Importantly, of over 1 million refugees and migrants who reached Europe via the Mediterranean in 2015 almost one-third were children (UNHCR, 2015a, 2015b).

In May 2015 the EU demanded that all its members should show solidarity and ease the burden on the countries severely affected in the unprecedented influx of asylum seekers by participating in the relocation scheme. The reduction of EU subsidies to the member states that opposed the EU refugee quotas has been proposed by the German interior minister, Thomas de Maizière, and financial penalties for the EU member states opposing the resettlement of refugees have been suggested. The request to accommodate quotas of refugees and prospects of financial punishment in the event of failing to meet this requirement gave rise to a heated debate on the European integrity both on the global and the EU scale. The Visegrád Group (Poland, Hungary, Czechia and Slovakia) together with the Baltic states (Estonia, Latvia and Lithuania) objected to accepting suggested quotas of refugees and spoke against the EU forcing such a solution regardless of a particular country's national interests. Slovak and Polish governments refused to accept Muslims in their country, giving a reluctant consent to a limited number of Christians (Dragostinova, 2016). In Czechia, media reports describing police officers writing registration numbers on refugees' wrists and arms with permanent markers 'summoned memories of the Nazi era' (Bilefsky, 2015). Additionally, some countries within the Schengen Area reintroduced border controls, and others (e.g. Austria and Hungary) decided to build a fence along their borders to prevent further illegal migrants' arrivals.[2] In consequence, Central and Eastern Europe started to be regarded as more xenophobic than the rest of Europe and the countries in question have been criticised, particularly by Germany and France, for not understanding how European solidarity works. Security concerns grew in strength after the Paris attacks on 13 November 2015 and after the Cologne sexual harassment cases on New Year's Eve 2015. Media reports of the latter resulted in a wave of anti-refugee protests across Europe and voices that 'refugees' should not be offered unconditional help but rather undergo effective procedures of identity control. The controversial EU–Turkey Refugee Agreement signed on 18 March 2016, according to which migrants who arrive in Greece may be sent back to Turkey, raised questions about its legality and viability, 'undermining Europe's human-rights commitments' (Collet, 2016). Likewise, the dismantling of refugee camps in the border towns of Idomeni in Greece and Calais in France evoked contradictory reactions, lessening local resentment but undermining empathy (Margaronis, 2016).

While both the media and politicians have used the terms 'migrant/ immigrant' and 'refugee' interchangeably, a distinction between political refugees (those trying to escape persecution) and economic immigrants (those in search of better living conditions) is crucial both because of a different legal status of the two groups and, what is more relevant for us here, because of differences in public perception as regards entitlement to help and protection.

The 1951 United Nations Convention relating to the Status of Refugees, ratified by all European states, defines 'a refugee' as a person who 'owing to a well-founded fear of being persecuted for reasons of race, religion, nationality, membership of a particular social group, or political opinion, is outside the country of his nationality, and is unable to or, owing to such fear, is unwilling to avail himself of the protection of that country...' (UNHCR, 1967). 'Migrants are persons who choose to move not because of a direct threat of persecution or death, but mainly to improve their lives by finding work, or in some cases for education, family reunion or other reasons. Unlike refugees who cannot safely return home, migrants face no such impediment to return. If they choose to return home, they will continue to receive the protection of their government' (UNHCR, 2016). As can be seen from the above definitions, the label matters, entailing, as Searle (1995, 2010) would say (see Section 4), different status functions and deontic powers when it comes to legal protection and institutional care. With mass immigration being now far from popular in Europe, especially in countries like Britain or France, the distinction is also vital from the perspective of public cognitive-affective attitudes. On moral grounds, 'refugees' are perceived as 'deserving' and 'migrants', especially 'economic migrants', as 'not deserving' a compassionate approach. Due to competition in the labour market and scarcity of economic resources (e.g. in Central and Eastern Europe), the latter are also more likely to be considered a threat to the economic security of the state's welfare.

3. DISCOURSES ON MIGRATION

In the context of contradictory discourses surrounding migrants, asylum seekers and refugees media representation of the crisis and those involved in it is not without impact on public opinion. Its influence becomes even stronger when members of the audience have no direct experience (and contact with these groups) and rely in their judgements on images provided to them by TV, press or the Internet.

As shown in literature, media portrayals of migrants and refugees are predominantly negative and oftentimes highlight the threats posed by them to members of host societies. A report on immigrants in the Norwegian media in 2009 demonstrated that 71% of stories on immigration or integration tend to be problem-focused (Immigrants in Norwegian Media, 2010, p. 3). Klocker and Dunn (2003) analysed media representations of asylum seekers in Australia between August 2001 and January 2002 and found out that 90% of the descriptive terms used by the federal government and 76% of terms used by the print media to portray this group were negative, referring to asylum seekers as illegitimate, illegal and threatening and presenting them as terrorists or criminals. In a similar vein, Henry and Tator (2002, p. 111) pointed to a tendency to represent any issue dealing with immigration as a crisis, with recurring themes of 'bogus refugees' taking advantage of the social benefits system, potential terrorists entering the country and immigrants as sources of infectious diseases (see also Esses et al., 2013, p. 525).

Using a CDA approach Hart (2010) examined discursive representations of migrants in the UK press listing the most frequent topoi and their associations, namely: burden (the out-group needs to be supported by the in-group), character (the out-group has certain undesirable characteristics), crime (the out-group consists of criminals), culture (the out-group has different norms and values than the in-group and is unable to assimilate), danger (the out-group is dangerous), disadvantage (the out-group brings no advantages/is of no use to the in-group), disease (the out-group is dirty and carries infectious diseases), displacement (the out-group will eventually outnumber and/or dominate the in-group and will get privileged access to limited socio-economic resources, over and above the in-group) and exploitation (the out-group exploits the welfare system of the in-group) (Hart, 2010, p. 67). Hart (*ibid.*) also points to words frequently used in the British press, connected with the concept of physical or mental threat, e.g. 'damage', 'danger', 'threat', prone to generate fear and evoke strongly negative emotional responses towards migrants.

Mahtani and Mountz (2002) argue that another way to evoke negative attitudes and promote anxiety and panic is the use of metaphors conceptualizing immigration as an invasion and as flooding the country. Musolff (2012, 2014, 2015), in turn, discusses the role of 'parasite metaphor' in the construction of such negative portrayal of migrants and threat to the wellbeing of the host population. An interesting insight into immigration discourse was offered by Baker et al. (2008), who combined corpus linguistics methods with the framework of Discourse Historical Approach. Having qualitatively and qualitatively analysed a 140-million-word corpus of British press articles in terms of common categories of representation of refugees, asylum seekers, immigrants and migrants (collectively referred to as RASIM) they found out that these groups are represented in newspapers with a limited number of topics/categories and topoi, most of which convey a negative stance.

Richardson and Colombo (2013), in their analysis covering both verbal and visual aspects of anti-immigration rhetoric, focused on political arguments employed by the Italian extreme right party Lega Nord (The Northern League) in posters from political campaigns held between 2001 and 2008. Following Rydgren (2003), they list four arguments used in anti-immigration discourse: '(a) immigrants are a threat to ethno-national identity; (b) immigrants are a major cause of criminality and other kinds of social insecurity; (c) immigrants are a cause of unemployment; (d) and immigrants are abusers of the generosity of the welfare states of Western democracies'.

Lenette and Cleland, in their analysis of the visual representations of asylum seekers in 2015 list the following dominant themes: (1) women depicted as vulnerable mothers with children or babies ('Madonna and Child' pose), and *feminization* of refugee representations, (2) recurring images of children, often with dirty clothing, (3) unidentifiable masses or processions of people, (4) people with obscured or out of focus faces, (5) subdued facial expressions, (6) lack of easily identifiable focal point, (7) military personnel and warfare equipment and (8) desolate settings (Lenette & Cleland, 2016, p. 71; see also Bleiker, Campbell, Hutchison, & Nicholson, 2013; Johnson, 2011; Wright, 2000, 2002). As argued by the authors, such images have the potential to reinforce the image of the primitive Other (Bleiker et al., 2013) as diseased, uneducated and unable to assimilate (Wright, 2000), and trigger what Martin (2015) describes as 'moral panic'. In the words of Esses et al. (2013, p. 519), 'the media and political elites may take advantage of this uncertainty to create a crisis mentality in which immigrants and refugees are portrayed as "enemies at the gate", who are attempting to invade Western nations'. The results of an experimental study conducted by them (ibid.) suggest that the uncertainty surrounding immigration, coupled with media tendency to focus on negative rather than positive news stories, can lead to extreme negative reactions to immigrants and refugees. Additionally, through a series of experiments, they demonstrate that there exists a cause-and-effect relation between these negative media portrayals of immigrants and refugees and the dehumanization of these groups, which may serve to reduce uncertainty among the members of the host population, particularly those with no direct experience with migrants, by alerting them to potential physical, economic and cultural threats and providing answers as to how immigrants and refugees should be viewed and treated (ibid. 522). This, in turn results in preserving the current status quo and strengthening in-group—out-group boundaries.

As argued by Maskaliūnaitė (2015, p. 98), the current refugee crisis 'worked to entrench existing stereotypes, to rekindle nationalist and populist rhetoric and to increase the undercurrent of Euroscepticism'. With a plethora of arguments against accepting larger numbers of asylum seekers of the economic and cultural nature, migration emerged primarily as a security issue. Hence, in their analysis of late 2015 media debates in Latvia, Lulle and Ungure (2015) speak of emerging discourses of fear on the one hand and safety and security on the other. Similar conclusions are drawn by Maskaliūnaitė (2015) who, adopting Huysmans' (2006) securitization approach, examines discourse and institutional practices related to current migration crisis in Lithuania.

Importantly, terrorism and links to ISIS are only one aspect of the security-related threat. More often, as argued by Maskaliūnaitė (2015), securitization reflects cultural and identity fears. The concept of 'societal security', developed by the Copenhagen school, can be of use here (Buzan, Wæver, & de Wilde, 1998). According to Buzan et al. (1998), societal insecurities stem from whatever is perceived as a threat to collective identities and the survival of a community as a cohesive unit. Migrants and refugees – the Other – inevitably constitute such a threat. Coming from a predominantly Muslim background they are likely to bring in beliefs and traditions incompatible with the European Christian worldview. In this respect typical Muslim-related stereo-types come to the fore bringing into public discourse a whole range of issues concerning civil liberties, human rights, religion and, more importantly, security and terrorist threat (Kopytowska, 2010a, 2010b; Lewis, 1994; Poole, 2002; Poole & Richardson, 2006; Richardson, 2004). The press thus eagerly reports on 'no-go areas' created in the British or Swedish towns, the introduction of Sharia law or cases of violence against women. At the same time, however, safety and security is imagined through certain discursive representations of a desired refugee: family, children, real political refugee (not an economic migrant), who will work hard to prove his or her worth (Lulle & Ungure, 2015, p. 83). Economic security-wise, migrants are seen as competitors for the scarce (welfare) resources. The image of a migrant is that of a lazy person, looking for welfare benefits in a European country, and prone to have a large family (Lulle & Ungure, 2015, p. 77). Maskaliūnaitė (2015, p. 117), for example, argues that unwillingness to accept refugees in Lithuania and other Eastern European countries compared to those in the West might be mostly due to economy-related fears rather than extreme xenophobia.

4. MEDIATED CRISIS – SALIENCE, PROXIMIZATION AND SOCIAL CONSTRUCTION

Even though, as Section 3 demonstrated, the refugee crisis is undeniably a set of facts end events – with people, institutions and states being multi-dimensionally affected by mass migration movements – its discursive construc-tion by important political/social actors mediated by the institutions of mass communication plays an important role in shaping public attitudes, and, in consequence, decisions and actions. As pointed out by Lippmann (1922, p. 29) media create 'pictures in our heads' and by making certain events (or their aspects) more salient than others, have the potential to influence what issues people pay attention to, and determine the audience's judgments about policies, public problems and their remedies. They also provide the material out of which identities are constructed in terms of ethnicity, nationality and religion, or more broadly, help to negotiate, preserve or challenge the status quo of the in-group and its relationship with the out-group. Consequently, they can become powerful nation-state tools with which national identities can be imagined (Anderson, 1991).

As demonstrated by studies within agenda setting, priming and framing (see Scheufele & Tewksbury, 2007 for an overview of these three theoretical frameworks), what is prominent in media picture is likely to gain prominence in audience's mental representation, especially if viewers or readers have no direct experience concerning a given event, problem or group of people. The impact of instantaneous and continuous media coverage of a particular conflict, incident or problem on government decisions and its role in generating 'collective compassion' have been explained under the term 'the CNN effect' or, more recently, 'Al-Jazeera effect'.

A look at Berger and Luckmann's (1991/1966, p. 149) concept of 'social construction', Searle's (1995, 2010) theory of social ontology, and main tenets of CDA highlighting the role of discourse as a formative agent already shows how social reality is co-constructed by language. It is also important here to refer to the Cognitive Linguistics notion of a *conceptualization*, defined by Langacker (1990, p. 18) as 'the cognitive activity constituting our apprehension of the world', which explains the dynamic nature of concepts and the process of constructing them. The same situation in the world can be conceptualised in multiple ways, which is also captured in the theoretical notion of 'a linguistic view of the world' (*językowy obraz świata*), defined by Bartmiński (2010, p. 156) as a collection of judgments and evaluations of the people, artifacts, events or phenomena making up a subjective interpretation of the world recorded in language. As argued by Chlebda (2016), one of the most significant dichotomies which can be explored here is the opposition Our versus Foreign. Importantly, since '[m]ost concepts presuppose other concepts and cannot be adequately defined except by reference to them, be it implicit or explicit (Langacker, 1987, p. 147)', linguistic expressions will always function in a specific conceptual environment within which they will enable access to stored knowledge and experience, determining in this way further conceptualizations. The complex and dynamic nature of the interface between reality, conceptualizations and discursive representations has been investigated from various theoretical perspectives within humanities and social sciences. 'How is it possible that subjective meanings *become* objective facticities?' asked representatives of social constructivism, Berger and Luckmann (1991/1966, p. 30). 'How does a mental reality, a world of consciousness, intentionality and other mental phenomena, fit into a world consisting entirely of physical particles in fields of force?' queried Searle (1995, p. xi−xii). Both found the answer in the notion of language. If we look at the three dimensions of the sociopolitical reality distinguished by Kaid, Gerstlé, and Sanders (1991, cit. in McNair, 2003, p. 12), namely (a) an *objective* political reality, comprising events as they actually occur, (b) a *subjective* reality − the 'reality' of events as they are perceived by actors and citizens and (c) a *constructed* reality − events as they are covered by the media, we are faced with a similar question about the interface and mediating factor between these three. While acknowledging the constitutive potential of discourse in entrusting individuals, groups, phenomena and problems with quasi-status functions and deontic powers, which in consequence is likely to reconfigure social relations (including in-group versus out-group) and bring about material consequences, we posit a claim that the process of construction of mediated social reality is contingent on journalistic/media manipulation of distance in its various dimensions (spatiotemporal, epistemic, axiological, emotional, see Fig. 1) between the members of the audience and the elements of presented objective reality they frequently have no or limited direct access to, the process known under the term of 'proximization'. The concept itself, theorised by Chilton (2004, 2005, 2014), Cap (2006, 2008, 2010, 2013), and Hart (2010), relates to how individuals position various entities (people, events, ideological constructions, etc.) within discourse space in relation to themselves, that is the deictic centre (the Self − *I* or *we*), using background assumptions and indexical cues. To original axes of time, space and modality in Chilton's model, Cap added axiological dimension to explain how the perception of distance from the Self can be skilfully manipulated in political discourse to legitimise the actions to be taken by political

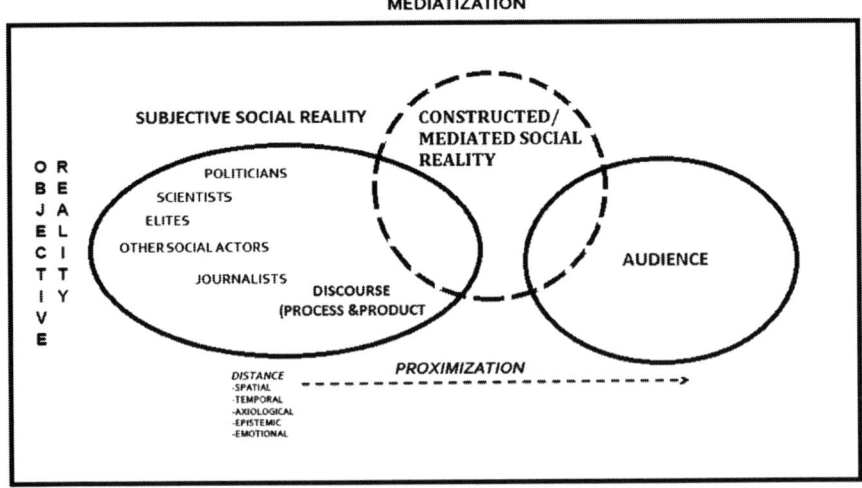

Fig. 1. Proximization Process and Mediated Social Reality (Kopytowska, 2015c, p. 139).

actors. Our approach goes beyond the legitimizing function and regards proximization as inherent in the very nature of mass-mediated communication and enabled by the semiotic properties of various media (for political blogs see Kopytowska, 2013; for television news see Kopytowska, 2014, 2015a; for press news see Kopytowska, 2015b). Whether it is about news discourse or other forms of mediated communication, entities from objective reality (events, groups, individuals, phenomena, both abstract and material), as they are perceived by influential social actors and journalists/media (subjective reality) are selected and brought closer to the media users. Harvey (1990) calls this process 'space-time compression', while for Thompson, media users 'become space-time travellers who are involved in negotiating between different space-time frameworks and relating their mediated experience of other times and places back to the context of their everyday lives' (Thompson, 1995, p. 94). While, as postulated elsewhere (Kopytowska, 2015a, 2015b, 2015c), reducing spatial and temporal dimensions of distance is key in proximization process and forms the basis for work on other distance dimensions, in this chapter we are going to focus on epistemic, axiological and emotional dimension.

The epistemic distance concerns the level of knowledge (or lack of it) of the audience. It is connected with media users' experience-based cognitive schema of interpretation and becomes particularly important in the case of news about unfamiliar problems or phenomena. In order to reduce this dimension of distance, journalists will rely on the mechanism of framing, that is using 'persistent patterns' of presentation, constructed to make the events more accessible to the public (Entman, 1991, p. 7). Frames will be constructed by providing and repeating certain words and visual images, and putting them in a particular context, which results in drawing attention to some aspects of reality while obscuring other elements (see Kopytowska, 2009). In order to contextualise new events journalists will refer to the existing news frames, involving *inter alia* topoi, metaphorical conceptualizations, stereotypes and keywords (and key images).

The concept of news as such is strongly related to the notions of 'deviance' (Shoemaker & Cohen, 2006) which involves both epistemic and axiological dimension. Similarly, Hartmann and Husband (1976, p. 276) argue that two kinds of characteristics that make events newsworthy are conflict, threat and deviance, and the potential to be interpreted within a familiar framework or in terms of existing images, stereotypes and expectations. In view of what was written in the previous paragraph we can thus expect interesting dynamics here: The media will rely on stereotypical representations (the audience is already used to), but at the same time they will highly value anything that is likely to clash with familiar standards, norms and expectations.

The axiological distance is contingent on differences in cultural values, beliefs and practices and often involves the opposition of us versus them, or us versus the Other. Cognitive-discursive operations related to values will have three functions, varying according to the physical and cultural proximity of the event/problem presented in the news and a potential threat it causes:

(1) establishing axiological status: 'our' values/norms;
(2) delineating axiological conflict: incompatibility of 'our' values/norms with 'their' values/norms;
(3) conveying axiological urgency: responding to a threat posed (often by 'their' actions) to 'our' values/norms and accepting moral responsibility to act (Kopytowska, 2015b);

Esses, Hodson, Veenvliet, and Mihic (2008), for example, examined the dehumanization of refugees through the use of the moral dimension. In their experimental study they combined the value attribution system concerning pro-social values suggested by Schwartz, Struch, and Bilsky (1990)[3] with an assess-ment of the enemy/barbarian image (Alexander, Brewer, & Herrmann, 1999) involving perceptions of a group as immoral. Haslam, Loughnan, and Kashima (2008) also demonstrate that dehumanization is characterised by a perception that the dehumanised lack such characteristics as refinement, civility, morality, self-control and cognitive sophistication.

Finally, emotional distance is connected with various degrees of emotional involvement on the part of the audience. The newsworthiness of such negative events as crisis, conflict, death, disease and destruction resides in their strong emotional appeal. Hence, negative events and incidents will not only be selected but also construed as more negative with the use of negatively loaded lexis, along with metaphorical conceptualizations. In times of crisis and conflict, fear of the Other and his/her actions will be one of the most frequent emotions at work.

5. METHODOLOGY, RESEARCH MATERIAL AND TOOLS

In this chapter, combining CDA and corpus linguistics methodology, our aim is to analyse the image of refugees and immigrants constructed in the Polish right-wing media discourse in terms of proximization strategies and the result-ing salience of aspects/problems related to this group of people and the migra-tion crisis as such. We depart from the assumption that corpus linguistics,[4] in particular when used in combination with qualitative approaches, is a valuable tool for discourse analysis as it, first, allows for the quantification of recurring linguistic features necessary to substantiate qualitative insights and, second, enables reliable generalizations concerning the effects of various linguistic choices (O'Keeffe, 2006, pp. 51, 158; Stubbs, 1997, pp. 107, 111, see also Baker, 2006; Baker et al., 2008). As a method it has been used by a growing number of media researchers, mostly in corpus-based analyses of the press language (e.g. Baker et al., 2008; Caldas-Coulthard, 1993; Gabrielatos & Baker, 2008;

Jeffries, 2003; Kopytowska, 2009, 2015a, 2015b; O'Keeffe's, 2002, 2003, 2005). Most of these studies rely on word frequency list generation and concordancing. Since in this chapter we treat corpus linguistics as a methodology for data analysis rather than as a distinct approach to study language, then this chapter can be described as a corpus-based rather than a corpus-driven one, among other reasons (using annotated corpora, pre-selecting search words, preselecting syntactic patterns in which they occur, etc.).[5]

Given the fact that news texts tend to render a particular meaning system through keywords combined in a specific form, the frequency of certain lexical items, which is 'an essential feature for making general claims about the discourse' (Teubert, 2005, p. 5), can serve as a starting point for identifying patterns within discursive representation. It is our assumption that this discursive representation (linguistic view) reflects the standpoint of editors, journalists and readers of *Rzeczpospolita* daily and *Niezalezna.pl*, their judgments and evaluations of the refugee crisis, but at the same time is likely to be constitutive for the public perception of the crisis.[6] Our aim is to explore the role of lexico-grammatical proximization triggers in the form of word co-occurrence patterns in the construction of refugee crisis. To that end, we focused on lexical associations of two nouns, that is, *uchodźca* 'refugee' and *imigrant* 'immigrant', as occurring in two custom-designed corpora of press articles published by *Rzeczpospolita* daily and *Niezależna.pl*, an online news portal. The study corpora were analysed in quantitative terms regarding the frequencies and distributions of the said nouns, and later they were studied qualitatively in terms of their use in selected lexical and grammatical patterns, called collocations and colligations respectively, as well as in larger co-text and context. Needless to say, collocations are identified statistically by corpus linguists in order to establish whether two words occur together systematically or by chance. Likewise, colligations are explored in this study using the words that occur with high frequency in a given syntactic pattern.

As for the research material, we decided to focus on *Rzeczpospolita* daily and *Niezależna.pl*. The former is a Polish broadsheet, with a circulation of 94,000, and a moderately conservative ideology.[7] According to the Institute of Media Monitoring, *Rzeczpospolita* was the first influential opinion-forming medium in Poland in 2016 (IMM 2016), and ranked second in 2015 (IMM 2015). The latter, much more explicit in its right-wing and nationalistic ideology, is the leader among conservative web portals in Poland (http://niezalezna. pl/63258-niezaleznapl-nadal-liderem-wsrod-prawicowych-portali).

When compiling the study corpora,[8] we employed two different procedures. For the *Rzeczpospolita* corpus, we used The EMM News Brief,[9] a search engine custom-designed for searching news stories from all over the world. After selecting *Rzeczpospolita* daily, we then specified *uchodźcy* 'refugees' as a search word in order to elicit links to the relevant press articles published in the years 2015–2016, that is the time when the refugee crisis in Europe started and reached its peak. Then we used the Compile Corpora facility of the

SketchEngine software (Kilgarriff et al., 2014). More specifically, by providing the links to the press articles, the programme compiled and tagged the corpus of press articles. As *Niezależna.pl* is not indexed by the EMM News Brief, we used an in-built search engine on the niezależna.pl website in order to identify — by keying in the search word *uchodźcy* 'refugees' — and further retrieve relevant articles on refugees published in the years 2015—2016. As the number of texts, as well as their length, dealing with refugee crisis varied between the newspapers, the study corpora are not equal in terms of their size (Table 1).

The varying size of the corpora has important implications for the interpretation of the frequency information. In terms of raw figures, the lemmas *uchodźca* ('refugee') and *imigrant* ('immigrant') are more frequently used in the *Rzeczpospolita* corpus, yet considering the normalised figures (i.e. per million words), the finding is the opposite (Table 2). Due to the fact that the *Niezależna.pl* corpus size is well below 100,000 word tokens (let alone 1,000,000 normalization threshold), and since the distribution of lemmas is not linear, we decided to provide raw frequency information throughout the analyses.

In order to analyse word co-occurrence patterns, we used two computer programs custom-designed for text analysis, namely SketchEngine (Kilgarriff et al., 2014) and GraphColl (Brezina, McEnery, & Wattam, 2015). Using SketchEngine, we generated the so-called word sketches, that is, lexical profiles featuring the most important grammatical and collocational relations of words. This has been possible because the study corpora were loaded into the software and subsequently tagged and parsed, that is, the words included in the corpus were provided with information regarding their morphology and syntax.

To further explore collocational relations between words, we used GraphColl software (Brezina et al., 2015), which enables one to identify frequently co-occurring words (nodes) and their collocates, followed by further retrieval of the collocates of their collocates, the phenomenon referred to by Sinclair (2005, cited in Warren, 2011, p. 121) as 'intercollocation of collocates'.

Table 1. Study Corpora in Terms of Their Size.

Corpus Name	Corpus Size in Word Tokens	Number of Articles
Rzeczpospolita (RP)	507,545	718
Niezalezna.pl (NZ)	31,229	95

Table 2. Raw and Normalised Frequency of Lemmas under Scrutiny.

Lemma	Frequency (Raw/Normalised) in Rzeczpospolita	Frequency (Raw/Normalised) in Niezależna.pl
Uchodźca	4,010/6,815	523/13,768
Imigrant	905/1,538	210/5,528

In other words, the software allows to explore cross-associations between lexical items as well as to identify the whole variety of collocational networks in texts, and this way explore the meanings that emerge from these complex lexical associations and networks. More details regarding the parameters used for identification of collocations are provided in the empirical part of this chapter.

6. RESULTS

In order to see which aspects of the crisis are made salient in the discursive representation of *refugees* and *migrants* and how the security problem is constructed in *Rzeczpospolita* daily and *Niezależna.pl*, we focused on naming and reference as well as predication patterns in terms of their epistemic, axiological and emotional potential. To this end we identified and scrutinised collocations of the said two nouns (in all their inflectional forms), as attested in the so-called word sketches provided by SketchEngine (Kilgarriff et al., 2014) in the following grammatical constructions: (1) adjectival modifiers + *uchodźca/imigrant*; (2) *uchodźca/imigrant* + preposition *z* 'from'; (3) *uchodźca/imigrant* in the subject position + verb; (4) verb + *uchodźca/imigrant* in the object position. Our intention was to find out whether any distinctions are made between these two groups of individuals, what traits and actions are attributed to them, and what actions they are subject to. While the epistemic dimension is related to how knowledge about them (and their status) is constructed by relying on culturally embedded stereotypes (see Section 3), facts and figures, as well as opinions mentioned, axiological proximization triggers include either explicit or implicit negative evaluations of character traits or actions. The emotional dimension of proximization, being in a way a consequence of both knowledge and moral judgement, consists in evoking emotions of fear and anger, or, alternatively, empathy and compassion.

In the analysis, we focused on the top 10 collocates (or fewer, depending on data availability) as computed by the software using a modified logDice score (Rychlý, 2008), with later modifications. Also, we decided to filter out those collocates that occur in the study corpora only once, so that no idiosyncratic uses impact the results of the qualitative analysis. In the tables presented below, the collocates of both node words (*uchodźca* and *imigrant*) are sorted according to logDice score, yet for the sake of clarity we also provide frequencies of the collocates.

The analysis of the first construction (adjectival modifiers + *uchodźca/imigrant*) shows a number of similarities when it comes to the two subcorpora (Table 3). The modifiers are used with factual and evaluative functions, but even the former are likely to evoke particular stereotypical frames and judgements. In both newspapers under scrutiny, immigrants are presented as illegal (*nielegalny*) or economic (*ekonomiczny/zarobkowy*) ones, the labels that are not

Table 3. Adjectival Modifiers + *Uchodźca/Imigrant.*

Uchodźca 'refugee' in Rzeczpospolita		Uchodźca 'refugee' in *Niezależna*		Imigrant 'immigrant' in Rzeczpospolita		Imigrant 'immigrant' in Niezależna	
Collocate	Freq.	Collocate	Freq.	Collocate	Freq.	Collocate	Freq.
syryjski	21	syryjski	8	nielegalny	57	nielegalny	11
nieletni	12	islamski	4	ekonomiczny	20	islamski	4
młody	8	tzw.	2	syryjski	5	ekonomiczny	2
potencjalny	7	afgański	2	afgański	3	młody	2
prawdziwy	6	arabski	2	kolejny	5		
dodatkowy	6			zarobkowy	3		
wewnętrzny	7			muzułmański	2		
nowy	14						
muzułmański	5						
chrześcijański	5						

used with reference to refugees. Differences, however, can be seen when concordances are examined. While *Rzeczpospolita* writes about 'illegal immigrants' and 'economic migrants', a distinction between them and 'refugees' seems to be maintained. It is even mentioned in one article that such a distinction is important for 'true refugees'. In contrast to this, *Niezależna.pl* in most cases lumps these two into one 'illegal' category, which is made explicit in the following example (1):

(1) Rozstrzyganie problemów definicyjnych typu, kto to jest uchodźca, a kto jest **imigrantem** ekonomicznym, ma z pewnością znaczenie dla władz Unii czy poszczególnych krajów, ma znaczenie dla określonych procedur administracyjnych, które będą stosowane. Ma natomiast znikome znaczenie dla wszystkich tych, pośród których będą owi 'nielegalni' ludzie mieszkali. [Niezależna.pl, 16/09/2015]

'Resolving definitional problems, such as who is a refugee and who is an economic **immigrant**, is certainly important for the EU authorities and the individual countries, it is important for particular administrative procedures that will be applicable. It has but little importance for all those who will live right next to those "illegal" people'.

Interestingly, in most cases when the term 'refugee' appears, it is used in inverted commas to undermine the legal (and social) status of this particular group of individuals. Similar effect is achieved by using the word 'so-called' (*tzw.*) (2):

(2) Grupa tzw. "**uchodźców**" zaczęła zaczepiać tam młoda kobietę. [Niezależna. pl, 07/02/2016]

'A group of the so-called "**refugees**" began to bother a young woman there'.

If we look at it from the point of view of Searle's status functions and deontic powers, the 'so-called' status has two serious implications. First, not being 'real' refugees these people are not trustworthy; second, they are not entitled to expect help and European solidarity; third, they may be potential terrorists (see Section 3).

As for the adjectives used to describe the refugees, one may find references to their age (*młody* 'young') or status (*nowy* 'new', *wewnętrzny* 'internal', *dodatkowy* 'additional'), also subjectively evaluated (*potencjalny* 'potential', *prawdziwy* 'true'). 'Potential' and 'new' refugees used in *Rzeczpospolita* highlight the continuity of the crisis, with the former co-constructing the imagined crisis in the case of Poland (speculating about how potential refugees would and should behave). Both newspapers emphasise the refugees' and immigrants' provenance (from Syria, Afghanistan, Arab world) and religion (Islamic, Muslim). However, in *Rzeczpospolita* the term 'Muslim refugees' is typically used in quotations where they are presented (by politicians or experts) as a possible threat or linked to radicalization (3):

(3) Radykalni islamiści podejmują próby werbowania nowych zwolenników wśród muzułmańskich **uchodźców** przebywających w Niemczech – powiedział agencji dpa szef Urzędu Ochrony Konstytucji (AfV) Hans-Georg Maassen [Rzeczpospolita, 14/08/2016]

'Radical Islamists are attempting to recruit new followers among Muslim **refugees** in Germany – said Hans-Georg Maassen, head of the Office for the Protection of the Constitution (AfV), to the agency dpa'.

Also, it is only in this newspaper that the information about Christian (*chrześcijański*) refugees appears. In the other source, the notion of Christianity seems to be incompatible with the stereotypical representation of this group due to an axiological conflict between Christian values and the Muslim world. Hence, in *Niezalezna.pl* all occurrences of 'Islamic refugees' are linked to negative, morally unacceptable actions (axiological proximization) (4, 5), and a possible threat to the host population (6). They are presented as having no respect for human life in general and women in particular (frequent mentions of attacks directed at European women). Additionally, they are linked to terrorist activities.

(4) W Finlandii aresztowano islamskich **uchodźców**. W Iraku mordowali strzałem w tył głowy. [Niezależna.pl, 12/12/2015]

'In Finland, Muslim **refugees** were arrested. In Iraq, they killed with shot in the head'.

(5) Arabscy **uchodźcy** podejrzewani są o dokonanie przynajmniej 11 morderstw w ramach działań terrorystycznych. [Niezależna.pl, 12/12/2015]

'Arab **refugees** are suspected of perpetrating at least 11 murders in the context of terrorist activities'.

(6) Napady islamskich **uchodźców** na kobiety trwały w Niemczech już od mie-
sięcy, lecz były skutecznie skrywane przed opinią publiczną. [Niezależna.pl,
13/01/2016]

'Attacks by Islamic **refugees** on women in Germany lasted for months,
but they were effectively concealed from the public'.

'Afghan refugees' is also further modified by a negatively charged adjective
associated with the concept of violence, e.g. (7):

(7) Został zaczepiony przez dwóch agresywnych afgańskich **uchodźców**.
[Niezależna.pl, 30/07/2016]

'He was accosted by two aggressive Afghan **refugees**'.

More comprehensive information (Table 4) regarding the origin or migration
path of refugees and immigrants is conveyed by the construction with the preposition *z* 'from'. While *Niezależna.pl* focuses on immigrants and refugees from
Syria, Africa, Afghanistan or Middle East, *Rzeczpospolita* also describes the
story of refugees from Ukraine (more specifically, from Donbas region and the
city of Mariupol) or from refugee camps outside or within the EU (*obóz*
'camp'), e.g. Turkey, Italy, the Balkans. Since the preposition *z* is used in Polish
in instrumental case (*with* sth), it is used by *Niezależna.pl* to construct a stereotypical image of refugees as machete-wielding fighters (*uchodźcy z maczetami*),
bringing in associations with barbarity and primitive violence. The construction
thus acts as a proximization trigger within all three dimensions: Epistemically
and emotionally it conjures up a stereotypical image evoking fear, axiologically

Table 4. *Uchodźca/Imigrant* + Preposition *z* 'from'.

Uchodźca 'refugee' in *Rzeczpospolita*		*Uchodźca* 'refugee' in *Niezależna*		*Imigrant* 'immigrant' in *Rzeczpospolita*		*Imigrant* 'immigrant' in *Niezależna*	
Collocate	Freq.	Collocate	Freq.	Collocate	Freq.	Collocate	Freq.
Syria	98	*Syria*	11	*Afryka*	13	*Afryka*	11
wschód (Bliski Wschód i Afryka)	24	*Afryka*	5	*wschód*	4	*ośrodek*	2
obóz (spoza UE)	20	*Maczeta*	3	*Bałkany*	2	*wschód*	2
Ukraina	17	*Afganistan*	3	*Włochy*	2	*Afganistan*	2
Afryka	14	*obóz*	2	*obóz*	2		
Irak	9			*Syria*	2		
Donbas	8						
Mariupol	6						
Afganistan	6						
Turcja	6						

it is not only linked to the lack of respect for the value of life, but also to a somewhat lower category of tribal violence.

The verbs following nouns *refugee* and *immigrant* in the subject position are also revealing as far as the construction of agency of this group is concerned (Table 5). In *Rzeczpospolita* the majority of collocates are motion verbs that describe migration path of refugees and immigrants (e.g. *przedostawać* 'get through', *docierać* 'get', *dotrzeć* 'get', *przyjechać* 'arrive', *wyruszać* 'depart', *podróżować* 'travel') or their way of occupying space (*przebywać* 'stay', *koczować* 'encamp', *oblegać* 'besiege'). While the same verbs are used by *Niezalezna. pl*, the website also mentions criminal and violent actions undertaken by refugees (*zaatakować* 'attack', *napaść* 'assault', *zgwałcić* 'rape', *podpalić* 'set on fire', *zabić* 'kill'). The role of a victim is not without importance here as far as axiological and emotional proximization is concerned. In most cases, the victim of refugees' criminal act is either a woman or a child — their inscribed vulnerability emphasises the immorality of the attack, which is more likely to evoke negative emotional reactions, including anger and need for revenge, in the audience. Another strong emotional trigger is a reference to Polish people as victims of violent acts (9, 10, 12, 13, 14). Due to cultural affinity, the threat becomes more tangible and imminent. It is also likely to evoke stronger in-group—out-group tensions and, eventually, hostility. A critical point is reached when w victim, killed with a machete, turns out to be a woman, who is not only Polish but also pregnant (9, 10). Yet another example of a person fit for a perfect victim status is a Polish homeless man set on fire while asleep.

Table 5. *Uchodźca/Imigrant* in the Subject Position + Verb.

Uchodźca 'refugee' in *Rzeczpospolita*		*Uchodźca* 'refugee' in *Niezależna*		*Imigrant* 'immigrant' in *Rzeczpospolita*		*Imigrant* 'immigrant' in *Niezależna*	
Collocate	Freq.	Collocate	Freq.	Collocate	Freq.	Collocate	Freq.
przedostawać	11	**mieć**	9	*usiłować*	3	*przedostawać*	2
mieć	22	*trafić*	4	*pochodzić*	3	*wyruszać*	2
docierać	9	*otrzymywać*	3	*przyjechać*	3	*podróżować*	2
Znaleźć	8	*kosztować*	3	*oblegać*	2	*znaleźć*	2
Dotrzeć	7	*pochodzić*	3	*próbować*	2		
otrzymywać	7	*zaatakować*	3	*znaleźć*	2		
przekroczyć	6	*przyjechać*	3	**mieć**	6		
przebywać	6	*dodać*	3				
wyruszać	5	*utonąć*	2				
mieliby	5	*zabić*	2				
koczować	5						

(8) 23-letni islamski **uchodźca** napadł na 10-letnią uczennicę. [Niezależna.pl, 13/01/2016]

'23-year-old Muslim *refugee* attacked a 10-year-old student'.

(9) Kolejny dramat w Niemczech – syryjski **uchodźca** zabił maczetą kobietę. [Niezależna.pl, 26/07/2016]

'Another drama in Germany – a Syrian refugee killed a woman with a machete'.

(10) Ofiarą syryjskiego **uchodźcy** z maczetą była młoda Polka w ciąży. [Niezależna.pl, 24/07/2016]

'A victim of a Syrian *refugee* with a machete was a young Polish pregnant woman'.

(11) **Uchodźcy** zgwałcili tłumaczkę telewizyjnej ekipy w Calais. W Dżungli to nic nadzwyczajnego. [Niezależna.pl, 18/10/2016]

'*Refugees* raped an interpreter of a television crew in Calais. It is anything but extraordinary in The Jungle'.

(12) Afgańscy **uchodźcy** napadli na polską parę. Bili także kobietę z dzieckiem. [Niezależna.pl, 30/07/2016]

'Afghan *refugees* attacked a Polish couple. They beat the woman and her child'.

(13) **Uchodźcy** zaatakowali Polaka. Przy granicy polsko-niemieckiej doszło do tragedii. W niemieckiej części Zgorzelca dwóch imigrantów z Syrii napadło na Polaka. 21 i 18-latek w centrum handlowym za pomocą sygnetu do podcinania gardła zranili Polaka. [Niezależna.pl, 21/05/2016]

'*Refugees* attacked a Pole. At the German-Polish border a tragedy unfolded. In the German part of Zgorzelec, two immigrants from Syria attacked the Pole. Using a signet designed to undercut the throat, 21- and 18-year-old hurt the Pole at the mall'.

(14) **Uchodźcy** podpalili Polaka. Grupa siedmiu młodych uchodźców w Boże Narodzenie podpaliła bezdomnego mężczyznę – Polaka, który spał na stacji metra w Berlinie. [Niezależna.pl, 28/12/2016]

'*Refugees* set fire to a Pole. During Christmas, a group of seven young refugees set fire to a homeless man – a Pole, who was sleeping in an underground station in Berlin'.

Similarly negative actions, morally deplorable, are attributed to immigrants. In addition to anger, however, they are likely to evoke disgust as in (15). Since the man's behaviour is ironically referred to as yet another example of 'cultural enrichment', the readers are left with conclusions as to the moral values, or their lack, of the newcomers. Not only do immigrants pose a physical threat to human life and property as in previous examples, but they also constitute menace to European cultural and moral standards. Referring to research on the dehumanization of refugees (see Section 3), we can see that the way they are presented (with predications acting as proximization triggers), these people indeed lack refinement, civility, morality and self-control, which complements their already barbarian image.

(15) Ostatnio *imigranci* z ośrodka nieopodal Zwickau znów "ubogacili kulturowo" Niemców. Jeden z nich masturbował się w jacuzzi. [Niezależna.pl, 25/01/2016]

'Recently *immigrants* from the refugee centre near Zwickau once again "culturally enriched" the Germans. One of them masturbated in a jacuzzi'.

There are two more types of threats associated with refugees and immigrants (identified in previous research). One of them is related to health (16) and the other to the economic welfare of the host country. As regards the latter, the emphasis is placed on the cost associated with the maintenance of refugees, both in countries like Germany, in which case the financial deficit is expected, and potentially in Poland, which cannot afford it.

(16) Renomowany Instytut Roberta Kocha (RKI) po raz kolejny ostrzegł przed zagrożeniem rozprzestrzenienia się rzadkich i niebezpiecznych chorób, które do Niemiec przywożą *imigranci* z Afryki i Bliskiego Wschodu. [Niezależna.pl, 21/10/2015]

'The renowned Robert Koch Institute (RKI) once again warned against the threat of the spread of rare and dangerous diseases that are brought to Germany by immigrants from Africa and the Middle East'.

(17) *Uchodźcy* słono kosztują Niemców. Zabraknie gigantycznej kwoty na ich utrzymanie. [Niezależna.pl, 09/11/2016]

'*Refugees* dearly cost the Germans. The money for their maintenance will run out'.

(18) Każdy z *uchodźców* otrzymuje od rządu 135 euro zasiłku. [Niezależna.pl, 12/09/2015]

'Every refugee receives 135 euros from the government in the form of an allowance'.

(19) Tymczasem miesięczne utrzymanie jednego *uchodźcy* to koszt o kilkaset złotych większy. Jeżeli Polska przyjmie 10 tys. imigrantów — a od wczoraj mówi się o takiej właśnie liczbie — ich utrzymanie będzie kosztowało dużo ponad 100 milionów zł rocznie! [Niezależna.pl, 04/09/2015]

'Meanwhile, the monthly maintenance of one refugee costs hundreds of zlotys more. If Poland will accept 10 thousand immigrants — and such a number hss been debated since yesterday – their maintenance will cost much more than 100 million zloty per year!'

Interestingly, in *Rzeczpospolita* the verb *otrzymać* 'receive'/'be granted' is used not only with reference to a financial benefit but also to 'refugee status', 'documents' or 'support'.

The analysis of the nouns *refugee* and *immigrant* in the object position (Table 6) also shows some interesting regularities. On the surface, the noun *refugee* collocates with positive verbs like *przyjąć*, *przyjmować* ('welcome/accept') or *zapraszać* ('invite') (the former are also used with the noun *immigrant*). The analysis of concordances reveals that most occurrences refer to speculations about which country will or should accept refugees, and in the case of immigrants, refer to the lack of such acceptance (20, 21). Immigrants are additionally presented as being stopped by the authorities (*zatrzymać*) or 'send back' (*odsyłać*), which confirms their illegal status.

(20) Polska nie jest wstanie przyjąć **imigrantów** na swoim terytorium. [Rzeczpospolita, 29/03/2016]

'Poland is not able to accept immigrants on its territory'.

(21) Zieliński skomentował także wypowiedź Beaty Szydło, która powiedziała, że na tę chwilę nie widzi możliwości, by Polska przyjęła **imigrantów**. [Rzeczpospolita, 23/04/2016]

'Zieliński also commented on the statement by Beata Szydło, who said that at present we just do not see a possibility for Poland to adopt immigrants'.

In the last stage of the study, we used GraphColl software (Brezina et al., 2015) to further explore collocational relations of the nouns *uchodźca* 'refugee' and *imigrant* 'immigrant'. A similar attempt was recently made by Saridakis and Mouka (2016), who used the said software to explore discourse representation of immigrants, refugees and asylum seekers in Greece. Also, Baker (2016) used

Table 6. Verb + *Uchodźca/Imigrant* (Object Position).

Uchodźca 'refugee' in Rzeczpospolita		Uchodźca 'refugee' in Niezależna		Imigrant 'immigrant' in Rzeczpospolita		Imigrant 'immigrant' in Niezależna	
Collocate	Freq.	Collocate	Freq.	Collocate	Freq.	Collocate	Freq.
przyjąć	55	przyjąć	6	zatrzymać	5	przyjąć	2
przyjmować	28	zapraszać	3	przyjmować	5		
pomagać	13	odbierać	2	przyjąć	6		
pomóc	9			odsyłać	3		
				zaprosić	3		

GraphColl to study discourse representation of various social actors in a tailor-made corpus of newspaper articles about Muslims extracted from the conservative tabloid *The Sun*.

By identifying the whole variety of collocational networks in texts, we were able to explore the meanings and representations that emerge from these lexical associations. Due to the limited size of the corpus of *Niezależna.pl*, we decided to focus on the corpus of *Rzeczpospolita* in order to illustrate the potential of using the aforementioned software. As we were primarily interested in the collocations that occur relatively frequently in the study corpus, we decided to use MI3 statistic. In short, it compares the number of times the two words occur together and separately by giving more weight to frequent co-occurrences (Gomez, 2013, p. 208). In the analysis, we focused on collocations that occur within the span of three words (to the left and right) of the node word, and we set the minimum collocate frequency at 11 occurrences in the study corpus. We decided not to filter out function words as they provide additional information on the relations between co-occurring lexical items. All in all, we applied the following collocation settings (5-MI3, L3-R3, C11-NC0) presented in the format suggested by Brezina et al. (2015, p. 146) to ensure that the study be replicable in the future (Table 7).

By applying the settings presented above, we generated a graph illustrating selected collocational relationships of the nouns *uchodźcy* ('refugees') and *imigranci* 'immigrants'. Since the *Rzeczpospolita* corpus was loaded into the software and processed as unlemmatized, we focused on the two nouns in their plural form only. We started the analyses by identifying the first-order collocates of the noun *uchodźcy*. Among its collocates, we found the noun *imigranci* 'immigrants' and the adjective *młody* ('young'); we decided to explore their collocates as well (these are called second-order collocates of the noun *uchodźcy*). The results are visualised in Fig. 2.

The lexical cross-associations between the nouns *uchodźcy* and *imigranci* presented in Fig. 2 provide further insight into their discursive representation. Again (see Table 3), one can notice that the adjectives *zarobkowi, ekonomiczni* ('economic'), *nielegalni* ('illegal') are used with reference to immigrants rather than to refugees, a finding that reveals directionality of collocational relations. On the contrary, the adjective *młodzi* ('young', pl.) is used to describe refugees, and its collocates are two nouns, that is, 'men' and 'people' (*młodzi mężczyźni, młodzi ludzie*). This reveals a typical discursive strategy of presenting refugees as primarily young males in their prime. The proper noun *Africa*, however, is

Table 7. Settings for Collocation Identification.

Statistic ID	Statistic name	Statistic cut-off value	L and R span	Minimum collocate freq. (C)	Minimum collocation freq. (NC)	Filter
5	MI3	9	3-3 LR	11	–	–

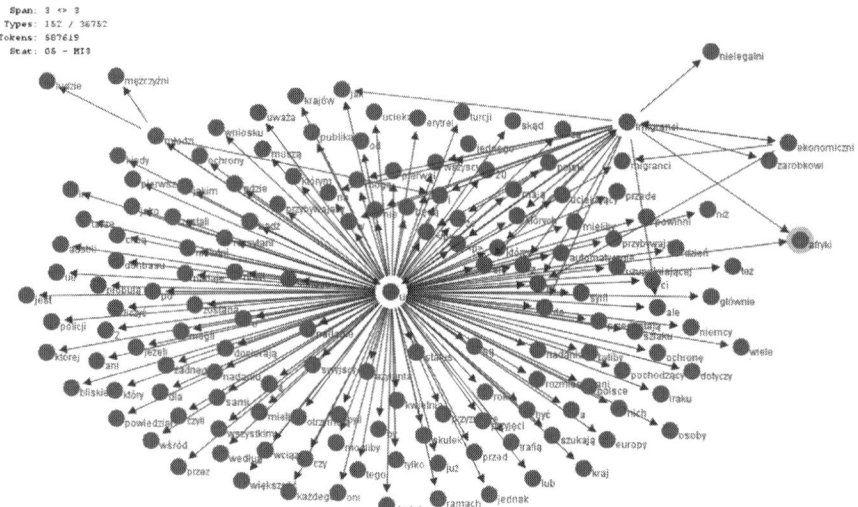

Fig. 2. First-Order and (Selected) Second-Order Collocates of the Noun *Uchodźcy* 'refugees'.

used to describe the provenance of both refugees and immigrants. Providing only a glimpse into the complex process of the construction of discourse on refugees and immigrants in the study corpora, these examples encourage further research using GraphColl software in the future.

7. CONCLUSIONS

While the current refugee crisis is undoubtedly a fact with its causes and consequences, the way it is perceived by the European and global public is considerably influenced by its media representation. The media construction of this phenomenon gains particular prominence in the case of countries like Poland, which have not been directly affected by the influx of refugees and, due to their ethnic and religious homogeneity, do not have much contact with either Muslim religion or culture of the Arab world.

Our quantitative and qualitative analysis — conducted from the perspective of MPA developed by Kopytowska (2015a, 2015b, 2015c) — has demonstrated that the lexico-grammatical patterns and their frequency can play an important role in the mediated construction of the refugee crisis through the attribution of character features, intentions and behaviour to its main social actors, namely migrants and the affected EU countries. By repeatedly referring to some aspects of migrant behaviour, the media proximize them epistemically, axiologically and emotionally. In the first case, they often rely on existing stereotypes and pre-conceptions concerning Muslims and, more generally, migrants from Africa and the Middle East. As far as axiology is concerned, in times of crisis and a real or imagined threat the in-group struggles to define and preserve its collective identity based on a shared system of values. One of the effective ways to do so is by juxtaposing such self-representation with the external Other and his or her worldview and norms. In the case of the media, this process is additionally reinforced by the search for *deviance* determining the newsworthiness of a given phenomenon. What is deviant from our norms and values becomes a threat to our status quo as it is both different and unfamiliar. In a similar way, a sense of fear is evoked by situations and phenomena which are unpredictable and beyond control. One might say that refugees and immigrants fulfil all these requirements and, more than that, the media make them do so. As in previous cases, the image of refugees and migrants tends to be negative and threat-construction related. Conservative broadsheets, like *Rzeczpospolita*, are far from adopting an explicitly xenophobic and alarmist perspective. Rather, they present possible threats by selecting and focusing on the factual information, and including (quoting) voices of those who are sceptical about refugees' relocation and integration. *Niezależna.pl*, in turn, is more overt in its nationalistic stance, building on the threat posed by the barbaric and uncivilised Other. To this end, it relies heavily on emotional proximization whose triggers include 'horror' stories involving Polish nationals, abounding with negatively charged adjectives and verbs denoting violent, life-threatening physical actions. The threat is constructed in all three domains, namely physical safety and health (in particular of women and children), morality and European cultural values, as well as economic security.

A study like this one, focusing on two custom-designed corpora of Polish press only, can be construed as a preliminary one only. More research is required in the future to further explore discursive representation of refugees and immigrants in the Polish press, both traditional and electronic one, and account for ideological differences. Finally, more comprehensive analysis of collocational patterns in texts, using the whole variety of measures of collocational strength, is required so that more subtle similarities and distinctions in the use and patterns of lexical items serving as proximization triggers are revealed.

NOTES

1. For empirical evidence see a study by Esses, Medianu, and Lawson (2013).

2. For details see 'Ten point action plan on migration' that was proposed at a joint meeting of Foreign and Interior Ministers in Luxembourg 20 April 2015 (European Commission, 2015).

3. 'Pro-social' values (e.g. equality, helpful, forgiving) are an example of such values because they 'reflect a conscious desire to promote the welfare of others' (Schwartz & Struch, 1989, p. 155). If people perceive that a group lacks pro-social values, then they will judge that group to be less human and thus less worthy of humane treatment.

4. According to McEnery and Wilson (1996, p. 1), corpus linguistics can be described as 'the study of language based on examples of "real life" language use'. Based on empirical observation of linguistic facts, corpus linguistics studies language primarily through description and explanation of linguistic patterns in texts (Kennedy, 1998, p. 8).

5. The distinction between a corpus-based and corpus-driven approach to study linguistic data is discussed in greater detail by Tognini-Bonelli (2001), McEnery and Gabrielatos (2008) or McEnery and Hardie (2011), among others.

6. A similar attempt to reconstruct a linguistic view of Europe recorded in the British National Corpus was conducted by Grabowski (2014).

7. The broadsheet itself characterizes its political stance as conservative-liberal.

8. The study corpora were compiled for personal non-commercial research. The texts included in the corpora are press articles freely available online.

9. The EMM News Brief search engine is freely available under the following link: http://emm.jrc.it.

ACKNOWLEDGEMENTS

This research is part of the project C.O.N.T.A.C.T. *Creating On-line Network, Monitoring Team and Phone App to Counter Hate Crime Tactics* 2015-2017 (reportinghate.eu), co-financed by the EU Commission (grant no. JUST/2014/RRAC/AG/HATE/6706).

REFERENCES

Alexander, M. G., Brewer, M. B., & Herrmann, R. K. (1999). Images and affect: A functional analysis of out-group stereotypes. *Journal of Personality and Social Psychology, 77*, 78−93.

Alfred, C. (2015, 12 September). What history can teach us about the worst refugee crisis since WWII. *Hungtonpost.com.au*. Retrieved from http://www.hungtonpost.com.au/entry/alexander-betts-refugees-wwii_55f30f7ce4b077ca094edaec?section=australia&adsSiteOverride=au. Accessed on December 15, 2016.

Anderson, B. (1991). *Imagined communities: Reflections on the origin and spread of nationalism.* London: Verso.

Bachman, B. (June 16, 2016). Diminishing solidarity: Polish attitudes toward the European migration and refugee crisis. *The Online Journal of the Migration Policy Institute*. Retrieved from http://www.migrationpolicy.org/article/diminishing-solidarity-polish-attitudes-toward-european-migration-and-refugee-crisis. Accessed on December 05, 2016.

Baker, P. (2006). *Using corpora in discourse analysis.* London: Continuum.

Baker, P. (2016). The shapes of collocation. *International Journal of Corpus Linguistics, 21*(2), 139−164.

Baker, P., Gabrielatos, C., Khosravinik, M., Krzyzanowski, M., McEnery, T., & Wodak, R. (2008). A useful methodological synergy? Combining critical discourse analysis and corpus linguistics to examine discourses of refugees and asylum seekers in the UK press. *Discourse & Society, 19*(3), 273−305.

Bartmiński, J. (2010). *Pojęcie językowego obrazu świata i sposoby jego operacjonalizacji*, [w:]. In P. Czapliński, A. Legeżyńska, & M. Telicki (Eds.), *Jaka antropologia literatury jest dzisiaj możliwa* (pp. 155−178). Poznań: Poznańskie Studia Polonistyczne.

Berger, P., & Luckmann, T. (1991/1966). *The social construction of reality. A treatise in the sociology of knowledge.* London: Penguin Books.

Bilefsky, D. (3 September, 2015). Numbering of migrants by Czechs brings outcry. *The New York Times*. Retrieved from https://www.nytimes.com/2015/09/04/world/europe/czech-republic-criticized-after-officers-mark-migrants-with-numbers.html Accessed on December 05, 2016.

Bleiker, R., Campbell, D., Hutchison, E., & Nicholson, X. (2013). The visual dehumanisation of refugees. *Australian Journal of Political Science*, *48*(4), 398–416.

Brezina, V., McEnery, T., & Wattam, S. (2015). Collocations in context. A new perspective on collocation networks. *International Journal of Corpus Linguistics*, *20*(2), 139–173. doi:10.1075/ijcl.20.2.01bre.

Buzan, B., Wæver, O., & de Wilde, J. (1998). *Security: A new framework for analysis*. London: Rienner.

Caldas-Coulthard, C. R. (1993). From discourse analysis to critical discourse analysis: The differential representation of women and men speaking in written news. In J. M. Sinclair, M. Hoey, & G. Fox (Eds.), *Techniques of description: Spoken and written discourse* (pp. 196–208). London: Routledge.

Cap, P. (2006). *Legitimisation in political discourse: A cross-disciplinary perspective on the modern US war rhetoric*. Newcastle: Cambridge Scholars Press.

Cap, P. (2008). Towards the proximization model of the analysis of legitimization in political discourse. *Journal of Pragmatics*, *40*, 17–41.

Cap, P. (2010). Axiological aspects of proximization. *Journal of Pragmatics*, *42*, 392–407.

Cap, P. (2013). *Proximization: The pragmatics of symbolic distance crossing*. Amsterdam: Benjamins.

Chilton, P. (2004). *Analysing political discourse: Theory and practice*. London: Routledge.

Chilton, P. (2005). Discourse space theory: Geometry, brain and shifting viewpoints. *Annual Review of Cognitive Linguistics*, *3*, 78–116.

Chilton, P. (2014). *Language, space and mind: The conceptual geometry of linguistic meaning*. Cambridge: Cambridge University Press.

Chlebda, W. (2016). Jak (w Polsce) zostać innym? Paper presented at the conference "OBCY, INNY w dyskursach publicznych" [OUR, FOREIGN in Public Discourses] in Chełm, Poland, 5 September 2016.

Collet, E. (March, 2016). The Paradox of the EU-Turkey Refugee Deal. *Migration Policy Institute*. Retrieved from http://www.migrationpolicy.org/news/paradox-eu-turkey-refugee-deal. Accessed on December 05, 2016.

Dragostinova, T. (2016). Refugees or immigrants? The migration crisis in Europe in historical perspective. *Origins: Current Events in Historical Perspective*, *9*(4). Retrieved from http://origins.osu.edu/article/refugees-or-immigrants-migration-crisis-europe-historical-perspective. Accessed on January 15, 2017.

Dzenovska, D. (2016). Eastern Europe, the moral subject of the migration/refugee crisis, and political futures. *Europe at a Crossroads: Near Futures Online 1*. Retrieved from http://nearfuturesonline.org/eastern-europe-the-moral-subject-of-the-migrationrefugee-crisis-and-political-futures/. Accessed on January 15, 2017.

Entman, R. M. (1991). Framing U.S. coverage of international news: Contrasts in narratives of KAL and Iran Air incidents. *Journal of Communication*, *41*, 6–27.

Esses, V., Hodson, G., Veenvliet, S., & Mihic, L. (2008). Justice, morality, and the dehumanization of refugees. *Social Justice Research*, *21*(1), 4–25.

Esses, V. Medianu, S., & Lawson, A. (2013). Uncertainty, threat, and the role of the media in promoting the dehumanization of immigrants and refugees. *Journal of Social Issues*, *69*(3), 518–536.

European Commission. (2015). Press release of Joint Foreign and Home Affairs Council: Ten point action plan on migration. Press Release Database. Retrieved from http://europa.eu/rapid/press-release_IP-15-4813_en.htm. Accessed on February 1, 2017.

Fairclough, N., & Wodak, R. (1997). Critical discourse analysis. In T. A. van Dijk (Ed.), *Discourse as social interaction* (pp. 14–31). London: Sage.

Gabrielatos, C., & Baker, P. (2008). Fleeing, sneaking, flooding: A corpus analysis of discursive constructions of refugees and asylum seekers in the UK Press 1996–2005. *Journal of English Linguistics*, *36*(1), 5–38.

Gomez, P. (2013). *Statistical methods in language and linguistic research*. London: Equinox.

Grabowski, Ł. (2014). Obraz Europy w Brytyjskim Korpusie Narodowym. In J. Bartmiński, S. Niebrzegowska-Bartmińska, & I. Bielińska-Gardziel (Eds.), *Wartości w językowo-kulturowym obrazie świata Słowian i ich sąsiadów II* (pp. 163–183). Lublin: Wydawnictwo UMCS.

Hart, C. (2010). *Critical discourse analysis and cognitive science: New perspectives on immigration discourse*. Basingstoke: Palgrave.

Hartmann, P., & Husband, C. (1976). The mass media and racial conflict. In S. Cohen & J. Young (Eds.), *The manufacture of news: Social problems, deviance and the mass media* (pp. 270–283). London: Constable.

Harvey, D. (1990). *The condition of postmodernity: An enquiry into the origins of cultural change*. Cambridge, MA: Blackwell.

Haslam, N., Loughnan, S., & Kashima, Y. (2008). Attributing and denying humanness to others. *European Review of Social Psychology, 19*, 55–85.

Henry, F., & Tator, C. (2002). *Discourses of domination: Racial bias in the Canadian English-language press*. Toronto: University of Toronto Press.

Huysmans, J. (2006). *The politics of insecurity. Fear, migration and asylum in the EU*. London and New York, NY: Routledge.

IMM. (2015). Najbardziej opiniotwórcze polskie media w 2016 roku. Retrieved from http://www.imm.com.pl/sites/default/files/raporty/najbardziej_opiniotworcze_media_w_2015.pdf. Accessed February 5, 2017.

IMM. (2016). Najbardziej opiniotwórcze polskie media w 2016 roku. Retrieved from http://www.imm.com.pl/sites/default/files/raporty/najbardziej_opiniotworcze_media_w_2016_0.pdf. Accessed February 5, 2017.

Immigrants in Norwegian Media (2010). Retrieved from https://www.imdi.no/globalassets/dokumenter/rapporter/2010/immigrants-in-norwegian-media-summary.pdf. Accessed January 15, 2017.

Jeffries, L. (2003). Not a drop to drink: Emerging meanings in local newspaper reporting of the 1995 water crisis in Yorkshire. *Text, 23*(4), 513–538.

Johnson, H. L. (2011). Click to donate: Visual images, constructing victims and imagining the female refugee. *Third World Quarterly, 32*(6), 1015–1037.

Kaid, L. L., Gerstlé, J., & Sanders, K. R. (Eds.). (1991). *Mediated politics in two cultures: Presidential campaigning in the United States and France*. New York, NY: Praeger.

Kennedy, G. (1998). *An introduction to corpus linguistics*. London: Longman.

Kilgarriff, A., Baisa, V., Bušta, J., Jakubíček, M., Kovář, V., Michelfeit, J. ... Suchomel, V. (2014). The Sketch Engine: ten years on. *Lexicography, 1*(1), 7–36. doi:10.1007/s40607-014-0009-9.

Klocker, N., & Dunn, K. (2003). Who's driving the asylum debate?: Newspaper and government representations of asylum seekers. *Media International Australia, Incorporating Culture & Policy, 109*, 71–92.

Kopytowska, M. (2009). Corpus linguistics and an eclectic approach to the study of news – The mechanism of framing. In B. Lewandowska-Tomaszczyk & K. Dziwirek (Eds.), *Studies in cognitive corpus linguistics* (pp. 83–109). Frankfurt am Main: Peter Lang.

Kopytowska, M. (2010a). Unveiling the Other – the pragmatics of infosuasion. *Lodz Papers in Pragmatics, 6*(2), 249–282.

Kopytowska, M. (2010b). Mass-mediated multiculturalism and identity – Representations of Muslims in the British press. In H. Pułaczewska (Ed.), *Intercultural Europe: Arenas of difference, communication, and mediation* (pp. 181–193). Stuttgart: Ibidem.

Kopytowska, M. (2013). Blogging as the mediatization of politics and a new form of social interaction. In P. Cap & U. Okulska (Eds.), *Analyzing genres in political communication* (pp. 379–421). Amsterdam: Benjamins.

Kopytowska, M. (2014). Pictures in our heads: Crisis, conflict, and drama. In Y. Kalyango & M. Kopytowska (Eds.), *Why discourse matters: Negotiating identity in the mediatized world* (pp. 89–109). New York, NY: Peter Lang.

Kopytowska, M. (2015a). Ideology of 'here and now'. Mediating distance in television news. *Critical Discourse Studies, 12*(3), 347–365.

Kopytowska, M. (2015b). Covering conflict: between universality and cultural specificity in news discourse genre and journalistic style. International Review of Pragmatics (Special Issue on *Communicative styles and genres: Between universality and culture-specificity*), 7, 308–339.

Kopytowska, M. (2015c). Mediating identity, ideology and values in the public sphere: Towards a new model of (constructed) social reality. *Lodz Papers in Pragmatics, 11*(2), 133–156.

Langacker, R. W. (1987). *Foundations of cognitive grammar. Theoretical prerequisites.* Stanford: Stanford University Press.

Langacker, R. W. (1990). *Concept, image and symbol. The cognitive basis of grammar.* Berlin: Mouton de Gruyter.

Lenette, C., & Cleland, S. (2016). Changing faces: Visual representations of asylum seekers in times of crisis. *Creative Approaches to Research, 9*(1), 68–83.

Lewis, B. (1994). *Islam and the West.* Oxford: Oxford University Press.

Lippmann, W. (1922). *Public opinion.* New York, NY: Harcourt, Brace and Co.

Lulle, A., & Ungure, E. (2015). Asylum seekers crisis in Europe 2015: Debating spaces of fear and security in Latvia. *Journal on Baltic Security, 1*(2), 62–95.

Mahtani, M., & Mountz, A. (2002). Immigration to British Columbia: Media representation and public opinion. *Research on Immigration and Integration in the Metropolis Working Paper Series*, No. 02-15. Retrieved from http://mbc.metropolis.net/assets/uploads/files/wp/2002/WP02-15.pdf. Accessed on January 15, 2017.

Margaronis, M. (Tuesday, 25 October, 2016). For Calais refugees, this is the bulldozing of hope as well as home. *The Guardian.* Retrieved from https://www.theguardian.com/commentisfree/2016/oct/25/calais-refugees-hope-home-camp-greece. Accessed on December 05, 2016.

Martin, G. (2015). Stop the boats! Moral panic in Australia over asylum seekers. *Continuum, 29*(3), 304–322.

Maskaliūnaité, A. (2015). Discursive and institutional management of refugees and their crisis in Lithuania. *Journal on Baltic Security, 1*(2), 96–124.

McEnery, T., & Gabrielatos, C. (2008). English corpus linguistics. In B. Aarts & A. McMahon (Eds.), *The handbook of English linguistics* (pp. 33–71). Oxford: Blackwell Publishing.

McEnery, T., & Hardie, A. (2011). *Corpus linguistics: Method, theory and practice.* Cambridge: Cambridge University Press.

McEnery, T., & Wilson, A. (1996). *Corpus linguistics.* Edinburgh: University Press.

Musolff, A. (2012). Immigrants and parasites: The history of a bio-social metaphor. In M. Messer, R. Schroeder, & R. Wodak (Eds.), *Migrations: Interdisciplinary perspectives* (pp. 249–258). Vienna: Springer.

Musolff, A. (2014). Metaphorical *parasites* and 'parasitic' metaphors: Semantic exchanges between political and scientific vocabularies. *Journal of Language and Politics, 13*(2), 218–233.

Musolff, A. (2015). Dehumanizing metaphors in UK immigrant debates in press and online media. *Journal of Language Aggression and Conflict, 3*(1), 41–56.

O'Keeffe, A. (2002). Exploring indices of national identity in corpus of radio phone-in data from Irish radio. In A. Sanches Macarro (Ed.), *Windows on the world. Media discourse in English* (pp. 91–113). Valencia: University of Valencia Press.

O'Keeffe, A. (2003). "Like the vise virgins and all that jazz" – Using a corpus to examine vague language and shared knowledge. In U. Connor & T. A. Upton (Eds.), *Applied corpus linguistics. A multidimensional perspective* (pp. 1–20). Amsterdam: Rodopi.

O'Keeffe, A. (2005). "You've a daughter yourself?" A corpus based look at question forms in an Irish radio phone-in. In K. P. Schneider & A. Barron (Eds.) *The pragmatics of Irish English* (pp. 339–366). Berlin: Mouton de Gruyter.

O'Keeffe, A. (2006). *Investigating media discourse.* New York, NY: Routledge.

Poole, E. (2002). *Reporting Islam. Media representations of British Muslims.* London: IB Tauris.

Poole, E., & Richardson, J. E. (2006). *Muslims and the News Media.* London: IB Tauris.

Richardson, J. E. (2004). *(Mis) Representing Islam. The racism and rhetoric of British Broadsheet newspapers.* Amsterdam: John Benjamins.

Richardson, J. E., & Colombo, M. (2013). Continuity and change in anti-immigrant discourse in Italy: An analysis of the visual propaganda of the Lega Nord. *Journal of Language and Politics, 12*(2), 180–202.

Rychlý, P. (2008). A lexicographer-friendly association score. In *Proceedings of Recent Advances in Slavonic Natural Language Processing,* RASLAN, 6–9.

Rydgren, J. (2003). Mesolevel causes of racism and xenophobia. *European Journal of Social Theory, 6*(1), 45–68.

Saridakis, I., & Mouka, E. (2016). Immigrants, refugees and asylum seekers in Greece. A critical corpus-driven analysis of journalistic discourse. Paper presented at the conference Europe in Discourse: Identity, Diversity Borders on 23–25 September 2016. Athens, Greece.

Scheufele, D. A., & Tewksbury, D. (2007). Framing, agenda setting, and priming: The evolution of three media effects models. *Journal of Communication, 57*(1), 9–20.

Schwartz, S. H., & Struch, N. (1989). Values, stereotypes, and intergroup antagonism. In D. Bar-Tal, C. G. Grauman, A. W. Kruglanski, & W. Stroebe (Eds.), *Stereotypes and prejudice: Changing conceptions* (pp. 151–167). New York, NY: Springer-Verlag.

Schwartz, S. H., Struch, N., & Bilsky, W. (1990). Values and intergroup social motives: A study of Israeli and German students. *Social Psychology Quarterly, 53,* 185–198.

Searle, J. (1995). *The construction of social reality.* London: The Penguin.

Searle, J. (2010). *Making the social world: The structure of human civilization.* Oxford: Oxford University Press.

Shoemaker, P., & Cohen, A. (Eds.). (2006). *News around the world. Content, practitioners, and the public.* New York, NY: Routledge.

Sinclair, J. (2005). Document relativity. Ms. Tuscan Word Centre. Italy.

Stubbs, M. (1997). Whorf 's children: Critical comments on critical discourse analysis (CDA). In A. Ryan & A. Wray (Eds.), *Evolving models of language* (pp. 110–116). Clevedon: BAAL in association with Multilingual Matters.

Teubert, W. (2005). My version of corpus linguistics. *International Journal of Corpus Linguistics, 10*(1), 1–13.

Thompson, J. B. (1995). *The media and modernity.* Cambridge: Polity Press.

Tognini-Bonelli, E. (2001). *Corpus linguistics at work.* Amsterdam: John Benjamins.

UNHCR. (1967). *Convention and protocol relating to the status of refugees, Geneva, Switzerland.* Office of the United Nations High Commissioner for Refugees (UNHCR), Communications and Public Information Service. Retrieved from http://www.unhcr.org/protect/PROTECTION/3b66c2aa10.pdf. Accessed on January 15, 2017.

UNHCR. (2016). UNHCR viewpoint: 'Refugee' or 'migrant' – Which is right? UNHCR 11 July 2016. Retrieved from http://www.unhcr.org/news/latest/2016/7/55df0e556/unhcr-viewpoint-refugee-migrant-right.html. Accessed on Janaury 15, 2017.

United Nations High Commissioner for Refugees. (2015a). Over one million sea arrivals reach Europe in 2015. Retrieved from http://www.unhcr.org/5683d0b56.html.

United Nations High Commissioner for Refugees (2015b). Mediterranean Sea arrivals 2015. Data by location, country of arrival, demographic and country of origin. Retrieved from http://data.unhcr.org/mediterranean/download.php?id 490. Accessed on January 15, 2017.

Veebel, V. (2015). Balancing between solidarity and responsibility: Estonia in the EU refugee crisis. *Journal on Baltic Security, 1*(2), 28–61.

Warren, M. (2011). Using corpora in the learning and teaching of phraseological variation. In G. Aston & L. Flowerdew (Eds.), *New trends in corpora and language learning* (pp. 153–166). London: Continuum.

Wright, T. (2000). *Refugees on screen.* Oxford, UK: Refugee Studies Centre.

Wright, T. (2002). Moving images: Thee media representation of refugees. *Visual Studies, 17*(1), 53–66.

EUROPE AND THE FRONT NATIONAL STANCE: SHIFTING THE BLAME

Fabienne Baider and Maria Constantinou

ABSTRACT

This chapter focuses on the anti-European stance as it unfolds in Marine Le Pen's and Jean-Marie Le Pen's discourses. As most far-right parties in Europe, both politicians focus on the notion of freedom and national sovereignty, asserting a strong anti-European Union stance; however, they construct their anti-European momentum by playing on different strategies and emotions. By using corpus linguistics tools, the present study examines and analyses the discourse of both politicians in interviews and debates. It concludes that if they share most issues on which they base their political agenda such as the fear of increasing immigration because of the Schengen's agreement, they differ as regards the ways they discursively address the same issue. Marine Le Pen relies more on a constructive/rational stance, by focusing on facts and figures as well as on solutions, while moving away from the strong and negative emotions which her father constantly used mainly as provocation strategies. This may have helped her build a favourable political momentum as witnessed in the 2014 European elections.

Keywords: Anti-Europe stance; discursive strategies; French National Front; national sovereignty; corpus linguistics

National Identity and Europe in Times of Crisis: Doing and Undoing Europe, 113–135

Copyright © 2017 by Emerald Publishing Limited
doi:10.1108/978-1-78714-513-920171006

1. INTRODUCTION

In the 2014 European parliamentary elections, Marine Le Pen succeeded in drawing a record score of 25% of the votes and gaining 24 of the 74 Parliament seats. This figure fits the trend of popularity for extreme-right parties across Europe whether in the same European parliamentary elections or in national elections such as in Sweden with the anti-immigrant Sweden Democrats in September 2014. As Mayer (2013) stated in her comments regarding an earlier success by the new Front National leader (during the 2012 French presidential elections) such a high score could be partly attributed to the de-demonization strategy implemented since her takeover from Jean-Marie Le Pen as well as to the 'shift in the whole space of political discourse' in France which includes now 'more readily FN themes and vocabulary' (Beauzamy, 2013, p. 182). Some other commentators have argued that her anti-European stance explains the party's popularity given the economic crisis (Taguieff, 2012). In this chapter, we examine the different discursive strategies used by both Front National leaders to understand how differently they construct an anti-European momentum.

2. 'EMOTIONAL ETHOS'

2.1 Affective Intelligence and Political Arguments

Smith (1992) and Wodak, de Cillia, Reisigl, and Liebhart (2009) identified the discursive construction of an imagined community and nationalistic discourse. Four important dimensions known to regulate this collective identity within the nation were put forward:

— a shared continuity;
— a shared memory;
— a common destiny (Smith, 1992, p. 58);
— and a relational dimension from the inside to the outside (de Cillia, Reisigl, & Wodak, 1999, p. 153; Martin, 1995, p. 12).

We focus on the fourth element, *the relational dimension* of the French National Front (henceforth FN) from the inside and outside. The adjective *relational* refers to the 'intersubjective shared emotional attitudes within a specific group of persons' towards the in-group and the out-group (de Cillia et al., 1999, p. 153). Therefore, emotions can prevent, foster or imply social interactions (Frijda, 2006, p. 85) and vice versa if emotions create social relationships, relationships shape emotions (Clore & Gasper, 2000; Fitzgerald, 2013; Marcus & Neuman, 2000). These intersubjective emotional attitudes are of special scientific interest and need to be further examined in politics since they drive to 'similar *behavioural* dispositions' towards especially the out-group (de Cillia et al. 1999, p. 153, our italics). Creating affects entails producing purposeful actions. Indeed, sharing on an emotional level was described in Aristotle (*Rhetorica* I, II, 5 cited by Frijda, Manstead, & Bem, 2000, p. 1) as fundamental in the art of persuasion and the formation of judgement:

> The orator persuades by means of his hearers, when they are roused to emotion by his speech; for the judgements we deliver are not the same when we are influenced by joy or sorrow, love or hate.

Within a cognitive perspective, Fridja explains further how emotions[1] in general derive from the appraisal of a situation:

> (...) emotions result from how the individual *believes* the world to be, how events are *believed* to have come about, and what implications events are *believed* to have. (Frijda et al., 2000, p. 1, our italics)

Affects will emerge then from a desire to act, i.e. from an urge to correct a perceived discrepancy between how the world is and how we believe it should be (Frijda, 2006).

Therefore, within this perspective we can state that cognition precedes and causes affects (Frijda, 2006; Panskepp, 1998). Hence, one of the key 'duties' of a politician is to describe reality, such as the European Union (EU) integration, in a way that will counter the expectations of the citizens of a specific country of what the EU's purpose should be. Such a discrepancy will mainly trigger anger or resentment. These emotions could, in turn, be translated into giving the mandate to a politician to correct the situation.

Since emotions are part of a politician's tools of persuasion in argumentative discourse and given the success of Marine Le Pen in all the elections in the last 3 years, the aim of this chapter is to understand how differently both FN leaders construct emotionally their political communication, almost always centred on the EU and Schengen, and what type of relationship they wish to create with the voters, while keeping a similar political agenda which still attests to the party's nationalistic agenda.

2.2 Indexing the Nationalistic Discourse

As Anderson (1983, p. 3) points out, 'since every search for identity includes differentiating oneself from what one is not, identity politics is always and necessarily a politics of the creation of difference'. However, within this creation of difference, Krzyżanowski and Wodak (2009) have noticed that in the current post-industrial societies, nationalism is no longer defined with regard to other nations, but increasingly 'nationalism is becoming more defensive and defined by reference to migrants and other marginalized groups' (cited in Costelloe, 2014, p. 21).

The new discursive strategies in the expression of negative views of the Other in the nationalistic discourse consist in the shift from biological racism to cultural difference in most EU extreme-right parties (Augoustinos & Every, 2007; Bar-On, 2007, 2013; Levy, 2015; Shields, 2013; Williams, 2011; Yilmaz, 2012). Contrary to their extremist right-wing forebears who claimed biological and racial superiority to legitimise 'intellectual and cultural hegemony' (Heinisch, 2013, pp. 49–50), the new far-right parties employ such concepts in their claim for cultural and national sovereignty. In this context, political scientists have pointed out (Mayer, 2013; Williams, 2011) that there has been a shift from the concept of 'racism', which implies a hierarchy among human beings because of the colour of their skin or other physical features, towards 'racialism', i.e. the difficult cohabitation of different cultures with different values. From this perspective, and since the Schengen agreement makes the European space more open, right-wing strategies are striving to present this openness as a threat. In particular, immigrants become 'an incompatible ontological category predicated on culture'; they also try to keep 'the focus on immigration as an imminent threat to "our common" achievements' (Yilmaz, 2012, p. 368), a threat which has to be present in their discourse since resistance is one of the mottos of the far-right populist parties.

In this postmodern racist discourse, a biological inferiority of migrants or Muslims is not at the centre of the argument, but discourse focuses on the right of a people to defend their collective identity. Therefore, in contrast with the 'old-fashioned racism' found in the FN discourse, which consisted in the use of blatant racist terms and intentional 'gaffes' regarding for instance Jews or Arabs (cf. J.-M. Le Pen numerous 'provocations'[2]), the FN discourse in the 90s had adopted what Taguieff (2012) has called 'new national-populism', with a focus on Islam and the Islamization of the West (Balent, 2013; Wollenberg, 2014). This new far-right national-populism is more associated with 'the fears sparked by globalization, European integration and mass immigration' as well as with 'a rejection of multiculturalism' (Taguieff, 2012), although keeping what Perrineau (1997, p. 178) had called the triad of 'unemployment, immigration and insecurity'. As a journalist from *Le Figaro* has recently pointed out:

> Le FN *new style* a su percevoir cette évolution et adapter son discours en conséquence. C'est pourquoi il est désormais rejoint par des militants de la cause homosexuelle, et gagne même une certaine sympathie dans les milieux juifs inquiets devant la hausse de l'antisémitisme.[3]

> [The FN *new style* has been able to perceive this evolution and adapt its discourse accordingly. This is why activists of the homosexual cause have now joined the party, and some sympathy has even been gained towards it within the Jewish community which is alarmed by the rise of anti-Semitism.]

Discourse as a social practice has played an important role in shaping this new national-populism, a more modern image of the party and in predetermining respectively its electoral victories and defeats.

2.3 France, the FN and the European Union

As it is true for many other ultra-nationalistic parties, the triad mentioned above has been reworked within a political agenda which used to be focused on a call for authoritarian politics (punitiveness), and the dislike of foreigners (Beauzamy, 2013, p. 182; Grunberg & Schweisguth, 2003) under Jean-Marie Le Pen's rule.

Most studies focusing on his discourse (for example, Beauzamy & Naves, 2010; Bernard, 2007; Souchard, Wahnich, Cuminal, & Wathier, 1997) analysed Le Pen's father's use of scandals and provocations, such as coining Vichyist metaphors, as a strategy to allow a constant media coverage, strategy which proved at times beneficial to the party (Beauzamy, 2013, p. 182; Bernard, 2007, p. 40). However, such aggressive behaviour made also reluctant other right-wing parties to be associated with the FN and no political alliance was possible until the change of the party's Presidence with Le Pen's daughter in 2011 when Jean-Marie Le Pen retired.

A lawyer like her father and adopting the same tribune style, Marine Le Pen is often presented as leading a 'modern' lifestyle (mainly because she has been twice divorced and did not marry her new companion), and being more open than her father on several cultural issues (gay marriage for instance), shying away as well from any anti-Semitic comment. She maintains though the strong anti-Islamic and anti-European integration stance dear to her father, since both positionings are endorsed by many French people.

As far as the anti-European stance is concerned and as far back as 2005, the French people voted with a big majority against the European Constitution, a vote which marked 'a reversal of its historical support for greater unity with its continental neighbours'.[4] If economic anxieties could explain the results, the fear of losing national sovereignty was as much a pull to the no vote. 'For me, the decisions should not be made by Europe, but by each nation. I want France to make decisions for herself' stated a French voter.[5]

Ten years later, a more recent survey by Pew Research Center,[6] focused on five European countries on European integration, has revealed that France and Spain were countries with the most people believing the European project has weakened their nation (Stokes, 2015). The euro-crisis is given as an explanation of such an anti-Brussels sentiment; this crisis gave way to the rise of Eurosceptic political parties on both the left and the right:

> Half or more of the publics in four of the six EU nations surveyed believe that these parties are good for their country because they raise important issues that are ignored by traditional parties. (Stokes, 2015, p. 4)

A recent survey conducted by Ipsos[7] has also shown that globalization is considered a threat to France (61%) while the majority draws inspiration from the values of the past (78%). As reported by journalists such figures are more acute among the lower paid, the jobless and the youth, a critical context which is a fertile environment likely to turn into 'a toxic recruitment ground for extremism',[8] an environment which benefits the FN. Indeed, this can be confirmed by the results of the 2014 European Parliament Election where 30% under 35 years old voted FN and 13% for the extreme left.[9]

Indeed, Marine Le Pen's efforts are focused on the appeal to French resentment against Brussels in order to transform the FN from a fringe movement into a party that could be trusted to govern.[10] To do so, she claims to speak to and for the social strata forgotten by the mainstream politics (Paxton, 2004; Shields, 2013), les 'oubliés' as Marine Le Pen calls them, and appears to have succeeded in winning on important aspects of a political persona, such as sincerity and benevolence, while her father failed to do so. This allows her to push her anti-EU agenda further.

3. METHODOLOGY RATIONAL, DATA, PROCEDURE

3.1. Methodological Rational: A Lexical Approach

In order to investigate the differences within the sentiment against the EU constructed through discursive representations in both Le Pens' discourse, we have relied on previous research which had identified specific emotions used in the rhetoric of the ultra-nationalist discourse in relation to the Other (Baider & Constantinou, 2014, 2015; Banks, 2007; Billig, 1978; Mayer, 2012; Shields, 2013) such as *fear, hatred, rage, anger*. We identify these lexical items in our data, by applying corpus-based methodologies, i.e. the use of corpus analysis tools such as AntConc. Given the limitations imposed by the size of the corpus which is thousand words big, we have opted for the lexical approach (Oster, 2010) which includes the extraction of statistical data, the identification of salient lexical information (collocates, keywords) and the examination of utterances contexts via the concordances (Baider, 2013; Bednarek, 2008; Kecskes, 2013). Utterance contexts reveal the salient semantic features of lexical units since these contexts describe the specific social experiences in which repetitive uses of language are anchored. Salience is the basis of conceptual associations, available to each speaker of that language community. Identifying lexical and conceptual salience allows discourse analysts then to detect an ideological positioning within the community.

3.2. Data

If most previous studies on the rhetoric of both politicians have focused on written data, our corpus consists of speeches and interviews involving both leaders, freely accessible on the Web. The data include Marine Le Pen's speeches and interviews focusing on Europe, France and its role in the EU as well as Jean-Marie Le Pen's speeches and interviews dealing with similar issues. Tables 1 and 2 provide information on the spoken data used in this chapter:

Table 3 illustrates the comparability criterion of both sub-corpora in terms of their volume.

Table 1. Data for Marine Le Pen.

	Title of the Video and Link	Date of Publication	Visited on
1	*Discours de Marine Le Pen et Aymeric Chauprade à Paris* http://www.frontnational.com/videos/discours-daymeric-chauprade-a-paris/	19.05.2014	22.05.2014
2	*GAD: une catastrophe annoncée* http://www.frontnational.com/videos/gad-une-catastrophe-annoncee/	16.10.2013	08.04.2014
3	*Marine Le Pen alerte les Français: nos libertés sont en péril!* http://www.youtube.com/watch?v=k_AcOLat8pk	13.01.2014	08.04.2014
4	*Enorme performance de Marine Le Pen face à des rafales de questions...* http://www.youtube.com/watch?v=VTBbTDMSLuM	14.02.2014	09.04.2014
5	*CLASH: Marine Le Pen en pleine forme!* http://www.youtube.com/watch?v=nYXete-s2Tg	22.10.2013	07.04.2014
6	*Marine Le Pen sur les Roms: 'il faut tous les renvoyer'* - http://www.youtube.com/watch?v=k_AcOLat8pk	26.09.2013	07.04.2014

Table 2. Data for Jean-Marie Le Pen.

	Title of the Video and Link	Date of Publication	Visited on
1	*Journal de bord No 311 de Jean-Marie Le Pen* http://www.youtube.com/watch?v=R8KqjoV5QNU	15.03.2013	12.04.2014
2	*Succès du FN: Jean-Marie le Pen répond aux questions des journalistes* http://www.youtube.com/watch?v=I7bkjX04HbU	23.03.2014	13.04.2014
3	*Jean-Marie Le Pen versus Noah, Bedos, Madonna, Bruel, Valls* http://www.youtube.com/watch?v=cs9ih-_H3W8	06.06.2014	13.06.2014
4	*Un des plus beaux discours de Jean-Marie Le Pen sur le mondialisme* http://www.youtube.com/watch?v=wnbDGUirz2k	28.02.2012	14.05.2014
5	*Emission intégrale: Jean-Marie Le Pen sur France 3 du 10 février* http://www.youtube.com/watch?v=yQIHdRjYrqI	11.02.2013	14.05.2014
6	*'L'ALGERIE NOUS ENVOIE SES RACAILLES' (sic) (JM LE PEN* http://www.youtube.com/watch?v=Zt-GzswDHjI	04.04.2012	14.05.2014

Table 3.   Volume of Data.

J.-M. Le Pen's interviews and speeches:
12,205 words
M. Le Pen's interviews and speeches:
12,024 words

3.3. Procedure: Emotion Words, Collocates, Concordances

As explained in Section 3.1, we focused our first search in the data by using relevant emotion words; however, analysing emotions in discourse entails several
strategies since emotions are not expressed usually by actually *saying* the emotions (*I am really angry*); they are more often indirectly expressed (*I was fuming*)
(cf. Fussell & Moss, 1998). Therefore, and as expected, very few hits of emotion
words have been found.

However, the few occurrences found for each emotion word gave typical
contexts of use and revealed lexical collocations and contextual specificities
(Blumenthal, 2002; Sinclair, 2004). The words associated with *anger* or *fear*, for
instance, corroborate what previous studies have identified as the most frequent
associations in the FN speeches. For instance, the word *colère* 'anger' in our
data is contextualized with lexical units such as *Europe, migrants, insécurité*
'insecurity', *frontières* 'borders'. These lexical units form then the conceptual
domain of the emotion of *anger* within the FN discourse (Banks, 2007). We
have found as well how differently the emotion of *fear* was indexed in both
data, i.e. a high frequency of collocates such as *immigration, immigrant*(s),
Arab(s), *parasite*(s), *Europe, Bruxelles* 'Brussels' in Jean-Marie Le Pen's data,
whereas for the same emotion, the words *immigrants* and *Arabs* had disap-
peared from Marine Le Pen's data.

Moreover, pronouns (Costelloe, 2014; van Dijk, 2006) such as *we/they* and
modality *should, must* were remarkable with their frequency. They play an
important role in constructing expectations for the electorate such as regarding
what French identity 'should' or 'must' be in the Le Pens' discourse as well as
to take a moral ground against the EU (see Section 4).

Finally we went back to concordances (context of the occurrence) to help us
refine the study and to identify the illocutionary force of the statements in
which these words had been used. For example, when expressing fear, the aims
could be as much to instil the idea of a threat (to fear the migrants) as to
express sympathy (to be frightened for the migrants) as we shall see in the next
section.

4. SHIFTING THE FOCUS: IMMIGRATION VERSUS IMMIGRANTS

In this section we examine how Marine Le Pen uses the same immigration theme as her father, but manages to construct discursively the issue in a positive relational way: She tries to build an emotional rapport with the audience (enhancing the emotion of empathy), and strives to appear coherent (referring to moral arguments and logic), while her father seems to strive to pull the audience away from the migrants (with the emotions of contempt and disgust), resorting to gross exaggerations.

4.1. Migration: From the Fear of a Tsunami to the Resentment of Illegality

Immigration and Europe have been traditionally the scapegoats of the FN's ire: They embody the enemy within the nation and the enemy outside the nation; anti-immigration and anti-Brussels/Europe stances had then been used in Le Pen's father's rhetoric as early as in 2007:

> (1) la France, qui a "bazardé (son) indépendance à un certain nombre de gnomes de Bruxelles". [France, which has sold off (its) independence to a number of gnomes of Brussels] (Libération, 20 April 2007)

The figures for the words *migrants* and *immigration* reveal qualitative differences between both Le Pens, even though references to the immigration phenomenon are comparable: The word *migrants* is almost unknown in the spoken data for Marine Le Pen as Table 4 shows.

When looking at the context, a different emotional stance is observed as well.

In Jean-Marie Le Pen's discourse (quotations 2 and 3) the linguistic context embedding the word *immigration* describes terror (*we are threatened, an astounding wave of a mass migration*):

> (2) je crois aussi, nous sommes *menacés* d'une *formidable* vague d'immigration *massive*. (J.-M. Le Pen, video 5) [=I believe also that We have been threatened by an astounding wave of mass migration]

Table 4. Occurrences of the Words *Immigration* and *Immigrés* 'Migrant'.

Data	Immigration/Immigré(s) (Migrants)
J.-M. Le Pen's interviews and speeches: 12,205 words	Immigration: 20 Immigrés/migrants: 7
M. Le Pen's interviews and speeches: 12,024 words	Immigration: 18 Immigrés: 1

Indeed, the threat being so huge (2), the door must be completely closed ('zero tolerance for migration') as he mentions in (3):

> (3) mais je crois que ce qui est essentiel maintenant c'est de fermer la porte. Immigration zéro doit être la politique. (J.-M. Le Pen, video 5) [=but I think that the most fundamental is now to close the door. Zero migration must be the policy to be adopted.]

The reason for this 'zero tolerance' is given with the quick but noticeable amalgam of *immigration* with *security* in (4):

> (4) et bien nous allons parler *de sécurité et d'immigration*, dans le temps qui nous reste (J.-M. Le Pen, video 6). [= well we are going to talk *about security and immigration* in the time left to us]

Marine Le Pen makes as well statements as below (5), consisting in the use of numbers to create probably an even more dramatic effect than her father's rhetoric; in (5) for instance, the expression 'a *terrifying figure slammed down*' could evoke the guillotine cleaver falling on French people heads:

> (5) *Un chiffre terrifiant qui vient de tomber: + 48% d'immigration illégale en Europe au cours de l'année qui vient.* (M. Le Pen, video 1) [= A terrifying figure that has just come down: 48% of illegal immigration in Europe in the coming year.]

However, since she chooses to focus on the phenomenon of migration and not on the people, the migrants, she appears to discuss more the problem itself rather than to target that group of people; such a strategy makes her positioning appear more rational than her father's. Second, contrary to her father who attacks verbally migrants but does not offer sufficient and realistic solutions (other than just to deport all migrants), she advocates a 'solution', recommending *assimilation*, as illustrated in the example below:

> (6) vous avez raison je ne veux pas d'immigration je veux de *l'assimilation*. (M. Le Pen, video 5) [=you are right I don't want immigration, I want *assimilation*]

Moreover, if in the same way as her father she amalgamates *security* and *migration* as in (7), she embeds both issues in an argument against the record of the Socialist Prime Minister, accusing then a political opponent of mishandling the situation while keeping away from putting the blame on migrants themselves:

> (7) (about Valls) Affaibli par un *très mauvais bilan en matière de sécurité et d'immigration*, il multiplie les provocations agressives. (M. Le Pen, video 3) [=Weakened by a very poor record on security and immigration, he (Valls) multiplies aggressive provocations]

We can also note the expression 'aggressive provocations' in the quotation above; this expression is generally used by journalists or FN opponents to denounce the FN leader's provocative statements. By describing the Socialist Minister in this light, it allows Marine Le Pen to reverse the stigmata, or at least to put both herself and her opponent on the same level, whereas she used to be described as a political and social pariah. This search for legitimation by resorting to careful discursive strategies is actually verified when studying statements made by politicians from the Sarkozy's conservative party for instance: Marine Le Pen makes less outrageous statements than they do; such a strategy helps her push further her agenda of 'mainstreaming' her party.[11] This appears to be even more powerful when we analyse the way she uses the terms *migrants* 'migrants' and *immigrés* 'immigrants'.

4.2. The Migrants: From Contempt to Compassion

In both data the word *immigration* is described as being 'massive' and 'a problem'; in both data, Brussels is the main culprit of all the ills occurring in Europe, the most frequent nominal collocates being *insécurité* 'insecurity' and *identité nationale* 'national identity' when referring to Europe.

As we have seen in Table 4, Jean-Marie Le Pen refers seven times more frequently to the migrants themselves (*émigrés*) than his daughter while Marine Le Pen restricts her references to the phenomenon by using the word *migration*. We have mentioned that this choice of words helps her to stay in the abstract, and to maintain a distance from personal labelling.

In contrast, Le Pen's father not only personalises the phenomenon, but the repetition of the word (*im*)*migrants* implies an agency which allows the politician to make them responsible for the existing/future social and financial destruction of France he is predicting, as illustrated in the quotations (8)–(11). Moreover, gross exaggerations point at an overt racist discourse since for Le Pen's father a 'typical migrant family' is a dad being a thief, and his son a serial killer as in (8):

> (8) En ce moment, ce qu'on appelle des chances pour la France... *le papa voleur, trafiquant de drogues, le fils assassin, multi assassin* (...) (J.-M. Le Pen, video 6). [=Now what we call opportunities for France ... *the thief dad, the drug dealer, the murderer son, multiple murderer* (...)]

Not only are migrants typically outlaws, but most of them are also taking advantage of financial assistance (*pour la plupart des chômeurs* 'most of whom are unemployed'); therefore, they do not contribute to but take advantage of the French society (9):

> (9) Nous avons accueilli des millions d'immigrés dans notre pays *qui sont pour la plupart des chômeurs* [=We have hosted millions of migrants in our country most of whom *are unemployed*]

Indeed, the context of the word *immigrés* 'migrants' in his speeches is typically associated with financial costs ('immigration costs us 70 billions'; '10 million migrants in 35 years') as in (10):

> (10) nous avons accueilli *10 millions d'immigrés* en 35 ans- L'immigration *nous coûte 70* milliards. [=We have hosted *10 million migrants* in 35 years - Migration *costs us* 70 billions]

His conclusion is that French society, instead of experiencing the migration phenomenon as an opportunity is actually being weakened ('society has been impoverished', a growing burden weighing on the shoulders of the nation[12]):

(11) La société *s'est appauvrie*, en raison notamment *du poids croissant* des immigrés qui *sont à sa charge* [= Society *has been impoverished*, particularly because of *the growing burden of immigrants* being *dependent on it*]

Consequently, the migrants are seen as leeches living on the back of the nation, very much the way Goebbels was describing the Jews in his speeches (Billig, 1978; Kohl, 2011; Musolff, 2008, 2010). More importantly, and in line with the new ultra-nationalistic agenda, this burden is not only social and financial; it is also cultural since migrants endanger the national values, put peace at risk, leading to the destruction of the whole country. In the quotation below, the accumulation of verbs (*challenged, saturated, threatened, explodes*) expresses a crescendo of negative consequences (and bad feelings):

(12) Nos valeurs et notre religion *sont remises en cause* par celles des *immigrants*, nos équipements collectifs, crèches, écoles, logements *sont saturés*, la paix civile est menacée partout, l'insécurité *explose*. (J.-M. Le Pen, video 5) [=Our values and religion *are being challenged* by the values of immigrants, our social facilities, nurseries, schools, homes *are saturated*, civil peace *is being threatened* everywhere, insecurity *is exploding*].

In contrast, Marine Le Pen is careful when using the adjective *illegal* in the rare instances she refers directly to the migrants, which her father does not do (cf. the quotation above); hence, the accumulated references to 'fake passports, fake visas'. This allows her to describe the illegal migrants (as in quote (13)) as breaking the law, and as being delinquents (*délinquant*). Therefore, they should be deported not because they are migrants but because they are firstly outlaws:

(13) Ce sont *des clandestins*, ils sont en *situation de clandestinité* ce sont des *délinquants*. M. Le Pen, video 6) [These are illegal, they are going underground, they are offenders.]

Her reasoning is based on logic, not on emotion as is the case with her father. Illegality of the migrants justifies as well better her resentment and the harsh measures she advocates.

Migration is also always used as an argument to destroy the ethos of her political opponents, describing them as being irresponsible since they encourage delinquency and criminality as in (14):

(14) La France est un pays d'immigration; *avec des clandestins...* vous, vous *encouragez la clandestinité*, [...] (M. Le Pen, video 5) [=France is a country of immigration; with *illegal immigrants...* you are *encouraging illegality*]

Claiming the moral high ground, she holds political opponents and Europe supporters accountable for the human catastrophes which are often the aftermath of illegal immigration:

(15) Ceux qui soutiennent encore Schengen, PS ou UMP, ceux qui encouragent l'immigration clandestine, *sont responsables de tout cela, sont coupables de ces drames humains* (M. Le Pen, video 1) [=Those who still support Schengen, PS or UMP, those who are

encouraging illegal immigration, *are responsible for this, are guilty of these human tragedie*s]

Hence and contrary to her father, she takes the responsibility away from the migrants' shoulders to shift it onto the mafia and, as we have seen above, onto Europe and its political supporters:

(16) Qui veut faire l'ange, fait la bête. *Cette immigration de masse entraîne des drames humains, avec ces noyés, ces disparus, ces bateaux pleins de migrants* prêts à risquer leur vie pour rejoindre ce qu'on leur vend à prix d'or comme un eldorado. (M. Le Pen, video 1) [=He who would act the angel acts the brute. This mass migration leads to human tragedies, with those drowned, missing people, and those boats full of migrants willing to risk their lives to reach what they are selling them at exorbitant prices as an Eldorado.]

Finally and most importantly, the extensive descriptions of the hardship experienced by the migrants drowning or enduring appalling conditions create a strong empathy towards them in (17), while Marine Le Pen appears then to be a compassionate soul:

(17) Dans *des conditions épouvantables*, ils organisent une immigration de masse vers l'Europe, et donc vers la France! (M. Le Pen, video 1) [=In such *appalling conditions*, they organize a mass migration to Europe, and so to France!]

4.3. A Different Rhetoric for the Same Argumentative Aim

The few examples given in the previous paragraphs have shown that despite fundamental similarities such as associating the migration phenomenon with danger and the EU with a catastrophic scenario, the discursive strategies used by both politicians are not only different, but almost divergent: Jean-Marie Le Pen makes personal judgements regarding immigration whereas Marine Le Pen puts the topic on a structural level (it is *out of control, illegal*), presenting the phenomenon as being badly regulated by the present politicians and the EU.

The *immigration* theme is then used in Marine le Pen's speeches to thrive for an image of a 'benevolent' protector of the nation and to appear as a potential legitimate leader of the country, while her father who did not really care to be elected was keen on making waves with shocking statements. She exploits the immigration theme to achieve her political aim and succeeds in shifting the gaze on her political competitors over the immigration 'topic', 'zooming' on them, while moving the focus away from the migrants themselves. Moreover, she has managed to construct a humane persona, thanks to the use of emotionally charged expressions such as *drames humains* 'human tragedies' (see quote (16)).

This stance is politically more useful and less costly than the one chosen by her father:

— She succeeds in channeling anger and resentment which is real among voters against her political opponents, helping her to get votes;

— Even though, the lexical associations are the same (*immigration* is linked to the words *insecurity*, *unemployment* and *national identity*), she tackles in a more acceptable way the same issue by using logic and targeting illegality, an important change since in order to win elections she needs the female and centre-right-line voters who had never appreciated the contempt displayed by her father towards migrants and towards his adversaries in general (Mayer, 2012; Shields, 2013).

Both viewpoints are also divergent on another dimension: Marine Le Pen, while focusing on the sufferings of the people (nation and migrants), has her gaze on the future, on how to rebuild the nation; Jean-Marie Le Pen's gaze focuses on a nostalgic glorious ideal of Europe as the next section explains.

5. EUROPE: THE AFFECTIVE POLITICS OF ANGER

In her effort to elaborate a more constructive stance than her father, mainly when referring to Europe and Brussels[13] Marine Le Pen seems to be creating a different political momentum, suggesting solutions and anchoring her speech on more positive emotions; she also moves the affective angers from Brussels to Germany, a historical strawman in France.

5.1. From Migration Problems to Brussels' Guilt

In Jean-Marie Le Pen's discourse, Europe is described as 'immigrationist' (18 and 19) as are the mainstream political parties in France, the opposite of the FN political stance:

(18) Toute la législation européenne est immigrationniste (J.-M. Le Pen, video 4) [=All European legislation is immigrationist]

(19) l'UMP (...) est *euro- mondialiste*, il est immigrationniste, *c'est à dire il est exactement l'adverse du Front*. (J.-M Le Pen, video 5) [UMP (...) is a *European globalist*, an *immigrationist*, i.e. it is exactly the opposite of the National Front.]

(20) Qui peut croire (...) que l'immigration est une chance pour la France? A part les politiciens européistes, personne! (J.-M. Le Pen, video 4) [=Who believes (...) that migration is a chance for France? Except for Europeanist politicians, no one!]

Quantitatively the data from Le Pen's father are much more focused on Europe than Marine Le Pen's, with almost three times more occurrences of lexical items referring to Europe (see Table 5).

The occurrences of *Europe, européen, européenne* in Jean-Marie Le Pen's interviews and speeches describe in context a polysemic entity: on the one hand, the new Europe (EU) and on the other the old Europe (before the EU).

Table 5. Comparative Numbers for Europe and Its Paradigm.

	Europe	European	Brussels
J.-M. Le Pen	66	55	7
M. Le Pen	16	25	2

The new Europe is as dangerous and incompetent as powerful and 'civilised' was the old one.

The old Europe is described as *grand* and *rich*, notably 'enriched by the Greek and Latin cultures', accentuating a nostalgic gaze of the 'European genius':

> (21) Cette Europe enrichie des cultures grecques et latines, magnifiée par le christianisme, sublimée par la Renaissance [...] (J.-M. Le Pen, video 4) [=That Europe enriched with Greek and Latin cultures, magnified by Christianity, sublimed by the Renaissance]

> (22) Nous revendiquons le génie européen, la civilisation de la liberté, le continent des hommes debout et des peuples libres, c'est-à-dire souverains. (J.-M. Le Pen, video 4) [= We claim for the European genius, for a civilization of freedom, the continent of men who stand up, that of free peoples, that is to say, the continent of sovereigns]

In contrast, the Europe created by Brussels has no soul, no identity, and is just a materialistic entity:

> (23) L' Europe de Bruxelles est sans âme, sans identité a rapidement fait place à une *Europe* économique et matérialiste (J.-M. Le Pen, video 4) [=the Europe of Brussels has no soul, no identity. It soon gave way to a financial and materialistic Europe]

This supra European state takes away the autonomy of each nation which as to adapt then to a 'European Soviet Union' (*union soviétique européenne*), which is part of a great plan of the conspiracy for 'a global Empire':

> (24) Mais l'Union européenne n'ayant pour vocation que d'être un morceau de l'Empire Global. (J.-M. Le Pen, video 4) [=But since the mission of the European Union is to be a piece of the Global Empire[...]]

Europe seen as being pro-immigration is also clear-cut in Marine Le Pen's data who advocates speaking for all French people on the issue:

> (25) Ils (les Français) ont d'abord compris le lien de plus *en plus évident entre l'Union européenne et l'immigration.* Tout le monde se plaint aujourd'hui de l'immigration de masse qui envahit la France. (M. Le Pen, video 1) [= They (French people) have first realized the link which is becoming more and more obvious between the European Union and immigration. Everyone is complaining today about mass migration that has invaded France.]

But unlike her father who constructed his argument on recriminations and a passéist vision, she builds a moral and political argument against her opponents. Again in (26) Europe is indirectly accused of encouraging criminal activities (mafia organising illegal migration):

(26) Mais il y a *surtout la conscience chez un nombre grandissant de Français* que ces fron-
     tières, si nous ne les avions pas laissées disparaître, nous ne connaîtrions pas tant les
     ravages causés par l'immigration clandestine et même légale. (M. Le Pen, video 1)
     [=But mainly a growing number of *French people have come to the realization* that
     these borders, if we had not let them go, we would have not known such a disaster
     caused by illegal and even legal immigration.]

If she expresses the same rejection of the EU, she accuses an 'Oligarchic
European Union' of enslaving and infantilising European nations, dropping the
'Soviet European Union' of her father, an expression which would have less
appeal to her electorate which includes nowadays as much the working-class
than the middle-class. However, her main argument is that Brussels had been
cheating the French people. The collocates for the noun *Europe* in her data
belong mostly to the lexical field of cheating and false promises ('tales and
legends of Europe', 'unreasonable expectations', 'lured with a more humanitarian Europe').

When using the same argument as her father (most French decisions are
orders from Brussels), Marine Le Pen explains as well solutions (referendum,
end of financial monopolies, etc.), whereas her father focused on regrets as we
can see in the two quotations below:

(27) je rappelle (...) 80% des lois qui s'appliquent en France viennent de Bruxelles et non
     pas de Paris. Ceci devrait justifier une mobilisation de l'opinion française. (J.-M. Le
     Pen, video 5) [= 80% of the legislation that is applicable in France comes from
     Brussels and not from Paris. This should justify the mobilization of the French public
     opinion.]

(28) C'est elle (Europe) qui décide de tout: 80% sont des transcriptions des directives eur-
     opéennes; je veux que les français décident, avoir des référendums, le vote à la propor-
     tionnelle et pas de technocrates, un état stratège, et pas de monopoles financiers (...)
     (M. Le Pen, video 5) [It is Europe that decides everything: 80% are transcriptions of
     European directives; I want the French to decide, to have referendums, I want a pro-
     portional vote and not technocrats, a strategist state, and not financial monopolies
     (...)]

Like when tackling the migration issue, she builds her anti-European stance
on appearing rational (the word *coherence* is prominent in her interviews), looking for solutions, focusing on the current problems, willing and able to build a
brighter future for France. Unlike her father, Marine Le Pen wants to establish
that *she stands to reason* against the *European folly*[14] — as she calls it. This
includes focusing again on more positive feelings and moral rectitude. For
example, she appeals to one's love for France by voting the FN:

(29) exprimons dans les urnes notre rejet de leur Europe et notre amour de la France (M.
     Le Pen, video 1) [= let air our rejection at the polls for their Europe and our love for
     France].

As for the moral ground, she refers to the 'totalitarian Europe' which
betrays and coerces France, clearly pointing at Germany as the main aggressor.
Among powerful expressions describing a punitive Europe in the quotation

below, we note the collocates which denote a 'totalitarian' and 'ultraliberal' Europe' resulting in an 'austerity' Europe, the expression of German origin *à la schlague* which echoes and intensifies the expression *Europe made the German way* in the same utterance (30) [15]:

(30) *"une Europe à la schlague, une Europe punitive, une Europe à l'allemande"* (Le Monde, 2 Decembre 2011) [=a Europe of harsh military punishment, a punitive Europe, a Europe in the German way].

The FN politician is then both implicitly and explicitly shifting the blame from impersonal Brussels onto Germany.

Furthermore, this correlation between punitive Europe, cruelty and Germany is strongly reminiscent of the Nazi past, especially when Marine Le Pen mentions the adjective 'totalitarian'. Indeed, the glimpse of hope she offers is materialised through the resistance she promotes, the word *resistance* being reminiscent of the Second World War. As a matter of fact, Marine Le Pen renamed the Front National 'le parti de la résistance', national independence being at the heart of the political battle: There are no more left- or right-wing parties but pro-globalization or pro-national sovereignty parties:

(31) a entonné son credo social sous le patronage de l'esprit de la "résistance". (Libération 2 May 2011) [=she struck up her social creed under the auspices of a resistance spirit]

Actually both FN leaders base their ideology on claiming sovereignty back, but one focuses on the confinement experienced by France within the EU and the other on reclaiming freedom for the nation away from Brussels.

5.2. From Confinement to Freedom

The statement below sums up the catastrophic scenario depicted by Jean-Marie Le Pen, when referring to the EU:

(32) NON à l'Europe supranationale et bureaucratique! NON à l'Europe de l'appauvrissement! NON au Traité de Lisbonne! NON à la Turquie dans l'Europe!

NON à Sarkozy! OUI à l'Europe des Nations et des peuples libres! (J.-M. Le Pen, video 4)

[=NO to a supranational and bureaucratic Europe! NO to Europe's impoverishment!

NO to Lisbon Treaty! No to Turkey in Europe! NO to Sarkozy! YES to Europe of Nations and of free peoples!]

In his speech the words *frontières* 'borders' and *souveraineté* 'sovereignty' are consistently associated with loss since the word *suppression* 'eradication' and its equivalent make 70% of the collocates. Consequently, his gaze is focused on a nation humiliated, ridiculed, even sold off by or to the EU. However, if the nation has been scorned, solutions do not abound in his speech to build a new hopeful future.

In contrast, in Marine Le Pen's data the word *nation*, still anchored in a negative discourse (*the nation is dismembered*), is used in a discourse which depicts the EU first as incompetent, mentioning for instance the powerlessness of Frontex because of lack of directives and of the laisser-faire on the part of the EU:

> (33) Ce n'est pas Frontex, cette agence *européenne sans moyens et sans directives politiques claires*, qui va protéger les frontières de l'Europe! Et ce n'est pas sans frontières nationales qu'on parviendra à nous protéger du *laxisme de l'Union* européenne et des autres pays. (M. Le Pen vide, video 1) [=It is not Frontex, the European agency with no means and with no clear policy guidelines that will protect the borders of Europe! And without borders we can't manage to protect ourselves from the laxity of the European Union and from other countries.]

Since there is incompetence and laisser-faire, she can then offer solutions to how to make the nation whole again; France will find again sovereignty by re-establishing borders and having tight controls. The verb *maîtriser* 'to control' describes an action and therefore dynamism which is positively connoted in (34). In contrast, Jean-Marie Le Pen's lexical choices (*suppression*) focuses on the negative result. We can also observe her concern about the control of *her* borders:

> (34) C'est-à-dire, permettez-moi, de maîitriser, supprimer Schengen, *maîtriser* mes (sic) frontières (M. Le Pen, video 4) [=That is to say, allow me to control, suppress Schengen, control my (sic) borders]

Moreover, Marine Le Pen focuses on the return to sovereignty more than on its loss as in (35) where the French legal system will supersede the European one:

> (35) [...] permettre aux lois françaises d'être supérieures aux lois européennes. (M. Le Pen, video 4) [=To allow French legislation to be superior to European legislation.]

The Second World War and Germany as the aggressor is again more or less subtly referred to with this 'resistance'; she also uses De Gaulle's motto *la France libre*, since Marine Le Pen is fighting for 'une France libre, pour la France libre', a very appealing slogan for the FN youth movement:

> (36) Le Front national de la jeunesse, (...) a ouvert le défilé avec des drapeaux frappés du mot "Libertés" aux cris de "Justice, honneur, la France aux travailleurs" ou encore "France, Marine, liberté". (Libération, 2 May 2011) [= The Youth National Front (...) opened the parade with flags stamped with the word "Freedom", shouting out "Justice, Honour, France to workers" or even "France, Marine, freedom."]

If the objective of nationalistic discourse is to define distinctive characteristics in order to incite or reinforce the unification of the nation (Smith, 1992, p. 61), Marine Le Pen's stance focuses on the nation's independence, freedom and autonomy, the most frequent collocates of *sovereignty* in her data:

> (37) *le retour de la souveraineté, de la liberté de la France.* (M. Le Pen, video 4) [= the return to sovereignty, to freedom of France.]

Table 6. Comparative Frequencies in Jean-Marie Le Pen's and Marine Le Pen's Discourse for Contingencies of Pain.

Keywords	Frontière(s) 'border(s)'	Nation(s) 'nation(s)'	Liberté 'freedom'	Souveraineté 'sovereignty
Jean-Marie Le Pen: interviews and talks	15	10	2	4
Marine Le Pen: interviews and talks	6	2	17	7

Table 6 summarises the shifts in the discourse related to the concept of 'sovereignty': the main axis developed by Marine Le Pen is about positive concepts and open space (freedom/sovereignty), while Jean-Marie Le Pen's data focus on confinement and close space (borders/nation). This change in discourse allows a shift of the emotional positioning, from confinement to freedom, from gloom to hope.

Therefore, when studying the syntactic and lexical choices of structuring her arguments, Marine Le Pen's strategy seems more turned towards the future, giving hope while inciting to action. Jean-Marie Le Pen's strategy seems to encourage a state of desperation, contempt of the Others, and a longing for a real or imagined glorious past.

6. CONCLUSION

As noted by political scientists (Mayer, 2013; Shields, 2013), external conditions were in place for the FN's victory in the 2014 European Parliament elections and for the departmental elections in March 2015, given the failure of the previous governments to tackle social exclusion, political corruption, insecurity and unemployment (Mohan, 2014; Shields, 1999; Taguieff, 2012). Obviously, EU scepticism is based on the real economic doldrums of countries such as Greece, Cyprus or Portugal which have disenchanted entire populations regarding the credibility of the EU and the euro. In this chapter, we have examined how the FN leaders used these external circumstances to undo discursively Europe. If both of them use the affective politics of anger, they adopt a different argumentative stance to address although the same issues. Keeping the affective politics of fear with new scapegoats such as Islam and older culprits such as Europe, Marine Le Pen works on a more constructive stance offering hope for a better future in order to build a favorable political momentum. As most politicians, her strategy is partially based on creating emotional ties between herself and the people who listen to her: We have observed a more frequent use of strategies aimed at establishing a *we*-group in her data (French people against the EU), at enhancing solidarity and union within the in-group, especially when referring to the notion of freedom and sovereignty. As far as the argument of immigration is concerned, shying away from her father contemptuous judgements against the migrants, Marine Le Pen uses the topic to show empathy with the sufferings of all people in order to underscore as well how badly regulated the EU is. Moreover, even though, their conclusion is the same (i.e. Schengen should be abolished), Jean-Marie Le Pen's argument for having borders is aimed at going back to an impossible past Europe. On the contrary, Marine Le Pen's viewpoint aims to build a future Europe of nations based on cultural values. Both politicians work on channeling anger which is real among voters. However, Jean-Marie Le Pen scattered his resentment against many enemies (Jews, Arabs, non-whites, Brussels, etc.), while Marine Le Pen focuses on Islam and Europe, fueling the conspiracy theory of Europe willing to dissolve identities and cultures in order to put in place globalization. Her discursive choices of a more empathetic and constructive stance are coherent with her aim to be elected since female and centre-right-line voters had never appreciated the scorn displayed by her father. These communicative strategies could therefore have contributed to establishing a different relationship with the public since, as far as our data indicate, they create a new 'emotional ethos' for the FN leader and her new victory in 2015 could be another step towards 'a new horizon of political opportunity' (Shields, 2013, p. 191). In this regard, the recent migration wave and the European reaction to it could very well become, as some EU politicians have already warned, a blessing ('du pain béni') for the FN and any extreme-right party as the statement below asserts:

> (38) Europe's refugee crisis is still far from settled, and tough decisions need to be made to ensure there is not a "surge of the extreme right" across the continent, EU leaders have warned.[16]

NOTES

1. We adopt here Frijda's typology (2006): the notion of 'affect' encompasses 'emotions' (which arise from interactions with the external environment) and 'feelings/moods'.

2. http://tempsreel.nouvelobs.com/politique/20091216.OBS0854/dix-ans-de-gaffes-bevues-et-boulettes-politiques.html.

3. http://www.lefigaro.fr/vox/politique/2015/09/24/31001-20150924ARTFIG00331-pourquoi-les-jeunes-sont-passes-a-droite.php.

4. http://www.washingtonpost.com/wp-dyn/content/article/2005/05/29/AR2005052900644.html.

5. http://www.washingtonpost.com/wp-dyn/content/article/2005/05/29/AR2005052900644_2.html.

6. http://www.pewglobal.org/2015/06/02/faith-in-european-project-reviving/.

7. http://www.franceinter.fr/sites/default/files/2014/01/20/821768/fichiers/Barom%C3%A8tre%20nouvelles%20fractures_2014%20vDEF.pdf.

8. http://www.theguardian.com/world/datablog/2015/jan/08/french-public-opinion-charlie-hebdo-attacks.

9. http://www.lefigaro.fr/vox/politique/2015/09/24/31001-20150924ARTFIG00331-pourquoi-les-jeunes-sont-passes-a-droite.php.

10. Jean-Marie Le Pen keeping up his anti-Semitic rhetoric has recently outraged the public including his daughter by minimising the significance of the Holocaust. This led to a family feud which resulted in a court dispute and her father's expulsion from the party.

11. http://www.lemonde.fr/les-decodeurs/reactions/2015/09/25/quiz-de-la-banalisation-du-discours-politique-du-front-national_4771768_4355770.html.

12. All these quotations are from Jean-Marie Le Pen, video 5.

13. http://www.lemonde.fr/politique/article/2015/09/24/l-allemagne-nouveau-bouc-emis saire-de-marine-le-pen_4770239_823448.html.

14. http://www.frontnational.com/le-projet-de-marine-le-pen/politique-etrangere/europe/.

15. In a recent interview (September 2015), she used the same expression: 'This Europe "à la schlague" (...). Whenever and for whatever, Germany imposes her views and laws (...) Germany considers as us as slaves because she gets what she asks (...) Germany appears big because we are on our knees' http://www.lemonde.fr/politique/article/2015/09/24/l-allemagne-nouveau-bouc-emissaire-de-marine-le-pen_4770239_823448.html#rox0v DXqEKWd9H0m.99.

16. http://www.independent.co.uk/news/world/europe/refugee-crisis-tough-decisions-needed-to-avoid-a-surge-of-the-extreme-right-across-europe-warn-eu-10515964.html.

REFERENCES

Anderson, B. (1983). *Imagined communities: Reflections on the origin and spread of nationalism.* London: Verso.

Augoustinos, M., & Every, D. (2007). The language of 'Race' and prejudice: A discourse of denial, reason, and liberal-practical politics. *Journal of Language and Social Psychology*, *26*, 123–141.

Baider, F. (2013). Hate: Saliency features in cross-cultural semantics. In I. Kecskes & J. Romero-Trillo (Eds.), *Linguistic aspects of intercultural pragmatics* (pp. 7–27). Berlin: Walter de Gruyter.

Baider, F., & Constantinou, M. (2014). How to make people feel good when wishing hell: Golden dawn and national front discourse, emotions and argumentation. In J. Romero-Trillo (Ed.), *New empirical and theoretical paradigms. Series: Yearbook of corpus linguistics and pragmatics*, *2* (pp. 179–210). Dordrecht: Springer.

Baider, F., & Constantinou, M. (2015). Jean-Marie Le Pen vs. Marine Le Pen: les deux 'ethos émotifs' d'un même pathos. *Studia Romanica Posnaniensia*, *42*(4), 3–19.

Balent, M. (2013). The French National Front from Jean-Marie to Marine Le Pen: Between change and continuity. In K. Grabow & F. Hartleb (Eds.), *Exposing the demagogues: Right-wing and National Populist Parties in Europe* (pp. 161–186). Brussels: Centre for European Studies (CES) and the Konrad-Adenauer-Stiftung (KAS).

Banks, D. (2007). Ideology, context and text in a systemic functional model. In G. Girard (Ed.), *Texte(s), contexte(s), hors-texte(s)* (pp. 179–191). St Etienne: Presses Universitaires de St Etienne.

Bar-On, T. (2007). *Where have all the fascists gone?* Aldershot: Ashgate.

Bar-On, T. (2013). *Rethinking the fascist new right: Alternatives to modernity.* London: Routledge.

Beauzamy, B. (2013). Explaining the Rise of the Front National to Electoral Prominence: Multi-faceted or Contradictory Models. In R. Wodak, M. KhosraviNik, & B. Mral (Eds.), *Right-*

Wing Populism in Europe: Politics and Discourse (pp. 177–190). New York: Bloomsbury Academic.

Beauzamy, B., & Naves, M.-C. (2010). Usages politiques des récits d'agressions antisémites et de violences policières. De la rumeur à la mobilisation. *Mots. Les langages du politique*. URL: http://mots.revues.org/19445.

Bednarek, M. (2008). *Emotion talk across corpora*. Basingstoke, New York, NY: Palgrave Macmillan.

Bernard, M. (2007). Le Pen, un provocateur en politique (1984-2002). *Vingtième Siècle. Revue d'Histoire, 93*, 37–45.

Billig, M. (1978). *Fascists: A social psychological view of the National Front*. London: Harcourt Brace Jovanovich.

Blumenthal, P. (2002). Profil combinatoire des noms. Synonymie distinctive et analyse contrastive. *Zeitschriftfür Französische Sprache und Literatur, 112*, 115–138.

Clore Gerald, L., & Gasper, K. (2000). Feeling is believing: Some affective influences on belief. In N. H. Frijda, A. Manstead, & S. Bem (Eds.), *Emotions and beliefs* (pp. 10–44). Cambridge: Cambridge University Press.

Costelloe, L. (2014). Discourses of sameness: Expressions of nationalism in newspaper discourse on French urban violence in 2005. *Discourse & Society, 25*(3), 315–340.

de Cillia, R., Reisigl, M., & Wodak, R. (1999). The discursive construction of national identities. *Discourse Society, 10*(2), 149–172.

FitzGerald, C. (2013). Prejudice and empathy in political discourse: A look into language used by politicians in the asylum seeker debate. *Macquarie Matrix, 3*(1), 1–28.

Frijda, N. H. (2006). *The laws of emotions*. Mahwah, NJ, London: Lawrence Erlbaum.

Frijda, N. H., Manstead, A., & Bem, S. (2000). *Emotions and belief*. Cambridge: Cambridge University Press.

Fussell, S. R., & Moss, M. M. (1998). Figurative language in emotional communication. In S. R. Fussell & R. J. Kreuz (Eds.), *Social and cognitive approaches to interpersonal communication* (pp. 113–141). Mahwah, NJ: Lawrence Erlbaum Associations.

Grunberg, G., & Schweisguth, E. (2003). French political space: Two, three or four blocs? *French Politics, 1*(3), 331–347.

Heinisch, R. (2013). Austrian right-wing populism: A surprising comeback under a new leader. In K. Grabow & F. Hartleb (Eds.), *Exposing the demagogues: Right-wing and National Populist Parties in Europe* (pp. 47–80). Brussels: Centre for European Studies (CES) and the Konrad-Adenauer-Stiftung (KAS).

Kecskes, I. (2013). *Intercultural pragmatics*. USA: Oxford University Press.

Kohl, D. (2011). The presentation of 'self' and 'other' in Nazi propaganda. *Psychology and Society, 4*(1), 7–26.

Krzyzanowski, M. R. (2009). *The politics of exclusion: Debating migration in Austria*. New Brunswick, NJ: Transaction Publishers.

Levy, C. (2015). Racism, immigration and new identities in Italy. In A. Mammone, E. G. Parini, & G. A. Veltri (Eds.), *The Routledge handbook of contemporary Italy: History, politics, society* (pp. 49–63). UK: Routledge.

Marcus, G. E., & Neuman, W. R. (2000). *Affective Intelligence and Political Judgment*. Chicago, IL: University of Chicago Press.

Martin, D. C. (1995). The choices of identity. *Social Identities, 1*(1), 5–20.

Mayer, N. (2012). De Jean-Marie à Marine Le Pen: l'électorat du Front national a-t-il changé? In P. Delwit (Ed.), *Le Front national. Mutations de l'extrême droite française* (pp. 143–160). Brussels: Editions Université de Bruxelles.

Mayer, N. (2013). From Jean-Marie to Marine Le Pen: Electoral change on the far right. *Parliamentary Affairs, 66*(1), 160–178.

Mohan, A. (2014). The breakthrough of neo-fascism in Europe: A case of mistaken identity. *Foreign Policy Journal, April 22*, 1–15.

Musolff, A. (2008). What can critical metaphor analysis add to the understanding of racist ideology? Recent studies of Hitler's anti-semitic metaphors. *Critical Approaches to Discourse Analysis Across Disciplines*, *2*(2), 1–10. [online]. http://cadaad.org/ejournal.

Musolff, A. (2010). *Metaphor, nation and the holocaust: The concept of the body politic*. New York, NY: Routledge.

Oster, U. (2010). Using corpus methodology for semantic and pragmatic analyses: What can corpora tell us about the linguistic expression of emotions? *Cognitive Linguistics*, *4*, 727–763.

Panskepp, J. (1998). *Affective neuroscience: The foundations of human and animal emotions*. Oxford: Oxford University Press.

Paxton, R. O. (2004). *The anatomy of fascism*. London: Penguin.

Perrineau, P. (1997). *Le symptôme Le Pen. Radiographie des électeurs du Front national*. Paris: Fayard.

Shields, J. (1999). The FN industry—No recession here. *Modern and Contemporary France*, *7*(3), 377–382.

Shields, J. (2013). Marine Le Pen and the 'New' FN: A change of style or of substance? *Parliamentary Affairs*, *66*(1), 179–196.

Sinclair, J. (2004). *Trust the text: Language corpus and discourse*. London: Routledge.

Smith, A. D. (1992). National identity and the idea of European unity. *International Affairs*, *68*(1), 55–76.

Souchard, M., Wahnich, S., Cuminal, I., & Wathier, V. (1997). *Le Pen: Les mots. Analyse d'un discours d'extrême droite*. Paris: Le Monde Editions.

Stokes, B. (2015). Faith in European project reviving. *Pew Research Center*. http://www.pewglobal.org/2015/06/02/faith-in-european-project-reviving/.

Taguieff, P.-A. (2012). *Le nouveau national-populisme*. Paris: CNRS Editions.

Van Dijk, T. A. (2006). Racism and the press in Spain. In J. L. Blas, M. Casanova, M. Velando, & J. Vellón (Eds.), *Discurso y Sociedad II. Nuevas contribuciuones al estudio de la lengua en un contexto* (pp. 59–99). Castelló de la Plana: Universitat Jaume I. http://www.discursos.org/unpublished%20articles/Racism%20and%20the%20press%20in%20Spain.htm.

Williams, M. H. (2011). A new era for French far right politics? *Análise Social XLVI*, *201*, 679–695.

Wodak, R., de Cillia, R., Reisigl, M., & Liebhart, K. (2009). *The discursive construction of national identity* (2nd ed.). Edinburgh: Edinburgh University Press.

Wollenberg, D. (2014). Defending the West: Cultural racism and Pan-Europeanism on the far-right. *Postmedieval: A Journal of Medieval Cultural Studies*, *5*, 308–319.

Yilmaz, F. (2012). Right-wing hegemony and immigration: How the populist far-right achieved hegemony through the immigration debate in Europe. *Current Sociology*, *60*(3), 368–381.

CIRCLING THE WAGONS: THE ALTERNATIVE FÜR DEUTSCHLAND AND THE RISE OF EUROSCEPTIC POPULISM IN GERMANY

Christian Nestler and Jan Rohgalf

ABSTRACT

This chapter enquires into the German right-wing populist party Alternative für Deutschland (AfD) and its narrative of the nation under attack. For two reasons, the AfD is a particular interesting case. Since its foundation in February 2013 the AfD was constantly extraordinarily successful in state, federal as well as European elections. The support garnered in their first elections is without precedent in German post-war history. What is more, no other populist party ever gained a similar backing in Germany. In contrast to other European countries, political culture in Germany for a long time entailed an anti-populist consensus which significantly curbed the outlook of populist parties. The rise of the AfD maybe indicates the erosion of this consensus. The chapter is based on the systematic analysis of all official party documents 2013/14.

Keywords: Alternative für Deutschland (AfD); right-wing populism; nation; party discourse; Euro-scepticism; Germany

National Identity and Europe in Times of Crisis: Doing and Undoing Europe, 137–159
Copyright © 2017 by Emerald Publishing Limited
All rights of reproduction in any form reserved
doi:10.1108/978-1-78714-513-920171007

1. INTRODUCTION

The European project is facing increasingly rough seas. Amid an unprecedented economic crisis, right-wing extremists and right-wing populist score in elections both national and European (Mudde, 2014, 2015). For sure, these parties do not form a unitary political bloc. Nonetheless, grave differences regarding their history and political creed notwithstanding, the French Front National, Britain's UKIP or the Alternative für Deutschland (AfD) in Germany agree upon the opposition against the EU. Yet, pitting the sovereign nation against the rule of an allegedly authoritarian European Union (EU) is not limited to the right. In promoting the dream of the nation 'liberated' from the burden of supra-national obligations and isolated from the turmoil of a globalised economy, the right converges with populists of the leftist denomination like Syriza in Greece or Die LINKE in Germany. This is by no means to suggest that the Europe as a political idea is by and large dead. However, today the process of European integration is seriously challenged. With EU-sceptics and outright EU-opponents on the rise throughout the continent, the European integration no longer appears as a one-way road to an ever closer union. Significant revisions or even the dissolution of the EU are on the agenda of political actors which cannot be ignored.

In this respect, we are witnessing the renationalisation of Europe or even the attempt to undo the Europe shaped by the advancement of European integration. A recent empirical study on the development of political conflict in Western Europe identifies the formation of a new cleavage (Kriesi, 2012): The conflict between those who are in favour of globalisation respectively transnational ties and those who wish to shield the nation against external influences and obligations more rigidly. The nationalism involved, usually comes in a defensive guise (Castells, 2010, Vol. 2; Kaschuba, 2000; Rohgalf, 2015a). Like any nationalism, while it claims to lend its voice to an already existing national identity, defensive nationalism is actively engaged in forging this identity in the first place (cf. the 'classics': Anderson, 2006; Hobsbawm, 1990; Smith, 1999). What makes this nationalism distinct from its 19th and 20th century predecessors is the way in which collective identity is construed: The nation and its sovereignty are first and foremost not to be preserved, revived or regained in the face of the onslaught by other nations. In this nationalism, the nation is said to have fallen prey to EU-authoritarianism. A rhetoric of self-victimisation blends seamlessly with the invocation of a national liberation from a foreign yoke. Obviously, this construction of a national identity relies on the construction of a specific image of Europe and the EU.

This chapter enquires into the German right-wing populist party AfD and its narrative of the nation under attack. For two reasons, the AfD is a particular interesting case. Since its foundation in February 2013 the AfD was constantly extraordinarily successful in state, federal as well as European elections.[1] The support garnered in their first elections is without precedent in German post-war history. What is more, no other populist party ever gained a similar backing in Germany.[2] In contrast to other European countries, political culture in Germany for a long time entailed an anti-populist consensus (Werz, 2013, p. 421) which significantly curbed the outlook of populist parties. The rise of the AfD maybe indicates the erosion of this consensus.

The following analysis focuses on the period between early 2013 (the foundation of the party) and May 2014 (the European election). It shows how the AfD disseminated a political narrative about Europe and the nation, skilfully weaving together a variety of concerns and grievances otherwise only loosely related. This narrative not only held together two factions of the party, usually characterised as the neo-liberal, Eurosceptic wing and the national-conservative wing.[3] Furthermore, it was decisive for the party's electoral success. It helped erecting a respectable façade which made the AfD attractive to both centrist and protest voters as well as the far right. Hence, dissecting the political narrative is prerequisite for understanding the rise of the AfD.

Since mid-2014, the party has seen an increasingly severe rift over leadership and ideological issues that resulted in the split of the party in July 2015. After the withdrawal of party founder Bernd Lucke and other senior party members as well as the dominance of the right-wing of the party, as of August 2015, the future prospects of the AfD are by and large unclear.

2. BASIC CONCEPTS

Before turning to the political narrative diffused by the AfD, it is imperative to have a glance at the basic concepts employed in the analysis.

2.1. Party Manifestos

The analysis focuses on the seven official documents put forth by the party from April 2013 (foundation of the party) to May 2014, when the European parliament was elected (see Table 1). These texts are the only liable sources which documents the official party doctrine in this period in contrast to the opinions of individual party members.[4] In addition, further texts, speeches and interviews by senior party members as well as journalistic commentaries and scholarly literature have been taken into account.

Scholarly literature distinguishes outward and inward oriented functions of party manifestos.[5]

Outward oriented functions include:

- advertisement
- provoking feedback

Table 1. Official AfD Documents Issued from April 2013 to May 2014.

Publication Date	Original Title/English Translation	Word Count	Shorthand
14.04.2013	Bundestagswahlprogramm/Federal election manifesto	871	P0
15.12.2013	Europawahlthesen Große Europakommission (GEK) I/ European election theses by the Great European commission I	1895	P1
25.01.2014	Europawahlthesen für den Aschaffenburger Parteitag (GEK II)/ European election theses for Aschaffenburg party convention (GEK II)	2403	P2
31.01.2014	66 Thesen zur Europawahl/66 theses for European election	3077	P3
01.03.2014	Mitgliederbefragung 2014/Member survey 2014	14361	P4
22.03.2014	Europawahlprogramm/European election manifesto	9587	P5
01.05.2014	Politische Leitlinien der Alternative für Deutschland /Policy guidelines of the Alternative for Germany	2935	P6

- confronting competitors, sharpening the party image
- agitation
- influencing public opinion and public agenda
- committing oneself to certain politics

Inward oriented functions are:

- sharpening self-understanding of the party
- integration and identification with the party
- mobilising party's rank and file
- disciplining dissenters

2.2. Political Narratives

In politics, making sense of a situation (framing) almost always has recourse to some kind of narrative, as dispersed and fragmented as it may be.[6] Political actors tell a story about the situation in which they act, about their motivations and goals. To be sure, politics is not solely about fiction or made-up worlds. However, narratives play an important role in organising political phenomena. They vigorously reduce the complexity of political reality by pointing out the decisive forces and dynamics whilst blanking out the rest. Although political narratives are rooted in reality, they can be heavily distorting – mirroring either the political actors' own limitations or their will to manipulate.

A narrative consists of a set of characters or roles, their relationship and a plot or a trajectory. Political actors refer to the roles the narrative provides to identify themselves and other actors with. Usually these roles recall in one way or another well-known, almost archetypical personae: the traitor, the oppressor, the victim, the rebel, the saviour etc. There is a tendency to reduce the complexity of political reality to the antagonism between two camps. The narrative's plot provides basic action models. Furthermore, the narrative potentially stirs emotions to act. Eventually it legitimises these actions as it draws on highly respected principles. In order to frame a situation, a minimal narrative may go as follows: The nation is under a foreign yoke but a band of brave patriots sets out to overthrow the oppressor and thus restores (the highly respected principles of) justice, liberty and popular sovereignty. Following Henry Tudor, we may think of the narrative as a practical argument as opposed to a scientific description:

> In their effort to understand this world of pragmata, of things endowed with moral or utilitarian value, men view their circumstances in the light of their purposes, and their explanations are simultaneously justifications or prescriptions. (Tudor, 1972, p. 123)

2.3. Self-Victimisation

In what follows, self-victimisation will be understood as a rhetorical device used to cause certain effects: The speaker presents herself to her audience as the victim of other individual or collective actors. More accurately, in order to become politically effective, the speaker not only refers to herself as a victim but also identifies herself as the member of a certain group. The experience of victimhood is not only an individual but a collective experience.

Self-victimisation is an attractive way of framing political issues, all the more in democracies which champion the critique and limitation of power in the name of human and civil rights.[7] More or less explicitly, self-victimisation recalls a well-known narrative which provides unambiguous roles to identify oneself and others with. Furthermore, the narrative clarifies the relationship between these roles as a clear-cut antagonism: On the one hand, we have got the righteous, yet powerless victims, on the other hand their malicious, overly powerful oppressors. In this kind of narrative, the latter are interested in maintaining power, suppression and exploitation, while the former demand nothing but liberation from oppression. Framing is not only used to make a situation graspable. What is more, it provides the justification for a revolt against the oppressors. Who would condemn a rebel with such a respectable cause as liberation?

2.4. Populism

In one guise or another, this mode of framing surfaces in populism of all shades. Like pretty much every concept in the social sciences, populism is a contested concept. Nonetheless, some core notions can – taken with a pinch of salt – be considered undisputed[8]:

The populist version of self-victimisation revolves around the betrayal of the 'elite' at the expense of 'the people'. 'The people' is threatened by 'the elite' and the populists lead the struggle in defence of 'the people'. This dichotomic constellation is usually coupled with other binary codes. As a result, the enormous complexity of political reality is reduced to this – apparently unquestionable – antagonism.[9] Priester (2008, pp. 32–33) lists some of the binary codes common in populism: hypocrisy/corruption vs. honesty/moral integrity, idleness vs. hard work, paternalism/arrogance vs. primordial wisdom of the people, but also codes like globalisation/supra-nationality vs. ethnic identity/national sovereignty.

Populism cultivates an anti-establishment attitude. The status as an outsider to the political system is the populists' political capital. It is this status which guarantees her moral integrity as opposed to the corrupted elite. Because of this, populist parties depend on being recognised as anti-party parties.

Yet, the antagonism depicted by populists is usually less clear than it may seem at first glance. Especially, the pivotal 'people' is a highly idealised entity that does not match an empirical reality. 'The people' appears as unduly homogenised, glossing over diverging opinions, interests and ends.[10] The honest people starring in the populist narrative are not to be mistaken for the whole population. Rather, it is only one part of the population (namely the populists' target audience) which counts as 'the people'. Hence, populism not only separates the people from the elite above. There is also a horizontal demarcation which distinguishes 'the people' and its others: for example, welfare recipients, homeless people, migrants, minorities or marginalised groups.

Populism condemns representative government for distorting or even neglecting the popular will. In contrast, populists claim to bypass the representative procedures and to speak directly to and in the name of the sovereign people. However, this does not imply public deliberation or the compromise between conflicting views and interests among the people. On the contrary, the popular will is not the *a posteriori* product of bargaining and discussion but is supposed to be an *a priori* property of the people, thought to be based on common sense, traditions, morals or even some biological qualities. As such the popular will is only to be 'discovered' and uttered (by the populist) in the purest form possible, unbiased by conflicting interests.[11] Far from being an emancipatory concept, popular sovereignty serves as a means to absolutize the lifestyle and interests of a certain part of society.

We can conclude that populist self-victimisation is in the end not aimed at challenging a congealed political system. It is not concerned with openness, but with closure (Rosanvallon, 2010, p. 266). It promises to preserve and to fend off external threats. Populists mobilise what Manuel Castells (2010) has called *resistance identities*. They suggest circling the wagons around allegedly (socially, culturally, ethnically etc.) homogeneous communities and to stubbornly defend the wagon fort against the outside world.

2.5. EU(ro)(pe)-Scepticism and Renationalisation

After 1945, and thus the demise of National Socialism and World War II, the nation was delegitimised in Germany. Following the unconditional surrender, the country was divided into four occupational sectors, three of which established a parliamentary democracy. Due to the experience of the Weimar Republic, Western Germany committed itself to a 'freiheitlich demokratische Grundordnung' (Bleek, Gawrich, & Sontheimer, 2007; Bracher, 1955; Herbert, 2014), entailing an anti-totalitarian, anti-extremist (Jesse, 1998) and (progressively eroding) anti-populist consensus (Nestler & Rohgalf, 2014; Werz, 2013). The preservation of the constitution was moved to the pre-parliamentary field. Through the possibility of a party ban, its protectors have a sharp sword at hand (Leggewie & Meier, 1995, 2012). Nationalism was generally frowned upon in society and politics, especially among intellectuals (Kroll & Reitz, 2013; Leggewie, 2009). Four decades later, the discourse on constitutional patriotism – 'Verfassungspatriotismus' – and a new constitution for the reunified German nation had a renaissance (Habermas, 1992; Sternberger, 1990). Viewed through the lens of European history and developments since 1945, one has to speak about normalisation.

The ever extending European integration (Wirsching, 2012, p. 401), German reunification and the Maastricht treaty (1992), the latter initiating a monetary union, provoked new nationalist sentiments. In the face of European integration (e.g., by territorial enlargement, market liberalisation, monetary union) the nation seemed to lose significance. This perception of loss was further nurtured by the so-called there-is-no-alternative-politics –'alternativlos' – of Chancellor Angela Merkel and her government throughout the Euro-crisis (Nestler & Rohgalf, 2014, pp. 398–399). National politics and parliaments appeared overwhelmed and deprived of power vis-à-vis the EU-institutions.

Despite the rise of nationalist sentiment, 'renationalisation' is not used in meaningful discourse fragments. In its place 'subsidiarity' is used as a camouflage to talk about perceived problems. Underlying this term is the concept of a Europe of nations and less charged with Euro-scepticism or EU(ro)(pe)scepticism, as we would like to put it (Nestler & Schütt, 2014).

The scientific processing of the term Euro-scepticism goes back to the first journalistic use in the United Kingdom. Therefore, the debate on the definition of options is mainly influenced by the Anglo-American understanding of the term. In this context, the term lacks a clear distinction between negative attitude towards the EU, Euro or Europe. This non-restrictiveness can be traced in its usage in English- as well as in German-speaking countries (Harmsen & Spiering, 2004, p. 16; Leconte, 2010, p. 5). Furthermore, the variety of options that have been offered to make the concept scientifically useful, have multiplied over the last 20 years, accompanied with growing sophistication. The value of a more natural approach is seconded because the journalistic use has developed into a battle cry, which is sometimes shared within the scientific community (Harmsen & Spiering, 2004, pp. 18–19).

The term euro-scepticism comprises a host of notions. Thus, further differentiation is needed. For this purpose we like to introduce a three-dimensional concept (see Table 2). These dimensions mirror an escalating denial of the benefits of an integrated Europe (Harmsen & Spiering, 2004, p. 19; Jopp & Tekin, 2014).

First, a party could reject the current EU in its seemingly top-down model, its too fast or too slow integration, its foreign policy or even the question if some kind of United States of Europe is the ultimate goal. This list could be extended further. However, the bottom line is that it is a common educated opinion to have a constructive critical view on this matter, and therefore it is normal for parties to be EU-sceptic. A second group will argue especially against the Euro as single currency. The culprit is not the single market, but its possible negative aspects revealed during the Euro-crisis. Financially strong member states, like Germany, had to keep Greece, Ireland, Portugal and Cyprus afloat. As will be shown below, the AfD — especially in 2013 and 2014 — can be counted among these Euro-sceptic parties. Exceeding this amount of criticism are, third, parties which in any case put their respective nation first. The idea of a 'Europe of sovereign nations' has an ethno-pluralist tenor and includes racism or in- and out-group-thinking in their programmatic. These parties have to be labelled Europe-sceptic.

Proposing this concept of EU(ro)(pe)-scepticism, no step towards German scientific exceptionalism is taken, but an intuitively usable and easily translatable and transferable way to catch subjective perceptions of speakers in their possible escalating criticism or outright rejection of Europe.

Table 2. Dimensions of EU(ro)(pe)-scepticism.

Dimension	Against	For
EU-sceptic	Current development of the EU	Divers
Euro-sceptic	(Further) integration through the Euro, pitfalls of solidarity	Europe of sovereign nations (subsidiarity)
Europe-sceptic	Multiculturalism	pure nations, ethno pluralism

Source: Own representation based on Nestler and Schütt (2014, p. 19).

3. US AND THEM – GERMANY AS AN ENDANGERED NATION

As mentioned above, renationalisation is not a common phrase in public discourse. However, the AfD is certain that the nation has to be protected from measures aiming at its dissolution. Culprit of these actions is the political class in Germany and Europe that implemented the EU as well as its institutions and uses them to their own advantage against the will of the people. Therefore the wagons have to be circled around the people, but even more so around the supposedly existing ideal nation. The AfD is not only able to disclose mismanagement and aberration, but is also willing to voice the opinion of the disgruntled, unheard and ignored people. The main conflict can be summarised as follows: sovereign nation vs. EUSSR. Where the first part doesn't need any explanation, the second one is an acronym constructed from EU and USSR, thus the former Soviet Union. This implies that the EU is not only a central but also a totalitarian state.

This section follows the thought of renationalisation through the proxy 'subsidiarity' aka Euro-scepticism. By doing this the populist black and white-thinking is revealed. Four facets are frequently evoked:

3.1. Europe as Centralist, Quasi Totalitarian Regime

AfD activists, members, and particularly its leaders, have a history of opposing the EU but even more so the Euro. But the first brought the second and a lot of seemingly pointless EU-directives with it. Well-known is the case of the 'bendy banana law' that requires the named product to be of the highest quality without being overly curved when imported (Commission Regulation, No 2267/94). This part of the law was reported by the media with verve and passion, whilst the part specifying that the banana has to be 'fit for human consumption, not rotten, clean and free of pests, and damage from pests' (*ibid*) is largely ignored. For the AfD, this overregulation manifests the conflict between the nation and a centralist European state:

> We insist in the unbridled budgetary powers of the national parliaments. We categorically reject a transfer union or even a centralised European state. (P0)

In the first party manifesto the conflict is touched upon rather lightly. 'Budgetary powers' belong to national parliaments and a transfer union and a centralised European state are rejected. In light of the Euro-crisis and the talk about Eurobonds, this notion is easily understood by a voter who happens to read it. But on another level, the reader is led astray, because the 'budgetary powers' still remain with national parliaments. Germany, the biggest net payer, only gives around 3.84% (2012) of its yearly expenses to the EU. In the following statement a potential 'transfer union', according to AfD propaganda caused by 'non-competitive Greeks and other lazy Southerners' (Lucke, 2013a), is directly connected to a centralised EU, as if the former needs the latter. With this in mind, the AfD describes the Union further as:

> The AfD opposes the gradual extension of competences of EU-institutions beyond the conditions laid down in the Treaties. What wasn't explicitly specified by the Treaties belongs exclusively within the competence of national states. (P1, P2, P3 almost identical in P4)

In German, the word 'schleichen' (to sneak) implies that the process is not widely known and breaks existing laws. Clearly the 'Brusselcrats' are doing something without public knowledge and again for their own benefit. Not only is this development not communicated, but it is also destructive to the achievements of European history. Therefore the conflict finally becomes completely obvious in the manifesto for the European Parliament elections. At the same time it is a good example for the 'respectability' practised by the party:

> The European unification made possible peace and growing prosperity because its member states implemented democracy, rule of law and social market economy. These successes are contrary to the excesses of the EU in the form of centralisation, bureaucracy and statism which increasingly threaten the historical achievements of Europe. (P5)

This suggests that, through the introduction of the Euro and even more so the Euro-crisis from 2008 onwards, the positive European developments since 1945 have been corrupted by politicians, who want to preserve something unreachable and are unable to make difficult decision because they fear getting voted out of office. A difficult decision would be a Greek exit from the Euro. Therefore the AfD wants to fight the EU from within:

> Together with like-minded people in the European Parliament, the AfD will fight against this super-state and against the Euro-debt policy. (P5)

3.2. The German Nation as an Ideal to be Preserved

With the enemy or, less martially spoken, the problem described, the question is, what kind of nation should be preserved. A lot of the leading party members have a past in the Christian Democratic Union (CDU) and tried to push the party to adopt a different strategy in economic and value questions. When they talk about a better Germany, they are not thinking Kaiser or Führer but 1950s and 1960s West Germany, roughly the Germany of the 'Wirtschaftswunder'.

> We affirm a Europe of sovereign states with a common market. We want to live together in friendship with our neighbours. (P0)

A 'Europe of sovereign states' is a positive 'respectable' way of advocating a 'Europa der Vaterländer'. The strongest supporter of this concept was Charles de Gaulle in the early phase of the European integration. From the 1970s onwards, the concept was mainly employed by populist and right-wing parties all over Europe. Apart from this concept, the AfD underlines the commitment to a common market and thus shows that she is not ready to leave the Union completely. They want all the advantages without the risks or being obliged to show solidarity with weaker countries.

> The AfD advocates a European Union of sovereign states. (P1, P2, P3 almost identical in P4)

This statement can be found in almost all party documents. But with the next quote, which is also included in almost all of the texts we analysed, we will see that the party implies that the integration, even the positive single market part, can't lead to the United States of Europe:

> Since there is neither a European identity nor a European people or a European nation, an idea of the United States of Europe is unrealistic. It is contrary to the culture and tradition of 2,000 years of European history. (P1, P2, P3 almost identical in P5)

This statement shows an extreme position that is not only a contrast to other examples but openly negates 2,000 years of history on the 'old' continent. Again 'nation' is employed as an unavoidable political reality to be recognised.

3.3. Single Currency Euro as a Battlefield

According to the last quote, the Euro appears to unnaturally chain together the sovereign nations in Europe. Therefore the AfD was willing to propose a German exit from the single currency:

> We call for an orderly dissolution of the Eurozone. Germany does not need the Euro. Other countries are harmed by the Euro. (P0)

For the general election 2013, a return to the former German currency Deutsche Mark (DM) was broadly advocated. Something that was laughable prior to 2008 was printed on posters, repeated in speeches, could be read in the party manifesto and became a beacon for economic naysayers as well as people with strong fears of economic relegation. Almost ironic is the last sentence, where the ailing economies in Southern Europe are symbolically supported. The logic is that the Euro was a carrot that couldn't be digested by these states. It now forces them to compete within a system in which they do not stand a chance of ever closing the existing gap:

> The introduction of the Euro was a purely political decision beyond economic reason. The Euro is undermining the EU's historic achievements. The 'no alternative' rescue of the Euro should no longer threaten the prosperity and the future of Germany. (P1, P2, P3) [In P5, the last sentence is substituted for:] For some time now, it is clear that the 'unity-Euro' destroys Europe's foundations. It causes controversy and the resurgence of national prejudices. Prosperity and peace among the member states in the Euro-zone are at risk. (P5)

Expressis verbis, the Euro becomes a tool of imperialism and suppression in the hand of Brussels and the EU. Therefore it is of utmost importance for Germany to either leave the Euro or at least reduce the group of participants to the well performing states.

3.4. Subsidiarity as a Proxy

In all this, renationalisation is not openly demanded and since the manifesto for the general election 2013 also a return to the DM has been abandoned. Instead, the AfD argues in favour of Euro-scepticism through the proxy of subsidiarity:

We will ensure that legislative powers are transferred back to the national parliaments. (P0)

In this first example from April 2013 it is just one of many other 'demands'. But it gains momentum in the process of formulating the manifesto for the European Parliament elections.

The EU shall only exercise competences when there is proof that the tasks in question cannot be accomplished better at the national level. Existing treaties should be reviewed and revised accordingly. (P1, P2, P3)

The party even calls for a court of justice for subsidiarity measures (P5):

To give Europe a prosperous future again, the AfD advocates a European Union that is based on subsidiarity and competition rather than on centralism, egalitarianism and harmonisation. (P5)

This last example brings us full circle. Subsidiarity is the measure that prevents the EU from getting overly centralistic. In all this we have to emphasise that subsidiarity is one of the cornerstones of all EU contracts. So the AfD can only argue against a supposedly wrong everyday practice. Out of this, the German media even argued that the AfD is not exactly Euro-sceptic. Justus Bender presumes that the party is mainly radical libertarian (2014). Connected to the issues discussed below (refers to Section 4, this paper), this does not seem that far off. But in light of the quotes concerning renationalisation, the rhetoric against further European integration and especially against the Euro is strong. Furthermore, the AfD's recent popularity in elections results from the party successfully positioning itself to the right of the CDU but still on democratic ground. The party is anchored there through two out of their three major internal currents (Korte, 2014). Where the right-wing populist current is garnering support even from the far right, the national-conservative and the neo-liberal currents are conjunct with a conservative-bourgeois milieu, especially in the Western European states. As a result we conclude that the party was — at least before the split in mid-2015 — in fact Euro-sceptic.

4. CONSERVATIVE REBELS IN A REPRESSIVE GERMANY?

The official documents we analysed conjure up the grim image of Germany as a repressive state. Due to the nature of the genre, this image is not depicted at length but rather hinted at in particular passages scattered across the party manifestos. In a nutshell, the party draws on the classical populist narrative of the treachery committed by the 'political system' and the mainstream media against 'the people'. Astonishingly, according to this narrative, the conspiracy is diffusely left-wing (pro-welfare, green, feminist, post-materialist etc.). The AfD stages itself as conservative rebels standing up against a repressive left-wing hegemony. In contrast, the traditional conservative forces in politics and the media are accused of having already surrendered. The narrative of the righteous victims that has its vantage point in Euro-scepticism is ultimately the narrative about circling the wagons around ultra-conservative visions of society and family values.

This section reconstructs the logic inherent to the rhetoric of self-victimisation. For this purpose, we start with significant claims in the party manifestos and look at the tacit assumptions underlying these claims. Furthermore, this section sheds light on the implications and consequences of these claims.

The rhetoric of self-victimisation frequently evokes four facets of the repressive Germany:

4.1. The Downfall of the Rule of Law

According to the AfD, the rule of law in Germany is in decline or has already vanished. In the party platforms, this view is represented in statements like:

> The actions of every German government are limited by the law of peoples, the constitution [Grundgesetz] and European treaties. These limitations are essential to our society and are to be respected without exception. (P0)

> The AfD demands contract fulfilment and the rule of law to be restored. State organs shall in no case breach laws and contracts, not even in isolated cases such as saving the single currency [Euro]. (P5)

Why does a party manifesto of hardly four pages (P0) remind the government of the basic standards of the rule of law? Apparently, the manifestos cited are not in the first place concerned with contracts and laws in general, but the no-bail-out-clause of the Maastricht (and later Lisbon) treaty in particular. This clause determines that the union will not take responsibility for the debts of its member states. For Euro-sceptics in Germany, this no-bail-out-clause has become a central indicator for the quality of the rule of law and democracy as such.[12]

For them, the measures taken in order to save the single currency during the Euro- and debt crisis since 2009 mark the bursting of a dam: the fundamental contract is broken and the EU is secretly rebuilt as a 'debt union' and 'transfer union'. If this fundamental contract is not valid any more what can one still rely on, whom of the politicians and parties can one still trust?[13]

The narrative of a betrayal of confidence committed by the 'political class' was the decisive stimulus to found the AfD.[14] For many years a number of now leading figures of the party have been active in various neo-liberal and Euro-critical think-tanks and lobbying organisations. Though there have already been civic associations dedicated to Euro-scepticism before the crisis, these were politically marginalised. Euro-scepticism had no representation in the party system (cf. esp. Plehwe & Schlögl, 2014).

Not only has Euro-scepticism gained momentum since then. The AfD also managed to translate the question of the no-bail-out clause into a symbol for the deceit of the 'political class' as such. This was a powerful symbol that reso-nated with a phenomenon known as *Politikverdrossenheit*, the disenchantment with the established political parties and politicians.[15] Hereby, the newly founded AfD could become a melting pot for (nearly) all sorts of grievances and discontent with the current state of society (cf. Honnigfort, 2014; Bender, 2014).

There is no doubt that the AfD touches a serious problem. The Euro-crisis and the measures taken indeed raise the question of democratic legitimacy and national sovereignty. However, the AfD is neither the first nor the only party to point out these issues.[16] Furthermore, the AfD deliberately blends this criticism with other grievances. Hereby, the party is rather nurturing a diffuse feeling of anger and disdain towards the 'political class.'

4.2. Surveillance, Intimidation, Ostracism

Furthermore, the AfD maintains that Germany is a far cry from a proper democracy because surveillance, intimidation and ostracism are common in politics today. With regard to the rhetoric, it is interesting that this far reaching criticism is introduced in laconic statements like:

> We vehemently oppose the surveillance of political groups just because they champion Europe- or Euro-sceptical ideas. (P1, P2, P3)

or:

> We vigorously oppose increasingly prevalent tendencies among self-proclaimed attitude watchdogs to intimidate dissenters or to ostracise them from the public. (P6)

Taken literally, in statements like this, the AfD condemns scandalous political practices that are commonly known and need no further explanation. These kind of practices would indeed be a political scandal. It is rather unlikely that – bad news are good news – none of the major newspapers and TV stations found this issue worthwhile reporting. Thus, the common knowledge that these statements assume has to be a knowledge not present in or even concealed by mainstream media. For this scenario to be consistent, the media, except some alternative sources,[17] are necessarily part of 'the system'.

Perhaps statements like these are less interesting with regard to their content. Rather we should look at the audience targeted and the way it is addressed. These statements presume an audience that might not have pondered the practices of surveillance, intimidation and ostracism yet. However, the presumed audience already distrusts the 'political class' and the media to an extent that it can easily *imagine* these practices to actually take place. The manifestos do not openly indulge in conspiracy theories but they are well capable of igniting the fantasy of an audience all too willing to believe in such theories.

4.3. *Political Correctness and Censorship*

Much of the political rhetoric of the AfD revolves around the rejection of political correctness. The party's rallying cry 'Mut zur Wahrheit'[18] suggests that democracy has declined into a regime of lies and that AfD solemnly demands freedom of speech and rejects censorship.

> We strongly support the open-ended discussion of unconventional opinions in public discourse as long as the constitution's [Grundgesetz] basic values are not violated. (P0)

> We demand that the media dedicate a reasonable share of their coverage to views beyond the corridor of opinions represented by the established political parties. Under no circumstances shall the freedom of the media be restricted. (P6)

The harshness of this critique notwithstanding, it remains largely unclear who really is accused of censoring public discourse. Does the 'cartel' of established parties exert influence on the media in order to curb the chances of newcomers to the party system or to conceal its own failures?[19] Do the media themselves act as censors as it has its own hidden agenda? Or, is the problem rooted in the dense entanglement of politics and the media?

Anyway, the topos of an inconvenient truth beyond a narrow 'corridor of opinions' accepted by the mainstream is a powerful political weapon. Not only does it claim that there are issues currently neglected by the political system and mass media – which is undoubtedly the case. Furthermore, it actually suggests that the most important, decisive issues are deliberately excluded from public discourse. Again, between the lines there is a neat little narrative of a conspiracy by the established parties and mainstream media. Against the backdrop of this narrative, any outlandish proposition is hailed as an inconvenient truth simply *because* none of the established parties and media outlets approve of this opinion.

Nonetheless, this narrative is only convincing if criticism is constantly mixed up with censorship. In fact, AfD spokespersons are frequently invited to all important (political) talk shows on German television. In addition, AfD leaders are not only interviewed by radio stations and major newspapers, some even write or previously wrote regularly for these papers. However, instead of engaging in political debates, AfD politicians usually dismiss critical questions and counter-arguments as attempts by the mainstream to muzzle Euro-sceptics. The charge of censorship is aimed at denouncing political opponents and their arguments in the first place. In contrast to their self-portrayal, the self-proclaimed defenders of the freedom of speech do not seek discussions but hegemony and acclamation.[20]

The attack on political correctness as censorship implies a rather peculiar (to say the least) understanding of the freedom of the media: Media would ultimately only be democratic if they presented any opinion (be it the report backed by evidence, the conspiracy theory or the outright lie) held in society as equally plausible and if they completely banned judgement and criticism.

4.4. 'Gender Ideology', Re-education and the Dream of a New (Androgynous) Man

Apart from the initial Euro-scepticism and immigration, the gender question has become one of the trademarks of the AfD.[21] The party suggests that ordinary citizens have become victims of aggressive politics of re-education that aim at nothing less than doing away with the fundamentals of any social order: the naturally determined differences between men and women. This re-education goes by the name of gender mainstreaming, 'gender ideology' or straightforward 'gender madness' (the latter does not appear in official documents):

> Gender roles are no subject of politics. The AfD dismisses socio-political re-education measures such as gender mainstreaming. We oppose any attempt by the EU to force these measures upon the nation states. (P1, P2, P4, almost identical in P5)

Interestingly gender mainstreaming, meant to provide equal opportunities for women and men, takes on a new meaning. Here, it encompasses everything from quotas and other affirmative action, academic gender studies to a nebulous 'dissolution of gender identities' (P4).

Again the AfD turns to the narrative of the righteous victim. Leftist politics had gone too far, resulting in a situation of reverse discrimination: Certain groups in society harassed and oppressed the vast majority.[22] Along the lines of this narrative, actually marginalised social groups striving for recognition, equal rights and chances are framed as oppressors. Discriminating against these marginalised groups is refashioned as liberation from oppression, denying equality is presented as an act of justice. At the end of the day, the AfD demands nothing less than the right to continue respectively restore discrimination. The charge of oppression turns out to be means of rationalising politics of resentment.[23]

Here, the wagons are not only circled around the sovereign nation besieged by supra-national institutions and obligations. As shown above, the circle of sameness becomes much tighter. It is confined to those who deem themselves the naturally decisive strata of society (the ordinary, 'normal' citizens maintaining the natural order of things) and who feel they are losing their position.

5. CONCLUSIONS: POPULISM IN AN AGE OF DISTRUST

The AfD and its rhetoric of self-victimisation is a novelty in Germany. For decades it has been part and parcel of radical left discourse to depict the German democracy as a (latent or manifest) authoritarian system. Now, we encounter a very similar narrative disseminated by self-proclaimed 'conservative rebels'. This is remarkable, as it was the conservative milieu of the population that steadfastly, at times uncritically, supported the socio-political order in Germany since 1949 – not least for the sake of anti-communism. In contrast the 'conservative rebels' suggest defending the nation against the 'political system'.

This phenomenon has to be assessed against the backdrop of the course which western democracies took roughly since the 1970s. According to Rosanvallon (2008, 2010), this new political setting is first and foremost characterised by the dominating role of *counter-democracy*. No doubt, the power of the civil society to counter the political system by criticism, by judgement or even by preventing certain policies is a landmark of modern democracy as such. However, it is due to the exhaustion of the grand ideologies and a new wave of individualisation that *counter-democracy* prevails. Scholarly literature has, for instance, pointed out the increase in protest movement in recent years of all sorts (e.g. Castells, 2012; Nestler, 2015; Walter, Geiges, Marg, & Butzlaff, 2013). In a 'society of particularities', it is much easier to forge a negative coalition than to group citizens around a common cause. Also, having neglected a particular group in society can become a serious charge made against politicians whose legitimacy increasingly relies on proximity towards the citizens. In this setting, populism is a successful strategy. Populists point the finger at 'the political class' or 'mainstream media'. They exploit the feeling of a lack of proximity on the side of their audience. However, populism is not about undoing the disenchantment with the political system as this grievance is the populists' political capital. On the contrary, populists must nurture disenchantment and disdain. Populists appeal to deprivation angst and the wish to circle the wagons around a community of sameness. Hence, populists are urged to stimulate an already existing grievance instead of solving a problem. In their narrative of self-victimisation, the AfD obviously exploits this prominent feature of contemporary democracies.

In addition, more recent factors serve the attractiveness of this narrative and hence the success of the AfD. First and foremost, the Euro and debt crisis unsettled significant parts of the German society, albeit the country's economy did comparably well. Not least, this crisis puts the European Union in its present form into question and urges for reforms. It goes without saying, that the European crisis is but a part of the multifaceted global economic crisis from 2007 — a global crisis that shook confidence in the present economic system. What is more, the trust in democratic governments to cope with these challenges has at the same time eroded. Colin Crouch's diagnosis of the coming age of post-democracy, as one-sided as it may be, is taken for granted by many (Crouch, 2010).[24] Further developments add to the clutter from which the AfD profits: The rise of the so-called Islamic State, the spectre of another Cold War between the West and Russia or the most dramatic migration crisis since World War II.

By combining self-victimisation and a defensive nationalism, the AfD successfully recommended itself as the political force to seriously address manifold uncertainties and grievances. From the very beginning, the AfD pursued a one-foot-in-one-foot-out-strategy. On the one hand, the party cultivated the status of an outsider to the political system. In this populist manner, the AfD engaged in opening up the political discourse (that which does count as a political argument) towards the right of the political spectrum. On the other hand, senior party politicians carefully tried to steer clear of outright extremism. In 2013/14, the AfD positioned itself beyond the alleged mainstream, yet on the side of democracy and respectable causes. The future will show the trajectory of this strategy. Although, the party had relatively successful elections in the city-states of Hamburg and Bremen, it failed to cope with the ideological rift which was formative to the AfD from the very beginning. The split in mid-2015 left behind two parties: On the one hand, headed by Lucke, the newly formed 'Allianz für Fortschritt und Aufbruch' (ALFA). On the other hand, by and large deprived of their neo-liberal wing.

NOTES

1. Federal election 2013: 4.7%; European election 2014: 7.1%; state elections: Hesse 2013: 4.1%, Saxony 2014: 9.7%, Thuringia 2014: 10.6%, Brandenburg 2014: 12.2%, Hamburg 2015: 6.1%, Bremen 2015: 5.5%.
2. Populist parties with a similar ideology like the Bund freier Bürger or Pro-DM never came close to 5%.
3. Korte (2014) aptly identifies a third current right of the national-conservative wing.

4. It comes as no surprise that the AfD party leadership has developed a certain division of labour in which each senior party member predominantly covers his or her respectively topics.

5. For a review of the literature on the function of party manifestos, see Kercher and Brettschneider (2013).

6. On political narratives cf. Tudor (1972), Flood (1996), Bottici (2007), Bigon and Nullmeier (2014), Viehöver (2014) and Rohgalf (2015b).

7. In democracies, self-victimisation appeals to what Rosanvallon (2008) described as counter-democracy.

8. For the following, cf. Holtmann, Krappidel and Rehse (2006), Priester (2008) and Rensmann (2006), who review the academic discussion.

9. On this aspect of the creation of collective identities cf. the excellent study by Giesen (1999).

10. Cf. Rensmann (2006, p. 65), Priester (2008, 21f.), and Rosanvallon (2010, p. 266).

11. Fraenkel (2011) noted the Rousseauean origin of the idea of the popular will *a priori* and opposed it to an *a posteriori* popular will, being the result of discussion, bargaining and compromise.

12. See, for instance, the programmatic speech by party spokesman Bernd Lucke (2013c) at the founding party convention (Berlin, 14 April 2013): 'The no-bail-out clause is a central provision of the Maastricht treaty. [...] The federal government has done away with this elementary part of the treaty like it was highly irrelevant. [...] We are not talking about a bagatelle or a political trick here but the fundamentals of the European and German rule of law. We are talking about the breach of a promise or even outright fraud. And thus, we are also talking about democracy. Democracy is government of the people, by the people, for the people, but the will of the people has been blatantly ignored'.

13. Cf. Lucke (2013b): 'Politicians shall serve the common good. Until recently, I believed that our politicians generally accomplished this task quite well. But then came the Euro crisis. [...] The CDU is the party that promised us that the introduction of the Euro will never result in us being liable for the debts of other countries. [...] The politicians who led us into the current mess shall in the future neither get our trust nor our vote'.

14. On the founding phase of the party, see Bebnowski and Kumlar (2013), Häusler (2013), Kemper (2013), Oppenhäuser (2013) or Plehwe and Schlögl (2014).

15. However, for a nuanced empirical assessment of this phenomenon in contemporary Germany see Petersen, Hierlemann, Vehrkamp and Wratil (2013).

16. Actually, members from all parties of the so-called 'political class' pointed to this issue. For instance, even Horst Seehofer, head of the conservative Bavarian CSU that is part of the governing coalition in Berlin, suggested a plebiscite on the rescue of the Euro one year prior to the foundation of the AfD, cf. Gaugele, Malzahn and Sturm (2012).

17. There are a number of these 'alternative' media sources that either openly support the AfD or to which high ranking AfD members contribute or that are often cited by supporters of the party on social media. Remarkably, these media outlets are scribed an almost samizdat-like character as they clearly position themselves as oppositional media that make public what the mainstream media tries to sweep under the carpet. See Häusler (2013, 76ff.) and Storz (2015) for a detailed analysis.

18. 'Dare to say the truth!' Whether the slogan deliberately resembles Vaclav Havel's 'Living in Truth' and thus likens the AfD to the civil society movement confronting the Soviet regime, remains speculation.

19. 'A large share of the population has the impression that the failure of the established parties is somehow connected to the growing limitations of open-ended public discussions (political correctness).' (P6)

20. An ultimately authoritarian longing which undoubtedly is not exclusively typical of the party in question here. Cf. Weiß (2011, pp. 89–106), Butterwegge (2013) or Zander (2013) who analyse this strategy with regard to Thilo Sarrazin.

21. For example in the manifesto for the Saxon elections 2014, the ideology 'genderism' is likened to 'Marxism-Leninism'. Later on, the manifesto opposes what it deems an 'indoctrination' of school curricula by 'LGBT-contents'. Or, see vice-spokesman Alexander Gauland (2013) who flatters those party members that regard 'gender mainstreaming, politically correct fairy tales and feminist bibles as mere brainchilds' of gooddoers. Beatrix von Storch, member of the European Parliament, is engaged in a host of activities and initiatives dedicated to ultra-conservative family values. On this topic see also the study conducted by Kemper (2014).

22. Cf. di Blasi (2014) for a similar observation of the discussion of sexism in Germany.

23. Similar to Pareto's (1983) theory of residues and derivations. According to Pareto, people turn to highly valued principles to rationalise their usually irrational motivations and causes.

24. For a critique of the diagnosis of post-democracy see e.g. Nolte (2011) or Rohgalf (2015c).

ACKNOWLEDGEMENT

The Authors thank Konstantin Sachariew and Antje Schröder for their support and insights.

REFERENCES

Anderson, B. (2006). Imagined Communitie. *Reflections on the origin and spread of nationalism.* London: Verso.

Bebnowski, D., & Kumlar, N. (2013). Jeder hat Angst, seinen Besitzstatus zu verlieren. Die Anti-Euro-Proteste. In F. Walter, et al. (Eds.), *Die neue Macht der Bürger. Was motiviert die Protestbewegungen* (pp. 219–249). Reinbek bei Hamburg: Rowohlt.

Bender, J. (2014). Alle eint der Groll. *Frankfurter Allgemeine Zeitung*, January 27.

Bigon, D., & Nullmeier, F. (2014). Narrationen über Narrationen. Stellenwert und Methodologie der Narrationsanalyse. In F. Gadinger, S. Jarzebski, & T. Yildiz (Eds.), *Politische Narrative. Konzepte – Analysen – Forschungspraxis* (pp. 39–66). Wiesbaden: Springer VS.

Bleek, W., Gawrich, A., & Sontheimer, K. (2007). *Grundzüge des politischen Systems Deutschlands.* München: Piper.

Bottici, C. (2007). *A philosophy of political myth.* Cambridge: Cambridge University Press.

Bracher, K. D. (1955). Die Auflösung der Weimarer Republik. *Eine Studie zum Problem des Machtverfalls in der Demokratie.* Stuttgart: Ring-Verlag.

Butterwegge, C. (2013). Sarrazynismus. Eine Katastrophe für die politische Kultur der Bundesrepublik und eine Gefahr für die Demokratie. In P. Bathke & A. Hoffstadt (Eds.), *Die neuen Rechten in Europa* (pp. 206–219). Köln: Zwischen Neoliberalismus und Rassismus.

Castells, M. (2010). *The information age.* (Vol. 3). Chichester: Wiley-Blackwell.

Castells, M. (2012). Networks of outrage and hope. *Social movements in the Internet age.* Cambridge: Polity Press.

Commission Regulation (EC) No 2257/94. September 16, (1994).

Crouch, C. (2010). *Post-democracy.* Cambridge: Polity Press.

Di Blasi, L. (2014). Die andere Sexismus-Debatte. In *Aus Politik und Zeitgeschichte* (8/2014, pp. 16–21).

Flood, C. (1996). *Political myth. A theoretical introduction.* New York, NY: Garland Publishing.

Fraenkel, E. (2011). Möglichkeiten und Grenzen politischer Mitarbeit der Bürger in modernen Demokratien. In A. von Brünneck (Ed.), *Deutschland und die westlichen Demokratien* (pp. 283–296). Baden-Baden: UTB.

Gaugele, J., Malzahn, C. C., & Sturm, D. F. (2012). Seehofer fordert Volksabstimmung über Euro-Rettung. In: *Die Welt*, February 12.

Gauland, A. (2013). Brief an konservative Parteifreunde. In *Website AfD*, December 29, accessed October 20, 2014. https://www.alternativefuer.de/2013/12/29/brief-an-konservative-parteifreunde/.

Giesen, B. (1999). *Kollektive Identität. Die Intellektuellen und die Nation 2.* Frankfurt/Main: Suhrkamp.

Habermas, J. (1992). Staatsbürgerschaft und nationale Identität. In J. Habermas (Ed.), *Faktizität und Geltung. Beiträge zur Diskurstheorie des Rechts und des demokratischen Rechtsstaats* (pp. 632–660). Frankfurt am Main: Suhrkamp.

Harmsen, R., & Spiering, M. (2004). Introduction. Euroscepticism and the evolution of European political debate. In R. Harmsen & M. Spiering (Eds.), *Euroscepticism. Party Politics, National Identity and European Integration* (pp. 13–35). Amsterdam: Rodopi.

Häusler, A. (2013). *Die Alternative für Deutschland: Eine neue rechtspopulistische Partei?.* Düsseldorf: Heinrich-Böll-Stiftung.

Herbert, U. (2014). *Europäische Geschichte im 20. Jahrhundert. Geschichte Deutschlands im 20. Jahrhundert.* München: C.H. Beck.

Hobsbawm, E. (1990). *Nation and Nationalism since 1780. Programme, Myth and Reality.* Cambridge: Cambridge University Press.

Holtmann, E., Krappidel, A., & Rehse, S. (2006). *Die Droge Populismus. Zur Kritik des politischen Vorurteils.* Wiesbaden: VS Verlag für Sozialwissenschaft.

Honnigfort, B. (2014). Kummerkasten AfD. In *Frankfurter Rundschau*, March 4.

Jesse, E. (1998). Antiextremistischer Konsens. Von der Weimarer Republik bis zur Gegenwart. In K. G. Kick, S. Weingarz, & U. Bartosch (Eds.), *Wandel durch Beständigkeit. Studien zur deutschen und internationalen Politik, Jens Hacker zum 65. Geburtstag* (pp. 151–169). Berlin: Duncker & Humblot.

Jopp, F., & Tekin, M. (2014). *Europas Wert. Studien zum materiellen und immateriellen Nutzen der europäischen Integration.* Baden-Baden: Nomos Verlagsgesellschaft.

Kaschuba, W. (2000). The emergence and transformation of foundation myths. In B. Stråth (Eds.), *Myth and Memory in the Construction of Community. Historical Patterns in Europe and Beyond* (pp. 217–226). Brussels: Peter Lang.

Kemper, A. (2013). Rechte Euro-Rebellion: Alternative für Deutschland und Zivile Koalition e. V. Münster: Edition Assemblage.

Kemper, A. (2014). *Keimzelle der Nation? Familien- und geschlechterpolitische Positionen der AfD — eine Expertise.* Berlin: Friedrich-Ebert-Stiftung.

Kercher, J., & Brettschneider, F. (2013). Wahlprogramme als Pflichtübung? Typen, Funktionen und Verständlichkeit der Bundestagswahlprogramme 1994–2009. In W. Bernhard et al. (Eds.), *Wahlen und Wähler. Analysen aus Anlass der Bundestagswahl 2009* (pp. 269–290). Wiesbaden: Springer VS.

Korte, K. R. (2014). Der Osten wählt immer wilder als der Westen. In *politik & kommunikation*, September 1, accessed November 18, 2014. http://www.politik-kommunikation.de/ressorts/artikel/der-osten-waehlt-immer-wilder-als-der-westen-14564.

Kriesi, H. -P. (2012). *Political conflict in Western Europe.* Cambridge: Cambridge University Press.

Kroll, T., & Reitz, T. (2013). *Intellektuelle in der Bundesrepublik. Verschiebungen im politischen Feld der 1960er und 1970er Jahre.* Göttingen: Vandenhoeck & Ruprecht.

Leconte, C. (2010). *Understanding Euroscepticism.* Basingstoke: Palgrave Macmillan.

Leggewie, C. (2009). West Germany. A return from cultural nostalgia to political analysis. *German Historical Institute Bulletin*, (Supplement 6), 239–243.

Leggewie, C., & Meier, H. (1995). *Republikschutz. Maßstäbe für die Verteidigung der Demokratie*. Reinbek bei Hamburg: Rowohlt.

Leggewie, C., & Meier, H. (2012). *Nach dem Verfassungsschutz. Plädoyer für eine neue Sicherheitsarchitektur der Berliner Republik*. Berlin: Archiv der Jugendkulturen Verlag.

Lucke, B. (2013a). AfD will nicht zurück zur D-Mark. *Frankfurter Allgemeine Sonntagszeitung*, May 19.

Lucke, B. (2013b). Lüneburger Rede. In *Website AfD*, accessed November 10, 2014. http://www.alternativefuer-bw.de/images/Dokumente/Bernd%20Lucke%20-%20L%C3%BCneburger%20Rede%2027.6.13.pdf.

Lucke, B. (2013c). Rede zum Gründungsparteitag 14.04.2013 in Berlin. In *Webseite AfD*, accessed November 10, 2014. http://deutsche-wirtschafts-nachrichten.de/wp-content/uploads/2013/04/Rede-Bernd-Lucke.pdf.

Mudde, C. (2014). Rechtsaußen, die Große Rezession und die Europawahl 2014. *Aus Politik und Zeitgeschichte*, *64*(12), 16–24.

Mudde, C. (2015). Local shocks. In *Eurozine*, March 13, accessed September 3, 2015. http://www.eurozine.com/articles/2015-03-13-mudde-en.html.

Nestler, C. (2015). Protest als Selbstzweck. In M. Kneuer (Eds.), *Standortbestimmung Deutschland: Innere Verfasstheit und internationale Verantwortung* (pp. 253–277). Baden-Baden: Nomos Verlagsgesellschaft.

Nestler, C., & Rohgalf, J. (2014). Eine deutsche Angst – Erfolgreiche Parteien rechts der Union. Zur AfD und den gegenwärtigen Gelegenheitsstrukturen des Parteienwettbewerbs. *Zeitschrift für Politik*, *61*(4), 389–413 (forthcoming).

Nestler, C., & Schütt, S. (2014). Die Europawahl 2014 in Mecklenburg-Vorpommern. In C. Nestler & C. Scheele (Eds.), *Die Kommunalwahlen 2014 in Mecklenburg-Vorpommern* (pp. 17–32). Rostock: Universität Rostock.

Nolte, P. (2011). Von der repräsentativen zur multiplen Demokratie. *Aus Politik und Zeitgeschichte*, *61*(1-2), 5–12.

Oppenhäuser, H. (2013). Demokratische Querfronten? Der neue Rechtspopulismus und die Ambivalenz der direkten Demokratie. *Prokla*, *43*(2), 277–295.

Pareto, V. (1983). *The Mind and Society. A Treatise on General Sociology*. (vol. 4). New York.

Petersen, T., Hierlemann, D., Vehrkamp, R. B., & Wratil, C. (2013). *Gespaltene Demokratie. Politische Partizipation und Demokratiezufriedenheit vor der Bundestagswahl 2013*. Gütersloh: Bertelsmann Stiftung.

Plehwe, D., & Schlögl, M. (2014). *Europäische und zivilgesellschaftliche Hintergründe der euo(pa) skeptischen Partei Alternative für Deutschland (AfD)*. Berlin: WZB.

Priester, K. (2008). Populismus als Protestbewegung. In A. Häusler (Eds.), *Rechtspopulismus als "Bürgerbewegung". Kampagnen gegen Islam und Moscheebau und kommunale Gegenstrategien* (pp. 19–36). Wiesbaden: VS Verlag für Sozialwissenschaften.

Rensmann, L. (2006). Populismus und Ideologie. In F. Decker (Eds.), *Populismus in Europa. Gefahr für die Demokratie oder nützliches Korrektiv?* (pp. 59–80). Wiesbaden: VS Verlag für Sozialwissenschaften.

Rohgalf, J. (2015a). Subsidiarität als Kampfbegriff. In K. R. Korte (Eds.), *Emotionen und Politik, Veröffentlichungen der Deutschen Gesellschaft für Politikwissenschaft (DGfP) Band 32* (pp. 297–316). Baden-Baden: Nomos.

Rohgalf, J. (2015b). *Jenseits der großen Erzählungen. Utopie und politischer Mythos in der Moderne und Spätmoderne*. Wiesbaden: Springer VS.

Rohgalf, J. (2015c). Der Körper des demos als Problemformel der Demokratie. In M. Doll & O. Kohns (Eds.), *Die zwei Körper der Nation. Ästhetische Figurationen des Politischen*. München: Fink. (forthcoming).

Rosanvallon, P. (2008). *Counter-democracy. Politics in an Age of Distrust*. Cambridge: Cambridge Univ. Press.

Rosanvallon, P. (2010). *Demokratische Legitimität. Unparteilichkeit — Reflexivität — Nähe.* Hamburg: Hamburger Edition.

Smith, A. (1999). *Myths and Memories of the Nation.* Oxford: Oxford Univ. Press.

Sternberger, D. (1990). *Verfassungspatriotismus.* Frankfurt am Main: Insel Verlag.

Storz, W. (2015). ...und meine Zielgruppe ist das Volk. *Querfront — Karriere eines politisch-publizistischen Netzwerks.* Frankfurt/Main: Otto Brenner-Stiftung.

Tudor, H. (1972). *Political Myth.* New York: Praeger Publishers.

Viehöver, W. (2014). Erzählungen im Feld der Politik. Politik durch Erzählungen. Überlegungen zur Rolle der Narrationen in den politischen Wissenschaften. In F. Gadinger, S. Jarzebski, & T. Yildiz (Eds.), *Politische Narrative. Konzepte — Analysen — Forschungspraxis* (pp. 67—92). Wiesbaden: Springer VS.

Walter, F., Geiges, L., Marg, S., & Butzlaff, F. (2013). *Die neue Macht der Bürger. Was motiviert die Protestbewegungen.* Reinbek bei Hamburg: Rowohlt.

Weiß, V. (2011). *Deutschlands Neue Rechte. Angriff der Eliten. Von Spengler bis Sarrazin.* Paderborn: Schöningh.

Werz, N. (2013). Erscheinungsformen und Debatten um den 'Populismus' in Deutschland. In A. Gallus, T. Schubert, & T. Thieme (Eds.), *Deutsche Kontroversen: Festschrift für Eckhard Jesse* (pp. 421—433). Baden-Baden: Nomos Verlagsgesellschaft.

Wirsching, A. (2012). Der Preis der Freiheit. *Geschichte Europas in unserer Zeit.* München: C.H. Beck.

Zander, M. (2013). Gespielte Ohnmacht. Das politische Programm des Thilo Sarrazin. In P. Bathke & A. Hoffstadt (Eds.), *Die neuen Rechten in Europa. Zwischen Neoliberalismus und Rassismus* (pp. 220—229). Köln: PapyRossa.

FROM NATIONAL CONSENSUS TO A NEW CLEAVAGE? THE DISCURSIVE NEGOTIATION OF EUROPE IN THE GREEK PUBLIC DEBATE DURING THE ECONOMIC CRISIS, 2010–2015

Zinovia Lialiouti

ABSTRACT

EU membership has been for the greater part of the post-authoritarian period (1974–2010) an important element of the Greek national consensus. Europe was commonly associated in public discourse with geopolitical security, democratic institutions and economic prosperity. Moreover, accession to the European Monetary Union in 2001 was celebrated as proof of a successful national course and as promise for economic growth. Nevertheless, challenges to pro-Europeanism both from the left and from the extreme right have risen in the context of the economic crisis (2010–2015). While Eurosceptical attitudes are still a minority within Greek society — but significantly increased in relation to past trends — the discursive negotiation of Europe in the Greek public debate is characterized by ambiguity and has acquired various negative connotations (e.g. austerity policies, authoritarianism, German hegemony, democratic deficit in decision-making). In the highly-polarized Greek political debate, a new cleavage has emerged based on the acceptance or rejection of the loan agreements and the austerity policies associated with them (the so-called pro- vs. anti-memorandum cleavage)

National Identity and Europe in Times of Crisis: Doing and Undoing Europe, 161–185
Copyright © 2017 by Emerald Publishing Limited
All rights of reproduction in any form reserved
doi:10.1108/978-1-78714-513-920171008

which have also transformed traditional Left vs. Right cleavage thus allowing for political alliances between left-ward and right-ward parties. It remains to be seen whether the new cleavage will take the form of a clash between pro-Europeanists vs. Euroscepticists as it is often argued in the context of Grexit scenarios. While this new dichotomy can be misleading especially if it is unambiguously interpreted in cultural terms, it describes a newly formed social and political tension that is under process. A special chapter in this respect is the currency debate; the dilemma between the euro and the drachma represents distinct ideological paradigms and power structures. The present chapter explores the discursive negotiation of Europe in the context of the Greek public debate analysing discourses produced both by political elites and mass media with special focus on the 2015 referendum campaign and the implications of the July 2015 Greece-EU agreement.

Keywords: Greece; cleavages; Euroscepticism; austerity; victimization; historical analogies

1. INTRODUCTION: AIMS AND METHODOLOGICAL REMARKS

This chapter explores the discursive negotiation of the European Union in the context of the Greek public debate during the economic crisis (2010–2015) with emphasis on elements of discontinuity in relation to the post-authoritarian period, the so-called *Metapolitefsi* (1974–2010). The temporal focus of the present essay is on the first 6 months of the coalition government between SYRIZA ('Coalition of Radical Left') and ANEL ('Independent Greeks') that was formed after the national elections of January 25, 2015 with the explicit goal of putting an end to the austerity policies implemented within the framework of the loan agreements between Greece and her creditors (International Monetary Fund, European Commission, European Central Bank) and to renegotiate the terms of Greece's lending programme. A landmark in this 6-month period was the referendum on July 5th on the question of approval of the proposed agreement by the three creditor institutions on June 25th. In Greek political practice, referenda are extremely rare and had been almost exclusively reserved for constitutional matters or the choice of the head of state. Thus, the recent referendum was of particular political importance and generated ideological trends that are worth exploring.

Against the purposes of the present study, the focus on the referendum electoral campaign and the public debate it triggered sheds light on the interaction between elite and mass perceptions of Europe and of the national self-image. It builds on the concept of 'communities of discourse' (Van Dijk, 2006, pp. 115–140) which captures the interplay between discourse and ideology in order to reconstruct the distinct discourses formulated in the process of transformation of existing political cleavages which is under way since the outbreak of the Greek economic crisis. This transformation involves the reshaping of the cleavage Right vs. Left (or anti-Right) into the cleavage pro-memorandum vs. anti-memorandum based on the acceptance or rejection of the loan agreements and the austerity policies associated with them. It has been argued that the new cleavage could evolve into a clash between pro-Europeanists vs. Eurosceptics. While the referendum provided some evidence in this direction, such a cleavage on Europe has not been consolidated. It remains to be seen whether the ground for such a cleavage has been set or is already in the making. The content and the features of cleavages in Greek politics, after the experience of the crisis, is an open question in the literature (Bosco & Verney 2012, pp. 129–154; Serrichio, Tsakatika, & Quagli, 2013, pp. 51–63; Teperoglou & Tsatsanis, 2014, pp. 222–242; Vasilopoulou, Halikiopoulou, & Exadaktylos, 2014, pp. 388–402). In any case, the experience of the crisis and austerity in Greece has resulted in the transformation in both contentious and conventional politics (Kousis & Kanellopoulos, 2014). The rise of right-wing extremism as represented by the neo-Nazi party of Golden Dawn has been another important aspect of the political setting of the crisis years (Dinas et al., 2013; Georgiadou, 2013, pp. 75–102)

In parallel, theoretical and methodological elaborations on Euroscepticism have provided new insights into the phenomenon, emphasizing the importance of distinctions in: (a) the levels of focus − 'authorities,' 'regime', or 'community', (b) the type − 'diffuse' vs. 'specific' Euroscepticism − and (c) the agents of Euroscepticism − political parties, public opinion (Boomgaarden, Schuck, Elenbaas, & De Vreese, 2010; Kopecký & Mudde, 2002; Krouwel & Abts, 2007; Leconte, 2010; Szczerbiak & Taggart, 2008; Taggart, 1998, pp. 297–326; Vasilopoulou, 2013, pp. 153–168; Wessels, 2007). The first category tries to capture differentiations between negative attitudes which are centred on EU officials and institution representatives, those which express opposition towards the European value and normative systems, and others which target the European people (or certain parts of it) as a collectivity (Wessels, 2007, p. 289). Moreover, opposition might be specific when it is focused on the particular embodiment of the EU in the present context or diffuse when it involves the project of European integration as such (Kopecký & Mudde, pp. 297–326).

Despite the analytical value of such distinctions, Euroscepticism develops in a cumulative way and can evolve from specific to diffuse and from authority or regime to community oriented (Serrichio et al., 2013, p. 52; Wessels, 2007, p. 290). Recent scholarship has incorporated the crisis dimension in its conceptualization of the rise of Euroscepticism (Serrichio et al., 2013, pp. 51–64). A most interesting finding is that even though Euroscepticism in on the rise in countries most seriously affected by the economic crisis, nevertheless, the worsening of economic conditions does not seem to be the main explanatory factor for such a rise. It is the prevailing of a strong, exclusivist national identity and a low level of trust in national political institutions that are positively correlated with the growth of Euroscepticism. In this vein, it has been argued that Euroscepticism 'is rooted in national contexts' (Serrichio et al., 2013, p. 61). The links between nationalism and Euroscepticism have also been established in relation to extreme right-wing and extreme left-wing parties (Halikiopoulou, Nanou, & Vasilopoulou, 2012, pp. 504−539).

What we will contribute to these ongoing debates is an insight on aspects of the Greek national context focusing on the discursive legacy created in public debate and an analysis of its implications. The discursive legacy approach has been particularly fruitful in the study of ideologies and belief systems (e.g. the study of anti-Americanism) addressing the later as an 'accumulation of representations, myths and stereotypes that are available to the entire ideological spectrum' (Roger, 2002, pp. 18−19) or as a set of 'deeply-seated and long-lasting ideas, images and metaphors that assume the character of a comprehensive interpretation' (Diner, 1996, p. viii). Thus, the present essay aims to shed light precisely on the slow process of accumulation and on the constitutive elements of the discursive legacy on Europe that is formulated as a result of this process. Our analysis is grounded in the Critical Discourse Analysis (CDA) paradigm and aims to reconstruct the discursive strategies employed in the crisis context and to provide an understanding of their interaction with collective identities. Two special research interests are involved in this task: (a) the use of historical analogies and their ideological functions and (b) blame attribution discourses. Concerning the issue of historical analogies, we are mostly concerned with their cognitive and ideological functions especially in crises as they often serve as means of reducing complexity, encouraging political mobilization and providing legitimization (Karner & Mertens, 2013, pp. 9−11). In terms of methodology, the discourse-historical approach within the tradition of CDA highlights the importance of historical grounding and contextualization in the study of discursive acts (Boukala, 2014, pp. 483−499; Wodak, de Cillia, Reisigl & Liebhart,2009, pp. 7−48). As far as blame attribution processes are concerned, we are interested in their links with the hegemonic interpretive schemes in the Greek crisis debate and their normative implications. As Wodak and Angouri have remarked 'Blaming necessarily involves a normative stance: it has to be proven time and again that specific actors are blameworthy. And such a link involves explanations, justifications and argumentation, as well as shared values which are referred to' (Wodak & Angouri, 2014, p. 418).

In an effort to combine elements from a top-down and a bottom-up perspectives this chapter builds on three categories of empirical material: (i) political discourse as recorded in the print and digital media and (ii) opinion articles published in a broad spectrum of the Greek press: newspapers *Avgi, Efsyn, Ta Nea, Kathimerini, Demokratia, Rizospastis*, news webpages www.iefimerida.gr, www.protagon.gr, (iii) slogans, images and symbols employed in the context of the square mobilizations that took place during the 6-month period and, in particular, in the weeks before and after the referendum. This latter category of material is the product of onsite ethnographic research conducted by the author at the time of the mobilizations. The corpus of the empirical material is processed through qualitative content analysis, using *themes* and *concepts* as units of analysis (Berg, 2001, pp. 238–258).

2. FROM EU-PHILIA TO EUROSCEPTICISM: CRISIS, AUSTERITY AND THE GREEK PUBLIC DEBATE 2010–2015

Following the collapse of military dictatorship (1974), the goal of European integration acquired the status of national ideology – from a top-down perspective – under the premiership of Konstantinos Karamanlis, leader of the conservative party of New Democracy (ND) (1974–1981) (Botsiou, 2010, pp. 93–108).Greece's membership in the European Community became effective in 1981. In parallel, ND's contender to power, the Pan-Hellenic Socialist Movement (PASOK) moved gradually away from its anti-imperialist, anti-capitalist rhetoric which rejected EU membership and integrated the goal of Europeanization in its political agenda during successive government terms (Pantazopoulos, 2001, pp. 253–255; Voulgaris, 2013, p. 98). Moreover, under the premiership of Costas Simitis (1996–2004) Europeanization and especially the goal of accession to the Eurozone was an integral part of the so-called modernization movement (Eleftheriou & Tassis, 2013, pp. 122–134; Voulgaris, 2013, pp. 142–148).

In terms of popular and party attitudes towards Europe, Verney argues that after a period of widespread Euroscepticism (1974–1981), pro-Europeanism prevailed in Greece during the 1980s, while a 'limited resurgence' of Euroscepticism developed in the 1990s, which was mostly associated with smaller leftist and rightist parties. On the other hand, the two major governing parties, PASOK and ND, formed a bipartisan consensus on Greece's European course. Thus, adaptation to Economic and Monetary Union (EMU) accession criteria became an important part of the programmatic discourse of both the centre-left and the centre-right and a measure for evaluation of their government performance. Accession to EMU in 2001 was celebrated as proof of a successful national course and as promise for economic growth. In the first half of the 2000s Greek public opinion was strongly in favour of European integration and supported the common currency by great numbers. In the year 2000 Greek support for the euro reached 69% compared to a 58% EU average (Verney, 2011, pp. 51–79). However, it has been stressed that Greek pro-Europeanism of the period was mainly utilitarian and associated with the prospects of economic growth and political modernization (Vernardakis, 2007, pp. 147–164).

The economic crisis (2010–2015) has had a decisive influence on the development of Greek Euroscepticism which can be detected at three distinct-but interrelated-levels: mass attitudes as recorded in opinion polls, party political positions and media discursive practices. With the outbreak of the crisis, public opinion indices such as EU image and levels of trust in the EU attested some dramatic shifts; according to the Eurobarometer surveys, the positive image of the EU in Greek shrunk from 56% in 2009 to 16% in 2013, while trust in the EU dropped from 60% in 2009 to 21% in 2013 (Lialiouti & Bithymitris, 2014, p. 255). This trend was also combined with extremely low levels of trust for national political institutions (10% trust for the Greek government and 12% for the national Parliament, EB 80, 2013). Nevertheless, support for an EU exit scenario remained minority-though not negligible (38%, EB 80, 2013). Moreover, all opinion polls conducted at the national level have attested that the majority of the Greek people remain in favour of the country's EU membership.

In the interplay between political and mass media discourses, since the beginning of the Greek crisis, two interpretive repertoires have taken shape and compete for hegemony; they are inextricably linked to the formulation of the cleavage between pro-memorandum vs. anti-memorandum political forces. Schematically, the first interpretive scheme emphasizes the internal causes of the crisis, insisting on the flaws in the country's economic, political and social development and on a cultural divide between Greece and (Western) Europe mainly understood as a Greek exceptionalism and backwardness. It's most common discursive formulation in the political debate is the goal set by the pro-memorandum camp that Greece should become a 'normal country'. Despite the vagueness of the concept of normalcy, it served to explain current national misfortune, to justify unpopular austerity measures and to offer legitimization to the reform agenda elaborated by the country's creditors and Greek governing elites.

The second interpretive scheme, also here schematically summarized, associates the crisis mostly with external factors and attributes the worsening of economic and social conditions in Greece to the actions of 'external enemies' (e.g. the IMF policies dictated by neoliberal economic dogmas, Germany as a hegemonic power in the EU) and to the submissive attitude of the Greek governments, thus levelling accusations of 'traitorous behaviour' on their part. The dominant metaphor in this context is that of foreign occupation and the historical analogy of WWII and of Nazi occupation of Greece has been particularly popular in political, mass media and everyday discourses. WWII historical analogies are found in discursive practices that emphasize the victimization of the Greek people and the need for heroic resistance (Lialiouti & Bithymitris, 2013, pp. 155–172).

In short, two distinct blame attribution practices have been employed by the competing ideological blocks: For the pro-memorandum, 'reformist' block blame lies with the internal enemy which is identified with populism, while the anti-memorandum block prioritizes the external enemy and argues that the country has a status of limited sovereignty. This absolute dichotomy set aside, actual discourses formulated by political parties and mass media during the crisis years have incorporated hybrid narrative and interpretive schemes that combine public beliefs on victimization and guilt (Lialiouti & Bithymitris, 2014, 2017). Anti-German discourse could be perceived as the first manifestation of Euroscepticism in Greek political culture which intersected horizontally the left vs. right cleavage and was instrumentalised by the anti-memorandum camp (Lialiouti & Bithymitris, 2013, pp. 155–172).

The above tendencies developed further during recent EU and the national election campaigns (in spring 2014 and December 2014, January 2015 respectively). After the 2015 elections, a coalition government between SYRIZA and ANEL was formed with the proclaimed goal of renegotiating Greece's bailout programme and adopting a more independent stance towards her 'creditors'.

A revealing manifestation of these trends was the 'Breath of Dignity' (February 2015) campaign which was coordinated by social media and involved pro-government square mobilizations in the capital and other cities. The campaign was orchestrated as a means of supporting the government and to urge her not to 'give in to the creditors demands', using slogans such as the following: 'We will not be blackmailed. We will not surrender. We are not afraid. We won't retreat. We will win'. (https://www.facebook.com/events/145681454122 7075/). It portrayed itself as the unmediated involvement of the Greek people in the negotiations ('We take negotiations into our hands') and denounced the 'creditors' attitude as an 'asphyxiation' attempt, while proclaiming 'our lives do not belong to the creditors'. (http://www.facebook.com/events/ 112764409059937/). The themes of war, physical violence and blackmail link these demonstrations with the discursive formulation of the EU negotiations by the government and the main themes of the referendum campaign. Moreover, it should not be overlooked that as an agreement between Greece and the EU on the terms of the loan agreements was pending, the word 'creditors' with negative connotations substituted the word Europe in press accounts of the events, even in opposition publications. A malice Shylock metaphor underlay references to creditors.

On the opposite side, the 'staying in Europe' mobilization, that emerged soon afterwards, identified itself in the following words opting for a liberal, civil society perspective: 'We the citizens who demand Greece to remain in Europe and in the Eurozone, who demand to remain a member of the great Democratic Community, we must be again at Syntagma … holding only Greek and European flags and our whistles. The Initiative belongs exclusively to citizens and not to parties'. (https://www.facebook.com/events/46373553380 2343/). In terms of public discourse, pro-European columnists portrayed Europe as a self-evident identity, linking personal biographies to collective sense of belonging, but also emphasized the rejection of alternative identities based on geographical proximity or cultural affinity:

I was born, raised, educated, worked, and grew old in Europe. Leaving Europe is like asking me to leave my home ... Where else could I possibly belong to? To the Middle East? To the Russian Federation? I feel no affinity with these lands ... You might say: There is also the Balkans. But that's what we should escape from. (Dimou, 2015)

As tension in the public sphere grew, the President of the Republic, Prokopis Pavlopoulos declared that he 'wouldn't tolerate to be president in a country out of the Eurozone', acknowledging the safeguarding of Greece's membership in the Eurozone as his constitutional duty and as the only acceptable national course (Pavlopoulos, 2015).

3. AN EMERGING CLEAVAGE? THE 2015 GREEK REFERENDUM AND ITS AFTERMATH

On June 27th, Prime Minister Tsipras announced his decision to hold a referendum, 40 years after the previous one that abolished the institution of monarchy in Greece (1974). This was the first referendum in Greek political history that was associated with European issues. As soon as the referendum was announced, a battle on its framing began. The Prime Minister and his party emphatically opted for a NO vote to the referendum. The NO coalition was formed by the anti-memorandum parties- that are the governing partner, far-right ANEL and neo-Nazi Golden Dawn, while the Greek Communist Party (KKE) refused to adopt a yes or no stance and campaigned on the common rejection of the government's position and of the YES vote insisting that the real question for the Greek people should be EU membership itself. Its party newspaper, *Rizospastis*, rejected the double 'blackmail' and the 'false dilemmas' posed by the government and the EU (Rizospastis, 2015).

The YES coalition was formed by the pro-memorandum parties which presented themselves as a 'European front': conservative ND, centrist POTAMI, and social-democratic PASOK. The YES camp framed the campaign as a dilemma between the euro and return to the national currency or as an approval of Greece's EU membership. Their argumentation was mainly based on utilitarianism prioritizing economic prosperity, geopolitical security and democratic stability. The editorial of *Kathimerini* under the title 'Yes for Europe, democracy and security' summarized the YES argumentation, acknowledging the 'totally justifiable anger and rage of the Greek people' and attacking the prime minister for 'hypnotizing everybody in the road towards drachma' (Kathimerini, 2015).

On the other hand, supporters of YES depicted in the darkest colours the consequences of a NO vote. As eloquently put in the front-page of *Nea* a NO would bring: 'Chaos, Poverty and Drachma' (*Ta Nea*, 3 July 2015). *Kathimerini* also warned against the dangers of NO: 'It will turn us into a third world banana republic'. Moreover *Kathimerini* challenged the belief that the NO vote could have a social grounding:

> It's necessary for the vulnerable and the credulous who succumb to the sirens of populism to understand this reality. The desperate who have the illusion that they have nothing else to lose. The young who underestimate the dangers and do not know how low this country could drop without the European safety net. (*Kathimerini, ibid*)

ND's main campaign slogan was 'Yes to Greece, Yes to the Euro' identifying Europe mainly with the common currency and the common market, highlighting the legacy of economic nationalism structured upon Greece's accession to the Eurozone. Its TV spot was also explicit about the real stake of the election: 'The question on Sunday is clear. Do you want to stay in the Euro?' (ND, 2015). Nevertheless, in defending Greece's European course, ND felt obliged to incorporate elements of soft Euroscepticism. In his widely advertised message former Prime Minister Kostas Karamanlis admitted: 'There is no doubt that the EU has many weaknesses in its function and that obviously our partners have committed grave errors in dealing with the crisis, but so have we'. Nevertheless, he insisted that EU membership represented for Greece a 'vital need', building his argumentation on the goal of economic growth and social development, on geostrategic factors stressing that Greece is located in an 'unstable neighbourhood' and naming 'security' as the 'ultimate criterion'. He emphasized the disastrous consequences in case of a Greek exit, but also tried to highlight the emotional ties with Europe by employing the concept of 'European family' (ND, 2015) (Fig. 1).

Fig. 1. Poster from the YES Campaign: 'Yes to Greece. Yes to the Euro'. *Source*: Photo taken by author.

In the above poster, as in the greater part of the YES campaign, the common currency functions as a metonymy for Europe. Arguably, the YES campaign failed to incorporate effectively identity themes and emotional elements; the poverty of imagery in the campaign is revealing in this respect. The European flag by itself or alongside with the Greek flag were the – almost – exclusive images in the campaign.

While most columnists from the YES camp acknowledged the emergence of a new and painful divide (Iordanidis, 2015), they also interpreted the referendum as an act of self-awareness:

> The referendum, with all its dangers, forces us to think, perhaps for the first time, who we are, where we stand and where we want to go ... It will not only be a tragedy if we lose the security and prosperity we have had in recent decades because we deny to have an understanding between us - it will be a crime. This dangerous referendum allows us to know ourselves. But also to consider our responsibilities. (Konstantaras, 2015).

They also often employed the child metaphor in terms of the Greek people as they portrayed the referendum vote as a passage to adulthood. Specifically, the YES vote would constitute an act of maturity (Chomenidis, 2015).

The government rejected the reading of the referendum as a pro- or anti-European vote and insisted that the question was on the continuation of austerity policies and the safeguarding of national independence. SYRIZA even argued that a NO vote would enhance Greece's place in the European Union (*Avgi*, 2015a). The NO campaign was mostly based on emotional appeal emphasizing the need to restore dignity for the country and democracy both in the national and the European context. The dignity and democracy themes had their roots in SYRIZA's argumentation that austerity policies in Europe were an undermining factor both for national sovereignty and for the quality of democracy which had been put forth during the EU election campaign (spring 2014) as previously discussed. These central themes were dominant in SYRIZA's referendum spot. Its slogans were 'For a Greece of Dignity. For a Europe of Democracy', 'NO to Subjection, NO to Austerity, NO to Fear' and 'No to the authoritarianism of austerity'. The narration in one of SYRIZA's TV spot was also revealing for the construction of an external enemy concept in the representation of EU negotiations: 'They do not want a compromise. They want humiliation. They do not want a solution. They want the continuation of the slow death. They want abolition of democracy. Will you let them?' (SYRIZA, 2015) (Figs. 2 and 3).

Even before the proclamation of the referendum, as the tension in Greek-EU negotiations grew, each camp held two square mobilizations in Syntagma Square. After the proclamation of the referendum, both camps held massive demonstrations in the capital. The YES mobilization took place on July 2, while the NO demonstration took place the following day with the prime minister delivering a passionate speech. Party flags were absent from the YES mobilizations, while in the NO demonstrations party flags of SYRIZA, ANEL and

Fig. 2. Photo Taken During the NO Mobilizations. The Banners Read 'Democracy WILL NOT BE Blackmailed', 'Peoples WILL NOT BE Blackmailed. SYRIZA'. *Source*: Photo taken by author.

Fig. 3. A Poster from the SYRIZA 'No' Campaign: 'With Head Held High, Say NO. Democracy-Dignity-Solidarity'. *Source*: Photo taken by author.

ANTARSYA were abundant along with the national flag. Mobilizations continued after the election as the attainment of an agreement with the EU was pending. The NO camp demonstrated under the slogan: 'The great feast of NO. Hands off democracy' (Iefimerida, 2015).

Anti-German arguments were prominent in the NO campaign. Most of them targeted German hegemony in Europe, German insistence on the austerity paradigm and the country's political leadership with the Minister of Finance Wolfgang Schäuble being portrayed as a sworn enemy of Greece. The use of WWII memories and the occupation metaphor were also generalized during the campaign. Moreover, as the word 'NO' was the main symbol of the Greek Resistance in WWII, it facilitated an association between the NO vote and the concept of resistance (Figs. 4 and 5).

The symbolic association between the EU and Nazism is a recent — and not yet generalized — trend in the manifestations of Greek Euroscepticism. The background which allowed for this association is the anti-German discourse which targeted the austerity policies and the German hegemony in the EU, often with recourse to Nazi imagery in order to denounce the current German

Fig. 4.   Poster from the NO Campaign Depicting Wolfgang Schäuble: 'For 5 Years He Has been Sucking Your Blood. Now Tell Him NO'. *Source*: Photo taken by the author.

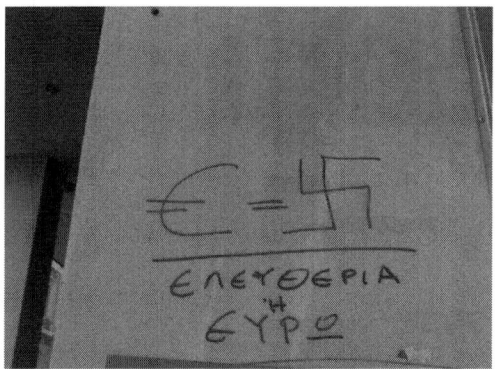

Fig. 5. Graffiti at Syntagma Square Equating the Euro with Swastika. Below the Slogan 'Liberty or Euro' Paraphrases the Emblematic Motto of the Greek War of Independence (1821−1829) 'Liberty or Death'. *Source*: Photo taken by author.

leadership and to the use of the Holocaust metaphor to describe the social and economic consequences of austerity (Lialiouti & Bithymitris, 2013, pp. 155−172). In this vein, after the announcement of the agreement, the front-line title of *Demokratia* was 'Greece at Auschwitz. Schauble seeks a Holocaust in the Eurozone' (*Demokratia*, 2015).

4. POLITICAL AND IDEOLOGICAL IMPLICATIONS OF THE REFERENDUM AND OF THE JULY 13 LOAN AGREEMENT

The outcome of the referendum, held with closed banks and capital controls, was an overwhelming victory for NO with a 61.3%, while the YES vote was limited to a 38.7%, to the surprise of many political analysts. The overwhelming victory of NO led to the resignation of former prime minister, and leader of the opposition, Antonis Samaras from the leadership of ND. It is worth commenting briefly on the socio-demographic features of the vote because they are particularly useful in shedding light on the origins of the emerging cleavage. The main finding of the electoral analyses in this respect is that the referendum portrays a deep generational and class divide with the youth and the lower social strata voting in impressive numbers for 'no'. Greeks under the age of 24 voted NO by 85%. Even though a thorough analysis of their electoral behaviour is in order, a first correlation with the 60% unemployment rate for the age group 18−24 can undoubtedly be seen as relevant (Louka, 2015).

The geographical distribution of the vote also highlights the emergence of a social divide. A comparison between the more privileged and the less privileged

areas of the wider capital district is revealing. In several popular neighbourhoods of Western Athens area, the NO vote scored at 67.5% and in the
Western Piraeus zone it reached a 72.5%. On the other hand, the northern,
middle and upper class Athens suburbs gave a YES majority – and even its
highest national score (Kifissia 63.9%, municipality of Ekali 84.6%).
Nikolakopoulos and Koustenis stress that the available data 'compose a picture
of class differentiation (with a socially structured No and an even more class
defined Yes) which ... is recorded to an unprecedented extent in post-civil war
electoral history'. Moreover, they argue that the result can be attributed to the
prevailing of the government's framing of the referendum as a pro- vs. anti-
memorandum dilemma – that is a vote on the continuation of austerity, while
the opposition failed to convince the electorate that their choice would be
between exit or stay in the Eurozone. (Nikolakopoulos & Koustenis, 2015) This
reading seems to be reinforced by opinion polls conducted after the referendum
according to which the overwhelming majority of the Greek people opted for
the Euro instead of a return to the national currency (Metron Analysis, 2015).
Finally, the referendum results seem to be related with the restructuring of the
party system under way since the outbreak of the crisis as the rather poor electoral attainment of YES was also interpreted as a rejection of the old political
personnel and of the established parties of the *Metapolitefsi* (1974–2010).

Political developments after the referendum influenced the content of the
public debate and the discourses employed. Despite the NO victory, the Prime
Minister continued negotiations with the EU seeking an agreement that would
allow the country's lending in the context of an austerity agenda. In trying to
defend this decision, which seemed contradictory, ministers and MPs emphasized the tremendous pressure Greece was put under by its European partners,
and most importantly Germany. As the minister for Culture stated 'We are facing very hard dilemmas. We are facing an intransigent Germany' (Xydakis,
2015).

Thus the YES camp avoided making a systematic and explicit account of its
electoral defeat promoting the goal of national unity and the absolute priority
of an agreement with the EU. Nevertheless, it is worth mentioning some self-
critical attempts from the YES camp stressing the individual and collective
responsibility in the development of the ideological trends that stemmed from
the period of crisis and were expressed by the NO vote. In this vein, a diplomat,
member of Potami and EU MP candidate described in an online article his personal and political state of 'depression':

> I admit that I feel weak. And rather guilty .... I feel standing in front of my children and my
> grandchildren as the representative of a generation that betrayed and has been
> betrayed ... The night of the referendum I understood how big my own mistake was. I used
> to speak before for the disaster of NO and the redemption of YES ... I thought: When Crete
> votes NO more than 70%, the right cannot be on my side. I do not know if someone has
> admitted that. It was a painful political defeat for the YES arguments. In reality, (a defeat)
> of the ideals and aspirations of a whole generation. (Mallias, 2015)

After the attainment of the agreement that put an end to the Grexit scenarios (13/7/2015), but involved particularly harsh austerity measures, public discourse was far from triumphalist. The concepts of defeat and humiliation prevailed in most narrations, while much of the blame for what was perceived as an extremely painful compromise was attributed to Germany, even by government opponents. A Euro-sceptical attitude, mainly focused on the German role — though not exclusively — and on the prevailing ideological paradigm in the EU, was dominant in most accounts of the events, while the concept of European solidarity was widely challenged and the concept of 'revenge' was in use.

The editorials of leftist pro-government newspapers denounced the role of Germany in the EU summit meeting:

> The Germans return, not by the force of arms, but by the power of their economy, seeking to impose their policies even to the governments of other countries of what euphemistically is now called 'united' Europe. What happened during the weekend in Brussels proves it. The vengeful Mr. Schäeuble unfolded his plans for Greek exit in five years' time from the Eurozone. The plan was distributed to his 'satellites' ... Greece has found some allies, albeit belatedly, the countries of the South. Their motives, of course, are related to internal political pressures on their governments, but also with the amount of their debts, which in some cases are larger than those of small Greece. The goal is obvious even to the most ignorant. Mr. Schäeuble and his faithful followers -Finland and others-do not want the change of power relations in Europe. They impose the law of the strong in every possible and impossible way. And Greece is the perfect guinea pig .... (*Efsyn*, 13 July 2015)

The belief that the terms of the agreement constituted national humiliation and a restraint on national sovereignty was widespread, but former Finance Minister Yanis Varoufakis went as far as to argue in the Parliament that the agreement was in essence another 'Versailles Treaty' (Varoufakis, 2015).

Former Minister and contender for the leadership of ND Nikos Dendias expressed discontent about the 'hostility towards our homeland' of 'smaller' EU-partners, such as the Baltic countries and Slovakia, in the EU negotiations. He acknowledged that there was not much Greece could do at the moment, but he insisted on the importance of 'institutional memory':

> We must remember who helped us in times of need, even with our own mistakes and who behaved in an intolerable way and tried to humiliate our country ... I even remember some of the ministers from these countries coming to Greece a few years ago asking for our help to bend accession criteria and join the EU and now they point a finger at us ... We have to tolerate stuff now, but we mustn't forget them. (Dendias, 2015)

The political debate on the approval of the agreement in the Parliament was characterized by a prima facie paradox. Apart from the two governing partners who were particularly critical of the agreement, also the parties that formed the YES camp — and particularly ND and PASOK — stressed that its terms were very unfavourable to the Greek side, while insisting that its approval was necessary for the country's survival. One conceptual implication of this political attitude was the acknowledgement of a divergence between justice and necessity.

Golden Dawn rejected the agreement and presented itself as the only genuine representative of the 'proud No of the National Resistance of the Greeks' (Golden Dawn, 2015a). Its leader characterized the agreement as an 'economic enslavement' and compared it to the German invasion of 1941 (Golden Dawn, 2015b).

A part of SYRIZA's MPs (almost 40 in a total of 149) rejected the agreement in the Parliament provoking a bitter split in the governing party. Moreover, they explicitly opted for an exit from the Eurozone and return to the national currency founding a new party ('Popular Unity'). The YES camp parties and the majority of broadcast networks argued that such a political stance was traitorous. Even before the schism, POTAMI had warned: 'If we do not hold on in Europe, that will be treason ... and it will be dealt as treason by the Greek people' (Theodorakis, 2015a). Later on, POTAMI leader coined the term 'drachma-gang' for the supporters of a Grexit scenario. The term could be associated with 'bandits', which was used in the context of the Greek Civil War to denounce pro-communist guerrillas (Theodorakis, 2015b).

5. THE USES OF HISTORICAL ANALOGIES

In the highly-charged public debates on the referendum, historical analogies gained prominence in the construction of political identities and in justifying and (de)-legitimizing patterns of political behaviour. In such a context of transformation of existing cleavages and political identities, historical analogies have particular normative functions and serve as means of orientation for collective and individual political behaviour. The choice of historical analogies employed in the referendum context is associated with the distinct interpretive schemes that prevailed during the Greece economic crisis. While the WWII historical analogy, previously discussed, did not lose its symbolic and emotional power, two other cases of historical analogies became particularly relevant during the referendum campaign.

The first was employed by the YES camp and it was based on the internal political confrontation, which almost turned into civil war, that preceded the 1922 Catastrophe in Asia Minor, a particularly painful historical memory for Greeks. In 1920, in the midst of a critical Greek military expedition in Asia Minor, as a result of the WWI peace accords with the allies of Entente, national elections were held. The Prime Minister, Eleftherios Venizelos, a bourgeois politician with international reputation and a mythical figure for Greek liberals and centrists to this day, was defeated by the unified opposition forces, which campaigned on the promise to terminate the expedition and bring back the Greek troops. This promise was of particular appeal to Greek public opinion since Greece had been on war mobilization since the Balkan wars of 1912–1914. Soon after the election, the new Greek government held a contested referendum that allowed the return to the throne of King Konstantine which was particularly unwelcome by the Entente allies. As a result, Greece lost the support of its allies when it was most needed. Moreover, the government did not fulfil its promises to end the expedition and made grave diplomatic and military mistakes that ultimately led to a military defeat and to the uprooting of the Greek-speaking population from Asia Minor (Mavrogordatos, 1983; Smith, 1998). The events of 1920–1922 are inscribed in the context of the National Schism (1914–1917), which created the cleavage between Venizelists vs. anti-Venizelist (or 'law-abiding' people), which in the post-war period was shaped into the cleavage between the 'nationally minded' vs. the 'non-nationally minded' (Mavrogordatos, 1983; Nikolakopoulos, 2001; Papadimitriou, 2006).

In our context, the important themes in the 1920 historical analogy are the following: populist politicians may deceive the electorate and lead to disastrous outcomes, the country's leadership should be likeable to international allies or else Greece risks isolation, and referenda can have unpredictable and disastrous outcomes- therefore the current referendum was commonly characterized as 'dangerous'. These themes combined with a reading of the pro-memorandum vs. anti-memorandum cleavage as a dichotomy between realism vs. irrationalism were employed to denounce the government's decision to hold a referendum and to urge for a YES vote. As a columnist put it 'With the referendum we go back to Sangarius river [i.e. the location of one of the critical battles in the Asia Minor expedition between the Greek and the Turkish army] ... Fifteen years since the turn of the century, we open a deep national wound ...' (Anastassakos, 2015).

An academic in his support for YES made thorough reference to the 1920 historical analogy insisting on the similarities with the 2015 referendum:

> A first similarity, thus, is the avoidance of responsibility for a dangerous decision and its transfer to the people – by a government that just won the elections. A second similarity is the deception of the people, taking advantage of their emotional charge and the hasty seizure of their vote .... Ultimately, the 1920 referendum was an opportunity not for sober and mature decision making, but for the explosive manifestation of the emotions of popular majority. (Mavrogordatos, 2015)

The second historical analogy employed by the NO camp, and particularly by SYRIZA and other leftist groups, is based on the political crisis of July 1965 that led to the downfall of the Papandreou government and to a period of social unrest and political instability that ended with the military coup of 1967. The crisis was triggered by the confrontation between King Konstantine and Prime Minister Georgios Papandreou on the constitutional limits of the Crown's powers and the government's desire to have control over the army. After Papandreou was forced to resign, the King imposed governments of his choice, which were short-lived, provoking popular outcry. An important element in the public perception of the political crisis was the allegation that the so-called 'American factor' was involved in the undermining of the lawfully elected government due to the independent stance of the Papandreou government in foreign policy issues. Although Centrist and anti-communist, Papandreou became a symbol of democracy for wider popular strata (Nikolakopoulos, 2001, pp. 339–352; Rizas, 2008, pp. 334–364). The July crisis and its aftermath was decisive in the transformation of the cleavage between the nationally minded vs. the non-nationally minded into the cleavage between Right vs. Anti-Right which became the prevailing cleavage after the restoration of democracy (1974) (Moschonas, 1994; Nikolakopoulos, 2001, pp. 163–169). In the following decades the July crisis – the so-called 'Iouliana' – with extensive references on the US role in the weakening of Greek democracy had a prominent place in public history and in the construction and reproduction of the identity of the Greek Center Left.

During the NO square mobilization held before and after the referendum, posters, banners and slogans made explicit reference to 'Iouliana' even more as this coincided with its 50-year anniversary (Fig. 6).

The July 1965 analogy and the coup theme gained a prominent place in the governing parties' political discourse after the attainment of a loan agreement between Greece and her creditors on the EU summit meeting of July 12. On the morning of the agreement, the themes of a cruel German hegemony, of a coup committed against the Greek government and a revengeful policy against Greece had a prominent place in the editorial of SYRIZA's party newspaper *Avgi*:

> The masks fell. In Brussels not only a criminal extortion is attempted to drag Greece into a disastrous agreement; a coup is underway in order to overthrow the lawfully elected government in Greece and the presumptuous Tsipras. Simultaneously a vindictive punishment of the Greek people is pursued, in a way that only Germany can perform, because with the referendum we did not comply with the instructions. Greece and the government of SYRIZA, if the plan succeeds, will be the first victims of a new European winter which will bury the postwar achievements of the continent and the hopes for a united democratic Europe. It may be the beginning of the end for the EU itself ... Germany is not entitled to destroy Europe for the third time in 100 years. (*Avgi*, 2015b)

In his statement on the announcement of the agreement Tsipras said that Greece would keep fighting to 'gain back her lost national sovereignty', while he argued that she had already gained her 'popular sovereignty' and had managed to spread the 'message of democracy, the message of dignity' throughout Europe (Tsipras, 2015a). In a TV interview Tsipras also said that he faced the 'revengeful stance' of EU-partners in the summit meeting and that he 'overestimated the power of a people's right' as well as the respect of Europeans towards democracy (Tsipras, 2015b). Repeatedly afterwards, he stressed that he was totally opposed to the content of the agreement, but he nonetheless was obliged to implement it because the country was threatened with destruction.

On the evening after the agreement, leftist extra-parliamentary groups, trade union organizations as well as SYRIZA's youth organization protested against

Fig. 6. Poster and Banner at Syntagma Square Advertising a Public Discussion on the July 1965 Crisis Held on July 16th Organized by a Leftist pro-SYRIZA Journal. The Event was Entitled 'Iouliana 1965–2015. About 70 Days During Which Everything was Possible, the Messages are Still Timely'. *Source*: Photos taken by author.

the agreement, which they framed as a European 'coup' and as 'process of humiliation', at Syntagma square under the slogan 'there is no future in the EU' (www.in.gr 2015). According to the declaration issued by SYRIZA's youth organization the protest aimed to oppose the 'coup committed by the political leadership of the Eurozone against our people' (SYRIZA Youth Organization, 2015). A similar demonstration took place 2 days later on the ratification of the agreement by the Parliament (Fig. 7).

Fig. 6. (*Continued*)

Fig. 7. Banner from the July 15 Mobilization Against the Agreement. It Reads: 'Greece is Not a Colony. NO. There is Another Way!' The Small Letter 'δ' is the Greek Initial For Drachma. *Source*: Photo taken by author.

The coup narrative was adapted to the internal political conditions created after the agreement. The austerity measures that should be implemented in its context represented a major political challenge for the coalition government of two anti-memorandum parties. The problem was more acute for SYRIZA with many of its members and MPs rejecting the agreement and threatening government stability. In this respect, a narration elaborated by SYRIZA argued that the rejection of the agreement in the Parliament would actually serve the creditors' plan to overthrow the government and would be tantamount to a coup. The statement made by the SYRIZA's parliamentary spokesman Nikos Filis is premised upon this equation:

> Today what matters is for the Parliament to express a response to the coup; to save the country from economic bankruptcy ... we will not collaborate in overthrowing the popular will of January. We will respond to the coup against the country ... The government has been threatened by forces abroad that did not forgive us for making a different choice. (Filis, 2015)

Serving similar purposes — that is justifying his stay in government despite his proclaimed disagreement with the terms of the agreement — P. Kammenos, leader of ANEL and Secretary of Defense, defended Tsipras' handlings in the EU summit meeting by arguing that the Greek Prime Minister 'faced a coup (committed) by Germany, and other countries as well such as Finland and the Baltic countries. A coup that went as far as to blackmail the Prime Minister with bank collapse and total haircut on deposits'. (Kammenos, 2015a) Later on the same day, he stressed that the attempted coup was still under way aiming to

Fig. 8. Poster at Syntagma Square at the Demonstration of the NO Camp Held After the Referendum. It Reads: 'When 63% say No, we Mean 100% No to the Memoranda, the Austerity, the Blackmails, the Debt, the Troika ...' *Source*: Photo taken by author.

'replace (the government) with one that is not the Greek people's choosing' (Kammenos, 2015b). Overall, the coup narrative combined connotations of victimization by foreigners and heroism (Fig. 8).

6. CONCLUDING REMARKS

To conclude, the 2015 referendum and the July 13 Greece-EU agreement are milestones in terms of existing cleavages and Greek Euroscepticism. The implementation of austerity policies in the context of the new agreement by an anti-memorandum coalition government is inevitably a challenge for the formulation and the representation of anti-austerity political views. In parallel, the experience of the referendum and the square mobilizations that addressed the issues of the loan agreements and relations with the EU has created an important ideological and discursive legacy. It is still an open question whether opposing views and confrontation on these issues can lead to the crystallization of a cleavage centred on Europe or on the currency. The aim of this chapter was to shed light on the discursive building materials that could structure this emerging cleavage and on the process of its formulation. In relation to this, it can be argued that the discursive negotiation of Europe in the Greek public debate is characterized by ambiguity and has acquired various negative connotations (e.g. 'Europe' being associated with austerity policies, German hegemony, authoritarianism and democratic deficit in decision-making). The set of themes, metaphors and historical analogies (e.g. blackmail, war, coup and physical abuse themes) employed point to elements of an enemy construction. Moreover, they shape a conceptual dichotomy between justice vs. injustice that associates Europe with the interpretive scheme of victimization.

REFERENCES

Anastassakos, Y. (2015). "Fliskouni ki agria menda", Protagon.gr. 28 June. Retrieved from http://www.protagon.gr/?i=protagon.el.article&id=41735. Accessed July 14, 2015.

Avgi. (2015a). Editorial: '5 July Referendum:NO', 5 July. Retrieved from https://www.frontpages.gr/d/20150704/13/%CE%91%CF%85%CE%B3%CE%AE. Accessed July 6, 2015.

Avgi (2015b). Editorial: "Thrice the same mistake?", 13 July.

Berg, B. L. (2001). *Qualitative Research Methods for the Social Sciences* (4th ed.). Boston and London: Pearson Education Company.

Boomgaarden, H., Schuck, A., Elenbaas, M., & De Vreese, C. H. (2010). Mapping EU Attitudes: Conceptual and empirical dimensions of Euroscepticism and EU support. *European Union Politics*, *12*(2), 241−266.

Botsiou, K. (2010). The origins of Greece's European policy. In *The Constantinos Karamanlis Institute for Democracy Yearbook 2010* (pp. 93−108). Heidelberg: Springer Berlin.

Bosco, A., & Verney, S. (2012). Electoral epidemic: The political cost of economic crisis in Southern Europe, 2010–2011. *South European Society and Politics*, *17*(2), 129−154.

Boukala, S. (2014). Waiting for democracy: Political crisis and the discursive (re)invention of the 'national enemy' in times of 'Grecovery'. *Discourse and Society*, *25*(4), 483–499.

Chomenidis, C. (2015). Adulthood or crush. *Ta Nea*, 3 July. Retrieved from http://www.tanea.gr/opinions/all-opinions/article/5254884/enhlikiwsh-h-syntribh/. Accessed July 6, 2015.

Demokratia. (2015). Editorial: 'Greece at Auschwitz', 13 July. Retrieved from http://www.dimokratianews.gr/protoselida. Accessed July 14, 2015.

Dendias, N. (2015). "TV interview", 13 July. Retrieved from http://dendias.gr/gr/read/1888/. Accessed July 13, 2015.

Dimou, N. (2015). "We stay home!", Protagon.gr. 22 June. Retrieved from http://www.protagon.gr/?i=protagon.el.ellada&id=41628. Accessed July 20, 2015.

Dinas, E., et al. (2013). From dusk to dawn local party organization and party success of right-wing extremism. *Party Politics*, 1354068813511381.

Diner, D. (1996). *America in the eyes of the Germans. An essay on anti-Americanism*. Princeton, NJ: Markus Wiener.

Efsyn. (2015). Editorial: "'No' to German Europe". July 13. Retrieved from http://www.efsyn.gr/arthro/ohi-sti-germaniki-eyropi. accessed July 13, 2015.

Eleftheriou, K., & Tassis, C. (2013). *PASOK. The rise and fall (?) of a hegemonic party*. Athens: Savvalas.

Eurobarometer.(2013). "Standard EB 80, November 2013". Retrieved from http://ec.europa.eu/public_opinion/archives/eb/eb80/eb80_en.htm. Accessed July 14, 2015.

Filis, N. (2015). "Statement", 14 July. Retrieved from http://www.iefimerida.gr/news/217087/o-filis-aporriptei-tin-kyvernisi-eidikoy-skopoy-den-prepei-na-yparxei-aristeri. Accessed July 14, 2015.

Georgiadou, V. (2013). Right-wing populism and extremism: The rapid rise of "golden dawn" in crisis-ridden Greece. In R. Melzer & S. Serafin (Eds.), *Right-wing extremism in Europe* (pp. 75–102). Bohn: FES.

Golden Dawn. (2015a). http://www.xryshaygh.com/deltiatypou/view/diaggelma-archhgou-chrushs-aughs-gia-to-ochi-sto-dhmopshfisma. Accessed July 20, 2015.

Golden Dawn. (2015b). http://www.xryshaygh.com/deltiatypou/view/mono-h-chrush-augh-ekfrazei-to-uperhfano-ochi-ths-ethnikhs-antistashs-. Accessed July 20, 2015.

Halikiopoulou, D., Nanou, K., & Vasilopoulou, S. (2012). The paradox of nationalism: The common denominator of radical right and radical left euroscepticism. *European Journal of Political Research*, *51*(4), 504–539.

Iefimerida. (2015). 10 July. http://www.iefimerida.gr/news/216455/ohi-apopse-pali-sto-syntagma-deite-ti-zitoyn. Accessed July 11, 2015.

Iordanidis, K. (2015). The new schism. *Kathimerini*, 28 June. Retrieved from http://www.kathimerini.gr/821277/opinion/epikairothta/politikh/o-neos-dixasmos. Accessed July 10, 2015.

Kammenos, P. (2015a). Statement, 14 July. Retrieved from http://www.iefimerida.gr/news/217017/rixi-stin-kyvernisi-o-kammenos-kataggellei-praxikopima. Accessed July 14, 2015.

Kammenos, P. (2015b). Statement, 14 July. Retrieved from http://news247.gr/eidiseis/politiki/sthrizei-me-asteriskoys-o-kammenos-de-tha-epitrepsoyme-praksikophma.3574122.html. Accessed July 15, 2015.

Karner, C., & Mertens, B. (2013). Introduction: Memories and analogies of World War II. In C. Karner & B. Mertens (Eds.), *The use and abuse of memory: interpreting World War II in contemporary European politics* (pp. 1–21). New Brunswick: Transaction Publishers.

Kathimerini. (2015). Editorial. In P. Kitromilides (ed.), Eleftherios Venizelos: The trials of statesmanship. Edinburgh: Edinburgh University Press.

Konstantaras, N. (2015). It's time to change our lives. *Kathimerini*, 4 July. Retrieved from http://www.kathimerini.gr/822252/opinion/epikairothta/politikh/wra-na-alla3oyme-zwh. Accessed July 6, 2015

Kopecký, P., & Mudde, C. (2002). The two sides of Euroscepticism: Party positions on European integration in East Central Europe. *European Union Politics*, *3*(3), 297–326.

Kousis, M., & Kanellopoulos, K. (2014). Democracy at a crossroads: Austerity, protest and politics in Greece. Paper presented at the SNES Conference "Elections and Democracy in Europe", Brussels, Belgium, April 7-9.

Krouwel, A., & Abts, K. (2007). Varieties of Euroscepticism and populist mobilization: Transforming attitudes from mild Euroscepticism to harsh Eurocynicism. *ActaPolitica, 42*, 252–270.

Leconte, C. (2010). *Understanding Euroscepticism*. Houndmills: Palgrave Macmillan.

Lialiouti, Z., & Bithymitris, G. (2013). 'The Nazis Strike Again': the concept of the 'German Enemy', party strategies and mass perceptions through the prism of the Greek economic crisis. In C. Karner & B. Mertens (Eds.), *The use and abuse of memory: Interpreting World War II in contemporary European politics* (pp. 155–172). New Jersey: Transaction Publishers.

Lialiouti, Z., & Bithymitris, G. (2014). Implications of the Greek crisis: Nationalism, enemy stereotypes, and the European Union. In B. Stefanova (Ed.), *The European Union beyond the crisis. Evolving governance, contested policies and disenchanted publics* (pp. 249–267). Lanham, MD: Lexington Books.

Lialiouti, Z., & Bithymitris, G. (2017). A nation under attack: Perceptions of enmity and victimhood in the context of the Greek crisis. *National Identities*, Special Issue: *Dividing United Europe*, 19(1), 53–71.

Louka, M. (2015). The new generation of 'NO'. *Vimagazino*, 12 July. Retrieved from http://www.tovima.gr/vimagazino/views/article/?aid=721833. Accessed July 15, 2015.

Mallias, A. (2015). Days of depression. Protagon.gr. 11 July. Retrieved from http://www.protagon.gr/?i=protagon.el.politiki&id=42056. Accessed July 15, 2015.

Mavrogordatos, G. (1983). *Stillborn republic. Social coalitions and party strategies, 1922-1936*. Berkeley, CA: University of California Press.

Mavrogordatos, G. (2015). Psomi, elia ke Kotsovasilia? Protagon.gr. 5 July. Retrieved from http://www.protagon.gr/?i=protagon.el.article&id=41931. Accessed July 14, 2015.

Metron Analysis. (2015). Pan-Hellenic public opinion research, July 11. Retrieved from http://www.politicometro.gr/timeline/polls/metronanalysis/20150711metron4parapolitika/. Accessed July 15, 2015.

Moschonas, G. (1994). The cleavage right vs. anti-right in the post-authoritarian period (1974-1990). In N. Demertzis (ed.), *Greek political culture today* (pp. 159–216). Athens: Odysseas. (in Greek).

ND. (2015). TV Spot. Retrieved from http://nd.gr//nai-stin-europi. Accessed July 8, 2015.

Nikolakopoulos, E. (2001). *Sickly democracy: Parties and elections 1946-1967*. Athens: Patakis.

Nikolakopoulos, E., & Koustenis, P. (2015). The 'No' X-Ray. *Ta Nea*, 11-12 July.

Pantazopoulos, A. (2001). *"For the People and the Nation". The Moment Andreas Papandreou*. Athens: Polis. (in Greek).

Papadimitriou, D. (2006). *From the law-abiding people to the nation of the nationally-minded. Conservative thought in Greece, 1922-1967*. Athens: Savvalas. (in Greek).

Pavlopoulos, P. (2015). Statement, 22 June. Retrieved from http://www.imerisia.gr/article.asp?catid=26509&subid=2&pubid=113558967. Accessed July 10, 2015.

Rizas, S. (2008). *Greek politics after the Civil War: Parliamentarism and dictatorship*. Athens: Kastaniotis. (in Greek).

Rizospastis. (2015). Editorial: 'We abolish the false dilemmas', 4–5 July. Retrieved from http://www.enikos.gr/media/327409/oi-politikes-efimerides-472015. Accessed July 6, 2015.

Roger, P. (2002). *L'Ennemi Americain. Genealogie de l' Antiamericanisme Francais*. Paris: Seuil.

Serrichio, F., Tsakatika, M., & Quagli, L. (2013). Euroscepticism and the global financial crisis. *Journal of Common Market Studies, 51*(1), 51–64.

Smith, M. L. (1998). *Ionian Vision: Greece in Asia Minor, 1919-1920*. London: Hurst&Co.

SYRIZA. (2015). TV Spot. Retrieved from http://www.syriza.gr/article/id/61871/1o-thleoptiko-spot-ths-kampanias-toy-OCHI.html#.VZ_HPJcXXCs. Accessed July 8, 2015.

SYRIZA Youth Organization. (2015). Announcement. Retrieved from http://neolaiasyriza.gr/%CE%B1%CE%BD%CE%B1%CE%BA%CE%BF%CE%AF%CE%BD%CF%89%CF%

83%CE%B7-%CE%BD%CE%B5%CE%BF%CE%BB%CE%B1%CE%AF%CE%B1%
CF%82-%CF%83%CF%85%CF%81%CE%B9%CE%B6%CE%B1/. Accessed July 14,
2015.

Szczerbiak, A., & Taggart, P. (2008). Theorizing party-based Euroscepticism: Problems of definition, measurement and causality. In A. Szczerbiak & P. Taggart (Eds.), *Opposing Europe? The comparative party politics of Euroscepticism. Volume 2: Comparative and theoretical perspectives* (pp. 238–262). Oxford: Oxford University Press.

Taggart, P. (1998). A touchstone of dissent: Euroscepticism in contemporary western European party system. *European Journal of Political Research, 33*(3), 363–388.

Teperoglou, E., & Tsatsanis, E. (2014). Dealignment, de-legitimation and the implosion of the two-party system in Greece: The earthquake election of 6 May 2012. *Journal of Elections, Public Opinion & Parties, 24*(2), 222–242.

Theodorakis, S. (2015a). Statement, 8 July. Retrieved from http://topotami.gr/nea/stavros-theodora-kis-an-den-kratithoume-stin-e-e-tha-ine-prodosia/. Accessed July 8, 2015.

Theodorakis, S. (2015b). Statement, 17 July. Retrieved from http://www.iefimerida.gr/news/217711/ theodorakis-elpizo-oi-anthropoi-tis-drahmosymmorias-na-loyfaxoyn. Accessed July 17, 2015.

Tsipras, A. (2015a). Statement, 8 July. Retrieved from http://www.stokokkino.gr/article/ 1000000000012739/SUNEXIS-ENIMEROSI-Sti-Bouli-i-elliniki-protasi–Tsipras-stin-KO-kai-ti-PG-tou-SURIZA-Ego-Papadimos-den-ginomai. Accessed July 8, 2015.

Tsipras, A. (2015b). Statement, 13 July. Retrieved from http://www.iefimerida.gr/news/216887/tsi-prasto-grexit-apotelei-parelthon-petyhame-polla-dyskoli-i-symfonia. Accessed July 13, 2015.

Van Dijk, T. A. (2006). Ideology and discourse analysis. *Journal of Political Ideologies, 11*(2), 115–140.

Varoufakis, Y. (2015). "Speech", 16 July. https://www.efsyn.gr/arthro/gianis-varoyfakis-nea-synthiki-ton-versalion, last accessed 21/07/2015.

Vasilopoulou, S. (2013). Continuity and change in the study of Euroscepticism: Plus ça change? *JCMS: Journal of Common Market Studies, 51*(1), 153–168.

Vasilopoulou, S., Halikiopoulou, D., & Exadaktylos, T. (2014). Greece in crisis: Austerity, populism and the politics of blame. *JCMS: Journal of Common Market Studies, 52*(2), 388–402.

Vernardakis, C. (2007). Pro-Europeanism and Euroscepticism in Greece. In C. Vernardakis (Ed.), *Public Opinion in Greece 2005-2006* (pp. 147–164). Athens: Savvalas.

Verney, S. (2011). An exceptional case? Party and popular Euroscepticism in Greece 1959-2009. *South European Society and Politics, 16,* 51–79.

Voulgaris, Y. (2013). *Post-authoritarian Greece 1974-2009.* Athens: Polis.

Wessels, B. (2007). Discontent and European identity: Three types of Euroscepticism. *ActaPolitica, 42,* 287–306.

Wodak, R., & Angouri, J. (2014). From Grexit to Grecovery: Euro/crisis discourses. *Discourse and Society, 25*(4), 417–423.

Wodak, R., de Cillia, R., Reisigl, M., & Liebhart, K. (2009). *The discursive construction of national identity.* A. Hirsch, R. Mitten, & J. W. Unger (Translated by) Edinburgh: Edinburgh University Press. https://www.facebook.com/events/1456814541227075/, last accessed 20/07/ 2015. http://www.facebook.com/events/112764409059937/, last accessed 20/07/2015. www.in. gr. (2015)13 July. http://news.in.gr/greece/article/?aid=1500012123, last accessed 14/07/2015.

Xydakis, N. (2015). Statement, 10 July. Retrieved from http://www.stokokkino.gr/article/100000 0000012739/SUNEXIS-ENIMEROSI-KSekinise-i-sunedriasi-tis-olomeleias-sti-Bouli–Tsipras-stin-KO-kai-ti-PG-tou-SURIZA-Ego-Papadimos-den-ginomai. Accessed July 14, 2015.

TOWARDS A (DIS)INTEGRATED EUROPE: THE CONSTRUCTS OF 'EUROPE' AND 'TROIKA' VERSUS 'PORTUGAL' AND 'THE PORTUGUESE' IN A CORPUS OF PORTUGUESE OPINION ARTICLES

Alexandra Pinto

ABSTRACT

Based on theoretical principles of Semantics, Pragmatics and Discourse Analysis/Discourse Studies, the present work analysed a corpus of opinion articles, published in Portuguese newspapers and news magazines from December 2011 to March 2013, in order to foreground the dominant social representations of 'Troika', 'The Portuguese Government' and 'The Portuguese' in these discourses.

A systematic analysis of discourse structures in the corpus was developed in order to examine their potential in the expression of ideological content. Concepts such as Semantic/Thematic Roles, Force Dynamics and Symmetry were combined with analytic models from Discourse Studies to illustrate the Ideological Discourse Representations and the Positions in the Discourse Space (DS) of Social Actors. The linguistic hypotheses and generalisations were generated bottom up, departing from the regular patterns observable in the empirical data and extracting conclusions from them. The interpretative practice was, therefore, made in adherence to corpus evidence.

National Identity and Europe in Times of Crisis: Doing and Undoing Europe, 187–209
doi:10.1108/978-1-78714-513-920171009

This integrated analysis has shown that the reconstruction of 'Portugal' and 'the Portuguese' vis-a-vis 'Europe', represented by 'Troika', corresponds to opponent positioning that polarise these entities, foregrounding the distance and the conflict between them and contributing to a vision of a disintegrated Europe. In fact, the reality depicted in the opinion articles analysed was a polarised reality, in the sense that these articles repeatedly used linguistic constructions that placed (through several rhetoric devices that will be ana- lysed) Europe and Troika on one 'pole' and 'The Portuguese' on the other 'pole', expressing, thus, the movement of the actors to polar opposites.

On the theoretical level, this chapter proposes an integrated approach towards opinion discourse in the press, combining Critical Discourse analytic and DS Theory perspectives with the insights from Socio-Cognitive approach by Van Dijk and aspects of Cognitive Linguistics by Talmy.

Keywords: Polarisation; *Troika*/Europe; the Portuguese; opinion articles; discourse structures; ideological content

1. INTRODUCTION

On 6 April 2011, the Portuguese Socialist Prime Minister, Mr. José Sócrates, announced that his government had sent a request for financial assistance to the European Commission (EC) to ensure financing for Portugal and its eco- nomic and financial system. Soon thereafter, a technical mission from the EC, the European Central Bank (ECB) and the International Monetary Fund (IMF) – the so-called 'Troika'[1] – arrived in Portugal to start negotiations on the financial aid programme for the country that began to be implemented in May 2011.

Together with the financial aid came the stringent austerity measures that deepened the Portuguese economic crisis and political disbelief. The spiralling growth of public debt, increasing unemployment, loss of competitiveness, the pressure of the financial markets and of European demands led Portugal to the understanding that the so-called adjustment and recovery programme was a remote and optimistic scenario that did not apply to the day-to-day life of the Portuguese people.

Soon, as the national government lost political and administrative auton- omy, the overall feeling of loss of sovereignty and public humiliation spread throughout the country and the European project entered an identity crisis. When the early parliamentary elections in 2011 and the presidential elections in 2012 in Portugal took place, people were already aware that the results were of minor consequence for the future of the country. That future was being decided by more distant entities, such as the ratings of the financial markets and the pressures by European partners and the IMF for Portugal to fulfil the agreement.

A generalised atmosphere of sadness and disbelief marked the social scenario in Portugal at the time, disaffecting people from the political processes, increasing their apathy and lowering voter turnout. Political leaders and the population had ambiguous feelings towards the Troika, conscious, on the one hand, of the vital issue of financial assistance, but angry and recalcitrant, on the other hand, because of the austerity measures imposed. The socio-economic context was, thus, dysphoric, contributing to a scenario of potential conflict among the actors involved − the Troika, Europe, the Portuguese and the Portuguese government − and to the coexistence of opposing feelings towards Europe and Troika.

No referendum on the Troika intervention in Portugal was ever held during the whole 3-year period of the bailout programme, a fact which makes it difficult to gauge public opinion towards Europe as represented by the Troika at this historic moment. Still, during this period, many articles about the European/IMF intervention in Portugal appeared in the Portuguese press, providing a very rich core of information to further comprehend this outstanding moment in the history of the country and Europe.

In order to assess the dominant social representations of 'Troika', 'the Portuguese Government' and 'the Portuguese' in media opinion discourse at the time of the bailout, the present study analyses a corpus of 62 opinion articles on the Troika intervention in Portugal, published in Portuguese newspapers from December 2011 to March 2013. The underlying conviction is that the dominant representations emerging from these public discourses can mirror the dominant public opinion about the matter.[2]

Taken from *general*-interest newspapers and news magazines in the Portuguese publishing market such as, *Jornal Expresso; Jornal Público; Revista Visão; Diário Económico e Jornal de Negócios,* the articles were written by journalists and commentators that represent a variety of political tendencies, from conservative right-wing to moderate and left-wing positions. In view of the general-interest nature of the publications consulted, no extremist positions, either to the left or to the right, were assumed by the political commentators and economic analysts of the articles chosen. *Jornal Expresso* is currently the most read weekly newspaper in Portugal, with a centre-right political orientation, while *Jornal Público*, the most widely read daily newspaper with national coverage, has a centre-left orientation. *Revista Visão* is the most read weekly news magazine in Portugal, with an overall liberal political leaning and regular contributions by centre-right as well as centre-left columnists. Finally, *Diário Económico* and *Jornal de Negócios* are the two leading daily business newspapers in Portugal, covering the specialised economic side of the Troika's presence in Portugal. The choice of the media was thus related to their capacity to represent the dominant public opinion at the time under analysis, taking into consideration that they are the most read publications in their respective target audiences.

The filter applied to the collection of opinion articles was a thematic filter led by lexical co-occurrences of the words 'troika' and 'Europe', on one side, and 'Portugal'/'Portuguese Government'/'Portuguese State'/'the Portuguese'/ 'Portuguese people', on the other side.[3] The corpus tool applied to analyse the data was VISL.[4]

This is a corpus-driven study[5] whose linguistic constructs have emerged from the analysis of the corpus and from the evidence that the dynamic of forces between the social and discursive actors 'the Troika/Europe' vs 'The Portuguese' was of a conflicting nature. In fact, the reality depicted in the opinion articles analysed was a polarised reality, in the sense that these articles repeatedly used linguistic constructions that placed (through several rhetoric devices that will be analysed) Europe and Troika on one 'pole' and 'The Portuguese' on the other 'pole', expressing, thus, the movement of the actors to polar opposites. By this definition, a polarised construct of Europe and the Portuguese means a divided reality in which Europe and the Portuguese occupy remote, extreme, not centrist, positions and increasing polarisation would indicate movement towards the poles.

The linguistic hypotheses and generalisations in this study were generated bottom up, departing from the regular patterns observable in the empirical data and extracting conclusions from them. Our interpretative practice was, therefore, made in adherence to corpus evidence. Semantic-pragmatic patterns such as the distribution of the thematic roles − in particular the question of *agency* − and the organisation of *deixis* in the discourse were some of the linguistic constructs that emerged from the empirical data, showing a recurrence of events in usage that was revealing. It will become clear in the process of the analysis that these two linguistic frames became important means to construct the polarisation of reality in the discourses studied.[6]

Furthermore, we believe, with Van Dijk and his socio-cognitive approach, that ideologies, as systems of fundamental social cognition that organise social representations shared by members of groups, are produced and reproduced in discourse (Van Dijk, 1995), namely by means of some of the semantic structures that function as vehicles carrying the ideological contents. Our analysis of recurrent discourse structures in the chosen corpus has, therefore, the objective of examining their potential for the expression of a particular ideological content.

In general, the analysis will demonstrate that the reconstruction of 'Portugal' and 'the Portuguese' as a nation, vis-a-vis 'Europe' − as represented by 'Troika' − corresponds to two opposing positions that polarise these entities, foregrounding the distance between them and contributing to a vision of a disintegrated Europe.

Our interpretation of the data available in the corpus is, thus, based on an eclectic approach derived from the theoretical and methodological principles of Semantics, Pragmatics and Discourse Analysis/Discourse Studies.

2. SEMANTIC ROLES; FORCE DYNAMICS AND IDEOLOGICAL POSITIONS

In order to ascertain the correspondences between the linguistic structures and their possible ideological values, we have adopted, in this section, a semantic-pragmatic perspective over the predicators, the arguments, and the semantic roles assigned to them in the discourse structures of the corpus studied. Our research goal was to examine how the concept of *troika* was dealt within the opinion articles collected and what relationship was established between the *troika*, *Portugal* and *the Portuguese*.

At this point of our study, the multidisciplinary project of socio-cognitive approach, which combines discourse structures with cognitive and the social structures, shows good potential for interpretative insight into our data. As Van Dijk has stated:

> Among the various levels of discourse at which ideologies may be seen to manifest them-
> selves, the level of meaning and reference plays a central role. Cognitive representations of
> attitudes and models may directly map onto semantic representations. (1995, p. 256)

And the same author further develops his thoughts thus:

> Schematic cognitive categories such as Setting (Place, Time), Circumstances, Actors, Actions,
> Processes, the involvement of the Social Actors in the processes, in particular positive or neg-
> ative events and different types or degrees of responsibility of the Social Actors are mental
> models that appear in the functional structure (semantic roles) of propositions expressed in
> the sentences. As such, propositional structures may also be ideologically controlled. (1995,
> p. 258)

The question of the mental model, as a cognitive structure of apprehending reality, is central in Van Dijk's socio-cognitive approach, in the sense that it is the means that permits the triangulation between cognitive structures, social structures and discourse structures ('the *triangulation* of *discourse, cognition* and *society*'; Van Dijk, 2006a, 2006b). Mental models are mental representations of situations and their categorisation into basic contents such as Time, Place, Participants and, according to Van Dijk, we can admit the existence of a social cognition in the cases in which the construction of the mental model is filtered through the beliefs, the knowledge, and the shared memories in the social group. Ideological social groups share what they experience to be 'true beliefs' about situations, these mental models being 'true' inside a certain epistemic community. Discourse is the expression of mental models and, as such, it can be the expression of ideological, socially construed, representations.

This seems to be the case in the opinion articles analysed in our study, where the discourse structures point to a recurrent mental model of the situations where *the troika* and *the Portuguese* interact as antagonists *Participants* in a *Time* and *Place*.

Therefore, our interpretation of these functional recurrences was based on corpus evidence of certain regular 'semantic representations' with regular distribution of semantic roles. The ideological potential of linguistic structures has been analysed through a synergetic approach of Van Dijk's socio-cognitive approach and Cognitive Linguistics, namely Talmy's approach to semantic roles and force dynamics. Further, in section 3, we also use analytic instruments from Critical Discourse Studies such as STA[7] to shed light on the data.

2.1. *Agent* versus *Patient*

Through the analysis conducted, it was possible to conclude that *the troika* was mirrored, in Portuguese opinion articles, as an agentive entity that controls and triggers changes in an affected entity, normally identified in sentences as *the Portuguese government/the Portuguese State/the Portuguese*.

Although, as Van Dijk maintained, 'Semantic agency as such is not ideological (...), it is a structural feature that may be used to express ideological positions by attributing specific kinds of involvement in, and responsibility for, good and bad action' (1995, p. 262), thus favouring the construction of preferred cognitive models. Agency as a linguistic category is not in itself a biased category. It may have an ideological biased treatment in the texts if it helps to construct an arbitrary shared mental model contributing to the formation of social stereotypes.

In fact, when the NP *the troika* appeared in the corpus as a subject of a sentence, typically it assumed the semantic role of AGENT, corresponding to a [+ HUMAN] argument, often as the subject of 'dicendi' verbs or verbs of verbal activity (*to say, to warn, to conclude, to suggest*); causative verbs (*to transform, to turn into, to require, to warn*),[8] coercive causative verbs (*to impose, to enforce*) and, eventually, verbs of cognitive or perceptive experience (*to recognise, to behave, to evaluate, to have the intention to*),[9] cases in which we can recognise also the presence of an EXPERIENCER and a STIMULUS, more than of a prototypical AGENT, following Talmy's terminology (1985).

It needs also be highlighted that *the troika* always appeared as a NP, constituted by DEF ART + N, and the noun *troika* almost never occurred in upper case.[10] This implies that the entity *the troika* is presented as a familiar and shared discourse referent by the addressee, placing the subject at a level of unquestionable sharing with the target discourse community. A means of 'claiming common ground with the addressee', a positive politeness strategy

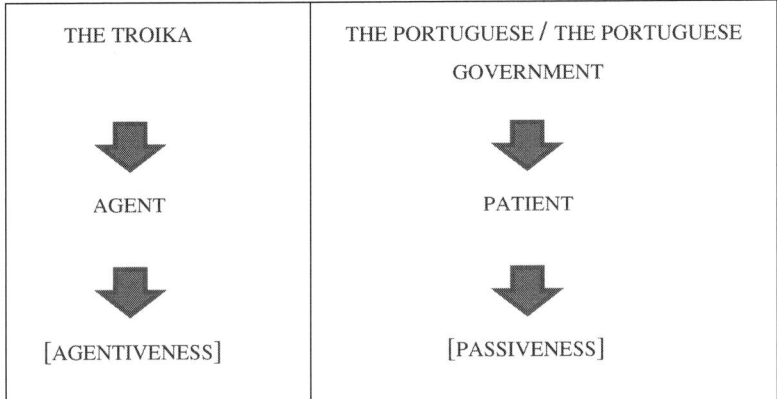

Fig 1. Distribution of Semantic Roles in Portuguese Media Discourse about *the Troika*.[14]

orientated to the addressee that counts as a manifestation of solidarity with him (Brown & Levinson, 1987).

A first axis that follows from the systematic distribution of the semantic roles AGENT/PATIENT[11] in the Portuguese media discourse about *the troika* is the opposition between the properties [AGENTIVENESS] *versus* [PASSIVENESS][12] associated to these realities, as illustrated in example (1) below, taken from the corpus:

(1) *The troika warned us well that one of the most serious problems of the country was the difficulty in dismissing people from public sector jobs.*[13] (*Visão*, 26 July 2012)

This systematic distribution of the semantic roles can be represented as follows in Fig. 1.

2.2. Lexical Causatives and Force Dynamics

This semantic-pragmatic configuration becomes particularly visible in lexical causative verbs, frequently occurring in the corpus with *the troika* as the AGENT, as can be seen in examples (2), (3) and (4) below:

(2) *The troika-that turned us into a protectorate-praised the Government. Small wonder....* (*Visão*, 15 July 2012)

(3) *Give or take, with more or less gaffes, the truth is that the Government had to walk the path we've travelled so far. Not because the revenue imposed by the troika was a miraculous revelation (...) but because (...).* (*Visão*, 15 June 2012)

(4) *(...) It is also true that Passos Coelho [Portuguese Prime Minister] has had time to realize his mistake in wanting to do more than was required by the troika.* (*Visão*, 25 May 2012)

As Talmy (2001) has shown, in the simplified schema in which linguistic constructions represent causation, we find a tripartite structure: 'a static prior state, a discrete state transition, and a static subsequent state'. In fact, in causative verbs a given CAUSATIVE ENTITY − a force-exerting entity − drives a change that affects a PATIENT ENTITY − a force-enduring entity. These verbs are dynamic configurations because they involve a transition of state. In the case of the examples (1), (2), (3) and (4) above, the verbs *warn; turn into, impose and require* can be summarised in the following formulas:

(1) WARN = [CAUSE TO KNOW];
(2) TURN INTO = [CAUSE TO BE/BECOME];
(3) IMPOSE = [CAUSE TO DO];
(4) REQUIRE = [CAUSE TO GIVE];

Lexical causatives are syntactic-semantic configurations adapted to delimit the *troika's* profile and the relationship between *the troika* and *the Portuguese/the Portuguese government*, in that they express, in a concentrated form, that a given AGENT-in this case, *the troika*−promotes a change that affects a PATIENT-in the current case, *the Portuguese/the Portuguese government*. This applies to either existential causatives: *transform/turn* [MAKE BECOME], and to experiential or cognitive causatives: *warn* [MAKE KNOW] or even to coercive causatives like *impose* [MAKE DO], *require* [MAKE GIVE] that configure a specific causativeness, leading to effective results (unlike, for example, *to prevent, to avoid*).[15]

If we look at the interaction between the participants of these statements, we find that each of the predicates involved refers to a set of reciprocal influences between the actants. It is possible to apply here what Fonseca (1999) has described as the force dynamics in the *feeling predicates*:

> (...) In this regard we still need to bear in mind that the 'presence/intervention of actant B in actant A' will not, in theory, go without any resistance on the part of the latter, who will see his territory threatened with invasion or his positive or negative face at risk of, in whole or in part, being affected.[16]

In all occurring causative verbs particularly salient are the dynamics of polarised forces around the terms CAUSATION/RESISTANCE and ANTAGONIST/AGONIST.[17] The one that CAUSES affects and invades the territory of the other, the one that suffers the effects of this invasion and this affectation.

We also see that, in many of the constructions where these conflicting realities are opposed, visible in examples such as (1) or (2) above, the ANTAGONIST identified with *the troika* is in the focal position, corresponding to the Subject of the sentence, thus in a foregrounded perspective.

Presented by Talmy (2001, p. 461) as one of the preeminent conceptual organising categories in language, the semantic category of force dynamics reveals itself as equally preeminent in the organisation of conflictual discourse as the one we are studying.

Fig. 2. Force-Dynamic Pattern. *Source*: Adapted from Talmy (2001, p. 415).

As a semantic category that seizes how entities interact with respect to force, including the exertion of force, the resistance to such a force, the overcoming of such a resistance, the blockage of the expression of force, the removal of such a blockage (Talmy, 2001, p. 410), this category allows for a global view on lexical items that:

> refer not only to physical force interactions but, by metaphoric extension, also to psychologi-
> cal and social interactions, conceived in terms of psychosocial 'pressures.' In addition, force-
> dynamic principles can be seen to operate in discourse, pre-eminently in directing patterns of
> argumentation, but also in guiding discourse expectations and their reversal. (Talmy, 2001,
> p. 409)

This extension of force dynamics to social force interaction, described by Talmy as *socio-dynamics* (2001, p. 438), applies to the characterisation of conflicting positions in discourse, such as is the case under study. In fact, the force-dynamic pattern dominantly operating in the corpus is one where an Agonist with an intrinsic tendency towards inaction – *the Portuguese* – is being opposed from outside by a stronger Antagonist– *the troika* – which thus overcomes its resistance and forces it to act. This schema involves necessarily two bodies in an opposition of force. It is possible to represent this conflict with the diagram proposed by Talmy in Fig. 2.

The fact that this propositional 'framing' is prevailing in the opinion pieces studied (consistently representing a conflictual situation in force dynamics where the stronger entity is *the troika* which affects the weaker entity, *the Portuguese*) makes it possible that such a frame itself adds to the negative portrayal of this invasive entity, gaining, therefore, an ideological basis, in the sense that it helps construct a stereotypical and evaluative image of *the troika* among Portuguese citizens.

2.3. Symmetry: Asymmetry and Co-Agency

Even in the cases where the AGENT *the troika* becomes CO-AGENT, the contexts in which it appears make it always retain its AGENTIVENESS, since it also participates with [VOLITIONAL INVOLVEMENT] and [CONTROL] in the process of *agreeing*,

negotiating, setting a goal, as can be illustrated in examples (5), (6) and (7) below:

(5) *The parties agreed with the troika[...].* (*Diário Económico*, 31 May 2011)

(6) *[...]the Government negotiated the most favourably possible with troika[...].* (*Expresso*, 12 April 2011)

(7) *[...]the goal the country has set with the troika[...].*[18] (*Público*, 5 July 2012)

In semantic terms it seems possible to include the predicates of the sentences (5), (6) and (7) above, respectively *agree, negotiate, set a goal,* in the class of symmetrical predicates[19] in the sense that they allow two alternative constructions, a transitive and an intransitive construction with a coordinated subject, and the *intransitive* version has a meaning close to the meaning of the corresponding *transitive* version (Gleitman et al., 1996) such as can be demonstrated by the examples below:

(5.a) The parties agreed with the troika.

(5.b) The parties and the troika agreed.

(6.a) The Government negotiated with the troika.

(6.b) The Government and the troika negotiated.

(7.a) The country has set a goal with the troika.

(7.b) The country and the troika have set a goal.

As described by Fonseca, the symmetrical predicates share the following properties:

(...) the reversibility of the NP's, having V as axis, translates at the surface the double orientation (= reciprocity) of the process linguistically conformed in V, articulated, as has been seen, with the mutual implication 'NP1 V (prep) NP2 ↔ NP2 V (prep) NP1'; on the other hand, the syntactic solution 'NP1 and NP2 V' represents a constructional variant of each of the other two schema (to which it relates by parassynonymy) (...)[20]

Notwithstanding, as several authors have noted, predicates such as *agreeing* can be perceived as symmetrical or asymmetrical according to the contexts of use. Dowty (1991, p. 583) notes that the asymmetry in these verbs arises when the criteria of 'who is responsible for the action' appears. In fact, it is not always evident that the solutions below are synonymous:

(i) X agreed with Y.
(ii) Y agreed with X.
(iii) X and Y agreed.

In verbs such as *agree* and *disagree,* as noted by Dowty, 'the relation may involve volition on the part of either one or of both parties, without the language, as it were, feeling the need for "independent" (more neutrally, "unrelated") lexemes to distinguish such subcases' (1991, p. 585). In these conditions the semantic selection of one of the two available entailments seems to be dependent on empirical contexts, such as is the case of the statements analysed about *the troika,* where the relevant reading is that *the troika* is volitionally involved and assuming control over the *agreement, the negotiation* or *the setting of goals* with *the Portuguese government*, thus configuring an instance of standard concomitant traditional Agency.

As such, if we take into account the statements under analysis and considering the question posed by Dowty:

> When confronted with a predicate denoting a kind of event that CAN reasonably be understood as either symmetrically or asymmetrically volitional (or motional) does the learner AUTOMATICALLY assume that the collective-subject version is symmetrically volitional (or motional) and the two-place version asymmetrically volitional (or motional), without requiring any specific empirical data to that effect? (1991, p. 586)

We could respond that only the contexts of usage give an answer to a correct reading. In the case of the solutions taken from the corpus with the partially symmetrical predicates *agree, negotiate, set a goal*, the semantic role of CO-AGENT played by the argument *the troika* shows that the pragmatic preeminence and hierarchy of *the troika* over *the Portuguese* in contextual ground imposes a semantic interpretation that gives *the troika* the properties of [+ VOLITIONAL INVOLVEMENT] and [+ CONTROL] over the processes asserted.

Talmy's proposal of the concepts 'FIGURE' and 'GROUND' (2001, pp. 312–344) as two fundamental cognitive functions, one that acts as a reference point or an anchor (GROUND) and the other that acts as the concept that needs anchoring (FIGURE), also allows us to explain the fact that some apparent symmetrical solutions are not understood as symmetrical, as can be illustrated by the examples given by Talmy 'She resembles him' versus 'He resembles her' (2001, p. 317).

As the author states:

> (...) not merely quantity of resemblance is being specified, but, additionally, one of the objects (the second-named one) is taken as a reference point and the other object (the first named one) is taken to have a variability whose particular value is at issue. (...) this asymmetry can be highlighted by choosing objects with different capacities to serve as a reference point.

> (12) a. My sister (F) resembles Madonna (G).

> b. Madonna (F) resembles my sister (G).

> And the asymmetry is unarguable for an analogue to a motion sentence − here, a change of relational state, as seen in (13).

> (13) She (F) grew to resemble him (G) ≠ He (F) grew to resemble her (G).[21]

The addition of these two analytical parameters of GROUND and FIGURE helps us to explain why in the sentences (5), (6) and (7) above we perceive the entity *the troika*, that appears as a CO-AGENT and in a background position, as a more forceful and stronger entity than the AGENT of the sentences itself. In fact, *the troika*, the second-named object acts as the GROUND, a cognitive entity taken as a reference point and *the parties, the government, the country*, the first named objects and the subjects of the sentences, are taken as the FIGURE, the entities that have a variability whose particular value is at issue.

This possibility of interpretation explains why the reader understands the semantic-pragmatic asymmetry present in these statements — that have potentially symmetric verbs as their predicates — as an asymmetry that opposes two unequal forces, in an asymmetric power and interdependence relation.

Fonseca also highlighted the fact that the difference of perspective established in discourse by the choice of one of the 'symmetrical' solutions is not irrelevant, since it corresponds to the selection of X or Y (or X and Y or, still, Y and X) to be the element that supports the predication (1993, pp. 146, 147). This prevents from accepting as not significant the various possibilities of arrangement of the nominal arguments X and Y around the vector V.

Furthermore, Fonseca notes that the characterisation of symmetrical predicates must take into account that language is used in social contexts and, as such, the socio-cultural properties are constitutive of its structure and functioning (1993, pp. 146, 147). This explains why the different arrangements of the arguments X and Y around V are not always possible. As the author states, cultural standards impose hierarchies between the elements, cancelling the possibility of some of the mentioned arrangements (1993, pp. 146, 147). This is applicable to the verb 'resemble' as in: The son resembles his father // The son and the father resemble each other; The father and the son resemble each other // (?) The father resembles his son.

> In short, it is a matter of bearing in mind that those socio-cultural properties are effectively constitutive of the structure and functioning of the language, not representing, thus, added dimensions to the grammatical organization, but dimensions fully integrated in it and, as it, equally codified. We are, after all, before an unequivocal proof of the strong inter-relation semantics-syntax-pragmatics.[22]

3. DISCOURSE REPRESENTATIONS OF *THE TROIKA* AND *THE PORTUGUESE* IN PORTUGUESE OPINION DISCOURSE

3.1. Semantic Roles, Force Dynamics and Discourse Representations

Returning to the oppositions of thematic roles, AGENT versus PATIENT and AGENTIVENESS versus PASSIVENESS, mentioned in section 2.1; the opposition of conflictual forces, FORCE versus RESISTANCE between ANTAGONIST and AGONIST, mentioned in section 2.2; and the ASYMMETRY between actants with unequal power and interdependence in section 2.3, we must draw conclusions about the social representations and the ideological positions of *the troika* and *the Portuguese* reflected/constructed by Portuguese opinion discourse.

One of the first conclusions to be drawn is that a prototypical AGENT, an over dynamic AGENT, present in the CAUSATIVE AGENT, has the effect of configuring a prototypical PATIENT, responding both of them positively to the various entailments of these thematic roles proposed by Dowty (1991):

Agent:

(a) volitional involvement in the event or state;
(b) sentience (and/or perception);
(c) causing an event or change of state in another participant;
(d) movement (relative to the position of another participant);
(e) exists independently of the event named by the verb.

Patient:

(a) undergoes change of state;
(b) incremental theme;
(c) causally affected by another participant;
(d) stationary relative to movement of another participant;
(e) (does not exist independently of the event, or not at all.)

In fact, the AGENT *the troika,* present in the corpus studied, is marked positively by all the properties listed above to the PROTO-AGENT. Also, the PATIENT affected by the causative predicates seen above in section 1, nominalised by such NP as *the government, the parties, the country, Passos Coelho* [Portuguese Prime Minister], amongst others and referred to by personal pronouns as *us*[23]is an entity affected, and in a certain way 'effected', by the CAUSATIVE AGENT that makes the PATIENT undergo a change of state to which she/he offered stronger or weaker resistance, through the form of inertia or of unwillingness, particularly visible in the forms of the coercive causatives such as *impose* or *enforce*.

We can thus focus AGENTIVENESS as a scalar concept that leads to degrees of AGENTIVENESS, according to more or less prototypical forms of AGENTS, where the CAUSATIVE AGENTS would be the most prototypical ones, responding positively to all of the properties of PROTO-AGENTS proposed by Dowty and, conversely, degrees of PATIENTNESS, according to the prototypicality of the PATIENT addressed, where the PATIENT of causatives would be one of the most prototypical ones.

Furthermore, as we have seen in sections 2.2 and 2.3, the force dynamics and the asymmetry that characterises the relation between these two entities often includes the interaction of opposite forces with the exertion of force on the part of the ANTAGONIST (the AGENT) over the AGONIST (the PATIENT) and the resistance to such a force on the part of the latter. This distribution of roles leads to the construal of *the troika* as the ANTAGONIST – the affecting entity

Table 1.   Representations of *the Troika* and *the Portuguese* in Portuguese
Opinion Articles.

THE TROIKA	THE PORTUGUESE
AGENTIVENESS/ACTION/ACTIVENESS	PATIENTNESS/INACTION/PASSIVENESS
EMPOWERMENT	POWERLESSNESS
AUTONOMY	DEPENDENCY
POTENCY	IMPOTENCY
DOMINANCE	SUBORDINATION
INVADER/AGGRESSOR/THREATEN	INVADED/VICTIM/THREATENED

Table 2.   Discourse Representations in Portuguese Opinion Articles:
Alienation vs. Participation.

VOLITIONAL INVOLVEMENT	VOLITIONAL UN-INVOLVEMENT
Participation − the capacity to transform our circumstances	Alienation − the incapacity to transform our circumstances
A positive state of social existence	A negative state of social existence

and the stronger entity − and *the Portuguese* as the AGONIST − the affected
entity and the weaker entity.

It follows that the images reflected in discourse of *the troika* and *the
Portuguese* and of the relationship between them is one that opposes two forces
of unequal power, as we have outlined above, leading to dichotomous rhetoric
representations, where *the Portuguese* are depicted as entities marked with
the properties of [− POWER]; [− CONTROL]; [+ INACTION]; [+ SUBORDINATION];
[+ DEPENDENCY]; [+ WEAKNESS] [+ VICTIM]; whereas *the troika* is depicted with
the inverse properties [+POWER]; [+ CONTROL]; [+ ACTION]; [+ DOMINANCE];
[− DEPENDENCY]; [+ STRENGTH], [+ AGGRESSOR], as is summarised in Table 1:

This schema is dynamic and symmetrical in the sense that it shows two
opposite and conflicting sides with scalar inverse entailments so that the more
dominance *the troika* exerts the more subordination *the Portuguese* endure.

By depicting *the Portuguese* as typically uninvolved volitionally in the
processes or either under the control of a more powerful entity, we can say
that, following Schweitzer (1992), discourse depicts reality as alien and beyond
people's grasp (in the current case, beyond Portuguese people's grasp) leading
to a sense of alienation, as schematised in Table 2.

3.2. Polarisation of Reality: The Troika and the Portuguese

Arising from the construals described in section 3.1 as well as contributing to
them, a second rhetorical pattern, present in the opinion discourses analysed, is

the polarisation of reality, offering a conceptualisation of US versus THEM; IN versus OUT as theorised by Cap (2008a, 2008b, 2010, 2013) and applied by Wieczorek (2008, 2009), Hart (2010) and Brokensha (2011), amongst others, to the analysis of political and other discourses.

Developed by Cap as an analytic model to serve as a viable handle on the post-9/11 war-on-terror rhetoric (2008a, p. 3), but applied afterwards by the author to other discourses and situations, the model is based on the 'simplistic dichotomy of "us and them"' (2008a, p. 2) used as a strategy of legitimisation in political discourse, with 'the latter party usually symbolising some kind of adversarial or plainly evil ideology that could potentially jeopardise [the former party]'. Based itself on the cognitive-pragmatic concept of proximisation that accounts for the symbolic construal of relations between entities within the Discourse Space (DS) (Chilton, 2005), the analytic model of STA is a combined model gathering three vectors: Space, Time and Ideological Values leading to a Spatial-Temporal-Axiological (STA) model of proximisation, where 'forced construals of THEM instigated events/actions as physically endangering US'; 'the NOW frame as the moment for US to start action to pre-empt the near future THEM invasive action'; as well as 'a gathering ideological conflict between US values and THEM values, eventually materialising in THEM physical impact upon US' (Cap, 2013), working altogether as a rhetorical organisation of argumentative discourses and as a strategy of legitimisation for pre-emptive action in crisis and conflict contexts.

The media-related version of Cap's STA model was developed by Kopytowska (2014, 2015) and Kalyango and Kopytowska (2014) showing that, 'A claim is made here that the mechanism, rather than performing only a legitimising function in public/political discourse, is inherent in the very nature of mass-mediated communication and enabled by the semiotic properties of various media' (Kopytowska, 2014, p. 77).

In the case of the opinion articles analysed in our work, although we are not before a state political discourse of legitimisation, we are, nonetheless, before a public space discourse and a mass-mediated discourse, where the authors, and the media they represent, are involved in an important process of social interventionism and regulation of public opinion. As such, the two main illocutionary values conveyed by these texts are the expressive-directive illocutionary value of criticism and censorship and the directive illocutionary value of incitement and exhortation to change (of mental states, convictions, behaviours).

As we have stated in the beginning of this chapter, the opinion articles gathered in our corpus were taken from *general*-interest newspapers and news magazines from the Portuguese publishing market and they reflect, thus, a variety of political positions and tendencies that range from centre-wright to centre-left, but do not include extremist positions in neither direction. The overall representation available opposes two entities, as schematised in Table 3.

The troika − THEM − is represented as a force coming to dominate and repress Portugal − US − and, thus, represented as a force opposed to US. *The*

Table 3. Portugal and the Troika.

Portugal/The Portuguese	The Troika/Europe
US	THEM[a]

Notes: [a]This dichotomy prevails, although in some centre-left articles we observe shifts of sides where *the troika* and *the Portuguese government* are on one side and *the Portuguese people*, on the other. In these cases, the polarisation is as follows: *the troika* and *the Portuguese government* — THEM/BAD — versus *the Portuguese people* — US/GOOD.

troika appears as a barrier to freedom, to self-determination and even to growth. This constant polarisation is used as a means of opposing different sides of a fragmented reality, as can be illustrated in example (8):

(8) *No matter how gigantic the task is, no matter how risky the taking off from **the orthodoxy of the troika** [THEM] is, the truth is that **the time** to give an independent political leadership to **the Government of Portugal**[US]**has come.**[NOW]* (*Visão*, 15 June 2012)

In this example we can see a typical DS organisation with the US at the centre of the Space and the NOW as the convergent Time towards which the motion in attracted: 'the time (...) has come'. It implies, thus a dynamic view of the DS, in the sense that it implies a motion and a change.

The US and THEM are identified through NP's that are axiologically neutral for the US and axiologically marked for the THEM — 'orthodoxy of the troika'-thus, conveying a negative judgement of the THEM.

The motion away from THEM (negative) towards US (positive) is described by the NP 'the taking off' that implies a necessary motion of detachment. This motion is characterised by means of NP's as 'gigantic task' and 'risky taking off'. The verb 'to give', a lexical causative verb decomposed in [CAUSE TO POSSESS], also implies a change of state from a state1 of [NOT POSSESSING] to a state2 of [POSSESSING], being, thus, a dynamic construction. The US starts having something that s/he did not have before. In this case '*independent political leadership*', a NP axiologically marked as positive.

Also the construction '**The truth is that** [the time (...) has come]' also contributes to the idea of the emergency of NOW, since it attributes the enunciative responsibility of the utterance '[the time (...) has come]' to the generic and abstract entity 'The truth', an unquestionable and credible source.

We can see, therefore, the legitimisation strategy at work by means of a THEM vs US opposition and the construal of positive and negative values around these vectors, as well as a dynamic configuration of the DS, where a motion of moving away from the THEM is conveyed as necessary, and, furthermore, legitimised with the stamp of 'The truth'.

Although it is not possible, for lack of space, to explore further, in this chapter, this analytical problem of the polarisation and the proximisation as strategies of legitimising the dominating *doxa* of *troika* as an antagonist vs. *the*

Table 4. Lexical expressions of *the Troika* and *the Portuguese* in Opinion Articles.

The Portuguese	The troika
Portugal	Europe
The country	The inspectors
The parties	The Commissioners
The prime minister; The president[a]	

Note: [a]In these more neutral nominalisations are included the proper nouns of the political individuals.

Portuguese as the agonist, we will still foreground below the lexical choices as forms of social categorisation.

In fact, the lexical expressions chosen for the two opponent forces confronted in the texts constitute relevant linguistic material for our analysis, in the sense that they also convey strong axiological distinctions. We leave aside the more neutral referent expressions of the entities Agonist and Antagonist, such as the ones identified in Table 4.

As Van Leeuwen has proven,[24] even amongst the more neutral ways of nominalising an entity, we can discover relevant differences that support social and ideological categorisations. Nonetheless, it is amongst the more marked lexicalisations that we find the heavier ideological load, such as happens in the examples in Table 5.

One aspect that becomes salient from the list above is that several NPs connected to the description of *the troika* explore very strong religious associations that carry, in the context, negative implications. Such is the case of 'Orthodoxy of the troika' 'Inflexible orthodoxy', 'Augustinian saints of economic and financial sin', 'The Moses trio', 'The sacred commandments', 'The bulk of the letter', 'Severe commissioners'.

The way the identity of *the troika* as the Opponent is reflected/construed in this dichotomous DS, already described in sections above, is, thus, also enhanced by the strong lexical choices used to describe this entity.

As Van Dijk has stated:

> (...) if a social group is consistently described as being the responsible agent of negative action (like crime or violence), or even as 'being involved' in such action, as is often the case for young black males in crime, drugs or 'riot' reporting, then we may assume that such propositional 'framing' itself adds to the negative portrayal of such a group, and therefore has an ideological basis. (1995, p. 261)

Sometimes, in ironic samples, *the troika* is even depicted as something alien, obscure, retaining magical powers, such as is the case in the instances below:

> (13) *Give or take, with more or less gaffes, the truth is that the Government had to walk the path we've travelled so far. Not because the revenue imposed by the troika was a **miraculous revelation of the tablets of the law** (...) but because there was no other option (...). (Visão,* 15 July 2012)

Table 5.   Lexical expressions of *the Troika* and *the Portuguese* in Portuguese
Opinion Articles.

The Troika/The Rules from the Troika/Europe	The Portuguese/Portugal and Its Allies
THEM	US
Orthodoxy of the troika	This strip of territory
Shock therapy	
The disreputable markets	The southern sinners of Europe
The inspectors from the International Monetary Fund, European Central Bank and European Commission	This land of the troika
Inflexible orthodoxy	Lax cultural impulses of a South European country
The Moses trio	
The sacred commandments	
The bulk of the letter	Our life style 'à tripa-forra' [with unnecessary expenditures and excesses]
Severe commissioners	Such a stupid people
Augustinian saints of economic and financial sin	
True decisions (...) taken by others that are not even elected	Little popular sovereignty that elects a little government capable of taking little decisions
The thing	
The recipe of the troika[a]	

Note: [a]The multi-word expressions used to identify *the troika* and *the Portuguese* were taken from several editions of the years of 2011 and 2012 of the newspapers *Expresso* and *Público* and from two editions of 2012 of the *Newsmagazine Visão*.

> (14) *(...) the big question that arises -the great political questions which existed from the start—is whether the Government has diligently applied the recipe of the troika, because they had no choice or because they genuinely believe in **the magical power of redemption of the thing**. (...)*. (*Visão*, 15 July 2012)

> (15) *(...) the problem of Portugal is not in the government's ability to meet the **bulk of the letter** of the sacred commandments boards but in the **inflexible orthodoxy of the Moses trio** that brought the sacred commandments to earth;* (*Visão*, 7 September 2012)

We must also mention that the lexical choices applied to the identification of Portugal or the Portuguese government/people summarised in Table 5 are also often used in an ironic sense. NPs such as 'the southern sinners of Europe'; 'lax cultural impulses of a South European country'; 'our life style "à tripa-forra" [with unnecessary expenditures and excesses]'; 'such a stupid people' have to be interpreted as integrated in the polarised vision of *Troika* versus Portugal, in the sense that these epithets, that imply criticism, translate the dysphoric view that *the troika* has about Portugal and not the view of the Portuguese about themselves. Thus, the pragmatic potential strategic benefits of irony in the naming of Portugal in this context is that it favours a construal of *the troika* as an enemy of Portugal and a construal of the Portuguese as a victim of *the troika*.

Going back to the hypothesis of our work summarised in the title '*Towards a (dis)integrated Europe: the constructs of « Europe » — as represented by « Troika » — versus « Portugal » and « The Portuguese » in a corpus of Portuguese opinion articles*' we conclude that the polarisation reflected does not favour the concept of a united Europe, demonstrating wholesomeness and promoting solidarity between the member States and European citizens. On the contrary, it depicts the image of a disintegrated Europe.

Furthermore, if we agree on the fact that, to some extent, *the troika* represents Europe (or, at least, a certain Europe) if *the troika* is depicted/is perceived as alien and hostile, it follows that Europe is depicted/is perceived as alien and hostile too. Therefore, we have a reconceptualisation of the meronymy/holonymy relationship between PORTUGAL and EUROPE, being that in discursive representations of Portuguese opinion articles, Portugal is depicted as not being a part of Europe, as we can schematise in Fig 3.

Van Dijk has stressed the evaluative nature of ideology as 'basic frameworks of social cognition, shared by members of social groups':

> Unlike knowledge, ideologies as defined here—are systems of social cognition that are essentially *evaluative:* They provide the basis for judgements about what is good or bad, right or wrong, and thus also provide basic guidelines for social perception and interaction. (1995, p. 248)

Public space discourse is particularly active in generating social impressions or images (that come to be) shared by the in-group — US. It normally helps in the reinforcement of judgments, opinions and attitudes that become ideological in the sense that they work as an 'informational glue'[25] that binds together the members of the in-group — US — and affect their social attitude towards members of the out-group — THEM.

In the opinion articles studied, the image of Portugal as the in-group, where a discourse of national cohesion and identity is active — we saw the number of instances where the nominalisations of the US group have positive interpretations and the first person plural deictics have inclusive significance, involving

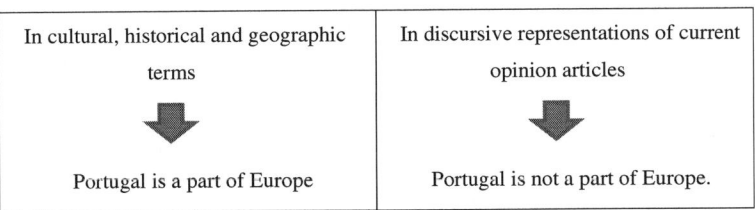

Fig. 3. Portugal and Europe — Holonymy and Meronymy.

the author and the readers – contrasts with the image of Europe as the out-group, the THEM group, that is distant and hostile, a group where Portugal does not fit and a group that menaces the in-group identity.[26]

4. CONCLUSIONS

In summary, it was possible to conclude from the corpus analysed that the semantic role played by the NP *the troika*[27] is mainly the role of the AGENT, nor-mally a CAUSATIVE AGENT that motivates a change affecting a PATIENT. Invariably this PATIENT is *the Portuguese government* or *the Portuguese*. Even when the entity *the troika* assumes other semantic roles such as CO-AGENT or TARGET it maintains the semantic property [+ CONTROL], that gives it some degree of AGENTIVENESS in the process.

Together with this semantic pattern we could see that the deictic material – pronouns – and also lexical expressions help to enforce a construal of US ver-sus THEM in polarised positions.

On the whole of the media taken into account in this study, the representa-tion delivered by newspapers opinion discourse in Portugal, whether humoristic or serious, is that of an opposition between Portugal and Europe, leading to an extremist construal of Portugal as not being a part of Europe. Also the domi-nant representation points to a conflict between an AGENT – Europe as repre-sented by *the troika* – that operates a change – the passage from a state of *not-experiencing intervention* to a state of *experiencing intervention* and being under the effect of the austerity measures – and a PATIENT – Portugal – that is affected by the change.[28] The PATIENT or OBJECT is represented as POWERLESS, deprived of its capacity to react. In a scalar construal of AGENTIVENESS/PASSIVENESS the PATIENT is represented as alienated.

This construal derives from and, simultaneously, helps to generate contra-dictory historical conditions, viewing that alienation can be a source of stability but also a source of potential conflict. These discourses thus projected an image of a fragmented and (dis)integrated Europe and, as language is power, it is not possible to measure the damage that these consistent representations, repro-duced and enforced in discourse, have caused to the future of Europe.

NOTES

1. The 'troika' is a term popularised during the eurozone crisis to describe the group formed by the European Commission, the International Monetary Fund and the European Central Bank as the group of lenders that imposed austerity measures on indebted European states – such as Ireland, Portugal, Cyprus and Greece – in exchange for the bailouts provided.

2. The intervention of the Troika in Portugal, as in other countries in Europe, led to the application of very tough and radical austerity measures, which although understood and defended as necessary by the Government and even by columnists that, for a short period of time until April 2011, defended in their opinion articles the idea of sacrifice, guilt, inevitability and resignation towards the intervention, were seen as abusive and excessive by the majority of the people and by columnists and analysts, even those who wrote for newspapers more closely linked to official political stance. We can, thus, say that the dominant public opinion on the matter of the Troika intervention in Portugal, even for those voters from centre wright wing, tends to be a negative one.

3. The slash (/) indicates lexical alternatives.

4. VISL is the acronym of 'Visual Interactive Syntax Learning'. To learn more about the analytical tools provided by the system, please confront: http://beta.visl.sdu.dk

5. 'In a corpus-driven approach the commitment of the linguist is to the integrity of the data as a whole, and descriptions aim to be comprehensive with respect to corpus evidence' (Tognini-Bonelli, 2001, p. 84).

6. Although the corpus is constituted of 62 opinion articles where the lexical co-occurrences mentioned took place, the analysis presented here can only include some of the examples found.

7. See further section 3.

8. As proposed by Dowty (1991, p. 572), this thematic role of Agent (Proto-Agent), assumed by the entity *the troika* in the statements analysed, possesses some of the entailments that characterize this role type: volitional involvement in the event or state; sentience (and/or perception); causing an event or change of state in another participant; movement (relative to the position of another participant); exists independently of the event named by the verb. In the case of the psychological predicates or mental verbs we can also consider the subject an *Experiencer* or a *Stimulus* (Dowty, 1991, p. 579).

9. All of the predicators mentioned have occurred in our corpus in sentences with *the troika as* a subject.

10. This aspect explains why we will, from this moment on in our work, refer to *Troika* with the same syntactic structure that it appears within the corpus: *the troika*.

11. Cf. Dowty (1991, p. 572): 'Contributing properties for the Patient Proto-Role: a. undergoes change of state b. incremental theme c. causally affected by another participant d. stationary relative to movement of another participant (e. does not exist independently of the event, or not at all)'.

12. We interpret [PASSIVENESS] here in the sense of 'the quality of being a patient', not necessarily related to the syntactic structure of the passive voice.

13. The examples taken from the corpus were translated into English and the comments added to the original text of the articles are signalled with *square brackets*.

14. The schemata provided reflect the dominant semantic axes of the texts analysed. We observed no substantial differences between particular papers in this respect.

15. Anna Wierzbicka distinguishes the *make* and the *have* causatives as far as the semantic property [WILL OF THE RECEIVER] is concerned: 'the make causative implies that the causee is acting against his or her will. The have causative doesn't imply that; here the causee is expected to comply with the causers will and there is no assumption, or expectation, of unwillingness on his or her part' (1988, p. 241). Due to the power relation and the force dynamics referred to, in the statements under analysis in this work we could paraphrase the lexical causatives with the verb TO MAKE, rather than with the verb TO HAVE.

16. Adapted from Fonseca (1999, p. 243).

17. According to Talmy (1976, 1985) and Fonseca (1999).

18. The original versions of the examples were translated and adapted.

19. According to Borillo (1971), Fonseca (1993), Gleitman, Gleitman, Miller, and Ostrin (1996), and Partee (2008).

20. Adapted from Fonseca (1993, p. 134).
21. We should note that Dowty (1991, p. 563) proposes to rule out these cognitive categories of GROUND and FIGURE from the concepts of thematic roles: 'I want to suggest that we rule out such perspective-dependent notions as Figure/Ground and Gruber's stative Theme as candidates for thematic roles. This is not to deny the existence of these distinctions or their importance, but to propose only that thematic role is the wrong rubric for them.'
22. Adapted from Fonseca (1993, p. 147).
23. For the analysis of *us*, see section 3.2.
24. Cf. the framework proposed by Van Leeuwen for analysing how the participants of social practices can be, and are, represented in discourse (1997, 2008).
25. Cf. the sense of ideology proposed by Althusser (1976, p. 105) as a material apparatus from which the human beings cannot escape simply because they are social beings. Cf. also the concept of ideological constructs in Advertising Discourse in Pinto (1997).
26. A similar polarisation can be confronted in Portuguese Presidential Manifestos in Pinto (2013).
27. See in the Introduction of this study the contextual background of the Troika intervention in Portugal from May 2011 to May 2014.
28. We adopt here the concept of 'change' as a central cognitive-semantic category of Talmy's cognitive approach to causation, force dynamics and to the basic conceptualization of events and thematic roles. For further detail, see section 2.

REFERENCES

Althusser, L. (1976). *Positions*. Paris: Éditions Sociales.
Borillo, A. (1971). Remarques sur les verbes symétriques. *Langue Française, 11*, 17−31.
Brokensha, S. (2011). Noticing *us* and *them* constructions: The pedagogical implications of a critical discourse analysis of referring in political discourse. *Per Linguam, 27*(1), 56−73.
Brown, P., & Levinson, S. C. (1987). *Politeness: Some universals in language usage*. Cambridge: Cambridge University Press.
Cap, P. (2008a). *Legitimisation in political discourse: A cross-disciplinary perspective on the modern US war rhetoric* (2nd ed.). Cambridge: Cambridge Scholars Publishing.
Cap, P. (2008b). Towards the proximization model of the analysis of legitimization in political discourse. *Journal of Pragmatics, 40*, 17−41.
Cap, P. (2010). Axiological aspects of proximization. *Journal of Pragmatics, 42*, 392−407.
Cap, P. (2013). *Proximization: The pragmatics of symbolic distance crossing*. Amsterdam: Benjamins.
Chilton, P. (2005). Discourse space theory: Geometry, brain and shifting viewpoints. *Annual Review of Cognitive Linguistics, 3*, 78−116.
Dowty, D. (1991). Thematic proto-roles and argument selection. *Language, 67*(3), 547−617.
Fonseca, J. (1993). Verbos simétricos. *Estudos de Sintaxe-Semântica e Pragmática do Português* (pp. 127−148). Porto: Porto Editora.
Fonseca, J. (1999). Aspectos centrais da semântica-sintaxe e pragmática dos predicados de sentimento. *Diacrítica, 13*(14), 237−278.
Gleitman, L. R., Gleitman, H., Miller, C., & Ostrin, R. (1996). Similar, and similar concept. *Cognition, 58*, 321−376.
Hart, C. (2010). *Critical discourse analysis and cognitive science: New perspectives on immigration discourse*. Basingstoke: Palgrave Macmillan.
Kalyango, Y., & Kopytowska, M. (Eds.) (2014). *Why discourse matters: Negotiating identity in the mediatized world*. New York, NY: Peter Lang.
Kerbrat-Orechionni, C. (2006). *Análise da Conversação, princípios e métodos*. (Translation of *La Conversation*. Paris: Éditions du Seuil, 1996). São Paulo: Parábola Editorial.

Kopytowska, M. (2014). Modality, distance, and the television news genre. *REDIS – Revista de Estudos do Discurso* (Vol. 3, 68–92). Porto: FLUP.

Kopytowska, M. (2015). Ideology of 'here and now'. *Critical Discourse Studies*, *12*(3).

Partee, B. H. (2008). Symmetry and symmetrical predicates. *Philpapers, Philosophical Research Online*, http://philpapers.org/rec/PARSAS

Pinto, A. (1997). *Publicidade: um discurso de sedução*. Porto: Porto Editora.

Pinto, A. (2013). Dialogismo, polifonia e heterogeneidade enunciativa nos manifestos políticos das presidenciais de 2011. *Estudos Linguísticos, Gramática e Texto*, *8*, 195–212.

Schweitzer, D. (1992). Marxist theories of alienation and reification: The response to capitalism, state socialism and the advent of postmodernity. In F. Geyer & W. R. Heinz (Eds.), Alienation, Society and the individual – continuity and change in theory and research. New Jersey: Transaction Publishers.

Talmy, L. (1976). Semantic causative types. In M. Shibatani (Ed.), *Syntax and semantics (vol.6): The grammar of causative constructions*. New York, NY: Academic Press.

Talmy, L. (1985). Force dynamics in language and thought. *Papers from the Twenty-First Regional Meeting of the Chicago Linguistic Society*. Chicago, IL: Chicago Linguistic Society.

Talmy, L. (2001). *Toward a cognitive semantics* (Vol. I). Massachusetts: MIT Press.

Tognini-Bonelli, E. (2001). Corpus linguistics at work. *Studies in Corpus Linguistics* 6. Amsterdam/ Philadelphia.

Van Dijk, T. A. (1995). Discourse semantics and ideology. *Discourse & society*, *6*(2), 243–289.

Van Dijk, T. A. (2006a). Discourse and manipulation. *Discourse & Society*, *17*(2), 359–383.

Van Dijk, T. A. (2006b). Ideology and discourse analysis. *Journal of Political Ideologies*, *11*(2), 115–140.

Van Leeuwen, T. (1997). A representação dos atores sociais. In E. R. Pedro (Ed.), *Análise Crítica do Discurso: uma perspectiva sociopolítica e funcional* (pp. 169–222). Lisboa: Caminho.

Van Leeuwen, T. (2008). *Discourse and practice: New tools for critical discourse analysis*. New York, NY: Oxford University Press.

Wieczorek, A. E. (2008). Proximisation, common ground, and assertion-based patterns for legitimisation in political discourse. *CADAAD. Critical Approaches to Discourse Analysis across Disciplines*, *2*(1), 31–48.

Wieczorek, A. E. (2009). This is to say you're either in or out: some remarks on clusivity. *CADAAD, Critical Approaches to Discourse Analysis across Disciplines*, *3*(2), 118–129.

Wierzbicka, A. (1988). *The semantics of grammar*. Amsterdam: John Benjamins.

DOING OR UNDOING EUROPE CRITICALLY IN THE LISBON TREATY DEBATE: A CORPUS-BASED ANALYSIS OF BRITISH NEWSPAPERS

Chiara Nasti

ABSTRACT

The referendum debate in Ireland on whether voting in favour of the Lisbon Treaty has filled the pages of newspapers and the online media. Several anti-EU campaigns have emerged and politicians have shown their own attitudes towards the ratification process. Being our first contact with reality newspapers enable potential readers to better understand their lives and socio-political events (Van Dijk, 1991; Richardson, 2007). It has been argued that newspapers construe public identities for individuals and social groups through specific textual strategies and contribute to our understanding of belonging to a community (Fairclough, 1995a). Some scholars have proved that, in reporting on European matters, British newspapers are mainly Eurosceptic and tend to depict EU leaders in a negative light (Musolff, 2004; Nasti, 2012). It has also been demonstrated that when reporting on European integration newspapers tend to define what it means to be a European citizen by construing their own images of Europe. By doing so, newspapers have the power to support or subvert the feeling of European belonging by showing desired or unwanted scenarios. In his analysis of newspaper discourse, Fowler (1991) points out how transitivity is of great interest in newspaper analysis as it is a potential tool to investigate the same event in

National Identity and Europe in Times of Crisis: Doing and Undoing Europe, 211–235
Copyright © 2017 by Emerald Publishing Limited
All rights of reproduction in any form reserved
doi:10.1108/978-1-78714-513-920171010

different ways, thus providing different views on the social and political events reported.

Against this framework, the present chapter aims to analyse, by combining a quantitative and a qualitative approach, how newspapers construct professional, social and private identity of the European politicians involved in the Lisbon Treaty debate following the features introduced by Fairclough (1995b) and Halliday and Matthiessen (2004) transitivity model. This study also investigates what qualities and features are attributed to EU leaders and to what extent the stereotyped roles of previous studies are also revealed through the analysis of material, mental and verbal processes.

Keywords: Social and private identities; corpus-assisted discourse studies; transitivity; Euroscepticism; newspaper discourse; European integration

1. INTRODUCTION: THE EUROPEAN DISCOURSE

European debates on the reform process have largely been the interest of newspapers and online media, which have expressed different viewpoints on the issue. More recently, the Lisbon Treaty reform process has brought new debates to the fore especially due to the fact that its enforcement was not approved and passed via referenda in all the European countries. Scholars have analysed the European discourse from different perspectives and methodologies investigating how the media employ various textual, cognitive and lexico-grammar strategies (Musolff, Good, Points, & Wittlinger, 2001; Nasti & Venuti, 2014). In particular it has been revealed that the British press is predominantly Eurosceptic and tends to portray European leaders as being somewhat heedless of democratic values. The following section examines some of the studies conducted on the press analysing how it construes identities when reporting on European debates and goes on to illustrate the goals of the present paper.

1.1. Previous Research Orientation

Previous studies on newspapers discourse have shown how the British press tends to be Eurosceptic, endorsing a negative view of European leaders and issues (Anderson & Weymouth, 1999; Musolff, 2004; Musolff et al., 2001). These studies have pointed out that when reporting on European integration newspapers are inclined to define what being a European citizen means by construing their own images of Europe. By doing so, newspapers have the power to support or subvert the feeling of European belonging by presenting both desired and unwanted scenarios (Nasti & Venuti, 2014). In particular, Nasti (2012) demonstrated that the British press in reporting on the Treaty debate uses movement and conflict metaphors, evoking a negative description of the EU leaders' actions aiming at implementing the treaty and getting it passed. The study in fact shows that EU ministers are described in terms of enforcers who are to some extent unmindful of democracy. A recent study (Nasti & Venuti, 2014) on the evaluation resources used by the press to describe the Lisbon Treaty debate has also revealed that EU leaders and pro-European politicians are depicted as aggressors who use bullying tactics while Ireland and the Irish people are described as being victims of EU leaders' behaviour and actions.

The media, seem to have a central role in construing and proposing a shared image of European leaders. As Fairclough (1995a, p. 233) points out the mass media are the most important social institution in achieving consensus, transmitting ideologies and construing identities, values and practices.

Other scholars (Van Dijk, 1991; Van Leeuwen, 1996) have also proved that the media play a crucial role in the construction, reconstruction and deconstruction of social identities. Richardson (2007) states that newspaper readers assume that the message and information conveyed in newspapers is an accurate portrayal of society. Van Dijk (1991) also says that newspapers are our mirror on the world and as a result, they shape our understanding of it. This affects readers' view of society and creates what Richardson calls the (re)production of social reality (2007, pp. 10–14). By reproducing social realities the media can manipulate people's attitudes and opinions.

As a result, the media's use of specific textual and rhetorical strategies might reveal peculiar identities and implicitly or explicitly construe politicians' roles.

1.2. Goals

As pointed out in the previous paragraph, the press construes public identities for individuals and social groups through specific textual and rhetorical strategies, and contributes to our understanding of belonging to a community; furthermore 'the relations between voices in public political discourse take the form of a conversation' (Mehan et al., 1990, in Fairclough, 1995a, p. 216), a dialogue, in which discourse strategies or moves on the part of one organisation provoke responses from others. Starting from these premises, this chapter seeks to analyse how newspapers construct the professional, social and private identity of the European politicians involved in the Lisbon Treaty debate, following the features introduced by Fairclough (1995b) and Halliday and Matthiessen (2004) transitivity model.

Transitivity generally refers to how meaning is represented in the clause and shows how speakers encode their mental picture of reality in language and how they account for their experience of the world around them. The investigation of transitivity has a central role in the scope of critical discourse analysis as it is a means of uncovering the links between language and ideology (Fairclough, 1992). It has been demonstrated that transitivity choices are fundamental to understand writers' opinions and points of view and are primarily concerned with the role of human participants in discourse (Mills, 1995). Fowler (1991) also proved that transitivity is of great interest in newspaper analysis as it is a potential tool to analyse the same event in different ways, thus providing different views on the social and political events reported.

A very important concern in analysing transitivity is whether agency and responsibility are made clear in the text. To analyse relations of agency and investigate ideological and political factors in the debate over the Lisbon Treaty, I examined material, mental and verbal processes and the passive used when referring to the three EU actors.

In the analysis of these processes, only three European Leaders have been considered – Sarkozy, Barroso and Klaus – because of their prominent institutional roles within the EU at the time of the first and second Irish referendum. Sarkozy took over the EU presidency on 1 July 2008 followed by Klaus who became President on 1 January 2009, while Barroso was the President of the EU commission.

The present chapter also attempts to identify what qualities and features are attributed to EU leaders and to what extent the stereotyped roles highlighted by previous studies, also emerge through the analysis of specific textual strategies.

2. POLITICAL AND HISTORICAL BACKGROUND

2.1. From the Drafting to the First Irish Referendum on the Lisbon Treaty

In October 2007 at an informal summit in Lisbon EU leaders drew up and adopted a Reform Treaty, in place of the European Constitution which was rejected by the Netherlands and France in 2005.[1] The Treaty of Lisbon, as it was called, was finally signed in Lisbon on 13 December 2007 by the representatives of the 27 Member States. The ratification process was mainly carried out in the member states parliaments except for Ireland where the country's constitution required a referendum. The treaty was contested by three countries – Ireland, Poland and the Czech Republic. The first Irish referendum, which was held on 12 June 2008, expressed a negative response with 53.4% voting 'no', despite the fact that European leaders encouraged the voters to vote in favour of the treaty arguing that it would have no effect on major concerns, these being taxation, neutrality and abortion. The rebuff of the Irish voters made the Polish and Czech Presidents hopeful that they could stop the ratification in their countries, as they were not very keen to sign the treaty. The Irish 'NO' was warmly welcomed by the British who had campaigned for a referendum in Britain. Therefore, the EU leaders' plans to have the Treaty enforced by 1 January 2009 failed.

2.2. The Ratification Process after the Irish 'NO'

At the following European Council, on 19–20 June 2008, EU leaders discussed what solution they could find to crack the ratification impasse and agreed that the Irish government would work both internally and with other Member States in order to put forward a common solution. Soon after the European Council, the Irish government decided to analyse the negative outcome of the Lisbon referendum in depth, by commissioning a research project aimed at evaluating the reasons underlying the rejection of the treaty. Sarkozy, who was in charge of the EU rotating presidency in the second semester of 2008, visited the Irish Prime Minister, Brian Cowen on 21 July, to discuss the reasons for the Irish rebuff. At the European Summit of October, Cowen presented the issues raised by Ireland to EU representatives in order to pass the Treaty. In November 2008, the Czech Constitutional Court decided that the treaty was compatible with the Czech constitutional order; however, to complete the ratification process, the approval of the two Czech houses of parliament was necessary, and this required more time.

The Council of June 2009 granted Ireland legal guarantees in terms of neutrality, right to life and tax autonomy, reassuring the Irish people that the treaty would not infringe on the government's authority in these domains. The Council also agreed that Ireland would hold a referendum in the autumn 2009. Therefore, the Irish Prime Minister decided to hold another referendum in Ireland on 2 October 2009, insisting that 'Doubts raised about certain issues have been put to rest once and for all' (*Mail on Sunday*, 20 June 2009).

This time the ballot result was positive, the Irish electorate voted with a majority of 67.13% in favour of the ratification of the Lisbon Treaty with a turnout of 59%. A few days later the Polish President, Lech Kaczynski signed the treaty saying that 'The fact that the Irish people changed their minds meant the revival of the treaty, and there are no longer any obstacles to its ratification' (*The Daily Telegraph*, 10 October 2009). Only the Czech President, Vaclav Klaus, a fervent opponent of further integration, continued to oppose the treaty. He also asked for opt-outs from the European Charter of Human Rights, which forms part of the Lisbon Treaty text. On 1 January 2009, the Czech Republic took over the Presidency of the EU and on 18 February the lower house of its parliament approved the treaty with 125 votes in favour.

On 3 November, despite Czech senators' complaints about the legitimacy of the Lisbon Treaty, the Czech Constitutional Court cleared the way for its ratification and on the same day, the Czech President signed the Treaty, which was enforced on 1 December 2009.

2.3. The Ratification in Britain and the Impact of the Irish Referenda

Britain has never truly favoured European integration (Anderson & Weymouth, 1999; Musolff, 2004). Since the negotiation on the Maastricht Treaty British politicians and citizens have tried to oppose further integration by choosing to opt out in certain areas. A poll carried out in December 2007 showed that British people were still sceptical towards the EU and the new treaty which was described as being a 'repackaged' or 'disguised' constitution.

What the British people found objectionable was the Labour party's refusal to hold a referendum. In its manifesto of 2005 Labour had promised a referendum on any other constitution or constitutional treaty. Indeed, the protocols of the new treaty were only discussed by parliamentary ministers and this was not only criticised by newspapers that fervently argued for a referendum such as *The Sun*, *The Daily Telegraph* and *The Times* but also by some politicians who did not support the treaty and the EU policy.

On 5 March 2008, the Conservatives tried to oppose the parliamentary procedure and proposed an amendment calling for a referendum which was defeated by 311 votes to 248. On 11 March, on the third reading, the treaty was approved by the members of the House of Commons and then passed onto the Lords.[2] Many hoped that the Lords would change the course of the ratification and even pro-Europeans staunchly criticised the government's actions.

Soon after the signing ceremony in Lisbon, the British multi-millionaire Stuart Wheeler brought an action questioning the legality of approving the treaty without a referendum before the High Court. Wheeler argued that the Labour party had promised a referendum on the Constitutional Treaty which was not in any way different from the Lisbon Treaty and therefore was obliged to keep its promise. This case urged many Tories to propose a suspension of the ratification and take time, thereby forcing Brown to proceed more slowly. Against this framework, the Irish referendum rebuff highlighted for British citizens the injustice that they had been denied a referendum. As *The Daily Telegraph* (14 June 2008) pointed out the Irish NO had serious consequences on Brown's position. On the one hand he was being pressured by EU leaders to continue with ratification while on the other hand, he was deeply disappointed and worried about the protests of British citizens. However, the British Prime Minister continued with the ratification process in spite of Wheeler's petition and the Irish negative turnout. Brown's decision was probably due to EU leaders' insistence on ratification. Moreover, EU ministers, especially the French

Prime Minister, Nicolas Sarkozy, who at that time, was about to take over the presidency of the EU, the German Chancellor, Angela Merkel, and the President of the EU Commission, Manuel Barroso claimed that a new referendum was the right solution in response to the chaos created by the rejection of the treaty. The British Prime Minister, Gordon Brown and the Foreign Secretary David Miliband, seemed to support EU leaders' advocacy for a referendum, they had never publicly admitted that the Lisbon Treaty needed to be revised or suspended, even though they stated that the Irish vote should be respected. The position of the two British leaders caused scathing reactions from the Conservatives. The Tory Leader David Cameron questioned Gordon Brown's position by saying that 'it would be ridiculous to ask the Irish to vote twice, when we haven't even been allowed to vote once' (*The Times*, 19 June 2008). Nevertheless, the Lords passed the treaty on June 18, and the following day the bill was given Royal assent. The final stage of the ratification was completed on July 16 when the instruments of ratification were deposited in Rome.

The official claim concerning the second referendum in Ireland following the guarantees agreed upon at the EU Summit in June 2009, initiated a new debate in Britain, as to whether those guarantees were legally binding, and a referendum was really necessary.

The Conservative Party immediately declared that their government would hold a referendum in Britain if the Conservatives were elected to government in 2010, as long as ratification had not been completed by then, in all the other Member States. In order to reach his goal, David Cameron wrote to the Czech President, Klaus asking him to help his party hold the referendum. He asked Klaus to delay ratification further until the British elections had been held (*Daily Mail*, 23 September 2009). His intention was to bring decision-making powers back as he thought these powers should be at a national, not a European level.

Unfortunately, Cameron's plans were soon dashed when the Czech President finally signed the document on 3 November. The ratification process was drawing to its completion in all Member States and the Lisbon Treaty was going to come into effect.

3. METHODOLOGY, DATA AND EMPIRICAL ANALYSIS

3.1. Corpus-Assisted Discourse Studies

The analysis presented in this chapter combines a more quantitative approach with a qualitative investigation of the corpus following the corpus-assisted discourse studies methodology (CADS). Partington (2004) points out how these two approaches serve analysts to explore linguistic features of a specific discourse type not only by concordancing data, reading small parts of texts but also by relying on external data such as the wider context in which the text is produced and on the analysts' own intuition. Other scholars have also demonstrated the validity of corpus tools in discourse studies pointing out how the corpus linguistics approach to discourse analysis helps to restrict bias and highlights specific discourse features (Baker, 2006; Mautner, 2009) The following paragraphs describe the data collection and size and the analysis of the corpus.

3.2. The Corpus

The corpus consists of 1,861 articles taken from 14 newspapers, three tabloids and four broadsheets plus their Sunday editions.[3] The corpus' full size consists of 914,602 running words. The articles were downloaded from the online database Lexis Nexis that provides researchers with a number of different resources.[4] The articles were saved in txt format, in order to be processed by WordSmith Tools (Scott, 2008), and then chronologically ordered and divided into subcoprora, with each newspaper being a subcorpus. Table 1 shows the number of articles, and the number of running words per newspaper, to provide an overview of the corpus size.

Table 1.   Description of the Corpus — Time Span, Articles and Tokens.

Newspaper	No. Articles	No. Tokens
Daily Mail	357	199,903
The Sunday Times	164	124,904
The Times	199	113,129
Guardian	151	92,779
The Daily Telegraph	161	90,092
The Independent	118	75,580
The Sun	309	66,225
Mirror	199	42,249
The Sunday Telegraph	53	39,275
The Observer	37	30,120
Independent on Sunday	18	13,940
Mail on Sunday	14	10,236
Sunday Mirror	50	10,866
News of the World	31	5,304

Note: The newspapers are ordered by the number of tokens.

3.3. Analysis of Data

In order to proceed with the analysis, it was decided firstly, to create a concordance list for each participant — Sarkozy, Barroso and Klaus — then to expand the concordance and analyse its co-text. Those concordances not strictly related to the debate over Lisbon were eliminated from the list. Before proceeding with the analysis of each concordance, collocates were investigated to see the relationship between the node word and the other lexemes in the corpus. Collocates also help us in the attempt to understand how the participants are referred to in the corpus, what verbs are used to talk about participants and what participants do or how they act. At a second stage concordances were expanded to explore the context and analyse the processes and participants involved in the debate, following the features introduced by Fairclough (1995b) and Halliday and Matthiessen (2004) transitivity model. In the analysis of transitivity only material, verbal and mental processes will be explored in order to investigate the (de)construction of European leaders' public and private identities. Table 2 shows the total number of occurrences per participant.

As can be seen in Table 2, Sarkozy has the highest number of concordances and this might be due to the fact that he was in charge of the rotating presidency at that time.

The following paragraphs provide a detailed analysis of the collocates and concordances in the co-text of each participant who is being investigated in this study.

3.4. Sarkozy: Analysis of Material, Mental and Verbal Processes

In order to have an overview of what the newspapers say about Sakozy, it was deemed necessary to analyse Sarkozy's collocates in detail.

As can be seen from Table 3, it emerged that Merkel, who is also referred to as Angela, German and Chancellor, is one of the most frequent collocates of Sarkozy. Other frequent collocates refer to Sarkozy's nationality and his national role as President while other collocates reveal his love affair with Carla Bruni. Other politicians are also frequent collocates of Sarkozy such as Mendelson and Cowen.

Table 2. Number of Concordances per Participant.

Concordances	Total Occurrences
Sarkozy	740
Klaus	427
Barroso	265

Table 3. Sarkozy Collocates Ordered by Relation.

Word	Relation	Word	Relation
PRESIDENT[a]	58,17	DUBLIN	6,06
FRENCH[a]	48,91	TOLD[b]	5,62
MERKEL[c]	39,58	MEETING[a]	5,39
MR	33,57	DESCRIBED[b]	4,90
ANGELA[c]	24,48	DETERMINED [d]	4,82
NICHOLAS[a]	21,68	MEET[e]	4,55
PARIS[a]	18,66	TAKES[e]	3,65
BRUNI[f]	14,80	HAS	3,60
CARLA[f]	14,49	EU'S[a]	2,84
FRANCE[a]	14,41	ACCUSED[b]	2,75
CHANCELLOR[c]	13,50	PLANS[a]	2,62
FRANCE'S[a]	12,33	PRESIDENCY[a]	2,45
TRAVEL[e]	9,52	LEADER[a]	2,25
MANDELSON	9,27	COWEN	1,78
HOLDS[a]	7,45	PLAN[a]	1,65
SAID[b]	7,44	ASKED[b]	1,29
VISIT	7,30	SAYING[b]	1,27
GERMAN[c]	6,96	BECOME	1,08
KEEN[d]	6,75	SUMMIT[a]	1,04
WIFE[f]	6,35		
WANTS[d]	6,13		

Notes:
[a]Referring to Sarkozy's National and Institutional roles.
[b]Referring to reporting verbs.
[c]Referring to Merkel.
[d]Referring to mental verbs.
[e]Referring to material verbs.
[f]Referring to his love affair.
For space constraint the Table excludes collocates with relation inferior to 1.

There are references to Sarkozy's plan, probably his plan as president of the EU and other references to his role as EU president such as 'summit', and 'meeting'.

As far as the verbs are concerned, among the reporting verbs greater frequency have the verbs 'told', 'said' and 'accused'. The verb accused is not used by Sarkozy but by other sayers. Among the mental verbs we have the verbs 'want', 'determined', the adjective 'keen' which seem to indicate a firm desire and intense devotion to the Lisbon cause and among the material verbs we have the verbs 'visit', 'meet' and 'takes' referring to things that Sarkozy did during his presidency. Looking at these transitivity patterns is important to understand how much responsibility is assigned to Sarkozy in his official role as EU President. However, to provide a better frame for interpretation it is necessary to investigate concordances and explore the co-text.

Table 4 shows the actors and goals which emerged from the analysis of the concordances of the node word 'Sarkozy'. For space constraint only goals with a minimum of three occurrences are shown. As is visible in Table 4, there are references to Sarkozy's visit to Dublin and Prague and references to his institutional role in the EU.

The expression 'He/Sarkozy takes over/holds the EU presidency' frequently occurs, as was the case in the previously observed collocates (Table 3). It also emerged that there are references to Sarkozy's push on Warsaw and Prague and more in general on the ratification of the treaty and its implementation in order to persuade the Irish people. Sarkozy appears to be intent on reaching the ratification deal as Examples 1, 2 and 3 show.

(1) Mr Sarkozy visits Ireland this week in an attempt to begin the process of persuading them to hold a second referendum in which they change their minds. (*The Sunday Telegraph*, 10 July 2008)

(2) EU BIGWIGS led by French leader Nicolas Sarkozy last night tried to BULLY the plucky Irish into overturning their historic 'no' vote on the Lisbon Treaty. (*The Sun*, 20 June 2008)

(3) Nicolas Sarkozy, the president of France, is travelling to Prague to put pressure on the Czech government to continue its ratification process. (*The Daily Telegraph*, 16 June 2008)

It is clear that in all the Examples, Sarkozy's visit as EU president to Ireland and Prague is described as being an attempt to convince the Irish and the Czech governments to continue the ratification process. In Examples 1 and 2, the Irish people are the goals of Sarkozy and the EU leaders' forceful actions while in Example 3 the Czech government is the target having to face Sarkozy's 'pressure'. The verbs 'persuade', 'bully', in Examples 1 and 2, and the noun 'pressure' in Example 3, place emphasis on the influential role of those in power who try to reach their own purposes, often without considering the perspectives of those in a weaker position.

Table 4. Actors and Goals in Sarkozy's Concordances. Concordances Were Calculated Manually.

Actor	N	Goal	N
Sarkozy	78	Ireland/Dublin/us/foreign capital/the country/on our (Irish) shores	23
		EU presidency	10
		Treaty/Lisbon/ratification/ new mission/a document	5
		Prague/Warsaw and Prague	3

While analysing the occurrences related to material processes, a very interesting and vivid metaphor emerged — the food metaphor — which clearly
expresses part of the British press' attitude towards Sarkozy's actions. As many
scholars have proved (Musolff et al., 2001; Nasti, 2012; Semino, 2002) metaphors play an important role in understanding social and political realities and
for this reason they are worth exploring. Metaphors are a very potential tool
that can help journalism to fulfil what Richardson (2007, p. 7) claims to be its
true function, that is 'to enable citizens to better understand their lives and their
position(s) in the world.' By presenting complex and abstract situations in more
simple and familiar terms metaphors enable readers to understand very complex political issues. The metaphor in Example 4 has this equation: Sarkozy's
ideas and plans are food prepared to be served up to unknowing EU citizens.

(4) Nicolas Sarkozy has been cooking up ideas for a grand menu of achievements for
France to munch through during its six-month presidency of the European Union,
which starts today. With the Lisbon Treaty as its main course, he had planned, as a sort
of mezze, a dish of his own invention, a 'Union of the Mediterranean'. Yet, if we poor
EU referendum-starved geese are worried that we might end up being force-fed by Mr
Sarkozy, we should take comfort. Think what he promised before he was elected
President of France. With his whirlwind reputation, the French expected economic,
social and labour reforms to be served up piping hot. Fourteen months later, voters
look up unfed, as the promised courses congeal in the kitchen. So, by the end of his six-
month EU shift, Mr Sarkozy will be lucky to have warmed up the oven. (*The Daily
Telegraph*, 1 July 2008)

Example 4 clearly expresses strong condemnation of the French Prime
Minister who seems determined to effect his own interests during his six-month
presidency without necessarily maintaining his promises. Sarkozy is described
as a leader unable to fulfil his promises as evident in the expression 'the promised courses congeal in the kitchen', in this case Lisbon and all its provisions.
The metaphor also provides irony that is reinforced by the prepositional phrase
'with his whirlwind reputation', all the passage seems to suggest that Sarkozy is
all talk and no action.

As far as verbal processes are concerned, Table 5 below illustrates the verbiage of communicative verbs when Sarkozy or his allies are the Sayers of the
clause. Table 5 provides examples with a minimum of two occurrences.

From the analysis it emerged that there was a volition to solve the problem
created by the Irish referendum result as the expressions 'find a solution' and
'minimise the Irish problem' reveal, this solution seems to be achievable by urging ratification and a second vote in Ireland. *The Sunday Times* (26 June 2008)
in fact hints at the ambiguity in Sarkozy's approach, in that his promises are
different from his actions:

(5) At last week's summit in Brussels, Sarkozy promised to 'keep the (European) family
together', but once he arrives in Dublin he will be pressing for a second referendum'.
(*The Sunday Times*, 26 June 2008)

Table 5. Verbiage of Verbal Processes Emerged from the Analysis of Sarkozy's Concordances.

Sayer (Sarkozy or His Allies/Office)	N	Verbiage	N
Sarkozy(he) President' con science	132	Urge ratification	15
(Close) allies to Sarkozy	7	Urging/option of a second referendum in Ireland as a possible solution/as necessary	13
Alain Lamassoure, a French MEP	3	No reworking of the document/no renegotiation/No treaty part III/the treaty could not be reopened/No plan C/It's either Lisbon, or it's Nice/there will be no new treaty	11
French president's (Sarkozy's) office	2	Negation of bullying Irish/of saying Irish have to vote again	8
Sarkozy and Merkel	2	Blames EU trade policy for the no vote	8
Mr Poniatowski, a spokesman for Mr Sarkozy,	2	Finding a solution to the crisis	8
Sarkozy's Foreign Minister	1	Sarkozy is coming to listen to the Irish and not to make proposals	8
Dr Kouchner	1	Acknowledgement of problems within the EU	6
Barroso, Merkel and Sarkozy	1	EU's priorities	6
Merkel, Sarkozy and others	1	No ratification no further enlargement and negative consequences	10
Sarkozy, Merkel and Zapatero	1	Minimising/tackling the Irish problem	5
France	1	The dilemma (over the post as President of Europe)	5
Sarkozy and Berlusconi	1	Appraisal of Brown for going ahead with treaty ratification	4
Joseph Daul, the chairman of EPP, the MEP for Strasbourg	1	There would be no treaty with a referendum in Europe/France	4
Pierre Lellouche, France's Europe Minister	1	Seek unity in the European family	3
The Elysee Palace	1	References to the creation of an intervention force/European army	3
A spokesman for the Department of Foreign Affairs	1	Britain should become more integrated with the EU (Tories delay of ratification and referendum proposal)	3
		Benefits of the treaty	3
		We don't have a miracle solution/Ireland needs time	2
		Accept Irish no	2
		Providing guarantees	2
		Waiting before deciding what to do	2

The negative portrayal of the French Prime Minister is conveyed through the use of the contrastive evaluator 'but' which enhances the dichotomy between the verbal process 'promise' and the material process 'press'.

The analysis of the co-text also proved that Sarkozy and his allies emphasise that a lack of ratification could cause negative consequences, especially for Ireland and no further enlargement. As a result, the British advance in the ratification process is praised. The investigation also revealed that Sarkozy's allies focus on the fact that the President will not present proposals to the Irish but stresses his willingness to listen to what the Irish have to say. Other occurrences also show Sarkozy's denial of his statement about a second Irish vote. Sarkozy's allies seem to be presenting positive aspects of the French leader as a person who is willing to listen and then decide what to do. *The Times* (21 July 2008) for example reports the quotation of the left-wing star of Mr Sarkozy's cross-party Cabinet 'We are going there [Dublin] as the French presidency of the Union and not as "France, the giver of lessons". We will listen to all sides'.

When looking at the verbal processes of Sayers other than Sarkozy, it emerged that what they say construes a very negative evaluation of the French leader as a dictator who wants to tell the Irish what to do. They criticise Sarkozy for having said 'the Irish have to vote again' (Example 5).

> (6) FRENCH President Nicolas Sarkozy has vowed to listen to Irish people when he visits Dublin tomorrow - despite telling us to vote AGAIN on the Lisbon Treaty ... . He stated that he is a defender of the Irish people's right to say No ... 'I was one of the first leaders to say the democratic decision of the Irish people should be respected', he said. But he added that he needs to 'understand the message the Irish wanted to convey by voting No to a bond signed by 27 EU member states'. Mr Sarkozy also warned Ireland faces losing its power in Europe because of its vote last month. He said: 'By rejecting the Lisbon Treaty, the Irish have risked losing their commissioner in 2009 rather than 2014.' (*The News of the World*, 20 July 2008)

Example 6 clearly portrays the inconsistent ideas of the French leader. He appears as someone who pretends to listen to the Irish people while taking time to better understand how EU leaders can reach their deal. By using 'despite' and 'again' in capital letters, the noun 'defender' contrasting with Sarkozy's quotation, the newspaper stresses Sarkozy's ambivalence and inconsistency. Moreover, the newspaper seems to convey an image of the leader who is threatening and expressing his authority, as shown by the use of the verb 'warn'.

The analysis of passive voices seems to confirm the results which emerged from the analysis of the verbiage of Sarkozy's opponents. In fact the cluster *is/was accused of* occurs 3 times and its verbiage is Sarkozy's attempt to salvage Lisbon by urging its ratification.

Other occurrences also refer to Sarkozy's pressure on Ireland as something that must be stopped, even though more neutral verbs are used.

From the analysis of verbal processes, it emerged that among the reporting verbs those verbs expressing neutral opinion (81) such as 'say', 'tell', 'state', 'restate' have greater frequency than those verbs expressing a promise (11) such as 'vow', 'promise', 'pledge', followed by those expressing authority (10) such as 'insist', 'order', 'signal', 'demand', 'call for'. Other verbs are also frequent such as those expressing officiality (8) for example the expression 'issued a statement', the verbs 'declare', 'proclaim', 'announce', 'claim', those expressing evidentiality (7) such as 'making clear/plain', 'assure', 'reassure', 'confirm', those expressing disapproval (7) such as 'blame', 'complain', 'criticise', 'rail at', especially used by Sarkozy's opponents and approval (6) such as 'thank', 'praise', 'hail', the expression 'single out for thanks', especially with reference to Brown's ride for ratification in Britain and the ratification itself. Other recurring verbs are those verbs expressing warnings (5) such as 'warn' and 'threaten'.

Table 6 provides a summary of what emerged from the analysis of the concordances where Sarkozy is the Senser.

As Table 6 shows, Sarkozy's main concern is the second Irish referendum. He seems determined to have the Irish question settled and the treaty put in place by the end of the year, as shown in Example 7.

> (7) Because more than anyone else, it is Mr Sarkozy who is determined that the Irish must lie down to Lisbon. The French president is determined Lisbon will go through, despite even his own French people rejecting the same treaty in their constitutional referendum, despite the Dutch rejecting it - and certainly despite the insignificant Irish rejecting it. (*Daily Mail*, 4 December 2008)

In Example 7, the newspaper expresses its disapproval of Sarkozy's determination which is contrasted with the rejection of the treaty. This contrast in reinforced by the repetition of both the verbs 'determine', 'reject' and the adverbs 'certainly' expressing evidentiality. Sarkozy appears as a powerful and resolute leader mindless of the opinion of EU citizens and above all of democracy.

Table 6. Mental Verbs — For Space Constraint a Minimum of Three Occurrences Are Shown.

Senser: Sarkozy and EU Leaders	N	What	N
Sarkozy	24	The Irish to vote again/a new referendum/Ireland can be made to vote again in a few months/the Irish must lie down to Lisbon	5
Sarkozy and other EU big players	4	To have the Irish question settled/to find a way around the Irish vote/to ensure that a solution to keep the Lisbon Treaty alive is found/to unveil the deal	4
		The treaty in place by the end of the year/to press forward from the Lisbon base/to keep the ratification process moving/to use France's EU presidency to steamroller the treaty through	4
		To push his agenda ahead/to save the EU/to solve Europe's crisis of confidence	3
		An agreement to create a common intervention force/a unified defence policy/it (cooperation in defence policy) is the most exciting development in Europe for a long time	3

Other occurrences refer to the creation of a EU intervention force as something desirable and suggest that Sarkozy's goal is to save the EU by pushing his agenda ahead.

In order to have a wide spectrum on how the press construes Sarkozy's identity, predicates and attributes were investigated. It emerged that among the predicates he is described as being 'unpredictable', 'loco', 'one of the brokers of the mini-treaty', 'architect of the treaty', 'presidential playboy', 'political dilettante', 'a six-month irritant', 'little Napoleon', 'a man in a hurry', 'a militarist who is an enthusiast in spending money', 'as not a neutral conciliator', 'a though political operator'. On the other hand, the analysis proved that 'arrogant' is the only attribute collocating with Sarkozy, apart from the appositive noun clause French president.

What emerges is a negative picture of Sarkozy as a careless leader — as is evident in the use of the adjectives *arrogant, militarist* and the predicates *not a neutral conciliator, a though political operator*. The press also seems to mock Sarkozy when describing him as *a man in a hurry, presidential playboy, political dilettante* emphasising his inability to deal with important issues, a similar frame to the one portrayed by the food metaphor (Example 4).

To conclude, both the analyses of material and verbal processes revealed that British newspapers tend to describe Sarkozy as a powerful leader whose aim is to save the European Union from the Irish crisis. It is also clear that Sarkozy is the main actor of verbs which reflect his position as President of the European Union.

The most frequent verbs in the verbal processes showed that newspapers only report what the French leader says without expressing positive or negative evaluation but rather neutral opinions and in some occurrences authority, official statements and also the promises that Sarkozy makes — to keep the European family together or save the EU.

The press seems to ridicule or minimise Sarkozy's role by referring to his love affair with Carla Bruni, by using the food metaphor and adjectives such as *political dilettante* and *presidential playboy*.

3.5. Barroso: Analysis of Material, Mental and Verbal Processes

As in the previous analysis, the first step was to look at collocates in order to have an overview of what is referred to when talking of Barroso. Table 7 shows collocates ordered by relation.

As can be seen in Table 7, Barroso's collocates seem to suggest that the British press refers to Barroso's Institutional role within the EU as the President of the European Commission, and in its use of reporting verbs the British press seems to frequently use verbs expressing authority in virtue of

Table 7.   Barroso's Collocates.

Word	Relation	Word	Relation
COMMISSION[a]	79.71	BELIEVE[b]	4.64
PRESIDENT[a]	54.06	NIGHT	4.07
EUROPEAN[a]	26.58	COMMISSIONER[c]	3.93
MR	13.46	LAST	2.99
SAID[d]	8.48	YESTERDAY	2.98
INSISTED[d]	8.03	EU [a]	2.76
WARNED[d]	6.34	WEEK	2.04
CHIEF	5.90	OTHER	1.25
MERKEL[c]	5.29	AS	1.05
TOLD[d]	5.19		

Notes:
[a]Referring to his institutional role.
[b]Referring to mental verbs.
[c]Referring to other European ministers.
[d]Referring to reporting verbs.
The collocates are ordered by relation. The table excludes collocates with a relation inferior to 1.

Barroso's political role. However, to provide a better frame for interpretation it is necessary to investigate concordances and explore the co-text.

As in the analysis of Sarkozy's occurrences, the clauses where Barroso was Sayer and Target or part of the Verbiage were separated. Table 8 provides a summary of the verbiage resulting from the analysis of verbal processes in Barroso's concordances, when Barroso is the Sayer. Only the verbiage with a minimum occurrence of 2 is reported.

It emerged that when Barroso is the Sayer he urges ratification by pointing out that the *Treaty is not dead but still alive* and warns about the negative consequences that Ireland and Europe will face if Ireland and other countries do not pass Lisbon – 'We will all pay a price for it, Ireland included', he said (*The Daily Telegraph*, 31 May 2008).

> (8) Barroso, 55, has ordered other countries to push on with ratifying the pact - even though we gave it a big thumbs down. The EU chief even hinted red-faced Taoiseach Brian Cowen could be forced to hold a referendum RE-RUN to secure a Yes. (*The Sun*, 17 June 2008)

> (9) He said suggestions that the Lisbon treaty will impose a minimum wage in Ireland are 'absurd lies', and insisted that it would not affect Ireland's sovereignty over taxation, abortion and euthanasia. Barroso also warned that a No vote would damage the Irish economy and threaten jobs and investment. He claimed the only way for Ireland to ensure it keeps a commissioner is to vote Yes (*The Sunday Times*, 20 September 2009)

In Examples 8 and 9, the use of the reporting verbs 'order', 'insist', 'warn' clearly portray Barroso as an authoritarian leader intent on pursuing his aim,

Table 8.   Verbiage of Verbal Processes Emerged from the Analysis of
Sarkozy's Concordances.

Sayer	N	Verbiage	N
Barroso	129	Urging ratification (EU member states should act quickly)	13
Barroso, Merkel and Sarkozy	1	The treaty is not dead/it is still alive/the reform package is still alive	11
		Reassuring Ireland on tax veto (IRELAND will continue to have a veto on tax policies under the Lisbon Treaty)	7
		Europe and Ireland would 'pay a price' if the treaty is rejected	7
		No plan b/plan A would be resubmitted	6
		Not to rock the boat on the treaty/find a solution I believe we should now try to find a solution	4
		Unless he signs the Czechs will lose their Commissioner/the consequences for ten million Czechs if their leader refuses to give in	4
		A great day for Ireland and for Europe	3
		Demands to reopen negotiations on the revamped European Constitution were 'absurd'/any attempts by Mr Klaus to reopen the Lisbon Treaty	3
		This was not a vote against Europe	2
		Congratulated Britain (for treaty support)	2
		The No vote in Ireland has not solved the problems which the Lisbon Treaty is designed to solve.	2
		A no vote would be bad for the whole of Europe/A no vote would be catastrophic for Europe	2
		Made a plea for Ireland to a Yes	2
		Europe would be stronger and better equipped/the treaty is the next glorious stage in the EU future	2
		Ordered other countries to IGNORE our vote	2

this being the ratification of Lisbon. Moreover, the use of the expression 'the only way' in Example 9 also reveals Barroso's dictatorial leadership.

The analysis of the reporting verbs proved that the neutral verbs (62) are the most frequent, followed by those expressing authority and command (22), official statements (9), warnings (8), promise (5), approval (5), certainty (3). As a result, this investigation revealed that Barroso is in general depicted as a powerful leader whose only aim is the Lisbon Treaty whose ratification he imposes officially and authoritatively.

Looking at the reporting verbs when Barroso is target or part of the verbiage it has emerged that apart from neutral reporting verbs there are also verbs expressing negative connotation and disapproval of Barroso's actions such as 'accused of' and 'criticise'.

However, other verbs also acquire negative connotation because of their collocate, as shown in Example 10.

(10) Declan Ganley, the Libertas leader, called Barroso a coward for refusing to engage in a debate (*The Sunday Times*, 20 September 2009)

In Example 10, in fact the neutral verb 'call' collocates with 'coward' thus acquiring a negative connotation. However, it is important to notice that the Sayer of the proposition is Declan Ganley, the founding member of the anti-Lisbon movement Libertas.

When analysing mental processes, it emerged that Barroso is the Senser of the verb believe which often expresses a faith in the treaty and its ratification process and confidence that there will be no further delays. This is also expressed by the cluster 'is determined to' as is clear in Example 11.

(11) Mr Barroso is determined to plough on and Taoiseach Brian Cowen could be forced to hold a rerun of the referendum to get a yes vote (*The Sun*, 14 June 2008)

In Example 11, Barroso's determination is reinforced by the metaphorical verb *plough on* and the enforcing action, 'could be forced', of which Cowen is the goal.

As far as material processes are concerned, apart from verbs that indicate Barroso's movements/visits from one place to another there are three verbs that seem to support what emerged from the analysis of mental and verbal processes. In fact Barroso is the actor of the verb 'bully', Example 12, whose goal is the Irish people, actor of 'plug', Example 13, whose goal is the treaty and actor of the verb 'ignore', Example 14, whose goal is the result. These three verbs all occur in headlines and construe the image of Barroso as a powerful, mindless leader, who is disrespectful of democratic values.

(12) Barroso bullies the Irish (*The Daily Telegraph*, 28 May 2005)

(13) Barroso ignores result (*The Sun*, 14 June 2008)

(14) Sparks fly as Barroso plugs the treaty (*The Sunday Times*, 20 September 2009)

In order to have a wider perspective on how the press construes Barroso's identity, adjectives and predicates were examined. It emerged that the majority of the occurrences confirms the image of Barroso construed by the processes analysed herewith. The press refers to Barroso as 'arrogant', as a 'Boss' and ironically as an 'Anglophile president'. Moreover, anti-Lisbon leaders describe Barroso as a 'thug and bully' (McKenna in the *Mail*)[5] and an 'insignificant nobody' (Ganley in the *Mirror*).

In conclusion, the analysis proved that Barroso is described as a powerful leader, disrespectful of democracy and only concerned with the completion of the ratification

The analyses of the attributes, verbal and mental processes showed that the press mainly refers to Barroso's official role in the EU. There are frequent occurrences of verbs expressing official statements, authority and determination and the appositive noun clause *European Commission President.*

3.6. *Klaus: Analysis of Material, Mental and Verbal Processes*

As in the analyses of Sarkozy and Barroso, the investigation of Klaus's concordances started by looking at the collocates in order to have a general overview of what emerges when talking of Klaus. Table 9 shows the collocates ordered by relation.

Table 9.   Klaus' Collocates.

Word	Relation	Word	Relation
CZECH[a]	60.93	WHOSE	4.55
PRESIDENT[a]	59.77	LEADER	4.44
MR	22.42	SIGNED[b]	3.92
EUROSCEPTIC[c]	21.09	WHEN	3.90
SIGN	19.28	SAID[d]	3.86
PRAGUE	16.92	UNTIL	3.54
REPUBLIC[a]	14.11	RATIFICATION[c]	2.69
HOPED[e]	12.06	OUT	2.38
DEMANDED[d]	11.49	TOLD[d]	2.22
WROTE[b]	9.34	ADDED[d]	2.16
LETTER	8.50	STATE[d]	2.09
PRESSURE	6.76	PARLIAMENT	1.90
HAS	6.31	LAST	1.85
REFUSED[d]	5.75	BETWEEN	1.82
COUNTRY'S	5.73	NOT	1.78
HOPE[e]	5.68	HOLD[b]	1.75
HOLDING[b]	5.51	STILL	1.55
OPT	5.44	YET	1.53
FEARS[e]	5.43	AGAINST	1.46
HAD	5.06	BEEN	1.40
WHO	4.73	WEEK	1.30
HIS	4.58	HE	1.12

Notes:
[a]Referring to national/political role.
[b]Referring to material verbs.
[c]Referring to his position within the EU.
[d]Referring to reporting verbs.
[e]Referring to mental verbs.
Collocates are ordered by relation.

The analysis of collocates seems to suggest that the British press refers to Klaus' national, political role as the President of the Czech Republic, and his position within the EU as being a Eurosceptic. In the use of reporting verbs the British press frequently use verbs expressing authority and refusal in virtue of Klaus' political role. The mental verbs seem to convey Klaus' hopes and fears. There are also references to pressure on ratification. However, to provide a wider framework of analysis it is necessary to investigate concordances and the co-text. Table 10 shows the concordances with a minimum of 2 occurrences relative to verbal processes.

When looking at the verbal processes when Klaus is the Sayer, the most frequent occurrences refer to Klaus' refusal to sign the treaty because 'it is dead', 'it is not good for Europe', because it is senseless going ahead without Ireland. Other occurrences express Klaus' authority especially when demanding for opt-outs from the Charter of Fundamental Rights as something necessary for a possible change of mind. There are also references to Klaus' statement that the ratification process 'is a train that cannot be stopped' which expresses his reasons for signing the treaty (see paragraph 1.2).

The analysis of verbal processes demonstrated that the most frequent other sayers are Barroso, Cameron and Fisher. Barroso and Fisher put stress on a possible agreement with Klaus to complete ratification. Barroso in particular

Table 10. Verbiage of the Verbal Processes Emerged by the Analysis of Klaus' Concordances.

Sayer: Klaus or His Allies	N	Verbiage	N
Klaus	127	Refusal to sign (until deliberation)	27
Allies	1	Demands for opting out from the Charter of fundamental rights	21
his office	1	Continuing ratification after Irish no is senseless/pressing ratification would have Disastrous consequences/ratification only if Ireland ratifies	11
		The treaty is dead/he will not encourage ratification	9
		It is too late to stop ratification for Britain/he cannot wait until British referendum	6
		It is a train that cannot be stopped	6
		Praise and support for Libertas opinions/other MEPs	5
		Prepared to sign	4
		Czech Republic finishes to be a sovereign with Lisbon	4
		Treaty is not good for Europe	4
		'I only said that I had not experienced such an atmosphere, such a style of debate, in the Czech Republic in the last 19 years.'	4
		Satisfied with concessions	3
		Welcome the Irish no/support Irish stance	2

Table 11. Actors and Goals in Klaus' Concordances.

Actor	N	Goal	N
Klaus	54	Formal ratification (blocking)/has yet to sign/dragging his feet over ratification/has to sign/hold up the treaty (ratification)/threw a spanner/set to delay/has not signed/ hold out/final attempt to derail the treaty	17
		His signature/expected to sign/on the pint of ending his last stand/moved closer to sign	18
		Presidency of the EU	3
		EU flag	2

expresses his faith in a final positive outcome to the extent that he said 'he was confident that Mr Klaus would sign the treaty 'in the end' ' (*The Independent*, 5 October 2009). Fisher too seems to work in the direction Barroso indicated he says '… he would secure 'guarantees' from Klaus not to cause further delays …' (the *Guardian*, 13 October 2009)

While Cameron hoped that Klaus would not sign, he acknowledges that he is about to change his attitudes towards the Treaty.

As far as the material processes are concerned, the results indicate an equal number of references to when Klaus firmly opposes ratification and to when he is about to sign the Treaty, as shown in Table 11.

Klaus' firm opposition to ratification is often expressed by verbs such as 'block', 'derail', 'delay' and the verb 'threw' in the expression 'threw a spanner', indicating an obstacle, of which he is the actor. Other fewer occurrences refer to Klaus' role as president of the EU rotating presidency which started at the beginning of 2009.

The analysis of mental processes construes a similar image to what emerged from the verbal processes. The occurrences proved that Klaus' great desire is to gain an opt-out from the Charter of Fundamental Rights as he fears German property claims and for this reason he appears to be determined to block ratification and act in the interest of his own people. On the other hand, looking at mental processes where Klaus is not the Senser, the Conservatives were the most frequent Sensers and 'hope' the most frequent verb expressing the Tories' approval of Klaus' resistance to the Treaty.

In order to have a wider framework on how the press construes the identity of the Czech President, an analysis of attributes and predicates was carried out. It emerged that Klaus is described as a *Eurosceptic, sceptical, maverick* but there are also references to the unpredictability of his actions, on whether or not he will sign the treaty.

> (15) It emerged that a legal challenge against the treaty's validity was being 'fast-tracked' through the Czech courts. This means the country's Eurosceptic president Vaclav Klaus could be forced to ratify the European Constitution before the end of the year. (the *Daily Mail*, 7 October 2009)

Example 15, apart from describing the Czech leader as a Eurosceptic also reveals a negative picture of EU leaders as possible enforcers, as revealed by the use of the passive voice of the verb 'to force' and the modal 'could'.

The investigation has also shown that Klaus is metaphorically described in terms of *hurdle* or *obstacles* to overcome, which reiterates the portrayal of Klaus in the analysis of the material processes.

In conclusion, the investigation proved that Klaus is described as a Eurosceptic worried about the completion of the ratification and determined to block EU progress because he fears that the approval of Lisbon would lead to disastrous consequences for the Czech Republic as his main fear concerns German property claims.

The occurrences of verbal processes showed that the most frequent verbs following those expressing neutral opinion are those revealing authority and expressing official statements followed by those expressing refusal and disapproval which are indicative of Klaus' Euroscepticism.

The most frequent mental verbs 'want', 'fear' and the cluster 'is determined to' are indicative of Klaus' intention to pursue his only aim that is not to sign the treaty. However, in the end Klaus changed his mind not because of EU leaders' pressure but because of the guarantees on German land claims he obtained by the EU leaders, that is because of his own interests.

4. CONCLUSIONS

The analysis has revealed that the use of specific language patterns represent the public and private identity of EU politicians. All the politicians here investigated are depicted as powerful leaders because of their institutional/political role within the EU and this has been demonstrated by the use of verbs expressing authority and official statements.

The analysis has also shown how the media play a pivotal role in the construction and deconstruction of the public and private identity of EU politicians. As many discourse analysts (Fairclough, 1995b; Richardson, 2007; Van Dijk, 1991) pointed out the message conveyed by the press might influence readers' opinions and attitude towards a specific issue and as a result, might contribute to the construction of public consensus. In the case of the Lisbon Treaty debate the British press' construction of Barroso and Sarkozy's identity as powerful leaders intent on pursuing ratification at any cost might influence public perception of the two politicians and foster a negative opinion on EU integration. At the same time, when the British press ridicules Barroso and Sarkozy's private identities by referring to the French President's love affair with Carla Bruni and to him as a 'political dilettante' or to the President of the EU Commission as an 'Anglophile leader', it is reinforcing negative opinions and diminishing the EU leaders' roles. These discourse constitutive roles emerging from the representations of Sarkozy and Barroso have a negative impact on public decisions on EU matters.

The investigation has shown that only Klaus is described differently as a Eurosceptic leader who becomes an 'obstacle' when opposing ratification. The emphasis on the Czech Leader's Euroscepticism comes as no surprise considering that several scholars (Musolff et al., 2001; Nasti, 2012; Nasti & Venuti, 2014) have already discussed and proved that the general sentiment filling the pages of the British press when reporting on European issues is that of Euroscepticism. However, the British press put Klaus on the same level as all the other politicians here investigated, when he changed his mind due to the guarantees obtained. The Czech leader in fact seems to justify his position when he says 'it is a train that cannot be stopped' as if he was simply giving into the decision made by other EU countries. These (de)construction of identities seem to reflect contextual differences – Barroso and Sarkozy have always been in favour of European enlargement and integration due to their European institutional roles whereas Klaus never actively endorsed integration.

In conclusion, this chapter has proved how the representations of European politicians' identities are evidence of specific attitudes towards the ratification of the Lisbon Treaty, reflecting both discourse constituted and constitutive roles, the latter having a negative influence on the process of EU integration and helping to construe the press' opinions concerning each politician. This study also seems to confirm previous research which shows that EU leaders are portrayed as bullies and enforcers who are unmindful of democracy.

NOTES

1. For further references see Presidency Conclusions 21-22 June 2007 available at: http://www.consilium.europa.eu/uedocs/cms_data/docs/pressdata/en/ec/94932.pdf.
2. For further references to the complete stages of the ratification procedure in the UK see http://services.parliament.uk/bills/2007-08/europeanunionamendment/stages. html.
3. Three tabloids and their Sunday editions (*The Sun, News of The World, Daily Mail, Mail on Sunday, Mirror, Sunday Mirror*) and four broadsheets and their Sunday editions (*The Times, The Sunday Times, The Independent, The Independent on Sunday, Guardian, The Observer, The Daily Telegraph, The Sunday Telegraph*).
4. Further references available at www.lexisnexis.com
5. Patricia McKenna is an Irish independent politician. She served as a Green Party Member of the European Parliament (MEP) for the Dublin constituency from 1994 to 2004.

REFERENCES

Anderson, P. J., & Weymouth, T. (1999). *Insulting the public? The British press and the European Union*. New York, NY: Longman.

Baker, P. (2006). *Using corpora in discourse analysis*. New York, NY: Continuum.

Fairclough, N. (1992). *Discourse and social change*. Cambridge: Polity Press.

Fairclough, N. (1995a). *Media discourse*. London: Edward Arnold.

Fairclough, N. (1995b). *Critical discourse analysis: The critical study of language*. London: Longman.

Fowler, R. (1991). *Language in the news: Discourse and ideology in the press*. London: Routledge.

Halliday, M. A. K., & Matthiessen, C. (2004). *Introduction to functional grammar* (3rd ed.). London: Arnold.

Mautner, G. (2009). Corpora and critical discourse analysis. In P. Baker (Ed.), *Contemporary approaches to corpus linguistics* (pp. 32–46). London: Continuum.

Mills, S. (1995). *Feminist stylistics*. London: Routledge.

Musolff, A. (2004). *Metaphor and political discourse: Analogical reasoning in debates about Europe*. New York, NY: Palgrave Macmillan.

Musolff, A., Good, C., Points, P., & Wittlinger, R. (Eds.) (2001). *Attitudes towards Europe: language in the unification process*. Burlington, VT: Ashgate.

Nasti, C. (2012). *Images of the Lisbon treaty debate in the British press: A corpus-based approach to metaphor analysis*. Newcastle: Cambridge Scholars Publishing.

Nasti, C., & Venuti, M. (2014). The Lisbon treaty and the British press: A corpus-based contrastive analysis of evaluation resources. *Research in Language, 12*, 1.

Partington, A. (2004). Corpora and discourse, a most congruous beast. In A. Partington, J. Morley, & L. Haarman (Eds.), *Corpora and discourse* (pp. 11–19). Bern: Peter Lang.

Richardson, J. E. (2007). *Analysing newspapers: An approach from critical discourse analysis*. Basingstoke: Palgrave Macmillan.

Scott, M. (2008). *Wordsmith tools version 5*. Liverpool: Lexical Analysis Software Ltd.

Semino, E. (2002). A sturdy baby or a derailing train? Metaphorical representations of the euro in British and Italian newspapers. *Text, 22*(1), 107–139.

Van Dijk, T. A. (1991). *Racism and the press*. London: Routledge.

Van Leeuwen, T. (1996). The representation of social actors. In C. Caldas-Coulthard & M. Coulthard (Eds.), *Texts and practices: Readings in critical discourse analysis* (pp. 32–70). London: Routledge.

ONLINE REFERENCES

Presidency Conclusions 21-22 June 2007 http://www.consilium.europa.eu/uedocs/cms_data/docs/pressdata/en/ec/94932.pdf.

Stages of the ratification procedure in the UK http://services.parliament.uk/bills/2007-08/europeanunionamendment/stages.html

TORN BETWEEN AGENDAS: MACEDONIAN NATIONAL IDENTITY BETWEEN EUROPE AND ITS MULTICULTURAL AGENDAS

Maja Muhic

ABSTRACT

In the last two decades, the region of Southeast Europe, Republic of Macedonian included, has been marked by a politics based on the pronounced primacy of the issue of national identity over other socio-political questions. National identity as an issue per se *entails material, cultural and academic processes aiming at the construction and fixing of an idea and a sense of a collective. Ample evidence in terms of material culture (the architectural project Skopje 2014) and recorded public discourse supports the claim that the question of national identity determines the course of politics, nationally and internationally.*

The main focus of this chapter is to examine the different discourses regarding national identity, and the multicultural and cultural policies, formulated against the backdrop of the conditions set by the EU. Through a discursive analysis of some of the speeches and texts of Macedonian and Albanian political officials, this chapter will trace the various (re)constructions of national identity vis-à-vis Europe and Macedonia's aspirations for European Union (EU) accession. Additionally, Macedonia's complicated interethnic relations are analysed through the country's struggle with the name dispute with Greece and, through what is seen as a lack of loyalty from the Albanian political parties and citizens, which push for the change of the name for a

National Identity and Europe in Times of Crisis: Doing and Undoing Europe, 237–257
doi:10.1108/978-1-78714-513-920171011

faster EU accession. This further complicates the picture of the Macedonian
EU integration and creates a triangulation of discourses: one stemming from
the EU requirements, and two more, stemming from the two major ethnic
groups and political parties in Macedonia, namely the Macedonian and the
Albanian.

Keywords: Discourse; multiculturalism; segregation; nationalist;
narratives; EU integration

1. INTRODUCTION AND A NOTE ON METHODOLOGY

This chapter looks into the versatile discourses (in public speeches and statements) of representatives of the major political parties in the Republic of
Macedonia, which make reference to 'multiculturalism', 'tolerance', 'intercultural dialogue', 'interethnic cooperation', 'Ohrid Framework Agreement' and
'name dispute'. Most of these statements and speeches have nationalist overtones and are torn between several agendas. Although the Republic of
Macedonia is home to many different ethnic groups recognised fully and
equally with the Constitution and the amendments to its preamble made in
2001, the tensions, conflicts and reconciliations of the two major ethnic groups,
the majority Macedonians and the largest minority group, the Albanians, seem
to be dictating the overall climate in the country. The tensions of these two
groups construct and redefine the meaning of multiculturalism in the country,
both against the backdrop of EU and U.S. recommendations and pressures
and the multicultural reality of the country.

This chapter therefore offers a threefold way into the topic. It looks into the
discourses of the Macedonian officials including some material manifestation
of their views on the one hand, and the Albanian officials' opinions on the
other (including both the ruling and opposition parties' statements). It then
places these discourses against the backdrop of the EU requirements and attitudes regarding Macedonian's accession to EU, which additionally revolves
greatly around the name dispute with neighbouring Greece. To this end, this
chapter looks into several speeches and statements given by representatives of
the Macedonian Government (the President, the Prime Minister, Albanian
representatives constituting the Government of R. Macedonia and representatives of the Ministry of Foreign Affairs). The study also includes several statements coming from the EU officials, including the statements of some of the
Ambassadors to Macedonia, who have spoken about the name dispute and the
possible future solutions. The focus is mainly placed on the politicians' recent
statements and speeches (between the years 2011 and 2014) depending on the
specificity and references made to multiculturalism, interculturalism and the

name dispute of some of these statements. During this period, the government has underwent changes in terms of representatives, but some of the statements of what are now former representatives, still reflect the general attitude of the ruling and opposition parties.

1.1. Theoretical Framework

This study attempts to move the discussion regarding ethnic segregation and the efforts for social inclusion and ethnic integration beyond the exhausted discourses on multiculturalism propagated by authorities such as Will Kymlicka, Charles Taylor and others. While extremely important, these discourses focus on ethnic and national identity issues, tackling the idea of social transformation as one primarily defined by criteria of social in/equality and in/justice. Hence, this perspective loses from sight the sharpness and critical lens, which must account for both the different multi-ethnic contexts of countries, and the important contribution that can come from the areas such as cultural anthropology and political philosophy. Authorities such as Alex Callinicos (2009), David Harvey (2009, 2010), Bourdieu's notion of the *habitus* are often neglected, as is the importance of anthropological ethnographic work, which can reveal more about the actual state of affairs than the various exhausted narratives regarding identity and diversity policies. This chapter borrows much of its inspiration from Herzfeld's concept of *cultural intimacy*, using it as one of the main theoretical frameworks in the interpretation of the multiculturalism discourses in Macedonia but it also, generally tries to promote the ethnographic tools and anthropological perceptions of such complex issues.

2. THE MACEDONIAN MULTICULTURAL LANDSCAPE AND ITS CHALLENGES

Republic of Macedonia[1] is a multicultural country with ethnically and culturally heterogeneous population. It has gained its independence from the former Yugoslav federation with a referendum on 08.09.1991. In the last two decades, Macedonia has been marked by a politics based on the pronounced primacy of the issue of national identity over other socio-political questions. National identity, (and not cultural dialogue or recognition of diversity), entails material, cultural and academic processes aiming at the construction and fixing of an idea and a sense of a collective. The new architectonic Skopje 2014 project and the freezing of the Gender Department at State University Cyril and Methodius followed by the announcement for the launch of the Family Studies Institute instead, clearly speak of the strong nationalist politics and the patriarchal values being woven into the society. Ample evidence in terms of material culture and recorded public discourse supports the claim that the question of national identity determines the course of politics, nationally and internationally. The multicultural structure of Macedonian society is reflected in the variety of ethnicities, cultures and religions. According to the last census of 2002 Macedonia's population is as follows: Macedonians 64.2%, Albanians 25.2%, Turkish 3.9%, Roma 2.7%, Serb 1.8%, other 2.2%. According to the census of the same year, the religious groups representative of the country are as follows: Macedonian Orthodox 64.7%, Muslim 33.3%, other Christian 0.37%, other and unspecified 1.63%. The minority rights are regulated by the Constitution of 1991 which, among other things, proclaims that the citizens share the same freedoms and rights irrespective of their sex, race, colour of their skin, national and social background, political and religious attitudes, property and social status; freedom of citizens to gather together in order to realise and protect cultural and other rights and attitudes. Macedonia has ratified major international human rights treaties, including the European Convention for the Protection of Human Rights and Fundamental Freedoms and the Framework Convention for the Protection of National Minorities, and they take precedence over national legislation. It also adopted a new anti-discrimination Law in 2010, which prohibits discrimination on the basis of ethnicity, gender, race, social status, language, citizenship, religious conviction, political affiliation or disability.

In 2001 Macedonia was struck by an ethnic conflict, which brought an 8-month unrest and calamity in the region. The conflict expressed the grievances of the Albanian community as a marginalised group within Macedonia, and aimed to improve its participation in the society, and to strengthen their representation in politics and public administration. The Ohrid Framework Agreement (OFA) was signed on 13 August 2001, finally putting an end to the insurgencies and radically improving the conditions of the Albanian population in Macedonia. The OFA is the core framework, which lies behind the engagement of Macedonia to adjust its governance so as to allow the participation of minority groups in policy making and increase their presence and visibility in politics and public administration. OFA reacted to the 1991 Constitution[2] which defined the country as a 'national state of the Macedonian people' guaranteeing civil equality and co-existence of the Macedonian people with the Albanians, Turks, Vlachs, Roma and other nationalities, and 'called for the elimination of any reference to specific ethnic groups. Instead, it proposed language that only speaks of "citizens of Macedonia"' (Risteska, 2013, p. 28). With the amendments to the Constitution after the OFA, the following has also been provided for the nationalities: in the units of local self-government where at least 20% of the population speak a particular language, that language and its alphabet will be used as official, in addition to the Macedonian language and its Cyrillic alphabet.[3]

The multicultural reality in Macedonia is far from a simple one. Put briefly, the three major ethnic groups in Macedonia (Macedonians, Albanians and Turks) can all lay various claims on the present day territory of Macedonia.

While the Turks can lay the claim to the longest tradition of statehood, but suffer the handicap of small numbers in Macedonia, and the Albanians amortise the fact that they have never had a state on this territory with their claim that they have the longest continuous habitation in the Balkans tracing it back to the Illyrians, the Macedonians are the most numerous on the territory of Macedonia and have had their own state, which the Albanians in Macedonia have not (Muhić, 1994, p. 236). It is only fair to conclude that the multiculturalism in Macedonia is a natural model derived from the condition of the historical, demographical and cultural facts, but also one which forms the social reality (Sharlamanov & Stojanoski, 2012, p. 64). Unfortunately, as Janev (2009) observes, ethnonationalist politics dominate the public sphere in independent Macedonia and this is reflected in every aspect of social life. Ethnonationalist politicians have triggered the image of a deeply divided Macedonian society. As Janev further observes, the Macedonian public is already becoming used to the federalised structure of the territory, and the political, economic and public life in the country, while the Albanian public and elite are not showing much interest in processes that would soothe the separation and slowly bridge the divides challenged by current political representations that manipulate and single out only the negative aspects of Macedonia's diversity. The representations of the past, as given in the official Macedonian historiography, also fail to correct this distorted picture. These historians promote a paradigm that revolves around defence and promotion of their own national cause.

3. MACEDONIAN NARRATIVES AND STORIES

3.1. Multicultural Legacy

Although it was generally accepted that Macedonia was a unique former Yugoslav state due to its peaceful and bloodless secession from the Yugoslav Federation, in 2001 Macedonia was struck by an ethnic conflict, which brought an 8-month unrest in the region. The conflict started on 17 February 2001, when paramilitary Albanian groups (NLA-National Liberation Army) have entered the village of Tanusevci (in the mountain range of Skopska Crna Gora). In a short time span, the conflict between the Macedonian security forces and the NLA expanded to the North-western part of the country). The OFA was signed on 13 August 2001, finally putting an end to the insurgencies and aiming to improve the conditions of the Albanian population in Macedonia. The former NLA members together with their leader, Ali Ahmeti, established the Democratic Union for Integration (DUI) and entered the coalition with the then ruling parties SDSM (Social Democratic Union of Macedonia) and LDP (Liberal Democratic Party of Macedonia). Since the

2006 parliamentary elections, these parties became the opposition, and a new coalition government has been established, with VMRO-DPMNE (Internal Macedonian Revolutionary Organization) and DPA (Democratic Party of the Albanians) as its major constituents. However, after the 2008 and 2011 parliamentary elections, DUI again won the highest percentage of the Albanian electorate and continued to be part of the governmental coalition of VMRO-DPMNE. Following the breakup of Yugoslavia and the independence of Macedonia in 1991, a general trend in the shift between the majoritarian electoral model and the semi proportional one was at a rise. This model became fully proportional with the 2002 elections, following the signing of OFA, which insisted on the principle of proportionality. The result of this was that 'a coalition government, composed of the winners in both communities, the Macedonian and the Albanian one, in time became a custom, not an exception' (Maleska, 2013). The picture gets more complicated here, since the coalition forming the Government is not gathered around the same vision or ideology, but rather around ethnic lines, which have a far more disintegrative, rather than integrative influence on the Macedonia society. This fragmentation is visible at many levels, and is especially manifested in the highly-opposed and often conflicting narratives of the political party representatives regarding Macedonia's multiculturalism and the future path of the country.

The overall attitude of the ruling VMRO-DPMNE party is that Macedonia is a real example of a successful multicultural story, woven out of both a very long multicultural legacy and a successful multicultural presence sealed with the signing of OFA. At a lecture recently given at the McMaster University in Hamilton, Canada, the Macedonian President, Gjorgje Ivanov, stated that 'at present, when the multicultural model in Europe has failed because of the attitude towards the Muslims, Macedonia shows that Muslims and Christians have always lived there without prejudices or fears. Macedonia is a country which can be proud of its specific attitude towards diversity' (Ivanov, 20 April 2013).[4] He goes on to even recommend the Macedonian multicultural model as one of the most positive examples of multiculturalism for the countries in the region. Similar statements come from all other segments of the ruling party. In the addressing at the fifth meeting for the inclusion of Romas and Roma refugees, the Prime Minister, Nikola Gruevski stated that Macedonia is home to many diverse ethnic groups, languages and cultures. Hence, he added that it is 'our permanent endeavor to care about their equality, participation, emancipation, and integration in the Macedonian society' (Gruevski, 12 March 2014).

It is true that Macedonia has a long legacy of multiculturalism, which was vibrant during the Ottoman presence in the country. The Ottoman rule in the Balkans had its longest duration in the region which covers what is now the Republic of Macedonia, that is, from 1371 to 1913, a total of 542 years.[5] One element worth mentioning regarding the overall respect for diversity in the Ottoman Empire is the *millet*, which refers to the confessional communities in the Ottoman Empire. It also refers to the separate legal courts under which different communities were allowed to rule themselves under their own system. It is also closely linked to Islamic rules on the treatment of non-Muslim minorities. This system has been called an early example of pre-modern religious pluralism. The beginnings of Yugoslavia (SFRJ) on the other hand, produced a socialist agenda of brotherhood and unity, but did develop strategies to keep the Muslim population loyal. Moreover, the socialist regime was cautious against political and cultural movements that would carry a dose of nationalist overtones, thus threatening the brotherhood/unity ideology. The Yugoslav regime and the discourse on brotherhood carried tones of authoritarianism and set out to demonstrate this by shutting down movements with nationalist connotations, but it did succeed in creating a powerful Yugoslav identity which, due to a complex set of factors, saw its colossal fall in 1991. The historical facts support the overall argument, that Macedonia has a long history of multiculturalism both within the framework of the Ottoman Empire and during Yugoslavia. Since 1991, however, many things have changed, including the conflict in 2001, so to blatantly narrate that Macedonia is the best example for multiculturalism in the region as the ruling party VMRO does, becomes somewhat problematic. Holding this position is controversial in several aspects. Firstly, such argumentation lays its foundation in the multicultural past of the country, which very much stems from the particularities of the Ottoman Empire and the Yugoslav past, yet it neglects the current segregation process and the strong nationalist agenda of the ruling VMRO party, which is trying to obliterate much of both these pasts. Ample evidences of this obliteration can be found in the material and academic production; the architectural, and mainly monoethnic project Skopje 2014 being but one example.

To further support our claim that the ruling, Demo-Christian party VMRO-DPNE ironically promotes a discourse on the successful multicultural reality of the country while at the same time executing actions which support its nationalist agenda, let us turn to several more statements of some of its representatives. Although a somewhat older statement, than our general framework, former Minister of Foreign Affairs, Antonio Milososki, in his address in 2007 at the London School of Economics, holds on to the same historical multicultural constellation of Macedonia. Milososki notes that the hardest test for its ethnic diversity besieged the country in 2001, but fortunately a mature solution came with the signing of OFA. Hence he lightly concludes that 'The Republic of Macedonia has translated into a political document the centuries built tolerance and mutual respect, which are not just a *modus vivendi* of democracy in a multi-ethnic society but our *credo* as well' (Milososki, 18 October 2007).[6] Clearly then, similarly to the logic of president Ivanov about the inherent multiculturalism of the country, Milososki builds a logic whereby even the responsible decision of the political parties in the country to sign the OFA found its inspiration in the historical tolerance specific of Macedonia. Similar parallels drawn between the past and present versatile setting of the country and the region can be diagnosed in the words of the Deputy Prime Minister for European Affairs,

Fatmir Besimi. In his lecture at the University of Harvard, he stated that the region of the 'Western Balkans is a region with long history and religious diversity' (Besimi, 5 October 2012).

3.2. Ohrid Framework Agreement and the Tensions Surrounding It

These discourses are further shaped by both the attitude parties takes towards the overall importance and success/failure of OFA and by the Greek assertion that the Republic of Macedonia must change its constitutional name. The narratives of the ruling VMRO and the opposition SDSM (Socijal Democratski Sojuz na Makedonija) are partly diametrically opposed when it comes to these issues. At the 10th Anniversary of the Signing of OFA, Prime Minister Gruevski stated that the 'OFA is a source of equilibrium promoting both the principle of equality and the central position of the citizen on the one hand, while also promoting the cultures and political rights of the ethnic communities, on the other' (Gruevski, 5 September 2011). Though condemning the armed way that helped OFA come into being, Gruevski clearly provides a narrative, which locates the source of reconciliation of Macedonians and Albanians in the signing of this agreement. Praise of the agreement's strength to foster the multiculturalism and cooperation in a society whose intercultural reality is very fragile, comes also from the statements of EU representatives, such as the European Commissioner for Enlargement and European Neighbourhood Policy, Stefan Fule. As a guest at the OFA anniversary, Fule stated that the agreement is a celebration of the peace and tolerance over war. In addition, he also said that the agreement is a mark of the politicians' will to achieve compromise, thus 'enabling the country to develop and become a candidate for EU membership and NATO'[7] (Fule, 5 September 2011). Although unpopular among the Macedonian electorate, which identifies the OFA with the armed conflict of 2001 and thus brings bad memories, the discourse that the OFA is a proof of the capacity of the country's leaders for a compromise and mature decisions, which will enable its further growth and prospects is generally shared by both the leading VMRO and opposition SDSM party. This in no way means that both the parties and the Macedonian citizens truly believe in this narrative. Its drafting and signing was under strong mediation and control from EU and USA envoys (Javier Solana, Francois Leotar, Pieter Feith), but that in no way satisfied the Macedonian citizens, who considered it as unacceptable. They also thought of it as something attained by force and not consensus. Similar sentiments and public opinion resides today among both the Macedonian population and the smaller ethnic communities. The general feelings that the means used to achieve the signing of such an agreement was a form of capitulation on the Macedonian part are strong if tacit. We shall briefly discuss a few radical critiques to the agreement which stem from a more academic perspective.

Interestingly, the views regarding the agreement are more diverse and create a gap between both the Albanian parties and the Albanian citizens themselves including the members of other minority ethnic groups in Macedonia.

One of the problems with OFA is that its original aim was to provide ethnic balance in the constitution by accommodating the requirements of the Albanian community while avoiding the possible federalisation of the country. One of the requests was that the government must correct the ethnic imbalance by hiring members of the communities which are insufficiently represented. Risteska points out the many failures of the principles of the agreement, which instead of attaining ethnic neutrality towards all communities in Macedonia, ended favouring only the Albanian ethnic community (Risteska, 2013). She points out to the increase in the number of the Albanian participation in the civil service from 5.61% in 2004 to 24.18% in 2010, which is not the case with the other under-represented minority groups. Following Merton's (1973) theory on sociology of knowledge, the author sharply notices that the role of EU as a controlling mechanism, mediator and conflict resolution agent during the implementation of the agreement, that is, the outside role, functioned between 2004 and 2006, but that the recent years since 2007, have seen merely, the insider's doctrine, which stemmed from the Albanian partner in the Macedonian government, the DUI. This unequal representation of ethnicities is a source of grievance for the other smaller groups in Macedonia. Yet, what makes things even more interesting, is that the OFA is a source of unrest for the both the Albanian parties and Albanian citizens in general. Political analysts and researchers point to the problems with its full implementation and the strengthening of ethnic tensions in the country (Fouéré, 2006; Ordanoski & Matovski, 2007). The conflicting attitudes between the ruling DUI and opposition DPA regarding OFA lies mainly in the fact that the former praises the agreement and as Ziberi points out 'the Albanian party in government usually considers the agreement as a 'win' for them since they are the ones that initiated it during the conflict in 2001, while the Albanian political party in opposition considers OFA as a "loss"' (Ziberi, 2013, p. 12). Thus is mainly due to the fact that the EU public acclaims of the implementation of the agreement bring favourable points to DUI and fosters their future electoral victory. The grievance regarding the electoral failure of the opposition party, resulted in their complete rejection of OFA calling upon the need for a new agreement, which will foster what are now very fragile relations between the two major communities in the country.

4. PRESENTING OR INVENTING A NATION?

Several nation building stories are set against the backdrop of the OFA agreement, used by the political parties to create a narrative about the successful, mature, multicultural reality of Macedonia. As mentioned in the opening remarks to this text, Macedonia has been marked by a politics based on the pronounced primacy of the issue of national identity over other socio-political questions. National identity, (and not cultural dialogue or diversity) is fostered through material cultural and academic processes aiming at the construction and fixing of an idea and a sense of a collective. These processes clearly work in the country through the means of recognition, legitimisation and symbolic production that maintains, enriches and perpetuates the representation of the national self. One of the major material examples of this nation building policy comes from the latest architectural project Skopje 2014, which speaks both of the creation of the new nation myths by the ruling VMRO, and of the Macedonia's foreign policy and its relation with its southern neighbour. So far, this project has radically changed the face of the city, launching itself with the erection of a monumental statue of Alexander the Great, dubbed The warrior on a horse, at least 50 additional sculptures, bridges, churches and museums, including the Museum of Macedonian Struggle and of the Victims of Communism. Herzfeld (1991) brings into focus the concept of cultural intimacy that originated from his work on Greece, and Greek's obsession to hide anything that didn't look Ancient Greek due to the Western European insistence that they had to be like the Ancient Greeks. Cultural intimacy for Herzfeld is precisely the recognition of those aspects of a cultural identity that are considered a source of external embarrassment, and yet provide the insiders with their assurance of common sociality. The concepts of collective memory remembrance and especially cultural intimacy are of particular significance when discussing the Skopje 2014 project. One can perceive the Skopje 2014 as a historical reconstruction project aimed at creating a new collective memory, but likewise, of organised forgetting aimed at erasing aspects that are considered embarrassing. Ironically, the project commemorates all sorts of historical characters, thus creating confusion rather than a real some solidified identity. It goes from the Antique period: moves on to figures of early Christianity, notable historical figures who were born or ruled in or around Skopje, as well as a league of freedom fighters that fought for the Macedonian independence, but it aims at erasing both the socialist past and the Ottoman legacy in Macedonia while the nation building policy of VMRO bursts from everywhere. The Nazi aesthetics and logic is present not only in the statues but in things, such as the parliamentary election campaign, where some of the best opera singers of the Macedonian opera were gathered to perform in a choir and summon the Macedonians to vote.

Though the project and nation building politics deserves a much deeper discussion, one cannot but avoid the lucid point that Herzfeld makes when he says that the populace is devoid of agency in the act of monumentalising and formalising history by the conservators, who create 'traditional neighbourhoods and archaeological monuments of what, for the residents are the streets where their friends and enemies live and die' (Herzfeld, 1991, p. 6).

5. THE DIVERSE COURSE OF ALBANIAN DISCOURSE

The discrepancy between the Albanian parties regarding the success of OFA has been discussed above. Yet, it goes without saying that all Albanian parties consider the agreement as a victory on their part, though some debate its successful and full implementation. The Macedonian parties and citizens, as mentioned earlier, are far more inclined to look at is as something introduced by force from both the Albanian and EU/USA factors. The ethnic division and loyalty of ethnic groups to their homeland, a narrative often employed to criticise the lack of it thereof by the Albanians, is extremely prominent in the attitude of the Albanian side regarding the name issue. Several discourses collide in this respect, forming a triad of 'anti-but', 'pro-end of discussion', 'deaf to the local context and hypocritical attitudes'. In order of appearance these would be the Macedonian, Albanian and EU/international factors points of view. In his most recent statements, amidst all his fervour to not dare change the constitutional name of the country, the Prime Minister Gruevski gave a very controversial statement in which he refutes the request for a name change calling upon the fact that it is neither his nor his father's name on the one hand, yet on the other, he attempts to please the international community, and attain peace of mind by handing the responsibility of the final decision on to the people. Thus he states that 'we shall always have new reforms and will always be prepared to enter NATO and start the negotiations with the EU, once they are ready to accept us. This certainly means that we must, at all times, preserve full respect towards out identity and the name dispute we have with our southern neighbor' (Gruevski, 17 December 2013). Gruevski accentuates that there shall be no final solution to this problem unless it passes a public referendum with the citizens of Macedonia, because the name is neither his nor his father's, nor anyone's for that matter. Hence, he calls on a referendum if a compromise with Greece is achieved, so that all citizens can decide upon the future faith of their name and identity. Such statements are highly-manipulative and confirm that the only solution of the ruling party now, after the infamous membership in NATO under the provisional name FYROM (Former Yugoslav Republic of Macedonia) until final agreement is reached with Greece, is to transfer the load on to the people and let them decide on the future name of the country. A number of reactions and comments came as a result of this statement, mainly showing people's utter grievance as to why would they be called upon to decide on something that is their country's constitutional name. Additionally, as Muhić points out, 'Macedonia should immediately stop any further negotiations as per its constitutional name, and inform the international factors of this decision, who albeit our friends, unanimously support Greek's irrational request,[8] (Muhić, 11 June 2012). Reactions to the past decision of politicians came recently in the media around the 8 April, the day of the anniversary of Macedonia's acceptance into UN when back in 1993 the country was accepted under the provisional name FYROM. This is still the source of major unrests and political tensions between Macedonia and Greece.[9] Moving on to the Albanian block, regardless of whether we are talking about the ruling or opposition Albanian block, the overall sentiment among the parties and Albanian citizens is that the 'name dispute' Macedonian has with Greece should be resolved as soon as possible, so that the country can proceed with its membership in the EU and NATO. Statements from main representatives of the parties confirm the ease with which the Albanian block is prepared to accept alteration to the country's constitutional name. The leader of the ruling Albanian party, DUI, has recently stated that 'the priority in the new political agreement for the governing of the country jointly with the Macedonian partner, will be the country's membership in NATO, which means immediate solution of the name dispute' (Ahmeti, 28 February 2014). Moreover, Ahmeti puts forward a discourse which asserts that if only Macedonia changed its name, everything would be in perfect order, including Greece which will immediately change its attitude towards the country. The ease of this assumption is obvious in his statement given after his recent meeting with the Deputy Prime Minister of Greece, Evangelos Venizelos. In it, Ahmeti says that Greece is prepared to immediately aid Macedonia's aspirations to become an EU and NATO member, as long as we are prepared to solve the name dispute (Ahmeti, 20 February 2014). Ahmeti's discourse does not question any aspect of Greece's demand for Macedonia to change its constitutional name, but instead, alerts us of Greece's immediate preparedness to facilitate the country's future in EU, *as long as*, it proceeds as required. Similar discourses come from other Albanian segments as well. The competition between each party's capacity to accelerate the country's accession to EU and the solution of the name dispute, is further straightened through the discourses of the leader of the oppositional Albanian party, DPA, Menduh Taci, who stated in several occasions, that the name dispute must be solved, since it presents a big political problem both internally, within the country, and regionally (Taci, 31 December 2013). Taci, bluntly argues that when asked by the diplomats, how soon he thinks, it would take him to change the name of the country if he becomes part of the government again, had he been in the government, he would have solved the name dispute and changed the name of the country within 6 months (Taci, 9 April 2014). These attitudes clearly show the decisiveness for change and the reluctance on the part of the Albanians to empathise with the inner struggle and burden of Macedonians who feel very uncomfortable about having to change their constitutional name, after making amendments to the constitution to counter Greek allegation for alleged territorial pretensions,[10] and after changing the State's flag with an Interim Accord signed in New York on 13 September 1995. For the Albanians, the name Macedonia clearly bares ethnic connotation, hence identifying themselves as Macedonians instead of Albanians, despite the fact that they do hold Macedonian citizenship, is incomprehensible and extremely hard, just as it is extremely easy for that to throw away any arguments regarding the complexity of the name dispute and aim to move with galloping speed towards the EU.

6. EU NARRATIVES AND IMPERATIVES

So far, we have discussed the discourses of the Macedonian and Albanian political parties and representatives regarding the multicultural state of affairs in Macedonia, the OFA and the name dispute with Greece, which is in close correlation with Macedonians EU membership aspirations. We have diagnosed several clearly opposed views between the Macedonian and Albanian representatives regarding the multicultural atmosphere in the country; an overall public agreement on the success of OFA, though evidently the Macedonian side is more diplomatic than honest in its admiration for this document; a tension between the ruling and opposition Albanian blocks regarding the OFA, and a joint Macedonian and Albanian aspiration for EU membership spiced up with attempts on the Macedonian side to avoid responsibility regarding the possible results of the negotiations by transferring the final decision to the people, and the Albanians (both ruling and opposition) who are absolutely disinterested in questioning Greece's ultimatum, and disengaged from the overall complexity of changing the country's constitutional name, thrusting its desire to end this long negotiation process for once and move towards the EU. In the following section we will look at the intricacy of both Greece's and EU requirements, thus trying to achieve a more comprehensive understanding of the forces, tensions and discourses which shape much of the political ambient in the country.

As Lozanoska points out (2013), the Republic of Macedonia underwent a different if not unique treatment from EU in its process of gaining independence back in 1991. Both the EU and the UN shaped their attitudes towards Macedonia giving primacy to the Greek discontent regarding the name. As Lozanoska further notices, although the conventional criteria for statehood are included in the Montevideo Convention from 1933, 'the recognition process of the countries of ex-Yugoslavia was conditional upon satisfaction of additional criteria' (Lozanoska, 2013, p. 8).[11] Among the additional requirements, there were respect for democracy and rule of law, respect for the rights of ethnic groups and minorities, inviolability of borders that can be changed only by peaceful means, and others, and they were all fulfilled by the Republic of Macedonia. However, it is only in the Macedonian case that the EU decided to extend its requirements upon Greece's insistence. Hence, the European Commission (EC) adopted a decision, which stated that if the country were to be recognised, 'it should not contain the term Macedonia in its name'. This shows that the EC has been inconsistent with its requirements and decisions only in the case of the Republic of Macedonia, thus temporarily delaying its recognition, preventing it from seeking recognition by individual EC members, and making undergo a much more complicated course of action of what was an already defined process of recognition (Lozanoska, 2013, p. 9). Regarding Greece's insistence on exclusivity over the history and culture belonging to ancient Macedonia, we shall not deal with a number of historical inconsistencies, but rather just point out to one of the major arguments of Greece – namely, that first and foremost Greece officially used the name and symbols prior to their appropriation by the Macedonian authorities. Lozanoska correctly observes that if one goes back to the time when Yugoslavia, as a socialist federal state, was comprised of six republics and two autonomous units, such a claim can be easily refuted, simply by pointing out that the name of the Republic of Macedonia was then 'Socialist Republic of Macedonia'. Hence, it is easy to notice that what has been removed since the dissolution of Yugoslavia is the term 'Socialist', as a signifier of the political and economic constitution of the country. She also notices that Greece really started to 'Macedonia-nise' its northern province and use the symbols only in the nineties, just before the breakup of Yugoslavia.

Complications and inconsistencies in the discourses of the EC came forward in the process of gaining a UN membership as well. Again Greeks' demands were put in front of every other logical and legal framework and additional criteria came from the Security Council regarding Macedonia. As a result, in Res. 817 from 1993, the SC recommended to the UN General Assembly to admit to membership in the United Nations, 'this State [the Republic of Macedonia – our constitutional name] being provisionally referred to for all purposes within the United Nations as 'the former Yugoslav Republic of Macedonia' pending settlement of the difference that has arisen over the name of the State'. Going forward through time, in 2005 Macedonia became EU candidate country, but the development is almost non-existent as the Council of EU specified the utmost importance of arriving to a 'negotiated and mutually acceptable solution' regarding the name dispute. Several authors have referred to the incongruous nature of this resolution and the consequences for Macedonia therewith (Janev, 2002; Queneudec, 2013). These authors point out that such impositions of additional criteria for membership are a blatant infringement of the UN Charter, which caused sweeping consequences for the Republic of Macedonia and belittling its legal strength by making it operate in the UN under a provisional name.

Finally, after putting a lot of effort and undertaking a number of reforms, The Republic of Macedonia fulfilled the technical criteria for membership in NATO. Expecting an invitation to accede NATO, at the high-segment in Bucharest in 2008, Macedonia was faced with Greece's blockade. Greece thus, infringed the Interim Accord signed in 1995, in which it concurred in Article 11(1) that it would not object to the Republic of Macedonia's applications to join international and regional organisations under the provisional name the 'Former Yugoslav Republic of Macedonia'. Bittered by these events, Macedonian started a suit regarding the violation of this provision. On

5 December 2011, the International Court of Justice rendered its judgment in the case of Republic of Macedonia vs. Greece, where it found that Greece has breached Article 11(1) of the said Interim Accord.[12] As Lozanoska points out 'the Court rejected all objections, arguments which were at the core of Greek defence' (14).

This short background to the name dispute shows a number of inconsistencies that came from the additional requirements and decisions from the EC in the recognition process of Macedonia, the infringement of the UN Charter by adding further criteria for the country's membership in the organisation, and finally, the absurdity of the problem, revealed in the decision of the International Court of Justice (ICJ), which rejected the objections of Greece and found that the Interim Accord has been breached. The name dispute is one of the filters through which much of the multicultural realities of the country also come to the fore. We have mentioned earlier that in the midst of the strong nation building politics from the ruling VMRO party, present in the politicians' rhetoric, academic discourses and material culture, the name dispute comes as a spear tearing apart the country's identity and threatening the political power of VMRO in case of proceeding with such a change. This is one of the reasons for the Prime Ministers' decision call for a referendum and let the people decide. This insistence on the preservation of the name, which has ethnic connotations, unnerves much of the Albanian population and political parties, who see in its unwillingness to finalise the negotiations, nation building politics. Such politics, the Albanians believe gives primacy to the nationalist sentiments, thus blocking the country's accession into the EU and endangering the peace, stability and multi-ethnic cohabitation of its citizens. In a speech delivered at the 45th Munich Security Conference in 2009, lamenting over Greece's unfair requests put on Macedonia, Gruevski, among his statements analysed earlier, says:

> The Macedonian people have never escaped from their problems. Rather, we have learned to face them. There is no doubt that the engagement of the international community in the country (through the key international factors, the first preventive mission in the UN history-UNPREDEP and OSCE) had a significant role in the prevention of spilling over of the wars from the rest of former Yugoslavia. [...]It is unfortunate that, despite meeting all NATO requirements and receiving recognition from NATO for our military, political and social reforms, the Macedonian NATO invitation was placed on indefinite 'hold'. The reason for leaving more than two million people outside NATO's sphere of freedom, security and democracy? Our constitutional name. The assertion by Greece that the Republic of Macedonia threatens their national sovereignty is simply not true. We have changed our constitution and our national flag to meet their concerns and we remain committed to working with them on a compromise. (Gruevski, 2 September 2009)

He continues by asking, 'How to explain to the Macedonian people that their entry in the European home, a home of diversity of identities, will cost them their freedom to express who they are? Will cost them their identity?'(Gruevski, 2 September 2009). The statement both reveals elements of admiration and humbleness regarding the significance of the international factor, but it also questions some of the principles of the EU, since it did not show any mercy with the name dispute. Although some authors (Ziberi, 2013, p. 23), argue that contrary to this, the opposition party is mainly focused at the benefits of Macedonia's EU membership and hence, criticises the government for not finding a compromise with Greece, we would argue that such statements come more as a result of SDSM being in the opposition rather than their real preparedness to push for the name change. If it came to that, it could very likely guarantee them a political hara-kiri. As mentioned earlier, the Albanian side is not so concerned with the problem, but rather sees in it nationalist sentiments dangerous for the multicultural future of the country. Hence, they support all the signals coming from the EU, which call upon immediate resolution of the name dispute. The Republic of Macedonia is clearly under the pressure to finalise the negotiations and make changes to its constitutional name from the international factors. To support this claim, let us look at the following statements in addition to the overview of the name question presented earlier in the chapter. Recently, the former EU Ambassador in Skopje, Ervan Fuere, has declared that FYROM has no other alternatives for its integration in the European Union. 'FYR Macedonia must put emotions aside. We have often said that the name dispute doesn't relate to the identity, but to the name. The only way to resolve it is through dialogue. I'm sorry that the name dispute issue is being misused for domestic political benefits', declared Fouéré (Fouéré, 2 July 2013). Likewise, the current EU Enlargement Commissioner Stefan Fule urged stronger efforts from Greece and Macedonia to resolve the name dispute. A clear call for Macedonia to push for a compromise comes in his statement where he says:

I expressed my support for this process and again urged both sides to immediately do everything possible to resolve this issue. That is why the country cannot take the next step that the Commission again and again recommended, and it is open to negotiations. I do not want to pre-judge what will happen this year to their port on progress, but I think the time has come to resolve this issue. Not only to see the possible compromise but the price of not going forward and maintaining the status quo one or more years (Falaga, 2013).

Finally, it is interesting to point out that although 133 states including the United States, the United Kingdom, Russia, Canada and China recognized Macedonia under its constitutional name, the penitentially new agreed upon name between the Republic of Macedonia and Greece, which insists on the principle of erga omnes, would impose the obligation on all those States to accept the new reference.

7. CONCLUSIONS

This chapter analysed the contested landscape of discourses surrounding the Republic of Macedonia's multicultural setting drenched in the agendas regarding the OFA and the name dispute. We have looked into the discourses of the leading figures from the ruling and opposition parties, which belong to both the Macedonian and the Albanian blocks. We specified the different under-standing of multicultural settlement according to the Macedonians vis-a-vis the Albanians and finally, the other smaller minority groups in the country. We have noticed that the ruling VMRO party promotes Macedonia as a successful multi-cultural story mainly due to its long multicultural legacy. Ironically though, the same party is currently drenched into heavy nationalist politics, obliterating (in the material culture) much of what can be considered Ottoman or Yugoslav/socialist, while re-establishing business relations and strong investments with Turkey. Even outside this sphere, with regard to the analysis of OFA discourses it is obvious that the current government is forcing a politics based on the pro-nounced primacy of the issue of national (Macedonian, Orthodox Christian, mainly patriarchal) identity over other socio-political questions.

The Albanians in Macedonia empowered their status in the society through armed conflict and settled their requirements with the OFA. Although there is a tacit bitterness on the Macedonian part and a feeling of capitulation upon the signing of the Agreement, both the ruling and opposition Macedonian parties, consider it a successful outcome and a fruitful ground upon which to further the country's integration into the EU. It is obvious though that the Macedonian electorate finds the Agreement problematic, and a number of scholars (Lozanoska, 2011; Risteska, 2013) refer to it as an empowerment tool in the hands of the Albanians, but an unjust mechanism for the promotion of the smaller groups' rights, and a tool which merely led to the ethnicisation of public administration. The Albanian parties are, however, divided in their opinion as per this issue, and this, as Ziberi (2013) noticed, is greatly a result of whether the party is in the government or the opposition. The former applauds it and its power to solve all the conflicting issues with the minorities, preparing Macedonia for the EU, the letter condemns it as insufficient means for building a truly functional multicultural society in the country.

The final part of this chapter dealt with the complexities rising from the name dispute that Macedonia has with Greece. An overview of the problem was given along with several inconsistencies on the part of the EC and the SC decision to add a requirement for the country's membership to NATO, as well as Greece's ban on Macedonia's attempt to join NATO at the summit in Bucharest in 2008. This dispute was used to further complicate the multicul-tural situation in the country and the discourses, which evolve around this issue. It was noticed that there is a clear dissatisfaction among the ruling VMRO as per Greece's request, but no real reaction against it. On the contrary, the burden is to be set on the people having to decide through a referendum on whether they are who they think or feel they are. The oppositional SDSM is mellower in their approach, pushing for the country's accession into the EU, yet we have presupposed that this discourse is mainly due to the fact of their current place in the government. In other words, we have concluded that neither one of the parties is ready to take on the responsibility of changing the name and committing a political hara-kiri. We have placed the narratives of the Albanian parties and the EU representatives' statements against this backdrop only to conclude that the multicultural reality of the country suffers enormously from this dispute. The Albanians see in the unwillingness of the Macedonian factors to easily compromise on the name dispute, a pronounced nationalist politics, and people who are reluctant to join the EU and guarantee the safety and peaceful cohabitation in the country. The incapability of the Albanians to remotely identify with the name Macedonia and defend the cause, is labelled by the Macedonians as lack of loyalty on their part, as well as unpreparedness to share a joint life and work towards a prosperous future. The EU narratives complicate this scenario even further, by strengthening the Albanians' position as they do push for an immediate solution to the dispute.

To conclude, it is obvious that there are significantly opposed views regarding the multicultural reality of the country between Macedonians and Albanians, which are further complicated by the country's attempt to become EU member and the conditions set by the international factors to achieve this step. It seems obvious that Macedonia is in an extremely difficult position and its future is very uncertain. Both the political actors as well as the international factors are completely detached from the local context of the country. The former are selfishly focused on their own private interests while the latter are playing the role of a powerful force from the outside, which sets rules regardless of local context or the set of consequences that may result from it for Macedonia. Sad as this may seem, it is sometimes inspirational to see that perhaps a slightly different engagement with these issues, coming from sphere like cultural anthropology can diagnose neuralgic points and provide ways to solve problems, much better than a number of vacuous multiculturalism theories, hypocritical speeches and even more so hypocritical requirements and demands from the outside. Going back almost 10 years ago, the anthropologists Antonia Zhelyiazkova came up with a very accurate picture of social discourse after the OFA through talking to randomly chosen people in different regions in the country. Some of her conclusions were that:

1. The Macedonians have developed fatalistic attitudes and have sunk into apathy: In fact, the Macedonian public is already becoming used and reconciled to the federalised structure of the territory, as well as of political, economic and public life in the country.
2. The Albanians are self-confident, their life is normal, calm and optimistic. They are in no doubt that the future is theirs. They are advancing slowly but surely in all spheres of life: demographic, political, economic and social (Zhelyazkova, 2003, p. 13).

Perhaps, more studies like this one, can on the longer run, provide solid recommendations for the government of Macedonia to aim towards the establishment of a sensitive system of institutions that react to local problems, a plural decentralised state, that makes the majority accept the different value system of the minority, and that can consolidate opposing political views in order to react appropriately to inconsistent requirements imposed from stronger factors irrespectively of the local context.

NOTES

1. The territory of what is today Republic of Macedonia was until 1913 the last part of the Balkans ruled by the Ottoman Empire. After 1919, Macedonia entered the Kingdom of Yugoslavia under Serbian jurisdiction and without administrative autonomy. This Kingdom was defined as a Kingdom of Serbs, Croats and Slovenians, without mentioning the Macedonians. After 1945, Macedonia was constituted as the People's Republic of Macedonia within the framework of Yugoslavia. After the breakup of Yugoslavia, Macedonia was admitted to the UN on 8 April 1993 as the Former Yugoslav Republic of Macedonia (FYROM) until an agreement could be reached with Greece.

2. The Amendments of the Constitution of R. Macedonian are available at the following web site: Retrieved from http://eudo-citizenship.eu/NationalDB/docs/MAC%20Const%20Amendments%20IV-XVIII%20(English).pdf. Accessed on 17 October 2013.

3. See more in Art. 7 of the Constitution of RM regarding the language issue. While the official language in the country is Macedonian, other languages spoken by at least 20% of the population (in almost all cases, Albanian) are considered official and can be used for personal documents, civil and criminal proceedings, local self-government and communication between citizens and central government.

4. http://grid.mk/read/article/2591788/ivanov-vo-kanada-makedonija-primer-za-multi kulturalizam

5. A detailed chart of the duration of the Ottoman rule by country and region may be found in Brown's *Imperial Legacy* (1996).

6. http://www.lse.ac.uk/assets/richmedia/channels/publicLecturesAndEvents/transcri pts/20071018_Macedonia_tr.pdf

7. http://www.utrinski.mk/default.asp?ItemID=23BFC71B5D6F3E45B5DEECA E18ABF156

8. http://dnevnik.mk/?ItemID=1A418EF76CEED24C9CD7441086F253F1

9. See http://www.mkd.mk/kolumni/nikoj-ne-saka-da-se-navrakja-na-sramniot-priem-vo-oon) − an issue around which both the international community attitudes and the multicultural realities of the country revolve and mould themselves.

10. Amendment 1 reads as follows: 'The Republic of Macedonia has no territorial pretensions towards any neighboring state' (section 1) and 'The borders of the Republic could be only changed in accordance with the Constitution and on the principle of free will as well as in accordance with generally accepted international norms' (section 2), Official Gazette of the Republic of Macedonia No. 1/92. United Nations Security Council Resolution 817, 1993. United Nations Interim Accord between Hellenic Republic and Republic of Macedonia, September 15, 1995.

11. The EC adopted the Guidelines on the Recognition of New States and the Declaration on Yugoslavia on 16 December 1991.

12. International Court of Justice, Application of the Interim Accord of September 1995, Republic of Macedonia v. Greece, 17 November 2008.

REFERENCES

Besimi, F. (2012). *Одложување на процесот на евроатлански интеграции обезбедува основа за скептицизам. (The delay of the processes for euroatlantic integrations gives grounds for skepticism)*. A public lecture of the Minister of Defense of the Republic of Macedonia, Fatmir Besimi, at the University of Harvard, USA. Retrieved from http://morm.gov.mk/?mainnews=20898

Callinicos, A. (2009). *Imperialism and global political economy*. Cambridge: Polity Press.

Daily Macedonia. (2014). *Мухиќ за 'Граѓански': Македонија веднаш да ги прекине преговорите за името!*. Retrieved from http://daily.mk/vesti/muhikj-za-gragjanski-makedonija-vednash-da-gi-prekine-pregovorite. Accessed 27 November 2014.

Daily, M. K. (2013). *Иванов во Канада: Македонија пример за мултикултурализам*, April 20. Retrieved from http://daily.mk/makedonija/ivanov-vo-kanada-makedonija-primer-za-multikulturalizam

Falanga. (2013). *EU Enlargement Commissioner Stefan Fule welcomed the signing of the report*, August 27. Retrieved from http://falanga.com.au/en/eu-enlargement-commissioner-stefan-fule-welcomed-the-signing-of-the-report#

Fouéré, E. (2006). Macedonia's perspective of EU membership. *Südosteuropa Mitteilungen, 46*(5), 50−55.

Harvey, D. (2010). *A companion to Marx's capital*. London: Verso.

Herzfeld, M. (1991). *A place in history: Social and monumental time in a Cretan Town*. Princeton, NJ: Princeton University Press.

Iindependent Balkan News Agency. *Fuere: Skopje has no other alternatives for the EU*. Retrieved from http://old.balkaneu.com/fuere-skopje-alternatives-eu/

Janev, G. (2009). *Historical Lessons of Macedonian Multiculturalism*, Working Papers. Göttingen: Max Planck Institute for the Study of Religious and Ethnic Diversity.

Janev, I. (2002). Some remarks of The Legal Status Of Macedonia in the United Nations Organization. *Review of International Affairs, LIII*(1108).

Lozanoska, J. (2011). Principle of non-discrimination and equitable representation in framework agreement ten years after - Formal or substantive equality?! *Crossroads: The Macedonian Foreign Policy Journal, 2*(4), 183−189.

Lozanoska, J. (2013). The true substance of the name issue: Consequences of an invented dispute for the Republic of Macedonia. In Dzuvalekovska, Lozanoska et al. (eds.), *An Anthology of Academic Articles "The Name Issue − Revisited*. Skopje: Macedonian Information Center.

Maleska, M. (2013). Multiethnic democracy in Macedonia: Political analysis and emerging scenarios. *New Balkan Politics, 13*, 1−27.

Merton, R. K. (1973). *The sociology of science: Theoretical and empirical investigations*. Chicago, IL: University of Chicago Press.

Milososki, A. (2007). *The Republic of Macedonia − Tests passed and challenges ahead*, October 18. Speech presented at the London School of Economics, London, UK. Retrieved from https://docs.google.com/a/seeu.edu.mk/viewer?a=v&q=cache:kYwd8yzQ9scJ:www2.lse.ac.uk/assets/richmedia/channels/publicLecturesAndEvents/transcripts/20071018_Macedonia_tr.pdf+&hl=en&pid=bl&srcid=ADGEESg_Cov8ObMrxYYgEO__WS47F1oxcdPy0xkxz_G8RZhOAMdfztdeEDWJPc359cpK1BOtfuG1y8bKgQX_-hebQGIpmrxsSHP_yHRfy_veqYp36qNbEYWPNoiOIER_Lcmuqf58PCL&sig=AHIEtbRnrPXTCwmY8Uv9mUuEoreRyTelJw

MKD.MK. (2013). *2013 година на дискриминација на Албанците, 2014 ќе се реши проблемот со името*, December 31. Retrieved from http://www.mkd.mk/makedonija/partii/tachi-2013-godina-na-diskriminacija-na-albancija-2014-kje-se-reshi-problemot-so

MKD.MK. (2014). *Ако не се реши спорот со имено, по предвремените, може да има и вонредни избори*, February 28. Retrieved from http://www.mkd.mk/makedonija/partii/ahmeti-ako-ne-se-reshi-problemot-so-imeto-po-predvremenite-mozhe-da-ima-i-vonredni. Accessed on 24 June 2017.

MKD.MK. (2014). *Ако сум во влада за една година ќе го решам проблемот со името*, April 9. Retrieved from http://www.mkd.mk/makedonija/partii/tachi-ako-sum-vo-vlada-za-edna-godina-kje-go-resham-problemot-so-imeto

Muhić, F. C. (1994) *Macedonia: Clasp of the world*. Skopje: Tabernakul.

Ordanoski, S., & Matovski, A. (2007). Between Ohrid and Dayton: The future of Macedonia's framework agreement. *Südosteuropa Mitteilungen*, *47*(4), 46–59.

Queneudec, J.-P. (2013). The name and symbols of the state in international law. In Dzuvalekovska, L. et al. (Eds.), *An anthology of academic articles 'The name issue – Revisited'*. Skopje: Macedonian Information Center.

Risteska, M. (2013). Insiders and outsiders in the implementation of the principle of just and equitable representation of minority groups in public administration in Macedonia. *International Journal of Public Administration*, *36*, 26–34.

Sharlamanov, K., & Stojanoski, A. (2012). The multiculturalism in Republic of Macedonia, observed through the perceptions for the symbols of the other ethnic groups: Framework of the symbolic interactionism. *International Journal of Humanities & Social Science*, *2*(23), 64–70.

Utrinski Vesnik. (2011). Груевски се поклони на рамковниот, September 5. Retrieved from http://www.utrinski.mk/default.asp?ItemID=23BFC71B5D6F3E45B5DEECAE18ABF156. Accessed 24 June 2017.

Zhelyazkova, A. (2003). *Macedonia in April 2003. diagnosis: 'Cancer with galloping metastases'*. Sofia: International Centre for Minority Studies and Intercultural Relations (IMIR).

Ziberi, L. (2013). The rhetorical uses of multiculturalism: An ideographic analysis of the European Union and the Macedonian discourses in the dialogue for EU accession, PhD Thesis, Bowling Green State University.

WEBSITES

PRESS 24 MK. *Груевски: Името не е ниту мое ниту на татко ми – ќе го решиме проблемот со референдум* [Online]. Retrieved from http://www.press24.mk/gruevski-imeto-ne-e-nitu-moe-nitu-na-tatko-mi-kje-go-reshime-problemot-so-referendum. Accessed 27 November 2014.

DAILY MACEDONIA. Мухиќ за „Граѓански": Македонија веднаш да ги прекине преговорите за името! [Online]. Retrieved from http://daily.mk/vesti/muhikj-za-gragjanski-makedonija-vednash-da-gi-prekine-pregovorite. Accessed 27 November 2014.

GRID.MK. Компромисот меѓу Македонија и Грција ќе мора да се направи [Online]. Retrieved from http://grid.mk/read/news/506516451/5618999/kompromisot-megju-makedonija-i-grcija-kje-mora-da-se-napravi. Accessed 27 November 2014.

GRID.MK. Тачи: Ако сум во Влада за една година ќе го решам проблемот со името [Online]. Retrieved from http://grid.mk/read/article/6956165/tachi-ako-sum-vo-vlada-za-edna-godina-kje-go-resham-problemot-so-imeto. Accessed 27 November 2014.

MUNICH SECURITY CONFERENCE. Nikola Gruevski – Speech at the 45th Munich Security Conference [Online]. Retrieved from https://www.securityconference.de/en/activities/munich-security-conference/msc-2009/speeches/nikola-gruevski/. Accessed 27 November 2014.

SETTLING ACCOUNTS WITH THE TROUBLESOME PAST: SELF-CRITICISM IN POLAND AND EASTERN EUROPE

Magdalena Nowicka-Franczak

ABSTRACT

Public acts of self-criticism in Eastern Europe — a genre cultivated and extorted by the communist parties — did not disappear with the end of communism. In the young democracies of the region self-criticism has become an attempt to diagnose society's 'backward' character and to develop 'self-correction' scenarios in order to participate in the Western modernising discourse. On the one hand, conservative and right-wing elites suppose that public acts of self-criticism (performed by politicians, artists or scholars) can endow the vetting procedures of the ancien régime *with a sense of social* catharsis *and retroactive justice. On the other hand, liberal and left-wing intellectuals subject themselves to collective self-reckoning, not only with their choices made in the transition period, but also with the memory of WWII, in order to shape a civil society free of anti-Semitism and intolerance. An analysis based on the discourse-historical approach in critical discourse analysis, Reinhart Koselleck's historical semantics and Michel Foucault's notion of discourse, and carried out on the text corpus of selected acts of self-criticism in Poland, aims to diagnose the role these acts had in shaping public discourse on the troublesome past.*

Keywords: Self-criticism; discourse-historical approach; Foucault; historical semantics; discourse; Eastern Europe

National Identity and Europe in Times of Crisis: Doing and Undoing Europe, 259–283
Copyright © 2017 by Emerald Publishing Limited
doi:10.1108/978-1-78714-513-920171012

1. INTRODUCTION

'Return to Europe — yes, but only with our deceased', said Maria Janion (2000), the renowned theoretician of Romanticism literature, while pointing to the peculiar dilemma of Eastern European intellectualists: How to constitute a part of the idealised Western Europe without losing our sometimes inglorious and not always victorious past? According to Reinhart Koselleck (2000), ever since the 18th century Europeans have been sharing the conviction that they live in the so-called *saddle time* (German: *Sattelzeit*), which in Western Europe resulted in the sense of temporality due to the social bourgeois revolution, scientific advances and transformations in philosophical thought. *Saddle time* for Eastern Europe also began at the end of the 18th century, but the experience was of a significantly different nature: the absence of political and economic stability, and the lack of consent to the imposed sovereign (e.g. Russian Tsar or Austrian Emperor) expressed by some elites, who — in this region — were often named the 'intelligentsia'. This exceptional threshold time was spread over the period of Soviet rule in the territory, and thus the imitation of the Western European modus of modernisation was not possible before the democratic transformation of the late 1980s.

In the context of post-communist Eastern Europe modernisation can be understood as, first, a macro-social process, consisting in 'catching up' with the West, that is, governmental and non-governmental 'social engineering': adapting the social order to a Western model of civil society and implementing procedures of liberal democracy. Second, modernisation is a micro-social process of an individual's self-adapting to modern goals, social values and life-style. Therefore, modernisation in Eastern Europe can be compared to a form of Foucauldian *governmentality*, (neo)liberal power over individuals, shaping their self freely but according to given expectations (Foucault, 2006).

One of the preconditions of modernisation specific to Eastern Europe is the reckoning with the past. The need for settling accounts with the past results, to a certain degree, from the tension between different types of discourse of modernisation present in Eastern European public spheres. The first one sees the future of the countries in the region in the return to strong statehood and collective identity founded on post-Romantic patriotism. It is the national pride of the glorious and heroic past, not settlements with the troublesome and shameful past, that is to guarantee an international recognition for the society. The second type of discourse, left-wing and liberal, sees the settlement as evidence of democratic 'maturity' in a post-communist society. Both discourses are based on the conviction that the modernisation of Eastern Europe *for the future* cannot be performed without the *past*. Therefore, the Western European theories of modernisation such as Urlich Beck's and Anthony Giddens' concept of *reflexive modernisation* or Hartmut Rosa's concept of *acceleration* shaping time structures in late modernity, are largely inadequate for the research on

Eastern Europe. Giddens, Rosa and others link modernisation with going beyond the past and traditional identities, and drifting towards an individualised post-traditional society (Beck, Giddens, & Lash, 1994; Brock, 2014; Rosa, 2005), whereas in Eastern Europe the debate on collective identities, social transformations and the future of democracy is not conducted in isolation from the past, as the past constitutes an integral element of such a discussion.

In this chapter I would first like to address briefly what I understand as a troublesome past in the context of Eastern European debates on collective memory. Second, I reflect upon the concept of self-criticism as a tool of dealing with the past, from both the Koselleckian and Foucauldian perspectives. Finally, I present my analysis of selected acts of self-criticism in Poland in order to discuss discursive mechanisms of settling accounts with the troublesome past of WWII, communist times and the transition period.

2. EASTERN EUROPEAN TROUBLESOME PAST

Settling accounts with a troublesome past means striving to re-shape the collective memory of those events and processes which have been remembered by various members of society in a different or competitive manner. Naturally, the disputes over the shape of collective memory are not an exclusively Eastern European phenomenon. Since the late 1960s, we have observed, especially in France, Germany and later in Austria, a 'memory boom' (Huyssen, 1995, p. 9) or rather the 'revenge of memory' (Nora & Zakowski, 2002, pp. 59−64; Glondys, 2009), thus far excluded from the mainstream discourse. Not until a few decades after the termination of WWII did a widespread debate begin in these countries over the passive and active participation of Western European societies, and the so-called 'ordinary people', in the murderous Nazi policy, which involved denouncing and killing Jews.

In Eastern Europe the settling debate involves the two totalitarianisms: fascist and communist. In Poland the very first voices on the attitudes of Polish citizens towards Jews during WWII, and the involvement of Polish elites in the creation and development of communism, were expressed as early as the 1950s, and their number noticeably grew over time. Nevertheless, a global dispute was initiated a dozen or so years after the political transformation. This time shift in comparison to Western Europe stems from a number of reasons. First, as Bernard Wasserstein remarks (2007, p. 403), 'Liberation came at different times and in different ways to the peoples of occupied Europe'. It was the fall of the undesired and discredited communist regime that offered the societies liberty, which allowed them to scrutinise the history 'from an outside perspective' and to perform a relatively global judgment. Second, the first years after the transition from communism to democracy and capitalism were dominated by economic and social issues, which, at that time, required more attention than the reconstruction of collective memory. Only after the relative normalisation of living conditions could historical issues become a regular constituent of the public agenda. However, from the very beginning of the transition the past has been a tool of the 'politics of memory' utilised, at first, as a symbolic seal of the delegitimisation of the communist regime (Paczkowski, 2010; Tileagă, 2012). Third, after 1989, a vast part of the local elites, in order to rebuild a positive collective identity, resorted to the discourse of the heroic past and suppressed arguments challenging this line of reasoning. In Poland, even in the early 1990s, but especially in 2005−2007 (the right-wing government of the Law and Justice party), historical policy focused on commemorating and fossilising the martyrological line of Polish history and the heroic image of Poles as victims of Nazi and Soviet aggression.

This process was challenged, on the one hand, by articles, books and films arguing that during WWII, Poles also acted as *perpetrators* of other people's suffering: denouncing and murdering their Jewish compatriots (see Kowalska-Leder, 2014; Krupa, 2014). To use Raul Hilberg's (2003) classic triad of the participants in the Holocaust, the figure of a bystander of the Shoah has been revaluated. On the other hand, and not only in Poland, the new democratic elites, profoundly divided, started to disclose the past of their political opponents. As a result, many former opponents of the communist regime were accused of collaborating with the regime, as the term 'collaborator' can be interpreted in a very vague way. As Tony Judt (2006, p. 33) noted, 'wartime divisions and affiliations often carried local implications altogether more complicated and ambiguous that the simple postwar attributions − of "collaboration" and "resistance" − would imply'. What is more, 25 years after the fall of communism Eastern European public discourses become loaded as if settling accounts with the promises and hopes connected to the political transformation and expressing disillusionment with choices made by the leaders of the transition.

The dispute on collective memory led to a polarisation of the representatives of opposing moral reasoning and assessments of the past. It seems that Maurice Halbwachs' classic definition of collective memory is no longer an adequate term to describe this kind of public controversy over the past. For Halbwachs (1992, p. 38), collective memory is a set of perceptions and beliefs about the past common for members of a community, resulting from the fact that people − carriers of memory − are a part of a single society which formed the resources of their memory. Changes in the social structure and historical processes affect the shape of collective memory, but they do not destroy its core, which allows the public to celebrate their sense of community.

Discussing contemporary reckoning with the past, we should revise the very concept of collective memory. It functions not as a collective representation of past events, but as a discursive formation (in the Foucauldian sense, see below), as a strategic design: hegemonic, or claiming the hegemonic position in the public sphere − and thus consisting in the rivalry between the modes of commemoration, including the subversive ones, utilising the dominant channels of public debate to remind society of groups and events that have been forced out of official historical narratives. As Foucault (2003, p. 7) points out, in modern societies, an increasingly common phenomenon is the insurrection of subjugated knowledge, hidden under the functional wholes of historical power-knowledge (Foucault, 1979, pp. 27–28). Such anti-science is verbalised in a particular kind of discourse: counter-history. It reverses the interpretation of events, presents victories as defeats, victims as perpetrators and the defeated as heroes. Counter-history is an appeal for recognition of certain arguments and an instrument of criticism of historical power-knowledge (Foucault, 2003, pp. 70–71). Historical knowledge does not produce consensual normative symbolic resources, but provokes a fight for the re-evaluation of existing relations of power and morality (Medina, 2011, pp. 12–18). What we observe as a dispute on the troublesome past is the result of the clash of competing types of knowledge and discourse. Moreover, the reconfiguration of collective memory resources within the various domains of public discourse may gain equal rank in the debate and re-shape collective memories into instrumentalised public memory (Kwiatkowski, 2008, p. 442).

Today, settling with the past in Eastern Europe refers to both a distant and relatively recent past whose actors are still alive. The settlement debate can be divided into three variants, following the criterion of time and generation which is being morally scrutinised:

a. **WWII and its direct repercussions, that is, 'inherited responsibility'** — the subject of debate includes the attitudes and actions taken by the elites and so-called 'ordinary people' around the wartime period towards fellow citizens of Jewish, German and Romani origin and other ethnic minorities. The axis of debate is represented by the conviction (negated by some debaters) that 'the nation of today bears the same responsibility for its history as an individual for their own past' (Kołakowski, 1973, p. 5), and that the present generations 'inherit' the duty of settling accounts with the deeds of their ancestors. The most fiercely discussed issue is the attitudes towards Jews: ranging from complete indifference, denunciation and blackmailing, to pillages and pogroms. Upon publication of the book *Neighbors: The Destruction of the Jewish Community in Jedwabne, Poland* by the historian Jan T. Gross (2001, Polish edition 2000), a public debate was initiated in 2001 on the issue of Polish guilt towards Jews and the manner in which the victims should be commemorated. Another two volumes by Gross, regarding the subject of pillage and murder committed by the Polish on Jews — *Fear: Anti-Semitism in Poland After Auschwitz* (2007, Polish edition 2008) and *Golden Harvest* (2012, Polish edition 2011, co-written with Irena Grudzińska-Gross) — have also raised a controversy. The debate, continuing for over 10 years now, has been joined by numerous historians, journalists, publicists, politicians and clergymen. Presently, even if the majority of debaters have ceased to question the fact that the pogroms took place in Poland, there is still no consent on the perpetrators' motives and the moral responsibility of the Polish for the misdeeds. Meanwhile, in the Czech Republic a public debate was triggered over the liability for the violent expulsions of the Sudeten Germans between 1945 and 1946 and the confiscation of their property on the basis of the decrees issued by President Edvard Beneš. The attempts made by Vaclav Havel after 1989 to settle accounts with the issue of 'wild expulsions' (Czech: *divoký odsun*) of Sudeten Germans and their massacres performed by the Czech met with incomprehension on the side of political allies and public opinion. In Hungary the issue of the war alliance with the Third Reich and the persecution of Jews, Romani people and Slovaks has become a recurring constituent of historical debates, while in Ukraine there is an ongoing dispute over, for instance, the moral assessment of the actions taken by the Ukrainian Insurgent Army, which between 1943 and 1944 performed ethnic cleansings, killing approximately 100,000 Poles.

b. **The commitment of symbolic elites[1] in communism, or the wound left by the 'Hegelian bite'** – both former members of the communist party and informal collaborators with the security service are brought into moral judgment. The majority of the ex-communists who have decided to settle accounts with their past are intellectuals, and the 'victims' of what Czesław Miłosz recognised in his book *The Captive Mind* (1990 [1953]) as the 'Hegelian bite' – a belief that communism was a historical necessity. As far as settling accounts with the past is concerned, Polish intellectuals issued several groundbreaking publications, such as *A Poem for Adults* by Adam Ważyk in the 1950s, Czesław Miłosz's extended interview with Aleksander Wat entitled *My Century: The Odyssey of a Polish Intellectual* in the 1970s, and in the 1980s *Domestic Disgrace*, a collection of interviews conducted by Jacek Trznadel with authors on their attitudes during Stalinism. Such publications were quite uncommon in Czechoslovakia, where the intellectual discourse was significantly more ritualised than in Poland, and in Hungary, where criticism of the regime was suppressed by the self-censorship imposed by local intellectuals who were offered relatively decent financial conditions by the communist authorities under the leadership of János Kádár. However, critical remarks were occasionally verbalised or put in writing, for example, by Pavel Kohout, Karel Kosík, Milan Kundera, Agnes Heller and János Kis. After the transition, various institutions and committees were founded in the post-communist countries with the aim of settling accounts with the communist criminal heritage. In 1992 the 17th November Commission worked in the Czech Parliament, investigating the deeds of the communist security service, while in Poland the Institute of National Remembrance came into being in 1999, and in 2006 in Romania, President Traian Băsescu established the Presidential Commission for the Study of the Communist Dictatorship in Romania. Since the early 1990s, accusations of informal or secret collaboration with the communist security service have been also a fixed feature of the political game. The so-called 'Macierewicz List' and

'Wildstein List' in Poland, or 'Cibulka lists' in the Czech Republic contained the names both of actual and alleged former collaborators among politicians and journalists. Intellectuals and artists, e.g. Zygmunt Bauman, Zbigniew Herbert, Milan Kundera, Jaromír Nohavica and Ryszard Kapuściński, were also accused of collaboration with communists, and in the right-wing media the impersonal settlement with the *ancien régime* gave place to personal attacks on public figures.

c. **Social consequences of the democratic transition, or liberals' doubts** – the very recent past is also subject to settlement. Facing the crisis of democratic power, the growth of nationalistic, anti-Western and anti-EU attitudes, the repercussions of the global economic crisis and the insecure job market, symbolic elites are striving to assess their ideological and political choices made in the first years after the democratic transition. Some liberals, who in the 1990s initiated the transformation from the planned economy to capitalism, are settling accounts with the social consequences of the reforms and changes which they supported. Polish intellectual public figures speak about the fall of the 'Solidarity' ethos and announce the weakening of the communal social bonds over statutory divisions. In the famed 2014 interview entitled *We were stupid*, Marcin Król, a historian of ideas and a public intellectual, spoke of 'the illusion of free market' and 'the lack of imagination' on the side of the liberals who created capitalism, regarding social issues which nowadays result in the rise of radicalism in the public sphere (Król & Sroczyński, 2014). At the same time, Czech publicists proclaim the withdrawal from the heritage of dissidents and the Velvet Revolution, whereas some Hungarian authors are wondering why, in just 20 years after the transition, the state is governed by Prime Minister Viktor Orbán and his Fidesz Party, since their policy is leading to the restriction of individual liberties.

3. SELF-CRITICISM IN PUBLIC DISCOURSE

The aspect of settling accounts with the past which is of great interest to me is the self-critical dimension, since it refers to complexes, resentments and emotions governing the area of public communication and infrequently verbalised in the public discourse. In a general sense, self-criticism is a reckoning of the self, criticism directed at its own subject: an individual or collective 'I' (Nowicka, 2015). Self-criticism may have a total or a partial form. Total self-criticism means that its subjects negate the previous shape of their subjectivity and look for the causes of their mistakes directly in themselves, whereas in partial self-criticism the subjects criticise products of the self, their words, books, deeds, but not the very self.

For a scholar of social communication self-criticism means a discursive strategy, serving both to express oneself and to reach an audience. Therefore, a public act of self-criticism can be called a particular act of speech. Its perlocutionary dimension, as stated by Austin (1975, p. 109), lies in the fact that a public confession of guilt most often contains an appeal to the audience to join the act and a request to the victims to offer forgiveness. A public act of self-criticism is also a peculiar variant of *Face Threatening Acts* (Brown & Levinson, 1987, pp. 65–68), namely a self-deprecation performed in order to, paradoxically, save face by evoking compassion and the feeling of shared responsibility for confessing the guilt, and to motivate social actors to pursue settling accounts with the past. The perlocutionary effects of self-criticism at the level of social consciousness are extremely difficult to assess, but it is possible to research their public manifestations, that is, 'the verbally balanced reaction to the speaker's words' (Post, 2001, p. 138), for instance, the responses to someone's self-criticism which are published in the press.

In this article self-criticism is an umbrella term which covers the communicative and discursive features of the subjective account with the past. At the same time self-criticism is a sensitising concept which cannot be perceived as a finally defined term, but rather as one which 'gives the user a general sense of reference and guidance in approaching empirical instances' (Blumer, 1954, p. 7). Self-criticism does not always follow the same rules, as it may be of different gravity and might appeal to various types of audience. The variants of self-criticism in public discourse reflect the dynamics of historical and political processes which occur in any given society. I do not perceive self-criticism as the realisation of the agency of its subject, but as a type of discursive strategy and the resultant of anonymous rules of discourse. Therefore, my approach to self-criticism stems not only from Koselleckian historical semantics and discourse-historical analysis (DHA), but also from the Foucaultian concept of discourse.

3.1. Self-Criticism in Koselleckian and DHA Perspectives

The history of concepts by Reinhart Koselleck (2006, p. 9), that is, the research into the meaning of terms and their past, assumes that since any historical event has its own social and anthropological dimension, the terms and concepts which help us learn about history must also have a social and communicative genesis. Therefore, a universal *histoire totale* is impossible since the past is interpreted dynamically, implying alternations in the meaning of terms. The method utilised in conceptual history is historical semantics, which focuses on the social and political application of expressions and terms, their social and historical origin, paralinguistic content and attitude towards the described objects (Koselleck, 1979, p. 114). It seeks the conditions in which particular cases occurred and the long-term transformations of socio-political and conceptual structures (Koselleck, 2006, p. 24), as terms are temporary in nature, convey ideological contents and are prone to politicisation. The concept of self-criticism shares similar characteristics; despite the fact that the act of self-criticism had functioned *avant la lettre*, the term was not coined before the Enlightenment, when it was incorporated into the emancipatory ethos of the period, and the institutionalisation of self-criticism as a means of indoctrination was completed under communist rule (Nowicka, 2015). Today the concept of self-criticism is illustrated by the overlapping of various layers of time (Koselleck, 2000) in which it functioned. Thus, self-criticism may belong to the emancipatory and educational, political and ideological discourse, and it might serve as a strategy of public figures' media image management.

The subject of conceptual history explores the research territory of discourse analysis (Koselleck, 2006, p. 101), researching the intertextual and interdiscursive nature of communication, including its historical and ideological dimension. The critics of Koselleck point out that the sole conceptualisation of history via the analysis of terms (which are relatively stable structures of thinking) leads to the principal constraint of reflection upon the appearance of meanings in the processes of social communication (Busse, 1987). Therefore, discourse analysis is not a competitive but complementary approach to the history of concepts, from which it may derive the critical and historical research context. Methodological parallels are particularly visible between the discourse-historical approach (DHA) in critical discourse analysis (CDA) (see Reisigl & Wodak, 2009) and the history of concepts. They both focus on the issue of the socio-conceptual structure of collective identities in temporary, spatial and power-related dimensions (see Forchtner & Kølvraa, 2012; Krzyżanowski, 2010).

In the Koselleckian view self-criticism is, first of all, a term whose meaning depends on the transformations in the social space of experience and upon the horizon of expectation, nominating the tension between the social perception of the past and the vision of the future. Second, a public act of self-criticism most often refers to the opposition of one of our own versus an outsider, and utilises *asymmetrical counter-concepts*, which symbolically divide the community into two separate groups, e.g. Catholics and non-Catholics, or communists and anti-communists. Third, some terms are 'privileged' in debates on collective memory or identity. Thus, self-criticism in the context of settling accounts with the past uses, to a large degree, a set of recurrent concepts and rhetorical structures.

At the same time DHA focuses on the discursive construction of national sameness and the discursive construction of difference, as well as on hegemonic ways of coming to terms with a troublesome past aiming both at the preservation/reproduction of the narratives of collective identity and at the changing/reshaping of the collective narratives (Reisigl & Wodak, 2009). In view of this approach, self-criticism is a discursive strategy meant to affect social images and opinions of the past, and the determination of discursive means exploited in the Eastern European acts of self-criticism becomes the main research question here.

3.2. Self-Criticism in a Foucauldian Perspective

In the communicative dimension I understand self-criticism as a *discursive strategy*, defined by Michel Foucault as a mechanism intended to generate discourse which occurs in a specific set of anonymous relationships of social power. Discourse in Foucault's terms (1972, p. 117) is 'a group of statements insofar as they belong to the same discursive formation', where the discursive formation is a product of 'a group of relations established between authorities of emergence, delimitation and specification' (Foucault, 1972, p. 44). Discourse is thus a set of statements which are subject in every society to a specific order: procedures of control, selection, organisation and redistribution (Foucault, 1981, p. 52). In the context of settling accounts with troublesome memory, self-criticism means a strategy aimed at forming the discourse which, respectively, either contravenes or replicates the existing canons of power-knowledge related to the past of any given society. The important fact is that the discourse is not continuous and ritualised but coincidental and prone to ruptures and transitions.

My approach in the presented study derives not only from Koselleckian historical semantics or DHA, but also from post-Foucauldian discourse analysis posing the question of the conditions of the existence of certain discourses and the relations of social power that underlie communications and related social practices (see Diaz Bone et al., 2008; van Dyk & Angermüller, 2010). The aim of the analysis is a critical reconstruction of the conditions in which any given statements may occur, the determination of contents which have been excluded and the consideration of power relationships which manage discourse. This analysis focuses upon the following issues: (1) the concurrences in Eastern Europe that facilitate debates on the past and trigger public acts of self-criticism; (2) the procedures of discourse control utilised in acts of self-criticism and the argumentation and rhetoric applied in such acts and (3) the types of discourse generated in public acts of self-criticism.

4. SETTLING ACCOUNTS WITH THE TROUBLESOME PAST: THE CASE OF POLAND

The study of the history of Poland reveals in a nutshell the complex and repeatedly tragic vicissitudes in the region. In the 20th century Poland regained its independence after 123 years of partition, experienced the Nazi and Soviet aggression in 1939, endured four decades of communism and submission to the Soviet Union, saw a wave of workers' strikes and, finally, witnessed the 'bloodless transition' from a single-party system of a planned economy to liberal democracy and capitalism. Since 2004 Poland has been a member of the European Union and one of the largest beneficiaries of EU funds allocated to its modernisation. The country is praised for its fast pace of economic growth and educational boom, but its public sphere is, at the same time, criticised for the manifestations of anti-Semitism and nationalism. In Poland the past is a crucial but conflict-triggering and politicised subject of public debate, which is often used to shape current social reality.

The example of Polish public debate shall illustrate the three aforementioned variants of settling accounts with the past: the memory of WWII, the communist period and the transition. A qualitative analysis has been performed on 36 articles, declarations and speeches published in the national opinion-forming press between 2001 and 2014. A relatively short period of time renders it impossible to fully apply the Koselleckian approach, as it usually refers to a time perspective exceeding a hundred years. Nevertheless, the analysis incorporates the temporary and ideological dynamics managing the meaning of terms and concepts used in the scrutinised texts. The material is analysed with regard to the intertextual and interdiscursive contexts in which they function, and in respect of the discourse control procedures to which they are subjected. My sample is purposive, which means that I am choosing those materials which have caused some resonance and meet minimal demands of self-criticism, that is, their subject is an individual or collective 'I' which addresses a mistake, guilt or self-correction. For clarity of argument, in the presentation of conclusions presented below I shall focus on a detailed analysis of several selected examples.

4.1. A 'Difficult' Memory of the Wartime Polish−Jewish Relationships

After WWII, the memory of the Jewish fate had existed mainly as part of the collected memory of the Polish victims of Nazism. However, after the anti-Semitic persecution by the ruling communist party and the emigration of Polish Jews after 1968, harmful stereotypes of Jews as traitors of Poland were reinforced. Gradually, following the dissemination of the Western European discourse of the Holocaust memory, the tragedy of Jews as specific victims of Nazism started to be recognised. However, the 'comparative victimhood' between Poles and Jews continued to mark the image of WWII. In 1986 Claude Lanzmann's film *Shoah*, depicting Polish anti-Semitism in the countryside, was shown in Poland, and Lanzmann suggested that the Germans chose Poland as the location for concentration camps because of the anti-Semitism of the Polish society. A year later, the Catholic liberal weekly 'Tygodnik Powszechny' published an essay *The Poor Poles Look at the Ghetto* by Jan Błoński (1987), who problematised the wartime indifference and passivity of Poles towards the suffering of the Jews. Both oeuvres caused a violent debate, with anti-Semitic undertones, on Polish−Jewish relations during the war. Soon, in the democratic Poland, the image of Jewish tragedy and of Polish heroism (inter alia of Poles who saved Jews) became a subject discussed in school textbooks and presented in museums, where the unique scene of rituals of commemoration is the former Nazi concentration camp at Auschwitz-Birkenau.

It was not until 2000 that the strong claim of Polish counter-historical memory was made. In 2000, the historian Jan T. Gross published his book *Neighbors*, discussing the crime committed against the Jews by the Polish countrymen on 10 July 1941 in the town of Jedwabne during the Nazi occupation. The Jews were herded into a barn, which was then set on fire (Gross writes about there being 1600 victims, the report of the Institute of National Remembrance speaks of around 300 victims). As for the reasons for the pogrom, the author suggests both the cultural anti-Semitism in Polish society as well as wartime anomie and Nazi propaganda. Gross's work resonated strongly among the symbolic elites and the general public in Poland. An intensifying moment of the debate was the announcement of foreign translations of Gross's book, which led to the fear that Poland's external image would suffer. Gross's critical approach to historiography, addressing the dark pages in the history of Poles, did not go hand in hand with the political discourse. The ambitions to enter the structures of Western democracies and the motto of the 'return to Europe' placed emphasis on the narratives affirming our own national group as worthy of joining the ranks of the Western democracies. Moreover, *the Jedwabne debate* referred critically to the martyrological and heroic core of Polish collective memory and resulted in very emotional stances of the public – both supporting and denying the need for settling accounts with the shameful past (see Ciołkiewicz, 2003; Czyżewski, 2008; Forecki, 2010; Paczkowski, 2010).

The official celebration of the 60th anniversary of the Jedwabne pogrom, held in July 2001, was a symbolic closure of this stage of the public debate on Polish guilt towards Jews. Aleksander Kwaśniewski, Polish president of that time, made a speech in which he apologised to the Jewish community for the massacre and referred to the issue of Polish attitudes towards Jews. On the one hand, his address is an example of *speculative* or *soul-searching speeches*, which do not directly regard the current political game, but focus on the issue of collective values and the nature of the community being the subject of the speech (see Wodak & Weiss, 2004). On the other hand, Kwaśniewski's address is also an act of self-criticism expressed on behalf of one community – the Polish – and aimed at another one – the Jewish, in order to appeal to the conscience of the living and to demonstrate Polish openness to the issue of settling accounts with the past.

Opening his speech, Kwaśniewski (2001) reminds the audience that the massacre took place under German occupation. The reference to the external circumstances (wartime anomie, the pressure of anti-Semitic propaganda by Nazi occupants) allows the speaker to attach the Polish crime in Jedwabne to the global list of war atrocities and to depersonalise it, that is, to avoid nominating specific culprits and to point to general anti-values of 'hatred and cruelty'.

Next, the president speaks of the lack of knowledge on the massacre in Jedwabne:

> We know much about this crime, though not yet everything. Maybe we will never learn the whole truth. But this did not prevent us from being here today. To speak in an open voice. We know enough to stand here in truth – facing the pain, the cry and the suffering of those who were murdered here. Face to face with the victims' families who are here today. Before the judgment of our own conscience.

In this passage the concepts which constitute the argumentative foundations of the speech appear: 'knowledge', 'truth', 'conscience'. Knowledge is made equal to truth, and the latter to the examination of conscience. Despite being fragmentary at that time (the Polish *Historikerstreit* on pogroms and the investigation of the Institute of National Remembrance were in progress), the knowledge and truth on Jedwabne still 'force' people to settle accounts with the past, since they both play a role of counter-history – revealing the marginalised facts and events in Polish collective memory, which call into question the predominant picture of the past. In another, unquoted part of his speech, Kwaśniewski describes the details of the massacre and its cruelty, paving the way for the following declaration:

> We know with all the certainty that Poles were among the oppressors and assassins. We cannot have any doubts – here in Jedwabne citizens of the Republic of Poland died at the hands of other citizens of the Republic of Poland. It is people to people, neighbours to neighbours who forged such destiny.

The declaration opens with a moralised naming, with Poles presented as 'the oppressors and assassins', but the victims are not called Jews, but 'citizens of the Republic of Poland'. Instead of the asymmetrical counter-concepts of Jews/Poles the speaker uses the universal concept of 'people', when referring to both the culprits and their victims, and 'neighbours', which is an intertextual reference to Gross's book under the same title. Simultaneously, Kwaśniewski stresses that, at that time, the Polish state was to be 'wiped from the map of Europe':

> But the Republic of Poland should persist in the Polish hearts and minds. And the standards of a civilised state, the state with ages-old traditions of tolerance and amicable co-existence of nations and religions should be binding on its citizens. Those who killed, beat, took part in the dead set, set fire – committed a crime not only against their Jewish neighbours. They are also guilty towards the Republic of Poland, its history and glorious traditions.

In this passage the issue of guilt appears for the very first time, a guilt not only towards 'Jewish neighbours', but – above all – to the values and standards of the Republic of Poland. Kwaśniewski evokes a thread, idealised in Polish historical studies, of the 16th century religious tolerance, arguing that the pogrom of Jews is a betrayal of Polish 'glorious traditions'. This is an example of the rhetoric of guilt – pointing to the fall of general ethical injunctions, which burdens the conscience of the addressee (comp. Piotrowski, 1997).

Further on, Kwaśniewski states that the massacre in Jedwabne was an act of fratricide and that this was not the only pogrom committed by the Polish during WWII. He does distance himself from the postulate of collective responsibility which is inherited from ancestors, but not from the memory of the crime:

> The nation is a community. A community of individuals, a community of generations. And this is why we have to look the truth in the eye. Any truth. And say: it was, it happened. Our conscience will be clear if the memories of those days will forever evoke awe and moral indignation. We are here to make a collective self-examination. We are paying tribute to the victims and we are saying – never again.

The obligation to remember and commemorate is a community bond between individuals and generations. We face the recurrence of the concept of 'truth' here, which may 'purify the conscience' of the living as long as they undergo 'self-examination'. Kwaśniewski avoids the term 'self-criticism', discredited in Stalinism, but appeals for 'self-examination', which is meant to serve a similar purpose to the modernising auto-critique: to ensure a brighter future by settling accounts with the past. This appeal is expressed by a phrase borrowed from the anti-fascist discourse: 'never again'. In the next, unquoted extract the president universalises the felony as an expression of evil, which may take place in any nation, not only among the Polish, and he distances himself from national labels. 'Cain could have killed Abel anywhere', he says, referring to the Old Testament, the Holy Book of Jews and Christians.

Thanks to a great nation-wide debate regarding this crime committed in 1941, much has changed in our lives in 2001, the first year of the new millennium. Today's Poland has the courage to look into the eyes of the truth about a nightmare which gloomed one of the chapters in its history.

We have become aware of the responsibility for our attitude towards the dark pages in our history. We have understood that bad service is done to the nation by those who are impelling to renounce that past. Such an attitude leads to moral self-destruction.

The abovementioned extract refers to the debate on Jedwabne, presented as evidence of Polish 'courage' in settling accounts with a troublesome past. However, the speaker uses the *exclusive 'we'*, which incorporates only those who are ready for such a settlement. The rest are broadly referred to as those 'who are impelling to renounce that past' and, thus, symbolically excluded from the national community as those performing 'moral self-destruction'. Next, Kwaśniewski states that there is an army of people in Poland, including clergymen, who are willing to settle accounts with the past, pay homage to the victims and ask for forgiveness. And here comes the climax: 'This is why today, the President of the Republic of Poland, I beg pardon. I beg pardon in my own name and in the name of those Poles whose conscience is shattered by that crime'. Kwaśniewski emphasises that, using his official position, he wishes to speak out as a Pole and on behalf of the Polish. At the same time, he demonstrates, by negation, the rationale behind the account with the past on behalf of the collective 'we', which is neither limited to human decency nor a mere response to the external expectations of (Western) observers:

> We are saying today the words of sorrow and pain, not only because of human decency. And not only because others expect us to. Not because they will be compensation for the murdered. Not because the world is listening. We are saying these words because this is what we feel. Because we ourselves need them most of all.

The final part reveals the direct recipient of the speech, who − apart from Jews − are also those Poles who feel the need to settle accounts with the Polish−Jewish past. Despite the negation placed in the abovementioned extract, the European or even global audience still remains an indirect recipient of his address. This can be concluded from the numerous attempts to universalise guilt as a world-wide issue, with which Poland is supposed to be coping 'well', as far as international standards are concerned. On the one hand, Kwaśniewski's address has the features of *speculative speeches*: it evokes more values and emotions than strictly historical knowledge, and it is also more visionary, projecting the Polish collective consent to an open debate on the Polish−Jewish past. On the other hand, this self-criticism is a *normalisation* strategy, Foucauldian in its nature (2008) − in this case the desired model of Polishness is identified with that of a tolerant and cosmopolitan society propagated in the West, a society which is open to discussing the troublesome past (comp. Underhill, 2011, p. 589). The speech by Kwaśniewski dates back to the pre-EU period of Polish history, when Poland was assessed not only for its economic situation, but also for the state of its democracy, and the issue of anti-Semitism is, in Western Europe, perceived as a major determinant of social tolerance. This act of self-criticism is not only meant to settle accounts with the past, but it also serves the purpose of pro-European auto-presentation. Contrary to initial expectations, however, it has not become the subject of social content, but a source of numerous objections expressed by right-wing audiences.

4.2. Settling the Past of the Collaborators with the Communist Regime

As early as the 1950s Polish intellectuals began the process of settling accounts with their involvement in the development of communism. However, their voice was either restricted by censorship or available only through unofficial channels of distribution and the underground publishing movement, which was aimed at a relatively small audience. For these reasons, only after 1989 is there a profusion of biographies of intellectuals who had been seduced by communism, victims of what Miłosz called the 'Hegelian bite'. Their authors are both local writers and foreign observers willing to understand the ideological blindness of the intelligentsia (see Bikont & Szczęsna, 2006; Grochowska, 2012; Shore, 2006).

Nevertheless, in this part of the chapter I shall focus on political attempts to settle accounts with communism. Democratic Poland witnessed a partial exchange and reproduction of elites: in the early 1990s every fourth active politician was at some point a member of the communist party, and in the sphere of culture this referred to every third activist (Wnuk-Lipiński, 1996, p. 141). On the one hand, in public discourse communism was perceived as an externalised and illegitimised phenomenon of the past (Tileagă, 2012, p. 473). On the other hand, former apparatchiks were still present in public life. The so-called 'thick line' policy applied by Prime Minister Tadeusz Mazowiecki, namely the abandonment of a coordinated decommunisation, led to the situation in which individual parties and the mass media that supported them began to judge their political opponents in a self-appointed manner and on the basis of weak evidence. Lustration became a tool of political struggle, not only against the old elites, but also against the new elites. Even Lech Wałęsa, the legendary leader of the 'Solidarity' movement and the first democratically elected President of Poland, was accused of collaboration with the communist security service.

The lustration postulates issued by the right-wing elites did not translate into a readiness for self-criticism on the part of those people who actually participated in the morally dubious co-operation with the regime. One of the very few acts of self-criticism is the text written by Lesław Maleszka, a journalist working for *Gazeta Wyborcza*, which was published in the daily in 2001. Maleszka confessed that in his student years, after being threatened with expulsion from university in 1976, he signed a declaration of collaboration with the communist security service and reported on his colleagues from the student dissident organisation, including Stanisław Pyjas, who in 1977 died in mysterious circumstances, most probably killed by the security service. Even after Pyjas' death, Maleszka did not break the co-operation with the security service, for which he would be rewarded financially. As an operational pseudonym he chose the alias 'Ketman', taken from *The Captive Mind* by Czesław Miłosz, and referring to the attitude of a mental split: a public manifestation of opinions and beliefs with which one does not really identify himself, in the hope of playing his own intellectual game with the regime. In 2001 in his piece entitled *I was Ketman* (Polish: *Byłem Ketmanem*) Maleszka wrote:

> It's been 12 or maybe 16 years since my collaboration terminated, but this sin shall burden my conscience till the end of my days. And even if I have asked for forgiveness a hundred times, I shall understand those who still won't shake my hand any more.

> Weak is my faith, but God knows what a torture it is for me to write these words. I loathe pathos, but no words could express how much I regret what I have done. I very much wish I could recompense the evil I have inflicted − if only it were possible. Shame, shame on me.

> I am also ashamed of my incapacity to put this story in words or of my inability to reveal it to any friends after 1989. Once more I have turned out to be a coward.

Instead of emphasising the political context of his collaboration, Maleszka stresses the feeling which − as he claims − his past evokes. This type of self-criticism is founded on the *projecting of the intended audience* and rhetorical addressing of its predicted emotions. The author 'accepts' social ostracism, but − at the same time − he applies Christian lexis ('this sin will burden my conscience', 'God knows', 'I very much wish I could recompense the evil I have inflicted'), which implies an appeal for *mercy and forgiveness.* He states that his self-criticism comes too late and attaches to himself the badge of coward.

Maleszka's self-criticism does not serve its perlocutionary purposes. It summons the figure of Stanisław Pyjas, a legendary victim of the regime (although there is no clear evidence that Maleszka's denunciations directly contributed to his death), but this act of repentance is performed after the public disclosure of his collaboration with the communist secret service. Thus, the self-criticism turns out to be belated and overly defensive in Foucauldian terms, which means it belongs to a different *discursive formation* than the discourse of its audience. Nevertheless, a few years later the issue of the lustration of journalists returned to the public agenda in Poland. In 2006 the right-wing government formed by the Law and Justice (Polish: PIS) passed the lustration law, which obligated thousands of politicians, officials, scientists and journalists to submit lustration statements on their activities in the communist period. The truthfulness of these statements was to be verified and assessed by the Institute of National Remembrance, on the basis of communist security service documentation. Subsequently, the Institute was obligated to publish a catalogue of former informants and collaborators. The liberal and left-wing elites, however, associated the lustration requirement with the procedures of submission of self-critical reports during the Stalinist period. In 2007, when the law was about to come into effect, some journalists refused to submit their lustration statements. These were the same people who a few years earlier, upon the publication of Gross's book, had supported the idea of settling accounts with Polish guilt towards Jews. The context of settling the communist past was, however, significantly different for them. This time settling accounts with the past would be institutionalised and, thus, it would apply to the majority of public figures, regardless of their attitude during the communist period, and the arbitrary institution adjudicating upon their morality was the Institute of National Remembrance, strongly related to the governing party.

In 2007, in the left-liberal daily *Gazeta Wyborcza*, Dawid Warszawski [Konstanty Gebert], a publicist and a former member of the anti-communist opposition, wrote: 'I have no desire whatsoever to prove that I am not a camel. The people and institutions suspecting otherwise may as well lustrate me on their own and without the slightest difficulty'. He referred to a saying popular in the era of Soviet cleansings in the 1930s and to the absurdity of an individual submitting statements to institutions which already have access to the files on this individual. In 2007, in the same vein, Ewa Milewicz wrote in *Gazeta Wyborcza*:

I shall not submit my lustration statement, which is a legal requirement imposed on journalists by the lustration law. I shall not submit it, because I do not wish to explain and excuse my actions in the Polish People's Republic. If I had done something wrong, I will be placed in the catalogue of informal collaborators, prepared by the Institute of National Remembrance. And if I had done something good, I won't brag about it.

In the aforementioned quotations lustration is associated with the violence of the state, symbolised by the Institute of National Remembrance. It is not the justifiability of settling accounts with the communist past that is explicitly questioned, but the fashion in which the government desires to enforce it. In response to the actions taken by the authorities, the left-liberal elites, in their discourse, resorted to *antipatterning*, which is a rhetorical technique of reversing the scale of the issue raised by the opponent (Ibarra & Kitsuse, 1993, p. 45). In other words, the manner in which, 20 years after the fall of communism, the authorities intended to perform settling with the past was considered to be more of an issue than the process itself. Paradoxically, the clash of the discourse supporting and disapproving lustration resulted in a written appeal made by Adam Michnik (2007), the editor-in-chief of *Gazeta Wyborcza*, entitled *Let's open the files* (Polish: *Otwórzmy teczki*), who protested against using security service files for political purposes and suggested making them public:

In March 1968, when Władysław Gomułka – using security service files – cast wicked aspersions on Paweł Jasienica, it filled all good men with disgust. Today we must react in the same manner towards the imitators of the foul play. Therefore, these days all the files should be made public and available to anyone, regardless of the terrible consequences. It would still be better than what we are experiencing today. We must make these files public in order not to, paradoxically, live in the slavery of these documents, as now they are used for foul purposes, their contents 'leak out' now and again, and they have become a powerful tool in the game of politics.

The author is creating *a historical analogy* between the communist authorities (who in the 1960s accused the respectable historian Paweł Jasienica of being their informant in order to destroy his reputation among the intellectuals critical towards the regime) and the policy applied by the Law and Justice government. An indirect result of the analogy is the appeal to make the security service files public so that they would cease to be such a threat in the hands of politicians. His argumentation is based on the affirmation of democratic transparency, which is expected to contribute to the fair and just assessment of the representatives of the former regime, and on the assumption that the greater access to knowledge, the more rational its interpretation. Liberal values are employed here to discuss local issues, even though they do not cover the entire complexity of the problem (some security service files were counterfeit and their disclosure could have led to the authentication of groundless accusations).

Eventually, the Constitutional Tribunal judged numerous provisions within the lustration act to be unconstitutional, including the obligatory lustration of journalists. It remains, however, a recurring issue and it antagonises Polish political discourse, suspended in the deadlock of self-criticism which, on the one hand, is based on transparency and Western reasonability and, on the other hand, on local instrumentalisation of the process of settling accounts with the past.

4.3. The Profit and Loss Account of the Transformation

In Poland, 25 years after the change in 1989 there has been more and more criticism of the current shape of democracy and the transition model chosen by the leaders of the democratic changes. In the context of growing social and economic stratification, a split into so-called 'winners' and 'losers' of the transformation and in the shadow of global economic crisis, both the conservative and left-liberal elites started to articulate their disillusionment with copying the economic models from the West, which had been implemented rapidly in the early 1990s in Poland. In most cases it is not democracy *per se* becoming the object of the most severe critique but the long-term effects of the top-down imitative transition to capitalism which led to individualisation within the society and to the destruction of the legacy of the legendary movement 'Solidarity' fighting for workers' rights and social justice.

Right-wing politicians put the blame for the social consequences of the transition on their left-liberal opponents and on the figure identified with the difficult capitalistic reforms – the former Minister of Finance, Leszek Balcerowicz, who in the early 1990s implemented an economic transformation program based on a series of radical reforms which were painful for ordinary citizens. Since liberal politicians defend themselves by claiming that the right-wing discourse is becoming more and more populist, the subject of self-criticism, which mainly occurs not in the political but in the intellectual field, is the left-liberal intellectuals who in the late 1980s and early 1990s supported a quick transformation to the Western model of democracy and capitalism, and who, in the 25th anniversary of the transition, find it a pretext for a bitter settlement with the past. These are acts of *transition disillusionment's self-criticism*, to a degree reactionary towards the pro-Western modernisation, mostly within the sphere of the economy but also within the social discourse. An event which greatly reverberated in Poland was an interview We were stupid (Polish: *Byliśmy głupi*) published in *Gazeta Wyborcza* in 2014, in which Grzegorz Sroczyński talked to the liberal intellectual Marcin Król about the causes of growing dissatisfaction with the shape that Polish democracy has taken. An analysis of three self-critical extracts from the interview can be found below:

We were stupid.

In the 1980s we got infected with the ideology of neoliberalism, and indeed I had my share in this, I would talk Tusk, Bielecki and all that Gdańsk milieu into it. I would scrupulously give them Hayek's writings. We had similar views with Balcerowicz, today we have drifted apart.

This zeal died in me pretty quickly. I realized that liberalism was being dominated by the element of individualism, which was gradually pushing out other important values and killing the community.

The interview opens with a strong, self-critical declaration made by Król on behalf of the liberal intellectuals: 'We were stupid'. Neoliberalism, being the main source of inspiration for the intellectuals, is defined as an 'ideology', which in Polish discourse has a pejorative meaning, associated with the ideology of communism and fascism. The idea of defining neoliberalism as an ideology stems from the left-wing anti-capitalistic discourse, but Król neutralises the criticism by comparing neoliberalism to a contagious disease which can be contracted unwittingly. His self-criticism is partial in its nature: the author admits that he encouraged the liberal politicians (Donald Tusk, Jan Krzysztof Bielecki, Leszek Balcerowicz) to draw inspiration from the Western model of liberalism, but, at the same time, he emphasises the fact that soon (sooner than other liberals) he recognised the menace lurking in liberalism itself. Referring to the Kosselleckian category, one may argue that modern liberalism, based on individualism, works as an *agonistic asymmetrical counter-concept* to the concept of 'community', which can and should be 'regained' for the discourse of liberal democracy (also see Postoutenko, 1992).

We were living on another planet, out of touch with everyday problems. From our point of view, the whole revolution was about liberty, after all. Let's take a look at the example of censorship in communism. Who did it really bother? 97% Poles never treated is as a nuisance. And for us it was the most fundamental problem when the regime edited our texts or forbid us to publish them. Freedom was of utmost importance to us. And it was enough for us, whereas the issues of social solidarity, poverty in the countryside, state agricultural farms [Polish: PGR], inequality… We just lacked imagination.

In this extract the author applies the strategy of *blaming* (Angouri & Wodak, 2014, pp. 544–545) in a self-critical manner: the liberals who are guilty of disregarding 'everyday problems' become a collective subject here, but their fault is relativised by pointing to the discrepancy between social *metanarratives* – for the intelligentsia the transition meant no censorship combined with freedom of speech in the public sphere, whereas the great majority expected some measures to be taken to prevent poverty and economic inequality, which – according to Król – the leaders of the transition failed to do. Therefore, the final statement ('We just lacked imagination') is of a self-excusing rather than self-blaming nature, since it refers to the social non-knowledge of the expectations held by various social groups.

Before 1990, whenever a circle of intellectuals met, we did talk about serious issues. We would discuss possible solutions and Poland's priorities. And then it just stopped, since there was this conviction that the relationship between mind and power was broken. Why should I bother coping with the issues of this world when nobody is actually listening…

The issue of knowledge reoccurs in the extract devoted to the social role of intellectuals in Poland. Król highlights the severance, at the very beginning of the transition, of the relationship between mind, personified by intellectuals, and power, identified with the new political elites (throughout the whole interview). The 'we' used in the opening sentences of the extract eventually transforms into the isolated 'I', which illustrates the process which in Foucauldian terminology can be called subjugation of certain knowledge and its transformation into a type of intellectual *counter-history*, perceived by the authorities as an infantile and marginal perspective.

Despite the incompleteness of this self-account, Król's point of view was objected to by numerous intellectuals from his own liberal circles, who denied him the right to settle accounts with the transformation on their behalf and reproached him for joining the populist front, negating and rejecting the achievements of the transition. The discrepancies in the assessment of its consequences and ideological background largely stem from the fact that in Poland − the country of a relatively short liberal tradition − the concept of liberalism is perceived quite ambiguously, either as a Western attribute and a set of technical economic directives, or − less frequently − as a comprehensive political philosophy (Szacki, 1994, pp. 11−14). Thus, the criticism of liberalism is not exclusively the critique of the condition of Polish democracy, but also the assessment of Western European values as a certain ideal to which Eastern Europe is supposed to aspire.

5. CONCLUSIONS

In Eastern Europe settling accounts with the past is a work in progress, a process which does not lead to social consensus, but to pluralism and the fragmentation of collective memory. The growing number of public interpretations of the past is accompanied by an increased self-critical approach to historiography. However, in the case of the commemoration of WWII, the phase of 'debunking' memory is usually followed by a phase of glorification of the past of one's own group. What is more, the debate on WWII is performed largely in isolation from a historical context and constitutes an example of the recontextualisation of the future in order to dispute the modern meaning of such *basic concepts* as 'nation' or 'collective identity'. In all likelihood, the issue of Eastern Europeans' attitudes towards Jews is just the first chapter of the debate. Other problems that need addressing are, for instance, the wartime relations between different countries in the region, e.g. Poland and the Czech Republic, Ukraine or Lithuania − the issue which until today has been omitted in the name of political pragmatism. On the other hand, the debates on communism and transition primarily focus on the meaning of such concepts as 'democracy', 'capitalism' or 'liberalism', and pose questions about the selection of elites.

Self-criticism, which accompanies the process of settling accounts with the past in Eastern Europe, is strictly correlated with the current socio-political context. On the basis of the analysis of the text corpus related to Polish public discourse, initial conclusions may be drawn, but they will, however, require further study, encompassing other countries in the region. First, the further the subject is in time, the more often a local guilt (e.g. Poles towards Jews) is universalised and incorporated into the general narration on good and evil. The argumentation also includes the relativisation of collective responsibility through accentuating the uniqueness of Eastern European suffering against the history of Europe. Second, self-criticism utilises the constituents of both moral discourse, set in the Christian tradition (the recurring terms of 'guilt', 'shame', 'sin', 'truth'), and the discourse of a civil society (with such points of reference as 'liberty', 'knowledge', 'community', 'state' and 'civil rights'). Third, the subject of self-criticism is most frequently the intelligentsia, who − while settling accounts with the past − maintains its pervious role in the development of national identities. The settlements of former generations with their past constitute the intertextual context for the intelligentsia's self-criticism, whereas the interdiscursive context is represented, beside the current governmental policy of any given state, by Western discourses of liberal democracy and left-wing social critique.

The Eastern European debate on the past also leaves its stamp on the perception of Western Europe. Witold Morawski notes that 'copying Western models has ceased to be a large mobilising force' for East European societies, as 'the conviction is growing that there isn't one sole West' (2014, p. 448). Nowadays, only a few Western values constituting the European economic, moral and social sphere are found alluring by the majority of Eastern Europeans, while others arouse controversy. Moreover, there is a growing anticipation that Western Europe will also initiate a critical reflection on closer and further past of the countries which, for many years, have been a role model for their Eastern neighbours.

NOTE

1. The category of symbolic elites refers to those people whose statements shape the content and the scope of public discourse, influence the assessment of validity or invalidity of some subjects and form opinions and standpoints in public debate. Symbolic elites may be represented by scientists, intellectuals, experts, politicians and publicists (see van Dijk, 1993, pp. 46−47; Czyżewski, Franczak, Nowicka, & Stachowiak, 2014).

ACKNOWLEDGEMENTS

This study was supported by Bronisław Geremek Junior Visiting Fellowship, sponsored by the Institute for Human Sciences, Vienna, the Polish Ministry of Culture and National Heritage, Warsaw, and the Adam Mickiewicz Institute, Warsaw.

REFERENCES

Angouri, J., & Wodak, R. (2014). 'They became big in the shadow of the crisis': The Greek success story and the rise of the far right. *Discourse & Society, 25*(4), 540−565.

Austin, J. L. (1975). *How to do things with words.* Harvard, MA: Harvard University Press.

Beck, U., Giddens, A., & Lash, S. (1994). *Reflexive modernization: politics, tradition and aesthetics in the modern social order.* Redwood City, CA: Stanford University Press.

Bikont, A., & Szczęsna, J. (2006). *Lawina i kamienie: Pisarze wobec komunizmu.* Warszawa: Prószyński i S-ka.

Błoński, J. (1987). *Biedni Polacy patrza na getto,* 'Tygodnik Powszechny,' No. 2.

Blumer, H. (1954). What is wrong with social theory?. *American Sociological Review, 19*(1), 3−10.

Brock, D. (2014). *Die radikalisierte Moderne.* Moderne Gesellschaften: Zweiter Band; Wiesbaden: Springer VS.

Brown, P., & Levinson, S. C. (1987). *Politeness: Some universals in language usage.* Cambridge: Cambridge University Press.

Busse, D. (1987). *Historische Semantik. Analyse eines Programms.* Stuttgart: Klett-Cotta.

Ciołkiewicz, P. (2003). Debata publiczna na temat mordu w Jedwabnem w kontekście przeobrażeń pamięci zbiorowej. *Przeglad Socjologiczny, 1,* 285−306.

Czyżewski, M. (2008). Debata na temat Jedwabnego oraz spór o 'politykę historyczna' z punktu widzenia analizy dyskursu publicznego. In S. M. Nowinowski, J. Pomorski, & R. Stobiecki (Eds.), *Pamięć i polityka historyczna. Doświadczenia Polski i jej sasiadów* (pp. 117−140). Łódź: Instytut Pamięci Narodowej.

Czyżewski, M., Franczak, K., Nowicka, M., & Stachowiak, J. (2014). Wprowadzenie. In S. M. Nowinowski, J. Pomorski, & R. Stobiecki (Eds.), *Dyskurs elit symbolicznych* (pp. 7−14). Warszawa: Sedno.

Diaz-Bone, R., Bührmann, A. D., Rodrigez, E. G., Schneider, W., Kendall, G., & Tirado, F. (2008). The field of Foucaultian discourse analysis, structures, developments and perspectives. *Historical Social Research, 33*(1), 7−28.

Forchtner, B., & Kølvraa, C. (2012). Narrating a 'new Europe': From 'bitter past' to self-righteousness?. *Discourse & Society, 23*(4), 377−400.

Forecki, P. (2010). *Od Shoah do Strachu. Spory o polsko-żydowska przeszłość i pamięć w debatach publicznych.* Poznań: Wyd. Poznańskie.

Foucault, M. (1972). *The archaeology of knowledge.* New York, NY: Routledge.

Foucault, M. (1979). *Discipline and punish: The birth of the prison.* New York, NY: Vintage Books.

Foucault, M. (1981). The order of discourse. In R. Young (Ed.), *Untying the text: A post-structuralist reader.* London: Routledge.

Foucault, M. (2003). *Society must be defended.* New York, NY: Picador.

Foucault, M. (2006). Security, territory, population: Lectures at the Collège de France, *1977−1978.* New York, NY: Palgrave.

Foucault, M. (2008). *The birth of biopolitics: Lectures at the Collège de France 1978−1979.* New York, NY: Palgrave.

Glondys, D. (2009). The revenge of memory?. *Eurozine.* Retrieved from http://www.eurozine.com/articles/2009-10-22-glondys-en.html. Accessed April 15, 2015.

Grochowska, M. (2012). *Ćwiczenia z niemożliwego.* Warszawa: Wielka Litera.

Gross, J. T. (2001). *Neighbors: The destruction of the Jewish community in Jedwabne.* Princeton, NJ: Princeton University Press.

Gross, J. T. (2007). *Fear: Anti-semitism in Poland after Auschwitz.* New York, NY: Random House.

Gross, J. T., & Grudzińska-Gross, I. (2012). *Golden harvest.* New York, NY: Oxford University Press.

Halbwachs, M. (1992). *On collective memory.* Chicago, IL: University of Chicago Press.

Hilberg, R. (2003). *The destruction of the European Jews.* New Haven, CT: Yale University Press.

Huyssen, A. (1995). *Twilight memories: Marking time in a culture of amnesia*. New York, NY: Routledge.

Ibarra, P. R., & Kitsuse, J. I. (1993). Vernacular constituents of moral discourse: An interactionist proposal for the study of social problems. In A. J. Holstein & G. Miller (Eds.), *Reconsidering social constructionism: Debates in social problems theory* (pp. 25—58). New York, NY: De Gruyter.

Janion, M. (2000). *Do Europy tak, ale razem z naszymi umarłymi*. Warszawa: Wyd. Sic!.

Judt, T. (2006). *Postwar: A history of Europe since 1945*. London: Penguin Books.

Kołakowski, L. (1973). Sprawa polska. *Kultura*, (4), 4—13.

Koselleck, R. (1979). *Vergangene Zukunft. Zur Semantik geschichtlicher Zeiten*. Frankfurt am Main: Suhrkamp.

Koselleck, R. (2000). *Zeitschichten. Studien zur Historik. Mit einem Beitrag von Hans Georg Gadamer*. Frankfurt am Main: Suhrkamp.

Koselleck, R. (2006). *Begriffsgeschichten. Studien zur Semantik und Pragmatik der politischen und sozialen Sprache*. Frankfurt am Main: Suhrkamp.

Kowalska-Leder, J. (2014). Literatura polska ostatniego dziesięciolecia wobec Zagłady — próby odpowiedzi na nowe wyzwania. *Zagłada Żydów, 10*(2), 768—803.

Król, M., & Sroczyński, G. (2014). Byliśmy głupi. *Gazeta Wyborcza*, February 8.

Krupa, B. (2014). Historia krytyczna i jej 'gabinet cieni'. Historiografia polska wobec Zagłady 2003—2013. *Zagłada Żydów, 10*(2), 721—767.

Krzyżanowski, M. (2010). Discourses and concepts: Interfaces and synergies between Begriffsgeschichte and the discourse-historical approach in CDA. In R. De Cillia, H. Gruber, M. Krzyżanowski, & F. Menz (Eds.), Diskurs—Politik—Identität/Discourse—Politics—Identity (pp. 125—137). Tubingen: Stauffenburg Verlag.

Kwaśniewski, A. (2001). The official address delivered by the President of the Republic of Poland Mr. Aleksander Kwasniewski On July 10, 2001, in Jedwabne, Poland. Retrieved from http://www.dialog.org/hist/kwasniewski.html. Accessed April 23, 2015.

Kwiatkowski, P. T. (2008). *Pamięć zbiorowa społeczeństwa polskiego w okresie transformacji*. Warszawa: SCHOLAR.

Lesław, M. (2001). Byłem Ketmanem. *Gazeta Wyborcza*, November 13.

Medina, J. (2011). Toward a Foucaultian epistemology of resistance: Counter-memory, episte-mic friction, and guerrilla pluralism. *Foucault Studies, 12*, 9—35.

Michnik, A. (2007). Otwórzmy teczki. *Gazeta Wyborcza*, May 14.

Milewicz, E. (2007). Lustracji i tak nie uniknę. *Gazeta Wyborcza*, March 8.

Miłosz, C. (1990[1953]). *The captive mind*. New York, NY: Vintage.

Morawski, W. (2014). 'Path dependence': How geopolitics and culture shape divisions in Poland after the fall of communism. *Polish Sociological Review, 188*(4), 435—460.

Nora, P., & Zakowski, J. (2002). Epoka upamiętniania. In J. Zakowski *Rewanż pamięci*. Warszawa: Wyd. Sic!.

Nowicka, M. (2015). Self-criticism in public discourse: A device of modernization? The case of Eastern Europe. In S. Eich & P. Marczewski (Eds.), *Dimensions of modernity*. Vienna: Institute for Human Sciences.

Paczkowski, A. (2010). Upiory przeszłości: Jedwabne i Kielce. Zmagania z pamięcia. In M. Czyżewski, S. Kowalski, & T. Tabako (Eds.), *Retoryka i polityka. Dwudziestolecie polskiej transformacji* (pp. 195—213). Warszawa: Wyd. Akademickie i Profesjonalne.

Piotrowski, A. (1997). Tożsamość zbiorowa jak temat dyskursu polityki. Analiza przypadku. In M. Czyżewski, S. Kowalski, & A. Piotrowski (Eds.), *Rytualny chaos. Studium dyskursu publicznego*. Kraków: Aureus.

Post, M. (2001). Efekty i akty perlokucyjne. In W. Kubiński & D. Stanulewicz (Eds.), *Językoznawstwo kognitywne: II. Zjawiska pragmatyczne*. (pp. 135—147). Gdańsk: Wyd. Uniwersytetu Gdańskiego.

Postoutenko, K. (1992) Asymmetrical concepts and political asymmetries: A comparative glance at 20th century democracies and totalitarianisms from a discursive standpoint. In: K. Junge,

K. Postoutenko (Eds.), *Asymmetrical concepts after Reinhart Koselleck historical semantics and beyond.* Bielefeld: Transcript.

Reisigl, M., & Wodak, R. (2009). The discourse-historical approach. In R. Wodak & M. Meyer (Eds.), *Methods of critical discourse analysis* (pp. 87–121). London: Sage.

Rosa, H. (2005). *Beschleunigung. Die Veränderung der Zeitstrukturen in der Moderne.* Frankfurt am Main: Suhrkamp.

Shore, M. (2006). *Caviar and ashes: A Warsaw generation's life and death in Marxism, 1918–1968.* New Haven, CT: Yale University Press.

Szacki, J. (1994). *Liberalism after communism.* Budapest: CEU Press.

Tileagă, C. (2012). Communism in retrospect: The rhetoric of historical representation and writing the collective memory of recent past. *Memory Studies, 5*(4), 462–478.

Underhill, K. (2011). Next year in Drohobych: On the uses of Jewish absence. *East European Politics and Societies, 25*(3), 581–596.

Van Dijk, T. (1993). *Elite discourse and racism.* London: Sage.

Van Dyk, S., & Angermüller, J. (Eds.), (2010). *Diskursanalyse meets Gouvermentalitätsforschung. Perspektiven auf das Verhältnis von Subjekt, Sprache, Macht und Wissen.* Frankfurt: Campus.

Warszawski, D. (2007). Nie, nie zamierzam się lustrować. *Gazeta Wyborcza*, March 6.

Wasserstein, B. (2007). *Barbarism & civilization: A history of Europe in our times.* Oxford: Oxford University Press.

Wnuk-Lipiński, E. (1996). *Demokratyczna rekonstrukcja. Z socjologii radykalnej zmiany społecznej.* Warszawa: PWN.

Wodak, R., & Weiss, G. (2004). Visions, ideologies and utopias in the discursive construction of European identities: Organizing, representing and legitimizing Europe. In M. Pütz, J. van Aertselaer, & T. van Dijk (Eds.), *Communicating ideologies: Multidisciplinary perspectives on language, discourse, and social practice* (pp. 225–252). Brussels: Peter Lang.

EPILOGUE

Christian Karner and Monika Kopytowska

We started our introduction to this volume by commenting on some of the (many) centrifugal forces affecting existing political structures and institutional arrangements in Europe today. From there, we proceeded to make the conceptual case for paying close attention to the domain of language and other sign systems and their role both in reproducing and — particularly in times of acute crises — in challenging a status quo. Our contributors have done much to illuminate, across a diversity of national settings, the workings and effects of competing political discourses about Europe and the European Union (EU) articulated in the context of some of today's most profound challenges. As such, the findings presented and the arguments made in the preceding chapters need little further repetition or restatement here. Instead, we would like to bring this volume to a conclusion by merely placing its constitutive analyses into their wider, current context once again, and by thereby re-stating what is at stake in the study of political linguistics in general, and in its application to current European crises in particular.

To return to one of our conceptual points of departure cited in the introduction, significant parts of the present volume have followed and corroborated Krzyżanowski, Triandafyllidou and Wodak's methodological argument (2009, p. 4) that '[b]y analysing different discursive patterns of 'talking about Europe' in the national media over time' it is possible to also illuminate how crises impact on changing or competing conceptions of Europe, the nation state and the values they are held to represent. As we have seen here, national media indeed play a prominent role in the ideological contests unfolding across nation states and the EU, as the quintessential 'network state' (Castells, 2000), in the

National Identity and Europe in Times of Crisis: Doing and Undoing Europe, 285–288
doi:10.1108/978-1-78714-513-920171013

second decade of the twenty-first century. Yet, we have also seen that the media, whether local, regional, national or transnational (including, of course, the social media domain), are far from the only discursive sites where such contests unfold. Europe is currently also being *done, (re)done and at least partly undone* on many of its city squares, in (national) political manifestos as much as at increasingly frequent EU emergency summits, in the boardrooms of corporations and banks but also in the realms of education and civil society, in the writings by academics and public intellectuals as well as in the domain of the quotidian, where many lives have indeed become irrevocably transnational, often unrecognised though such 'banal Europeanism' (Cram, 2009) is.

At the outset, we set the scene for this volume by listing some of the many current crises facing the EU and its member states and by underlining that such a list could be added to at will. While this evidently remains true, we would like to briefly draw attention to some of the hallmarks of the crises captured by our contributors and/or accompanying the preparation of this volume. As mentioned, some of today's most profound challenges pertain to already steep and further widening inequalities of both wealth (see Piketty, 2014) and life chances, within nation states and globally. Such structural crises have obviously fed directly into some of the recent international stand-offs mentioned in the introduction, such as that pitting the governments of Germany (and other parts of the continent's 'north') against that of Greece, where the debt- and austerity crisis has left the deepest of wounds. Since the summer of 2015, a further intra-European 'axis' of difference (Brah, 1996) and confrontation has opened up. In the context of the humanitarian crisis triggered by unprecedented migratory flows of refugees from Syria and elsewhere to the EU, the EU's north–south divide so evident in the Greek debt crisis has been added to by other divides. With some Central- and Eastern European EU members opposing calls for an obligatory and proportional sharing of responsibility for asylum seekers across the EU – and, arguably, the United Kingdom's (UK's) position one of the outliers to this emerging 'west-east schema' insofar as the UK has also opposed compulsory quotas – much discursive energy has again been invested in what EU membership means or should mean, in how European solidarity and transnational responsibility are variously defined and, in some cases, refused. All along, nation states, including those whose governments are currently adhering to a definition of 'Europe' as entailing a commitment to the protection of universal human rights, are also internally divided between advocates and critics of a much narrower, national(ist) definition of the state's purported responsibilities.

Our approach to understanding the ongoing *doing and undoing of Europe* has consistently emphasised the role of language, texts and rhetoric in these processes. One of the key promises and benefits of the various approaches to political linguistics represented here is that they enable researchers to transcend the structure-agency dichotomies typical of many conceptualisations of our social and political worlds. In understanding language as 'social practice' (e.g. Chouliaraki & Fairclough, 1999; Fairclough, 1989; Weiss & Wodak, 2003), all statements, whether private or public, and texts become political, and are recognised for their active contributions either to structural reproduction or transformation. A further benefit of such approaches is that they encourage a heightened state of (self-) reflexivity regarding social research itself and its own political leanings. If all language is socially positioned and consequential, then so are our academic texts and analyses. To state what we hope is obvious, this volume does not come with a singular, dogmatic 'party line' on any of the complex questions pertaining to Europe's past, present and future. It would clearly not only be ethically deeply problematic but also intellectually highly counter-productive, not to say impossible, to assume or demand a uniformity of positions, explicit or implicit as they may be, in a project like ours. Take the question of a shared European historical consciousness, for example: at least one of the editors of this volume is a strong supporter of the notion that the EU both presumes and needs more post- and transnational memory of the continent's deeply troubled history (Karner, 2015). However, there are other academic voices that have questioned 'whether historical consciousness should be moved from a national to a European plane', where 'history as an anchor of identity' could, it has also been postulated, perhaps do 'still more damage' than it has done 'in conjunction with the idea of the nation' (Berger, 2010, p. 135). Surely more productive than a pre-determining quest for intellectual hegemony on questions of Europe is the provision of a space where alternative conceptions, understandings and ideas can be presented and debated. It is our hope that this volume will contribute and add to such spaces. What is more, the approaches to political linguistics employed here take the conversation one reflexive step further: encouraging a particularly active form of readership, they ask all of us to not only interrogate the politics of the texts and statements recorded here but also to reflect on the politics and positioning of those who have done the recording and analysing of others' positions. Put more simply: attentive readers should indeed also query where, how and to what effect we as authors, and they as readers, think, speak and write about the big questions facing us in and beyond the EU today.

Its methodological contributions and thematic findings aside, this volume also possesses much wider social scientific relevance. While (most of) our respective points of departure and research foci are evidently still oriented towards nation states, individually and collectively our chapters also add to the growing case against a 'methodological nationalism' (Wimmer & Glick-Schiller, 2002), or the often circular assumption that social life can be reduced to assumed national societies and publics. In clear departure from outdated approaches to studying social life in 'national containers' (see Beck, 2000), our contributors have provided much evidence of how transnational the life-worlds and orientations or, more accurately, the concerns, connections and conflicts of social and political actors across Europe have become. Yet, and to distil a further and obvious key insight emerging from the preceding pages and chapters, we are clearly here witnessing a conflictual transnationalism with uncertain outcomes. Analogous to Ulrich Beck's (2000) invocation of Roland Robertson's concept of 'glocalization' to capture the mutually transformative entanglements of global and local tendencies, Europeanisation is clearly not resulting in political or cultural uniformity. The network state (Castells, 2000) and its constitutive nation state members are engulfed in a process of multi-directional and multi-dimensional change. At present, different outcomes (or indeed no definitive outcome) are all perfectly thinkable: further European integration, or even the possibility of a truly 'postnational democracy' (Menasse, 2012, p. 117); or − and in moments of heightened crisis this can sometimes indeed appear far more plausible − further 're-nationalisation' (e.g. Hartleb, 2012), a retrenchment of national boundaries and self-interests, and perhaps indeed an eventual dismantling, a complete *undoing*, of European structures. Either or any way, what people say and write about Europe seems more consequential than perhaps ever before.

REFERENCES

Beck, U. (2000). *What is globalization?*. Cambridge, MA: Polity.
Berger, S. (2010). Remembering the Second World Wat in Western Europe, 1945-2005. In M. Pakier & B. Stråth (Eds.), *A European memory? Contested histories and politics of remembrance.* (pp. 119−136). New York, NY: Berghahn.
Brah, A. (1996). *Cartographies of diaspora.* New York, NY: Routledge.
Castells, M. (2000). *End of millennium.* Oxford: Blackwell.
Chouliaraki, L., & Fairclough, N. (1999). *Discourse in late modernity.* Edinburgh: Edinburgh University Press.
Cram, L. (2009). Introduction. *Nations and Nationalism, 15*(1), 101−108.
Fairclough, N. (1989). *Language and power.* London: Longman.
Hartleb, F. (2012). European project in danger? Understanding precisely the phenomena 'Euroscepticism, Populism and Extremism' in times of crisis. *Review of European Studies, 4*(5), 45−63.
Karner, C. (2015). Questioning memory nationalism. *Discover Society,* 21 (Focus), http://discoversociety.org/2015/06/01/focus-questioning-memory-nationalism/.
Krzyżanowski, M., Triandafyllidou, A., & Wodak, R. (2009). Introduction. In A. Triandafyllidou, R. Wodak, & M. Krzyżanowski (Eds.), *The European public sphere and the media: Europe in crisis* (pp. 1−12). Basingstoke: Palgrave.
Menasse, R. (2012). *Der europäische Landbote.* Vienna: Paul Zsolnay.
Piketty, T. (2014). *Capital in the twenty-first century.* Cambridge, MA: Belknap/Harvard.
Weiss, G., & Wodak, R. (2003). Introduction. In G. Weiss & R. Wodak (Eds.), *Critical discourse analysis* (pp. 1−31). Basingstoke: Palgrave.
Wimmer, A., & Glick-Schiller, N. (2002). Methodological nationalism and beyond. *Global Networks, 2*(4), 301−334.

INDEX